D1084764

EDUCATION FEVER

Hawai'i Studies on Korea

HAWAI'I STUDIES ON KOREA

Education Fever

Society, Politics, and the Pursuit of Schooling in South Korea

Michael J. Seth

University of Hawai'i Press, Honolulu
and
Center for Korean Studies, University of Hawai'i

Library of Congress Cataloging-in-Publication Data

Seth, Michael J.
    Education fever : society, politics, and the pursuit of schooling in South Korea /
Michael J. Seth.
        p. cm. — (Hawai'i studies on Korea)
    Includes bibliographical references and index.
    ISBN 0-8248-2534-9 (hardcover : alk. paper)
    1. Education—Korea (South) 2. Education—Social aspects—Korea (South)
3. Education and state—Korea (South) 4. Educational change—Korea (South)
I. Title. II. Series.
    LA1331 .S35 2002
    370'.5195—dc21

                                                                        2002004189

 The Center for Korean Studies was established in 1972 to coordinate and develop resources for the study of Korea at the University
of Hawai'i. Reflecting the diversity of the academic disciplines
represented by affiliated members of the university faculty, the
Center seeks especially to promote interdisciplinary and intercul-
tural studies. Hawai'i Studies on Korea, published jointly by the Center and the
University of Hawai'i Press, offers a forum for research in the social sciences and
humanities pertaining to Korea and its people.

Designed by inari
Printed by The Maple-Vail Book Manufacturing Group

Contents

Acknowledgments

I am indebted to the many people who have assisted in this book. The East–West Center supported much of my dissertation research, which provided some of the material for this work. The Korea Foundation, the Social Science Research Council, and James Madison University made it financially possible to further pursue my study of Korea's educational development through generous grants. There are so many people who assisted me in my research that I can name only a few: Kim Chong-so, Kim Yŏng-ch'ŏl, Ch'oe Myŏng-suk, Kim Kyŏng-sŏng, and Yu Sang Duk all shared their expertise with me. Lee Jae-kyŏng and the late Hong Ung-sŏn went out of their way to assist me in my research efforts. The staff at the Korean Educational Development Institute was patient, helpful, and kind. Yong-ho Choe and Joanne Charbonneau read two different drafts of my manuscript and offered helpful suggestions on style and content. Patricia Crosby and the staff of the University of Hawai'i Press helped walk me through the final stages of the manuscript.

Most of all I want to thank the scores of Korean parents, students, former students, teachers, educational officials, academics, and others whom I either formally interviewed or simply met by chance while researching this book. Their willingness to share their thoughts, personal experience, knowledge, and time in spite of their very busy lives made this study possible. Their goodwill, good humor, and encouragement made it fun.

Introduction

A great air of tension hovered throughout South Korea on 17 November 1999. A special task force had spent months planning for that day. The night before, President Kim Dae Jung had appeared on television to announce that the nation was prepared for the event. All nonessential governmental workers would report to work only later in the morning, as would employees of major firms. Thousands of special duty police were on hand in many cities; thirteen thousand police had been mobilized in Seoul alone. Flights at all the nation's airports had been restricted, and special efforts had been made to halt construction to avoid creating noise or commotion of any kind.[1] It was the day of the national university entrance examinations. For weeks Buddhist temples had been filled with hopeful parents and students; in fact, churches and temples received a large proportion of their annual revenues from the donations of these hopefuls. Shamans and vendors of amulets and "lucky" sticky candy had been doing a brisk business. It would be a day for which young men and women had prepared since elementary school, if not before, and for which parents had sacrificed a large portion of their income.

The college entrance examinations provide a vivid example of what Koreans sometimes call their "education fever" *(kyoyuk yŏlgi)*. Education is a national obsession in South Korea. Everywhere there are "cram schools" *(hagwŏn),* where elementary, middle, and high school students study late in the evening and on weekends. Every neighborhood has a store selling textbooks, supplementary readings, and guides to the entrance examinations. Adults, too, study at night schools, attempting to advance their education. Real estate prices depend

1

as much on the reputation of local schools as on the inherent desirability of the location or the quality of housing. South Korean families invest heavily in the education of their children, and children and young adults spend a huge portion of their time studying and preparing for examinations. Education pops up in conversation often, and the success of a son, daughter, or grandchild at entering a "good" school is a source of great pride. Although education is important in every nation, even casual visitors become aware of the intense preoccupation of South Koreans with schooling. This was certainly true of the author, who first arrived in Korea to take a job teaching English at a university in Seoul, with little knowledge of the country and its culture but with experience working in other developing nations. It did not take long to discover how important education was to the Koreans the author met. Later the author participated in a number of in-service training programs for middle and high school teachers and was invited to visit provincial urban and rural schools. It became apparent that the concern for educational attainment was not confined to the urban middle class of the capital but was an all-pervasive feature of South Korean society.

This obsession with formal learning has accompanied a remarkable educational transformation of South Korea in the half century after its liberation from Japan. In 1945, when the thirty-five-year Japanese colonial rule in South Korea ended, the majority of adult Koreans were illiterate. Mass primary education had only recently begun, and less than 5 percent of the adult population had more than an elementary school education. There was only one university in Korea, and most of its students were Japanese. Five decades later, virtually all South Koreans were literate, all young people attended primary and middle schools, and 90 percent graduated from high school. There were over 180 colleges and universities, and the proportion of college-age men and women who enrolled in higher education was greater than in most European nations. The quality of education was high as well—at least judging by comparative international tests. These tests usually rate the math and science skills of South Korean primary and secondary students as among the highest in the world.[2]

The rapid expansion of state-directed formal education in the second half of the twentieth century is not unique to South Korea. National educational systems developed at impressive rates during this period in both Koreas. The growth of formal schooling in South Korea was part of what has been called the "Educational Revolution," the global expansion of national education systems that occurred after World War II and was especially dramatic in the developing world. The post-1945 era saw the emergence of many new independent states and the general acceptance of universal literacy as a national goal in almost every state.[3] Yet even if we place South Korea's educational development within the context of this Educational Revolution, it stands out in terms of the intensity of its development. Indeed, since the 1950s South Korea has been on the extreme end of the correlation between the general level of education and the level of economic development, with a higher level of educational attainment than other nations of comparable per capita income.[4] As the country advanced economically into a major industrial power, the general level of educational attainment remained higher than in almost all other nations at a similar level of GNP per capita. That is, not only did education keep abreast with the nation's much admired rapid economic development, but it also kept ahead.

South Korean education also differed from that of most other developing nations in the sequential nature of its development. In other words, the emphasis was on bringing the entire school-age population up to a certain level before building up the higher tiers of the system, and there was greater stress on uniformity of content and quality. Only a few other nations—most notably Japan and the other "tigers" of East Asia (Taiwan, Singapore, and Hong Kong)—so consistently pursued these aims.[5] The nation's schooling was also characterized by long hours of study, strict discipline, educational advancement contingent on success in competitive entrance examinations, and a high level of competency among teachers, whose education followed a rigorous and rigorously enforced course of training.

While it may be impossible to establish precise causal links among economic, political, and educational development, South Korea's pursuit of education clearly contributed to its industrial transformation from the position it held as late as 1960 as one of the world's poorest nations to its membership in 1996 in the Organization for Economic Cooperation and Development (OECD), an organization of industrially advanced states. South Korea's educational system, with its stress on teacher authority and intense competitiveness, driven in part by very competitive school entrance examinations, produced a workforce that was highly literate and disciplined and a society ready for the competition characteristic of a capitalist industrial regime. This was especially true because the sequential nature of educational development and the wide diffusion of the values and goals that universal schooling achieved brought much of the population into this competitive struggle for educational advancement. The relative uniformity of educational standards and opportunity may also have accounted for the relatively equitable distribution of wealth in South Korea and prevented the creation of an underclass of ignorance and poverty that could breed discontent and social turmoil. South Korea has thus avoided the gaps in educational development that have characterized many developing nations, for the state has always stressed bringing the general population up to a shared standard of education rather than concentrating resources and efforts on creating a well-schooled elite. The uniformity of the educational system and the ability of a strong centralized state to impose uniformity of content at least assisted in adjusting education to developmental goals, as well as creating a sense of shared values.[6]

South Korea's achievements in education are all the more remarkable in view of its turbulent history. The sudden collapse of four decades of harsh occupation by Japan was followed by the division of the nation by the United States and the USSR and by internal unrest. The emergence of a new state, the Republic of Korea (ROK), after a brief three years of U.S. military government came at a time of widespread poverty and internal tensions, and it presented a government with questionable legitimacy and nationalist credentials. South Korea had to cope not only with the loss of markets and most of its modest industrial structure, which lie in the north, but also with an influx of refugees from North Korea and Japan. Most tragically, independence was soon followed by the horribly destructive Korean War (1950–1953). After a slow economic recovery real industrial growth began only in the early 1960s. But educational development proceeded rapidly from 1945 onward and continued uninterrupted, seemingly immune to the nation's political turmoil, economic chaos, and warfare that punctuated its history.

South Korea's educational development has been characterized by other features that are in some ways just as striking as its growth. Perhaps foremost is the pervasive preoccupation with competitive examinations—or as Koreans often term it, "examination mania." Observers of Japan have widely commented on that nation's phenomenon of "examination hell." South Korea too has its examination hell, and it has been no less important in shaping schooling and society. The entire educational system, from elementary school through high school, has focused on entrance examinations into higher levels of schooling. Both the public and officials have widely criticized examination preparation as the center of learning, which has deep roots in Korean history. Yet a half century of reform efforts has resulted in only an intensification of this phenomenon. Perhaps most interesting is the degree to which "examination mania" has come to embrace virtually the entire populace; families from all social or regional groupings make enormous sacrifices and go to great lengths to aid their children in the entrance exams. It could be argued that South Korea has become the most exam-obsessed culture in the world.

Another prominent feature of South Korea's educational development has been the continual, and to a considerable extent unsuccessful, attempts by the state to coordinate education with economic development needs. While South Korea is often seen as a model of successful state-directed economic development, state planners have been less successful in matching the curriculum with and shaping the school system to the economic development agenda. Although the creation of a well-educated and disciplined workforce was a major factor in accounting for South Korea's transformation into an industrial nation, educational development often took on a momentum of its own, driven by public demand for schooling and degrees rather than the practical requirements of industrialists and technocrats. As a result, government officials encountered difficulties in trying to promote technical and vocational training and direct enrollment growth in ways that met the assumed needs of the expanding industrial economy. Policy initiatives to coordinate education with economic goals generated tensions and met resistance when they ran counter to popular aspirations for educational attainment. The difficulties the state had in coordinating education with development strategies suggest limitations to its ability to control national development, and they underline the role of popular demand for schooling in shaping the nation's social transformation.

As striking as the rapid growth of schooling, the preoccupation with competitive exams, and the difficulty of a series of authoritarian, dirigiste regimes to direct educational development to meet economic objectives is the extraordinary cost of South Korean schooling. No nation in the world spends a larger share of its income on education. While this may seem admirable at first glance, less commendable is the fact that this cost has been progressively driven up for five decades by the relentless competition to score well on entrance exams. Competition for educational entry into higher levels of schooling and prestigious institutions has generated huge expenses for private tutoring, cram schools, and under-the-table payments to teachers and school officials. The scale of this problem cannot be precisely measured, but it is certainly enormous and has produced not only great financial hardship for millions of Koreans, but also many anomalies in both the educational system and the general economy. Another prominent feature of educational finance is the unusual degree to which the state has been able to transfer most of the cost of education directly to the students and their parents. Education has been publicly underfunded. The state instead has relied on the popular demand for schooling to pay for the greater portion of educational development.

Still more paradoxical has been the success of educational development in the face of an authoritarian state headed by a series of oppressive rulers who attempted to use education as a means of legitimizing the state and maintaining their control. Despite a centralized educational system, a highly politicized curriculum, and the regimented, militarized nature of South Korean schooling, the school system has produced dissident teachers and students who have helped to undermine the very regimes that sought to use them as instruments for political control. Furthermore, even though there was a long tradition of authoritarianism that characterized Korea both before and for decades after independence, the nation began a successful process of democratization with students and educators acting as a spearhead for democratic reform.

From the late 1980s, the pattern of educational development began to undergo some significant changes. The era of rapid educational expansion was over, and the emphasis had shifted primarily to improving standards. As South Korea underwent its transition to democracy, the most blatant use of the school system to achieve political objectives ended; schooling became less politicized and less regimented. Nongovernmental civic groups began to play a more significant part in shaping educational policies. Educators, officials, and the public discussed reforms, and in many cases these were implemented to solve some of the worst problems generated by four decades of frantic expansion and political tensions. Yet the national obsession with the attainment of education continued unabated, as much as ever defining the character of South Korean society.

This study argues that South Korea's "education fever" was the principal force that drove the country's extraordinary educational development. It further argues that this preoccupation with the pursuit of formal schooling was the product of the diffusion of traditional Confucian attitudes toward learning and status, new egalitarian ideas introduced from the West, and the complex, often contradictory ways in which new and old ideals and formulations interacted. The especially intense nature of the competition for educational attainment was also shaped by institutions and practices introduced by the Japanese and by the political and social turmoil that characterized Korea in the mid- and late twentieth century.

South Korea's extraordinary educational development and the national obsession with education have attracted the attention of many observers, but there has been no systematic treatment in English.[7] This book is intended to fill the void. Educational development has been central to the modern transformation of Korea; it has also been both a part and a product of the complex social and political changes that took place during the mid- and late twentieth century. Therefore, the examination of South Korea's obsession with education is an important part of its social history and provides a better understand of the nation's rapid economic, social, and political transformation. Furthermore, since South Korea has served as one of the developing world's "success stories," this topic has implications beyond the Korean Peninsula. This study should add to our understanding of the role of educational ideas and educational systems in economic and social development and in the transition from authoritarian to democratic societies.

To measure and probe the causes of South Korea's "education fever" this study takes a historical approach. Data are drawn from the secondary literature on educational development in English and Korean, from official government reports and statistics on education, and from formal interviews with more than sixty teachers and educational officials. Some material has been drawn from theses and dissertations on education in English and Korean. Additionally, public discussion of educational matters has been surveyed through newspapers, periodicals, National Assembly debates, and informal interviews with Koreans of various backgrounds. Opinions on education are easy to obtain. The preoccupation with educational matters is reflected in the prominence given to educational issues in the press. It is even more evidenced in conversations with Koreans. Not one out of the scores of Koreans the author interviewed ever displayed any hesitation in discussing educational matters or lacked strongly held views on the importance of education in their lives or in Korean society.

This study begins with a chronological background of Korean education in order to delineate the complex and contradictory inheritance that has shaped educational development in South Korea. Chapter 1 deals with the dynastic and Japanese colonial periods and examines their legacies on educational institutions and attitudes. It suggests that the Japanese colonial regime inaugurated a period of social turmoil that profoundly influenced educational and social development. Chapter 2 deals with the immediate years after the end of colonial rule in 1945, when Korea was divided and a three-year American occupation promoted concepts of education at variance with traditional and colonial concepts. The focus then shifts to the process by which the formal structure of schooling in South Korea was worked out from 1948 to 1951. The debates that accompanied this process reveal the range of ideas on education and their traditional, colonial, and American sources.

Educational development in the decades after independence in 1948 is then examined thematically. Chapter 3 measures the scope and nature of the rapid expansion of education that took place in the decades after 1945 and explores the social demand that drove much of this expansion. It suggests some of the reasons for the incessant demand for education. Chapter 4 deals with one of the tensions behind South Korean educational development: the often conflicting aims of a state that sought to coordinate educational development with economic growth strategies and parents who in the pursuit of high-status degrees for their offspring regarded technical training as an inferior form of schooling. Chapter 5 looks at the "examination mania" created by the highly competitive examinations that formed the main focus of schooling. Chapter 6 investigates the enormous cost of education, including the near-universal use of private, after-school lessons and tutoring. This chapter also analyzes the state's use of the public demand for education to shift the financial burden of schooling to students and their families. Chapter 7 describes how a succession of authoritarian regimes used education as a means of political indoctrination and control. In doing so, these regimes often ran into conflict with the goals of Korean families, who resented the time taken away from study. In addition, the discrepancy between the democratic ideals taught in school and the very undemocratic practices of the state generated cynicism and opposition among teacher and students. Chapter 8 examines the changes that took place in the late 1980s and 1990s as South Korea became more democratic and more prosperous. It also looks at the continuing contradictions and tensions generated by conflicting ideals and goals within the Korean public and between the state and society. It concludes by examining the challenges educational development faced at the start of the twenty-first century.

This account hopes to provide a better understanding of how South Korea succeeded in rapidly transforming itself into a well-schooled nation. It also is intended to contribute to our understanding of South Korea's rise from an impoverished and authoritarian nation to one of the most prosperous and democratic nations in Asia. The author hopes that this study will aid in understanding the connection between education and economic development and between education and democratization. But in addition, the South Korean obsession with formal education is a fascinating story that is worthy of being told for its own sake.

1 Korean Education until 1945

What are the origins of the national obsession with education? Koreans, both experts and laymen, most often attribute their "education fever" and the educational transformation of their society to their cultural heritage. Indeed, Korea entered the twentieth century with a centuries-old tradition in which formal learning and scholarship played a central role in society. This tradition, usually associated with Confucianism, entered Korea from China more than fifteen centuries ago. After the unification of the peninsula in the seventh century, Confucianism emerged as the central ideology of the state. A major theme of Confucianism is governance by men of merit—that is, men of talent and virtue. In order to recruit men into government, a civil examination system was adopted in Korea in 958 patterned on the system developed in China during the Tang dynasty. Subsequently, throughout the Koryŏ period (918–1392), a concern for education grew as a means of preparing men for the examinations and promoting Confucian learning and moral training. To aid in this task a national academy—the Kukchagam—was established in 982, and in 1127 King Injong ordered that each *chu* (prefecture) and *hyŏn* (district) establish a school.[1] With the establishment of the Chosŏn (Yi) dynasty (1392–1910), Confucian ideology was strengthened in the form referred to by Western scholars as Neo-Confucianism, and the examination system became virtually the only route to high government office.

Education in traditional Korea was valued as both a means of self-cultivation and a way of achieving status and power. An individual could become virtuous through the study of ethically oriented Confucian classics; he could then play an informal role as a moral exemplar and teacher and adviser to others, thus enhancing his status and influence in society. As did members of other East Asian societies, Koreans highly esteemed the written word and the prodigious efforts to master the accumulated body of literary and scholarly works. Furthermore, the examination system, based on the mastery of Chinese classics and literary skill, played a central role in allocating bureaucratic positions and the social status and privileges that were attached to them.

The early Chosŏn period leaders established a fairly comprehensive network of schools as a means of establishing loyalty, maintaining orthodoxy, and recruiting officials. Basic education was provided by village schools, known as *sŏdang* or *sŏjae,* and by private tutoring. The origins of the *sŏdang* are not known, but they appear to predate the Chosŏn period. The *sŏdang* was usually located in the house of the teacher and consisted of a small number of neighborhood boys, generally not more than ten or twelve, who entered at around the age of seven or eight. Each studied at his own pace for an indeterminate period usually lasting at least four or five years.[2] Although these schools were outside the official system of education, early Chosŏn rulers encouraged their formation, for they were seen as a means of selecting and preparing talented youths for entry into the official state schools.[3] The *sŏdang* remained the most common institution of formal education in Korea until well into the twentieth century.

At a more advanced level, a system of state-sponsored local schools called *hyanggyo* existed to prepare students for the civil examinations. These included the four *sahak,* organized in four of the five districts of Seoul, and schools established in each of the provinces. Each *sahak* accepted 160 and later just 100 students. There were over three hundred *hyanggyo* (the figure varied somewhat over time) throughout the countryside. The number of students assigned to these schools was fixed by law in the fifteenth century and ranged from 30 to 90 according to the type of local administrative unit (*mok, kun, hyŏn,* etc.). Students entered at around the age of sixteen and at about the age of eighteen or nineteen were allowed to sit for the lower-level civil exams *(sama).* Admittance to a *hyanggyo* brought with it the coveted status of *yuhak,* which included exemption from military duty and eligibility for taking the civil service exams. At the pinnacle of Chosŏn education were those who had passed the *sama* and had entered the National Academy (Sŏnggyun'gwan). These students were often eighteen or nineteen years old when admitted, and then at various ages, often between twenty and twenty-three, they would compete for the *munkwa,* the higher-level civil service examination.[4]

The basic structure of Chosŏn schooling was set up in the early fifteenth century; however, there were significant changes during subsequent centuries. The official schools experienced a gradual decline, and although they continued to function until the end of the nineteenth century, their role as agents of advanced schooling was challenged by the private academies, or *sŏwŏn,* which emerged in the middle of the sixteenth century. Unlike the *hyanggyo,* which were usually located in administrative centers, the *sŏwŏn* sprang up in the countryside and functioned as rural retreats for the literati, as shrines to honor scholars and officials, and as centers of learning. About 680 *sŏwŏn* had been founded by the end of the eighteenth century, and they served as important bases for political factions until most of them were closed in the decade after 1864 by the regent Taewŏn'gun in an effort to centralize authority.[5]

The legacy of premodern education was more than just an emphasis on formal learning. In many ways Chosŏn education resembled that of modern South Korean education. Perhaps the most striking point of resemblance is the degree to which both focused on preparing students for competitive examinations. While education was recognized as an end in itself, in practice it was generally seen as a means of social mobility and status selection. A series of highly competitive examinations served as the means of selection. In the lower-level examinations of the Chosŏn period, the *sama,* a student could choose to take either the classics *(saengwŏn)* or the literary *(chinsa)* exam. Passing these exams did not secure an official post, but it did bring certain privileges, such as eligibility for government office and exemption from military duties. Most important, it qualified those who passed for the higher civil exam, the *munkwa,* which was the real vehicle to high government office. In a society in which no other culturally sanctioned avenue to power and prestige existed, the exam system was of enormous importance. Historians disagree over how open the civil exams were to those of commoner status and whether exams served only to allocate official positions among members of the *yangban* aristocratic elite.[6] All agree, however, that the examination system acted as the main selection device for the limited number of government posts and that consequently formal education was largely organized around preparation for the exams.

Another feature of education during the Chosŏn period is the incongruity between the ideal of meritocracy implied by the system and a society emphasizing bloodlines and kinship and dominated by a hereditary aristocracy. Korea was the Confucian state par excellence. The Neo-Confucianism developed in

Song China, which became the reigning orthodoxy in Korea in the fourteenth century, emphasized the perfectibility of all men and assumed that each individual was capable of benefiting by education and achieving moral enlightenment. Talent and virtue could best be demonstrated by a mastery of the classics, self-discipline, and personal conduct. In conformity with this ideology, the schools and the civil examinations were theoretically open to all except outcast groups; however, a number of practices arose that limited access to both the state schools and the exams. In addition, preparing for the examinations required many years of study, so students whose parents could afford to finance lengthy studies and hire tutors had an enormous advantage. And as studies have shown, family lines, along with rank and hierarchy, were strongly emphasized in Korean society. In reality, therefore, the examination system and the schools associated with it primarily served as a means of allocating power, privilege, and status—all closely associated with officeholding—among members of the *yangban* aristocracy.

During the long Chosŏn period Korean society was dominated by this *yangban* class. A hereditary group, the *yangban* comprised the officialdom that ruled society, the scholars who reigned over intellectual life, and the principal landowners who controlled the economy. While this was largely a closed caste, the values of the *yangban*, who saw themselves as scholars and moral leaders, gradually permeated throughout society. The *yangban* ideal of a refined, elite individual or family whose virtue, moral excellence, and right to privilege was periodically reaffirmed through educational achievement would remain a model for aspiring middle- and even lower-class Koreans.

As a result of the Confucian ideology and the use of examinations as a social selection device, premodern Korea was a society in which formal learning was a major preoccupation. The first Western account of Korea, written in the seventeenth century by a shipwrecked Dutch merchant who spent thirteen years in the country, points this out: "The nobles and the free men take great care for the education of their children. They place their children under the direction of teachers to learn to read and write. The people of this country are very enthusiastic about [education] and the method they use is gentle and ingenious. Teachers offer their students the teaching of earlier scholars and constantly cite the example of those who attained fame through high scholarship. The boys devote their time to study day and night."[7] Literacy in Korea among males was probably high by premodern standards and most likely increased in the eighteenth and nineteenth centuries. An indication of this is the growth in private academies, which promoted education among the *yangban* class. There is also some evidence that the number of and enrollment in village schools expanded in the late Chosŏn period, but this area still awaits investigation. What is clear is that the elite families, at least, devoted a great deal of energy and expense to education and exam preparation. In this way they behaved much like modern South Korean families.

Another legacy of premodern Korea was the exalted position held by the scholar–teacher. Organized religion was peripheral to Chosŏn society; rather than the temple and the priest, it was the school and the teacher that served as the principal source of ethical counsel. Consequently, the scholar attained an almost sacred status. The learned man was more than a scholar or teacher: he was the moral arbiter of society and source of guidance at the village as well as the state level. Thus, the value placed on learning was extremely high.

The moral authority attached to teachers, scholars, and earnest students provided the basis for another legacy of premodern Korean education: the tradition of remonstrance. It was the duty of the scholar to criticize the actions of the government, including the king. Confucianism perceived the universe as a moral order; improper behavior on the part of officials and rulers threatened that order. Scholars and lower-ranking officials wrote memorandums critiquing the king and his ministers on ethical grounds. Students at the Sŏnggyun'gwan held protest demonstrations when they felt that those in positions of authority were not adhering to ethical standards or were improperly performing rituals. Academy students withdrew from school in mass protests periodically. Nineteen such incidents are recorded in the reign of King Sukchong (1674–1720) and twenty in the reign of King Sunjo (1800–1834).[8] This tradition of equating education and scholarship with moral authority, hence giving students and scholars the right and duty of remonstrance against officialdom, has been one of the most persistent features of Korean education.

Several other attributes of the pre-twentieth-century culture were to remain characteristic of South Korean schooling. The master–disciple relationship of the *sŏwŏn* echoed an ancient cultural pattern that has appeared in modern higher education. The emphasis on rote memorization, moral training, and the notion of schooling as basically a male activity all have continued to shape Korean education. Education in the dynastic period was also characterized by a disdain for the specialist and for technical training that has prevailed in modern Korea. Although specialized technical exams *(chapkwa)* existed for certifying doctors, astronomers, interpreters, and other needed professionals, they remained far less prestigious; education was basically of a nonspecialized, literary nature that has remained the preference of most Koreans.

Serving the state was the goal of the elite, for although the state lacked reliable communications and organizational efficiency, to a great extent it dominated Korean society. There was no major cultural or political center of significance other than Seoul, which was primarily an administrative rather than a commercial center. Nor were there any regional centers of political power of importance. Members of the *yangban* elite competed through the civil examinations and through capital intrigue for political posts that ultimately determined social rank and power and secured wealth and privilege. Lacking major secondary institutions such as independent religious or social groups, Korea was a state in which the central government was the vortex that drew nearly all of the upper classes.[9] Thus, as Korea entered into the modern era it brought with it a legacy in which formal education was of fundamental importance in allocating positions in government and in confirming or securing social status.

EARLY MODERNIZATION

Toward the end of the nineteenth century as a result of the sweeping changes brought about by the intrusion of foreign powers into Korea, the Chosŏn period dynasty began to implement the beginnings of a Western-style educational system. After the opening of Korea to international trade and diplomacy in the years following Japan's gunboat-style port opening in 1876, new types of schools appeared. Starting with the Wŏnsan Academy (Wŏnsan Haksa) in 1883, wealthy Koreans established privately organized schools offering nontraditional instruction, especially in the major ports.[10] The Korean government experimented with a number of educational institutions from 1881 on, attempting to introduce foreign knowledge and technical skills. Perhaps most significant, from the early 1880s, a group generally referred to as the Kaehwadang (Enlightenment Party) urged the establishment of a Western-style system of state-supported schools and the addition to or replacement of the Confucian-oriented learning with a modern curriculum. Efforts to reform education, however, were fitful and unsystematic before 1894. New patterns of thought and learning were mainly the result of the activities of the few Koreans who had traveled abroad, especially to Japan, and the efforts of foreign agents, mostly American missionaries, who, starting with the Paejae Academy in 1886, began to open schools.[11]

Significantly the two main foreign influences that have so profoundly shaped Korean education, the Japanese and the American, made their impact felt from the inauguration of Korea's modern era. The Japanese influence during the early period was the more important. Indeed, most of the reformers in Korean education, as well as in other areas, shared the experience of having spent some time in Japan; many had close contacts with Japanese educational reformers such as Fukuzawa Yukichi and his Keiō Academy. Japan became a model for a younger generation of Koreans. Furthermore, by 1894 large numbers of Japanese merchants and adventurers appeared in Korean cities and towns, and in some cases they came with their families and established Japanese schools.[12] Consequently, the Japanese model was not a remote concept but a visible demonstration of what a neighboring society with a partially shared cultural tradition was doing to modernize its educational institutions.

The American influence, while less penetrating, was nonetheless substantial. At first American missionaries had great difficulties in attracting students to their schools. Ewha Academy (Ihwa Haktan), which Mary Scranton established in 1886 as a school for girls, for example, initially was able to enroll only a single student, a young prostitute.[13] Gradually a few Koreans were attracted to mission schools, many becoming Christians and acting as major agents for educational reform in twentieth-century Korea. A trickle of Koreans also began to make their way to the United States, forming a small intelligentsia with first-hand experience in the American educational system. Among these pioneering students was Syngman Rhee (Yi Sŭng-man), the future South Korean president. But before 1945 the American influence on Korean education was modest compared to that of Japan.

Aside from a few experimental schools, the first effort to establish a modern national system of education took place between 1894 and 1906. The Japanese presence in Korea that accompanied the Sino-Japanese War (1894–1895) created a situation that was utilized by the Enlightenment Party. Korean reformers eager to emulate Japanese adoption of Western institutions and their Japanese supporters inaugurated the Kabo Reform of 1894.[14] The Kabo Reform reorganized the Korean governmental institutions along modern lines. As part of this reform an Office of Educational Affairs (Hangmu Amun) was established to oversee a national system of schools.[15] This organ, which the following year was renamed the Ministry of Education (Hakpu), was divided into a

School Bureau and a Compilation Bureau. The School Bureau set regulations and standards for a system of primary and secondary schools, while the Compilation Bureau prepared and approved textbooks.

Under this new system, *sohakkyo*, five- to six-year elementary schools were established by the state. These schools were divided into three years of ordinary and two to three years of higher education, thus allowing some flexibility in areas where a full six years of education might not be feasible. Secondary education was carried out by *chunghakkyo*, or middle schools, consisting of seven years: four years of ordinary and three years of higher education. There were also special four-year secondary schools for English and Japanese and five-year secondary schools for French, Russian, and German. The Seoul Teachers' School (Hansŏng Sabŏm Hakkyo) was established to train teachers for the new schools. This system was implemented slowly and gradually. The regulations for the new primary schools were issued in 1895, and the Seoul Teachers' School was established the same year, but regulations for secondary schools were not issued until four years later. In addition, several short-term technical schools were established, such as the Commercial and Technical School (Sanggong Hakkyo), the Electrical and Telegraph School (Chŏnmu Hakkyo), the Postal School (Umu Hakkyo), and, most influential, the Military School (Kunmu Hakkyo). These technical schools were created to meet the government's immediate need for the acquisition of modern technical skills and represented a less significant break with tradition than the radically new public schools.[16]

The new educational system that began to emerge reflected the influence of Japan, and many of its features foreshadowed the colonial education system that was to succeed it. In theory it was a highly centralized system, with the Ministry of Education defining curriculum, issuing and approving textbooks, certifying teachers, and issuing detailed regulations for the management of schools. Textbooks, for example, were divided into two categories: *kukchŏng*, government-issued, and *kŏminjŏng*, government-approved, a system that was still in use at the end of the twentieth century. In both cases the Compilation Bureau had direct control over the content of all texts. Schools were originally financed by the state, but soon a system of private contributions, tuition, and government grants took shape, inaugurating what became a familiar pattern of state regulation but private financial support.[17]

The achievements in these early years were modest. By 1904 public education was confined mainly to Seoul, and even in the capital it was on a very small scale. There were only seven or eight primary schools operating in Seoul, each with about forty to eighty boys, for a total enrollment of about five hundred, and only one secondary school, with about eight teachers and an average reported attendance of thirty boys.[18] In the next two years, a few new schools were established, and in 1906 seventy-two graduates of the Seoul Teachers' School were teaching in Korean schools.[19] But the new schools accounted for only a tiny proportion of all students; the vast majority were still attending *sŏdang* and other traditional institutions. Reform of public education came slowly and with difficulty. Expenditure on education was extremely modest; it was reported that the total budget of the Ministry of Education came to only $60,000 while that of the Army Ministry was $4,000,000 during 1903–1904.[20] The new public schools did not prove very popular and met with resistance not only from parents, but also from government officials.[21]

But Koreans were not resistant to education. On the contrary, amid the poverty and confusion of the period private education grew rapidly. After 1900 a number of private educational and cultural organizations were formed to set up and operate a vast number of schools. The Kyŏnggi–Ch'ungch'ŏng Educational Association (Kiho Hŭnghakhoe) and the Northwest Educational Association (Sŏbuk Chibang Hakhoe) were among the largest of these organizations, whose membership after 1905 rose to several thousand. The former, heavily supported by active and out-of-service officials, promoted a mixed style of education including traditional Confucian values, modern science, world history, and geography. There is evidence that it received considerable financial support from members of the royal family. The latter received support from both *yangban* and merchant elements from P'yŏngan Province.[22] The expansion of private schools occurred at the same time as a rapid expansion in American missionary activities and mission schools. As a result, by the end of 1909 there were about 1,300 "modern" private schools and 823 mission schools operating in Korea.[23]

The impressive growth in private education during the last years of the Yi dynasty must be seen in the context of several developments. The abolition of the civil examinations in 1894 dealt a severe blow to the old educational system, at least at the higher levels. Education could no longer function as the prime avenue of social and political advancement. The new educational system lacked prestige and purpose and floundered for lack of public support. Yet in addition to the concept of education as a means of moral cultivation, education was beginning to be seen as a method of national renewal. Indeed, one of the largest organizations for promoting education was the Korean Self-Strengthening Society (Taehan Chaganghoe), formed in 1905 (renamed the Korean Association [Taehan Hyŏphoe] the next year). This and other groups established a number of private schools that attempted to incorporate a modern curriculum. Drawn principally from elements of the *yangban* class, along with some nonaristocratic members of the business, professional, and religious communities, these individuals displayed considerable eagerness to modernize Korean education. So in spite of the modest achievements of the new, state-sponsored system, there was a growing support among educated Koreans for educational modernization and reform.

It is also worth noting that traditional values and attitudes about education remained strong. An examination of textbooks reveals the extent to which education during this early modernizing period was still rooted in inherited values. Textbook lessons were largely Confucian and ethical in tone and, except for some modern geographical information, were not radically different from traditional didactic works. The quality of paper and illustrations was high, reflecting a customary Korean respect for books and paper making.[24] The *sŏdang* too continued to function in villages and urban neighborhoods. One interesting development was the use of mixed script. The indigenous *han'gŭl* (Korean alphabet), which had long been held in low esteem, was used along with Chinese characters. The use of the easily mastered Korean alphabet would make acquiring basic literacy easier in the future.

The early experiment in modern education foreshadowed later attempts to find a suitable system for Korea. The government's modest attempts at modernizing education reflected the weakened condition of the Korean state. These contrasted with the efforts of progressive private groups and individuals, who were opening up hundreds of schools that introduced modern science and Western geography, history, culture, and languages. Both state and private educational reform programs, however, were overwhelmed by the efforts of the Japanese to organize Korean society to serve their own needs.

EDUCATION IN KOREA UNDER THE JAPANESE

Korea's forty-year occupation by Japan, first as a protectorate (1905–1910) and then as a colony under direct rule (1910–1945), is important for understanding South Korea's educational development because it was during Japanese rule that a comprehensive, modern national system of education was established. From the start the Japanese administration of Korean education was characterized by a high degree of centralization, careful planning, and professionalism among teachers and other educational personnel. Educational development was also sequential, with a concentration on basic education followed by a slow growth in the secondary and tertiary levels of schooling.

But the Japanese came as conquerors, outsiders who ruled over an often hostile Korean population in order to carry out policies that they thought beneficial to Japan. To secure their control, they created an elaborate bureaucratic apparatus staffed by tens of thousands of Japanese, a national gendarmerie with substations in almost every village and neighborhood, and a substantial military garrison.[25] The educational system the colonial authorities created became part of the strong, coercive, and exploitative state structure, and its primary purpose was to serve all the needs of the empire. These were not necessarily the perceived needs of the people they ruled. As a result, a pattern of tension over educational policies evolved between the Korean public and the state. Educational policies contributed to a legacy of bitterness among Koreans toward their colonial rulers that remained strong over a half century after it ended.

Two features of colonial educational policy contributed greatly to the anger and frustration that the Korean people felt toward the colonial state and would greatly influence South Korea's educational development. First, under the Japanese, access to education beyond the elementary level was restricted as part of Korea's subordinate status in the empire. Colonial planners did not see the need for most of their peninsular subjects to obtain more than basic literacy and numeracy. This restriction on higher education led to a pent-up demand for educational access that would burst into the open in South Korea when the Japanese empire collapsed. Second was the use of education to indoctrinate Koreans into being loyal subjects of the Japanese empire and later to assimilate them into Japanese culture. Forced assimilation left a nationalist anger, while the use of education as a political instrument by a powerful centralized state set a pattern that was followed by the governments of both North and South Korea.

Restricting Access to Education

By emphasizing lower-level, nonprofessional track schooling for Koreans, Japanese educational policies generated tensions and frustrations that would contribute greatly to the post-1945 mass pursuit of education. While emphasizing the importance of education at home and creating what would become a comprehensive system of public education in the peninsula, the colonial officials limited the access of Koreans to upper levels of schooling and assigned them to inferior schools. From the start the purpose was to create a system that was regarded as more "appropriate" for Korea's level of development. The dominant view among Japanese policymakers was that Korea was a backward society and that this backward society should occupy a subordinate position in the empire. Korea was to be a source of raw materials and cheap labor, as well as a market for Japanese products; therefore, basic education was all that was necessary for Koreans.

Shortly after the Japanese assumed direct rule of Korea under the Government-General of Chosen (Sōtokufu), they issued the Educational Ordinance of 1911, a comprehensive outline for a system of Korean education that could be described as separate and unequal. The newly organized Bureau of Education was to supervise two educational systems, one for Japanese residents and another for Koreans. The Japanese residents were to receive the same education as in the home country *(naichi)*—six years of compulsory primary education followed by five years of secondary or technical school and then three years of college preparatory or higher technical school, all using the same curriculum as in Japan. For Koreans, elementary education was to be limited to four years of "common school" *(futsū gakkō)*. After completing "common school," a student could attend a four-year "higher common school" or a four-year "industrial school." In contrast to the fourteen years of schooling available to Japanese, education for Koreans was to be limited to eight years, with the exception of one three-year "special higher school" designed to train civil servants.

According to the Educational Ordinance, the purpose of the educational system for Koreans was "to give the younger generations of Koreans such moral character and general knowledge as will make them loyal subjects of Japan, at the same time enabling them to cope with the present condition existing in the Peninsula."[26] This meant that education was intended not to prepare Koreans for professional or administrative positions, but to provide basic literacy and those "arts indispensable" for low-level technical tasks for men. For girls the purpose was "fostering . . . the feminine virtues such as constancy and domesticity."[27] Japanese teachers were recruited to teach in the schools, and their authority was emphasized by the regulation that they wear swords in class. No provision was made for training Korean teachers; in fact, the country's only modern teachers' college, Seoul Teachers' School, was closed. Japanese became the medium of instruction, and Japanese history and geography were introduced as required subjects. The curriculum, however, was not identical to that in the schools for Japanese students; for example, less class time was devoted to the liberal arts. Since education for Koreans did not have a very high priority at this time, the authorities built few "common schools" in the decade following the 1911 ordinance and even fewer "higher common schools."[28]

In the early years of the colonial occupation, the authorities showed more interest in securing control over the nation's schooling than in promoting learning. Toward that end the administration of Governor-General Terauchi Masatake on 20 October 1911 issued the "Regulations for Private Schools," placing all private schools under the supervision of the Bureau of Education. These included a number of schools established by Korean reformers in the last days of the dynasty, most offering modern subjects. Koreans were allowed to continue to operate and teach at these institutions but only if the Japanese language was used as well as Korean and if the teachers and textbooks were approved by the Bureau of Education. The regulations became increasingly burdensome, and between 1911 and 1920 the number of such schools gradually declined. This contrasted with the great mushrooming of such schools in the previous decade. Clearly a demand for modern schooling in Korea was being met by these private, Korean-run institutions but was continually hindered by colonial restrictions.

Mission schools run by Westerners fared a little better. An ordinance issued in 1915 and aimed at the mission schools required that teachers at all private schools have sufficient knowledge of Japanese to teach in that language, and it tightened supervision over curriculum, textbooks, and administration. Due to the strong reaction among foreign missionaries to the new regulation and perhaps Japan's wish to avoid a diplomatic incident, implementation of the ordinance was delayed for ten years.[29] But eventually foreign mission schools would be tightly regulated by the Japanese, and it became difficult to open new ones. Consequently, the first decade of colonial rule saw a big drop in the number of private schools; mission schools fell from 823 in 1909 to 279 in 1920, and nonmission schools from 1,300 to 410.[30] Smaller institutions were particularly hard hit since a series of regulations set fiscal and organizational requirements for schools that many were unable to meet. Constant pressure was placed on private schools that their instructors be proficient in Japanese, although few such persons could be found. The arrest and intimidation of prominent figures in Korean education, such as Yun Ch'i-ho, and the self-exile of other educators, such as An Ch'ang-ho, also hindered the operation of private educational associations that supported these schools.

A more comprehensive effort at educational development began with a policy devised in the 1920s. In the wake of 1 March 1919, when anti-Japanese, pro-independence demonstrations broke out in Korea, the Japanese inaugurated what they called their "culture policy" *(bunka seiji)*. As part of this new liberal policy, aimed at gaining the cooperation of moderate nationalist leaders in Korea, the government-general issued the Educational Ordinance of 1922. The ordinance reopened the Seoul Teachers' School, extended elementary education from four to six (sometimes five) years, extended secondary education to five years, and added a three-year college preparatory or advanced technical school. According to the ordinance, Koreans were to receive the same standard of education as Japanese residents. The basic principle would be separate but equal. Symbolic of this new liberal policy, the authorities discontinued the practice of having Japanese teachers wear swords in class. Regulations for private schools were revised as well, permitting the teaching of religion and allowing for the use of the Korean language and the introduction of special subjects related to Korean culture. All textbooks and teachers, however, still had to be approved by the Bureau of Education, and the Japanese language, Japanese ethics *(shūshin),* and Japanese history had to be taught at all levels.[31] The ordinance, in recognition of national sentiments in Korea, required that all schools, Japanese and Korean, institute courses in Korean history and geography.

Education for Koreans was not compulsory after 1922, but the colonial administration made efforts to expand the school system. These efforts emphasized basic education and were characterized by careful planning and modest expenditure. Educational expansion was carried out in accordance with a series of short-term plans. The first, 1922–1928, had the goal of one school per two townships *(myŏn)*. After this goal had been reached in 1929, a target of one school per township was declared, and it was close to completion by 1936.[32] As would be expected, educational development proceeded faster in urban areas, but efforts were made to avoid regional and urban–rural disparities. In the 1930s a rural simplified school system (the Nōson Kan'i Gakkō Seido) was introduced to assure some basic education by reducing the term and length of primary schooling in poorer and more remote areas.[33] By 1935, 17.6 percent of all Korean children of elementary school age were in officially recognized schools. In 1937, the new governor-general, Minami Jirō, had a five-year plan drawn up that called for a doubling of enrollment in elementary schools. This was to be followed by a ten-year plan that would achieve a 60 percent enrollment rate by 1953. The five-year plan also called for the elimination of the rural simplified school system, and all primary schools were to offer six years of instruction. The plan actually exceeded its target enrollment figure in 1942.[34]

While the new policy promised to provide greater educational opportunity to Koreans and made a few concessions to Korean ethnic sentiment, it continued to frustrate the demand. Schools were not constructed fast enough to enroll all those seeking an education. As a result, competition to enter elementary schools rose in the 1930s, especially in the cities, with many public schools requiring oral interviews.[35] Furthermore, the schools that were built were generally poorly funded and inferior in quality to the schools for Japanese residents. A Korean student after 1922 could attend a Japanese school in theory, but in practice relatively few were admitted to primary schools, although after 1930 admission to secondary schools became more common.[36]

One sign that educational expansion was not keeping up with demand was the creation of thousands of unlicensed schools. Some were one-teacher schools, perhaps conducted at home, offering a modern curriculum or vocational training. After 1920, many young graduates of the new government or mission institutions established night schools.[37] The largest number of private schools were *sŏdang,* the traditional village schools. Until the 1920s they remained the principal form of schooling for most Korean children; in fact, they increased in number. A survey in 1912 reported the existence of 16,450 traditional village schools, with 141,604 students. Seven years later, 23,556 *sŏdang* were counted, with 268,607 students. The government-general made an attempt to utilize the *sŏdang.* In 1918 it issued regulations requiring teachers to attend special classes in Japanese, but this and other attempts to "modernize" the *sŏdang* appear to have been largely ineffective.[38] The number of these schools continued to increase in the 1920s, with enrollment peaking in the 1930s.[39] The increase in these traditional schools and hundreds of other unlicensed schools reported to be supplying basic education indicated a rising demand for education in the 1920s and 1930s that Japan's deliberate pace of educational expansion was not satisfying. But unlicensed private schools could not issue certificates, and *sŏdang* were dead ends as far as a means of social advancement was concerned since only a modern-style education could provide opportunities for success in the new society.

Frustration at the gradualist approach to educational development was felt most keenly by members of the elite and the small but growing urban middle class. At the secondary and higher educational levels, the expansion of education proceeded even more slowly. This was in part a deliberate policy to reinforce the subordinate role of Koreans in the empire. The result of this policy was that in spite of onerous restrictions, private Korean and mission-run schools accounted for about half the secondary and most of the higher-level educational institutions in Korea. The higher-level schools were mostly *semmon gakkō*, a term for nonuniversity-track, technically oriented schools. These were modest in size, with enrollments that never exceeded more than two or three thousand, but they were to play important roles in post-independence South Korea. After 1945, Ewha Semmon Gakkō was to become the leading women's university; Posŏng Semmon Gakkō and Yŏnhŭi Semmon Gakkō became Korea (Koryŏ) University and Yonsei (Yŏnse) University respectively, the two leading private coed universities.

A central issue for upper-class and upwardly mobile Korean families was higher education. The colonial administration announced a plan in 1922 for the establishment of a university in Korea, to be open to Koreans and Japanese residents in Korea, and a university preparatory school.[40] Keijō Imperial University was established in 1925 and remained the sole university in Korea until after 1945. However, it became as much a symbol of resentment as one of opportunity for Koreans. The faculty was overwhelmingly Japanese, and the student body contained a disproportionate number of Japanese students. Thus, the pinnacle of the elite educational track was to be open to Koreans, but only to a few. Admission into the university was difficult; a mere 10 percent of Korean applicants were accepted, compared to a 40 percent admission rate for Japanese applicants.[41] This limited access to higher education generated great resentment among the Korean elite.

The restrictive policies of the colonial regime became linked with the tracking system. Schooling at the secondary level was divided into a narrow college-preparatory track and several terminal vocational tracks: technical, agricultural, fishing, and pedagogical. Korean critics saw this tracking system as a means of limiting economic and social advancement to a privileged few and placing unreasonable pressure on young children. It also may have acted to reinforce traditional attitudes toward technical education. In the strict hierarchical system created by the colonial regime those moved into technical schools were fated to lower-paying and lower-status positions. For ambitious families technical-track education meant failure. The struggle to overcome this perception was one of the greatest obstacles that later South Korean planners faced in their efforts to coordinate education with economic development schemes.

Overall, the Japanese record on providing opportunities for higher education for Koreans compares unfavorably with the British record in India or the American record in the Philippines.[42] Because the expansion of higher education was too slow to meet demand, an increasing number of Korean students sought schooling in Japan. In 1925, 13.8 percent of Korean students in higher education were in Japan. By 1935, the figure was 47.3 percent, and in 1940, 61.5 percent. In 1942, there were 6,771 Koreans attending institutes of higher education in Japan but only 4,234 in Korea. Also impressive was the number of Koreans attending secondary schools in Japan; in 1940, 71.6 percent of the 20,824 Korean students in Japan were enrolled at secondary schools. It should be pointed out that little assistance or encouragement was given by the Japanese government to this educational exodus, and the higher living costs were a heavy burden for most.[43] Yet rapidly increasing numbers of Koreans were overcoming linguistic handicaps and making financial sacrifices to obtain education because in their own country the rising demand for education was outstripping opportunities at all levels.

Limited access to higher education was paralleled by limited opportunities for Koreans to serve in administration and teaching. The bureaucracy remained dominated by Japanese. Of the *kotokan* (high officials) 29.9 percent were Korean in 1915 and 31.4 percent in 1920, but by 1935 the figure had fallen to 23.5 percent. Even at the middle level of the bureaucracy there was no increase in the percentage of positions occupied by Koreans.[44] In the schools for Koreans, Japanese teachers dominated, and the trend became worse, not better. In 1922, 29 percent of the instructors in public schools were Japanese; ten years later, 30 percent were Japanese; the figure rose to 44 percent in 1938.[45] This created serious problems after liberation. But the most serious problem for many individual Koreans and their families was being blocked from taking the traditional route to honor and privilege, advanced education, and appointment to government office. This frustration was aggravated by wartime policies after 1938 that further limited the number of schools of higher education (even as they expanded primary education) and redirected the curriculum away from literary to less prestigious technical education and vocational training. The result was anger, frustration, and an unsatisfied desire for schooling at all levels, especially at the higher levels. These are key factors in explaining the "education fever" of South Korea in the decades following World War II.

Education and Political Control

As noted, the strong ideological emphasis of Korean education during the colonial period was another important legacy. Education served national goals of enhancing state power and inculcating an ideology that demanded loyalty and obedience to the state. From the start a principal aim of colonial education was to indoctrinate young Koreans into the ideology of the Japanese imperial system. Officials were often frank about this. One government publication stated, "The aim of the common school is not to provide education but to make them [Koreans] into good and loyal citizens of the empire."[46] The government-general was often more concerned with the danger of "infusing disquieting thoughts in their [Koreans'] minds" than in promoting learning.[47]

Although a slightly more liberal and tolerant policy was pursued in the 1920s, after 1931, with the rise of militarism and foreign adventurism, the political and ideological nature of education was intensified. With the outbreak of the China War in 1937 an extraordinary effort was made to use education to create not just loyalty to the state, but also a new sense of identity. The government-general issued the Educational Ordinance of 1938, which revised the structure of education and aimed at the assimilation of Koreans into Japanese culture. The new ordinance declared the goals of education as threefold: (1) "The clarification of national policy" (kokutai no meicho); (2) "Japan and Tyosen [Chosen] as one body" (Naisen ittai); and (3) "endurance and training."[48] This meant that Korean schools were to be identical to Japanese in organization and closer in curriculum. Elementary schools, futsū gakkō, were renamed shōgakkō, and secondary schools, kōtō futsū gakkō, became chūgakkō, following the Japanese practice. Koreans were taught the same subjects as Japanese students, and the Korean language was limited to four hours a week for the first three years, two hours a week for the next three, and one or two hours a week in middle schools. By contrast, elementary students spent ten to twelve hours a week on the Japanese language, and secondary schools taught it six or seven hours a week. In 1941, the last minor concession to Korean identity was eliminated, and all Korean language instruction or even use on school grounds was prohibited. In the same year all primary schools, Japanese and Korean, were renamed *koku-min gakkō* (citizen schools).[49]

Education was now an instrument for the policy of forced assimilation. Japanese ultranationalism and militarization pervaded the entire school system, and the curriculum became stridently patriotic in tone.[50] Korean history was replaced by Japanese history, and greater emphasis was given to such subjects as *shūshin* (ethics), in which Japanese nationalist themes were zealously emphasized. Private schools were gradually forced to close down or were placed under Japanese supervision. The authorities prohibited the teaching of religion, required that all Koreans register at Shinto shrines, closed the mission schools, and expelled foreign missionaries. The prohibition against the use of the Korean language and its strict enforcement after 1940 meant that many Korean-operated schools were forced to close. Students were required to attend regular assemblies where the *Imperial Rescript on Education* was read and to give daily pledges of allegiance to the Japanese emperor. The subject matter of textbooks was dominated by patriotic themes, the time spent on liberal arts subjects was once again reduced, and more emphasis was placed on technical subjects. The Educational Ordinance of 1943 further prohibited all courses in the Korean language and shortened the middle schools to four years, with more emphasis on technical education. The new ordinance also required the *semmon gakkō* to change their names in order to rid them of any non-Japanese associations.

Education became highly militarized and regimented. Compulsory military drills were introduced to all middle and higher-level schools. Political rallies became a part of schooling, as did mass mobilization of Korean youth for the war effort. In incremental stages the colonial government brought the students into the war. In April 1938, the Japanese government organized a Special Student Volunteers unit for selected Korean students who wanted to participate in military duty. In May 1943, the state permitted all Korean students to volunteer for service in the army, and in October of that year, for the navy. Because the numbers volunteering proved to be modest, the state made registration for military service compulsory in November 1943.[51] In October 1940, all student organizations automatically became branches of the Citizens' Total Mobilization League. Students found their time increasingly occupied by extracurricular activities, such as collecting metal for the war effort and attending patriotic rallies.

College students were sent to the countryside to explain the war effort to farmers and rural folk. In the early 1940s, the school term was shortened, and secondary school students were required to work on military construction sites. After 1942, many students were conscripted to work in Japan, while at home *kinrōtai*, student labor groups, were formed to do "voluntary" work such as building airstrips and defense works.[52] By the spring of 1945, virtually all classroom instruction above the elementary level was suspended, and students were fully involved in labor and military service.[53] Thought control was maintained throughout the schools with the assistance of student police. A special "student section" of the Ministry of Education kept watch on Korean students in Japan.

The war years were only a culmination of the pattern by which the Japanese created a highly centralized educational system that served as an arm of a semi-totalitarian state with powerful coercive organs. The school network was dominated by the central bureaucracy, which extended its control down to the village school and the village or neighborhood police post. There was a close association among the Education Bureau (Gakumu Kyoku); the Interior Bureau (Naimu Kyoku), which controlled local government administration; and the Police Bureau (Keimu Kyoku). The concern of the Japanese authorities with internal security, their distrust of the Koreans, and the more authoritarian drift of the Japanese government at home and abroad after 1931 resulted in a system in which teachers reported to security officials, soldiers drilled students, and the lines among the organs of education, defense, and internal security were blurred.

Educational rules and regulations throughout the colonial period were made by professional civil servants and were handed down the bureaucratic chain of command without much consultation with subordinates. This chain of command ran from the Education Bureau to the provincial governor, *dōchiji* (Korean: *tojisa*), who wielded considerable power over local implementation through his administration of the education section of the provincial government. Below the provincial level, the *gunshu* (Korean: *kunsu*), or county chief, or the *fuin* (city mayors) presided over local education councils. The county chiefs and the city mayors had direct contact with school principals and higher-ranking educational personnel and are remembered by many Korean teachers as powerful, authoritative figures. Interior Bureau officials, who were responsible for the maintenance of law and order and who supervised the centralized and efficient police force, worked closely with education officials so that the school and the instruments of state control were closely intertwined.

Perhaps no less important in understanding Japan's colonial legacy is the size and nature of the centralized state it created. The Japanese greatly increased the power and efficiency of the centralized state, especially its police and surveillance apparatus. In contrast to the modest investment in personnel that the British and French made in their colonies, some 246,000 Japanese manned the civil service, the police, the army, and state-dependent businesses and organizations—more than ten times as many as the French needed to administer and control Vietnam, a colony of similar size and population.[54] As a result, they created a state that was largely alien from the society it governed. The extent to which the demands of society for educational and administrative advancement could be ignored testifies to both the autonomy of the state from the society and its exploitative character. Consequently, it left a legacy of what Hagen Koo has described as an antagonistic relationship between the state and society in Korea.[55] This too would have an important impact on educational development in post-liberation South Korea.

Other Legacies of Colonial Education

The Japanese administration influenced South Korea's educational development in a number of ways. Colonial education was well disciplined. Class instruction was based on rote memorization and choral recitation, methods not unfamiliar to Koreans, who had always equated learning with vigorous memorization of Chinese characters and the ability to quote from classical texts.[56] New elements were the Japanese concern for ritual performance, neat uniforms, lining up smartly at the morning assembly, and performing student duties, such as keeping classrooms and lavatories clean. All these promoted the school as a model of discipline, orderliness, and cleanliness. These practices would continue in South Korea, contributing to the regimented and disciplined nature of the nation's schooling.

Although the Japanese colonial administration expanded the educational system too slowly to satisfy many Koreans, it established an impressive level of professionalism. Teacher qualifications were of a high standard and rigorously enforced. By the 1930s, Korean teachers had to adhere to the same standards for qualification as their Japanese colleagues, which meant at the minimum attending a three-year educational secondary school (shihan gakkō). The high standards of teacher training served to strengthen traditional respect for teachers and enhanced the teacher's authority in the classroom. Perhaps just as significant for South Korea's future was the disciplined, almost martial quality of teacher training. To this day elderly Koreans recall their Japanese teachers with a sense of awe and respect.[57] Teacher training within Korea, as well as in Japan, was a closely supervised activity. *Shihan gakkō* were state-operated, and teacher training emphasized loyalty and discipline, characteristics deemed appropriate for instructors of the empire's youth. Great emphasis was placed on spiritual and physical training, with morning calisthenics led by military officers. The training carried over to the classroom, where teachers even in elementary schools stressed discipline, loyalty, and physical and spiritual cultivation. The system within its limitations operated with honesty and efficiency.

Several other features of Japanese education were to become important features of South Korean education: the importance of class bonding, the level of internal efficiency, and emphasis on extracurricular activities. Tight bonds among classmates had always been a trait of Korean education.[58] The close-knit relationships formed among students were reinforced by some of the other aspects of colonial education. Unlike schools in many colonial and developing societies, few students dropped out or fell behind once they started. (Students did fail, but the number was relative small.) Furthermore, students entered at about the same age. Both factors strengthened the ties among classmates. Indeed, the bonds remained lifelong ties of mutual aid and support. The forging of these bonds was assisted by the emphasis on extracurricular activity, which enabled academically weaker students to excel at something—sports, singing, art—and provided a basis for shared experiences and mutual respect among students.

Administratively, it was a uniform system, with all schools following the same curriculum and operating according to detailed regulations set down by the Education Bureau in Seoul. Education was developed sequentially—that is, the thrust of educational development was toward the creation of a uniform system of mass education. This emphasis on bringing everyone up to a certain level and the tight controls over curriculum, textbooks, and teacher training meant that educational standards were consistent. South Korean authorities continued this concern for creating a uniform basic education for all Koreans.

The Japanese also bequeathed a complex system of educational finance. While the separate educational system maintained for Japanese students was heavily subsidized from the state treasury, schools for Koreans relied on many sources of revenue. Income from the property of former *hyanggyo,* some money from the Imperial Donation Fund, tuition, donations, state subsidies, and local revenues all contributed to public schooling.[59] After 1920, with the expansion of the educational system, local supplementary "school" taxes, as well as portions of local revenues from taxes on buildings, households, and land, provided over half of the financial support for public education. Local taxes were collected by the School Expenditure Associations (Gakkōhikai), local fund-raising organizations, and city councils *(fukai)*, consisting of local men of property and prominence.[60] Yet the money raised locally was never sufficient, and only meager support was received from the government-general, which spent more on its police and its prisons than on education. For example, in the mid-1930s education made up only 6 percent of the central colonial government's budget.[61] Consequently considerable amounts of money had to come from tuition and private donations. When the South Koreans constructed their educational system after 1945, they inherited this pattern of underfunding and shifting costs to parents.

Another important feature of colonial education was the reliance on competitive entrance examinations. Students took exams to enter middle school, college, and university. Access to upper levels of instruction was restricted and competition was severe. Even at the primary school level, especially in the cities, oral interviews were given to parents and students to select pupils for limited places. Thus some sort of exam pressure was felt at every level.[62] Exam pressure was nothing new to Korean education, but under the Japanese, the scope and extent broadened. Japan's notorious "examination hell," which placed pressure on children still in primary school, was transplanted to Korea, at least to the urban elites, who saw in it the possibility of educational advancement. The pressure was intensified by the centralized, multitrack system of schooling (discussed above). Among ambitious families enormous pressure was placed on children in elementary school to do well and gain entry into the small, elite, university-bound track. The scores on middle school entrance exams largely determined a young person's life chances. The examinations gave the system a sense of fairness and served to enhance the authority of teachers and principals, but eventually the focus on entrance examinations would prove to be one of the central problems of Korean education.

The Japanese colonial authorities did not monopolize schooling in Korea. As noted, private schools, many operated by American missionaries or American-trained Koreans, survived. Since the Japanese state invested little in higher education for Koreans, private institutions were important at that level.

In 1935, 73.6 percent of post-secondary education was carried out by private, nonuniversity-track institutions.[63] These private colleges were regarded with suspicion by Japanese authorities, and most were eventually closed down. Those that survived owed their existence in part to the protection of foreign missionaries.[64] It is significant that a number of Koreans became exposed to Western ideas about education, society, and politics through these mission institutions. The existence of a countertradition of American-influenced schooling helped prepare the way for the reception of educational reforms promoted by the United States in South Korea after the end of World War II.

A SOCIETY IN TURMOIL: THE LEGACY OF WORLD WAR II

Korean education and society were profoundly impacted by the imperialist adventures and warfare that marked the last years of Japanese rule. The state became more coercive and education more politicized and militarized when Japan's imperialist adventure in China put the colony on a wartime basis. With the occupation of Manchuria in 1931 and the creation of the puppet Manchukuo state the following year, Korea's position in the Japanese empire changed from peripheral to central, as the peninsula became a bridge from the Japanese archipelago to the Chinese mainland. Industrial development in Korea increased, particularly in the north, and opportunities for employment in the newly industrializing centers in northern Korea and Manchuria became available to many Koreans, setting into motion a great social migration as hundreds of thousands left their villages to take advantage of these new opportunities. This process accelerated in 1937, when war broke out between Japan and the Republic of China. As the conflict escalated, the energies and resources of the Japanese empire, including colonial Korea, were harnessed for war. The colonial authorities undertook a major mobilization of Korean society for the war effort and directed education to serve war aims.[65]

No part of the Japanese legacy is more important for understanding South Korean educational development than this great social upheaval. The Japanese takeover of Manchuria inaugurated a vast internal and external migration.[66] Imperial need resulted in the decision to develop the mineral-rich northern part of the peninsula as well as Manchuria. The process of migration quickened with the invasion of China in 1937, which led to a huge demand for manpower of all sorts. At first the movement of farmers and laborers was mainly voluntary: many poor Koreans left their villages in search of employment in the mines and factories that were mushrooming in the north and in Manchuria, but this soon involved a forced mobilization of millions of Koreans to work where needed in Korea, Japan, China, and elsewhere in the expanding empire. The scale of this great social upheaval, which continued to accelerate in the early 1940s, is extraordinary. As Bruce Cumings has pointed out, by 1944, 11.6 percent of all Koreans were residing outside of Korea, and 20 percent were living abroad or in Korea but outside their home provinces.[67] By 1945 there were two million Koreans working in Japan, where they made up a quarter of the industrial labor force. According to Cumings, "forty percent of the adult population was part of this uprooting."[68]

This mass movement of people served to break down routines of ordinary life and open up new experiences and possibilities to millions of Koreans. Further studies of Korean society are needed before a comprehensive picture of social change in the twentieth century can emerge, but it is clear that Korea in 1945 was a society in social turmoil. Educational development after 1945 took place among a nation of millions of dislocated, restless citizens, most born into illiterate peasant households but many of whom had been exposed to urban life and industrial routines during the war. The last years of colonial rule had shaken up traditional Korean society, and this society would be further shaken by the political turmoil and civil war that followed liberation.

2 Establishing the Educational System, 1945–1951

The intense drive for educational attainment that has characterized South Korean society burst forth in the years immediately after the collapse of the Japanese colonial empire. The colonial restraints on access were removed, new ideas on education were introduced by Americans and American-educated Koreans, and the basic framework of the educational system was debated. The educational "reforms" carried out under the three-year American military occupation, 1945–1948, and the new school system created by the South Korean government in 1949–1951 would help set in motion and shape the course of South Korea's mass drive for educational attainment.

The 1945–1951 period was also a time of turmoil and rapid change. The surrender of Japan in August 1945 was accompanied by the partition of the Korean nation along the thirty-eighth parallel into American and Soviet occupational zones. U.S. forces arrived in the southern zone in September and set up the U.S. Military Government in Korea (USAMGIK). Under the supervision of the U.S. military a separate government in the south was organized that on 15 August 1948 became the independent Republic of Korea. A rival Democratic People's Republic of Korea was proclaimed in the north on 9 September of that year. Meanwhile, hundreds of thousands of Koreans returned from Japan, Manchuria, and North Korea seeking work in the impoverished new state, adding to the turmoil. The new South Korean state, with Syngman Rhee as its president, struggled with almost overwhelming economic difficulties, domestic political unrest, rebellions, and, in 1950, war. In the midst of these upheavals the structure of South Korea's educational system was worked out, and the popular demand for education, already stirring in the colonial era, emerged in full force.

THE AMERICAN OCCUPATION AND EDUCATIONAL DEVELOPMENT

The Americans occupied South Korea for only three years, yet their impact on education was considerable. One reason was that they made education a major priority. The Americans had two aims in this area, both stemming from the belief that educational systems determined the character of the state and society they served. One aim was to purge Korean schooling of the fascist, militarist, and totalitarian nature of imperial Japanese education and to Koreanize and democratize it. The second was to provide educational opportunity for all young people so that Korea could have the literate population needed to become a prosperous society and each individual could fulfill his or her potential. To achieve these goals the USAMGIK sought to promote American ideas of progressive education, produce suitable Korean-language textbooks and a Korean-oriented curriculum, and accommodate the great demand for education that immediately appeared when Japanese rule ended.

These tasks, however, were difficult because America was not prepared for the occupation of Korea. The sudden collapse of the Japanese empire caught both Koreans and Americans by surprise; as a result, as Bruce Cumings has made clear, the U.S. occupation of Korea was a contingency that had not been anticipated.[1] For example, when General John R. Hodge and his forces arrived in Korea on 6 September 1945, they had no Korean experts; in fact, General Hodge initially did not even have a Korean-speaking interpreter on his staff. Thus, Americans set out to reorganize and reform a society that they knew little about. Yet the Americans did have a basic vision: to create a peaceful, democratic, and anti-Communist society. Education was a crucial component of this vision. Subsequently, educational policies were central, not peripheral, concerns of the American military government. And there was a great deal of goodwill and support for the American efforts among the Korean people, who were generally eager to promote schooling and to consider new ideas.

The USAMGIK carried out educational policies based on those that the United States had formulated for the occupation of Germany and Japan. The underlying principle was that a system of democratic education was fundamental to creating a democratic society. In Korea, the effort to establish a democratic educational system became part of what came to be called the "New Education Movement" *(sae kyoyuk undong)*. The New Education Movement was rooted in the American progressive educational philosophy of John Dewey; it emphasized equal opportunity for all and the development of self-reliance and individual responsibility. It encouraged student participation in the classroom to stimulate active discovery, by which a student would learn that there was no absolute right or wrong answer to most questions; it also encouraged a pragmatic approach to problem solving. It was an educational philosophy that encouraged individual differences, the belief that students should be taught to think for themselves, and the idea that change was desirable. In Korea, advocates saw the New Education Movement as "providing a foundation for the reconstruction of the social order into a progressive cultural identity."[2]

The educational concepts that the Americans introduced were linked with their mission as bearers of democracy. An essential element in democratic schooling was the American experience with decentralized education. Local and community control of education, as opposed to the highly centralized and bureaucratic educational systems of Germany and Japan, was considered necessary for an educational system to be free from authoritarian controls. The American concept of progressive education envisioned a model in which parents, communities leaders, and teachers would decide what to teach and how to teach it. This meant that educational administration needed to be decentralized and teachers and schools had to be given considerable autonomy. The Americans, as well as many Korean educators, saw the educational system the Japanese had created in Korea as diametrically opposed to these progressive concepts. It stressed authority rather than questioning and conformity rather than individual development; it was elitist rather than democratic and centralized rather than allowing for local participation and local needs.

To administer educational reform, the USAMGIK set up a dual structure of authority, with Americans assuming the key administrative posts; the two most important were the Education Bureau director, E. N. Lockard, and the deputy director, Paul D. Ehret. Americans headed each department and the provincial education bureaus. Each, however, had a Korean counterpart who acted as an adviser. Since none of the American officials in the Education Bureau could speak Korean or had any background in Korean culture, they were dependent to a great extent on these advisers. At the start of the occupation, two English-speaking Korean educators sympathetic to the American educational aims were placed in key positions: Yu Ŏk-kyŏm was appointed adviser to Lockard, and O Ch'ŏn-sŏk (Auh Chun Suk), a graduate of Teachers College, Columbia University, adviser to Ehret.[3] Until his death in 1947, Yu was probably the single most influential Korean educator working with the Americans. The son of a noted scholar and reformer (Yu Kil-chun), he had a law degree from Tokyo University (1920) and had served as vice-president of Yŏnhŭi College from 1937 to 1945. He had long been active in both Christian and educational movements in Korea. He and O Ch'ŏn-sŏk were both familiar with and strong proponents of American progressive education. It was important to the American occupation that a small handful of English-speaking Korean educators understood and enthusiastically embraced the American educational ideals; the occupation authorities soon transferred responsibility for educational reform to them .

These Koreans had begun discussing the need to reorganize Korean education even before the Americans arrived. At the start of September 1945, Yu Ŏk-kyŏm, O Ch'ŏn-sŏk, and two other prominent, American-trained Korean educators, Paek Nak-chun (George Paik) and Kim Hwal-lan (Helen Kim), formed the Korean Committee on Education. Kim Sŏng-su, one of the country's wealthiest citizens and an educational philanthropist, served as the chairman. Although they met only several times, according to O Ch'ŏn-sŏk, they discussed plans for sweeping educational reform, including the implementation of a system of education patterned after that of the United States.[4] Kim Sŏng-su left the committee and Yu Ŏk-kyŏm succeeded him as chairman. The committee continued to meet until May 1946, serving as an advisory body to the Americans in the Education Bureau; recommending the bureau's reorganization; and advising on the reopening of schools, the dismissal of Japanese personnel, and the appointment of educational officers. At the recommendation of the committee, USAMGIK established the National Committee on Educational Planning, which met from November 1945 until the spring of 1946.[5] The purpose of the committee was to develop the "fundamental philosophy of Korean education based on democratic principles and practices" and to reorganize "Korean education in accordance with that philosophy." In order to carry this out, the committee's work was to be "predicated upon a balance between native cultural aims and modern American educational influences."[6] Ten subcommittees were formed whose heads formed a virtual "who's who of education" in postwar South Korea—for example,

Ch'oe Kyu-dong, Cho Tong-sik, Chang Il-ok, Yun Il-sŏn, and Ch'oe Hyŏn-bae (the last a distinguished scholar and promoter of *han'gŭl*).[7] The subcommittees deliberated for four months and in March 1946 began adopting reports that were, in general, approved by the USAMGIK and implemented in the course of that year. Thus, the educational reform efforts under the U.S. occupation were as much the product of a small, enthusiastic group of Korean educators as of the Americans.

The committee reports recommended changes that brought South Korean education closer to the American example. Most prominent was the proposed adoption of the 6-3-3-4-year educational system. Six years of primary education would be universal, followed by three years of middle school and three years of high school, leading to a four-year college education. The committee recommended that the two-track system of vocational and academic (university-bound) secondary schooling be abolished for a single track. This move was intended to bring the country's schooling in line with the principle of equal opportunity, regarded by advocates of progressive education as an essential feature of a democratic society. The Americans, upon endorsing these proposals, added their own recommendations for a unitary educational structure and a separate middle and high school, eliminating the old system whereby children decided their life's vocation when they finished elementary school. The Americans also proposed that no type of middle or high school, nor any type of course, was to be terminal so that a student in a technical program could switch to a college-bound one. This flexibility was in accordance with prevailing American educational theory, which stressed the need to give a child more freedom and responsibility, thus promoting individualism, the foundation of a democratic society. In addition, American advisers supported equal opportunity for girls at all levels and argued for the need of coeducation at the secondary school level.[8]

Perhaps the most important leader of the New Education Movement was O Ch'ŏn-sŏk. With the sponsorship of the Department of Education (formerly the Education Bureau—see below), O Ch'ŏn-sŏk ran a summer workshop at the former Keijō Imperial University in 1946.[9] The first of a series of similar programs, it introduced the concepts of progressive education to hundreds of Korean teachers. Another series of workshops, conducted by Hyojae Primary School principal Yun Chae-ch'ŏn, were designed to introduce these new educational concepts to elementary school teachers.[10] Since there was a widespread fascination with the new educational theory among Korean educators, workshops, seminars, and manuals were eagerly received.

Little, however, was actually done during the occupation to put the ideas of democratic education into practice or to implement the reforms proposed by the National Committee on Educational Planning. Not only did the Americans not implement any radical changes in the structure of schooling created by the Japanese, but they also maintained the authoritarian, centralized educational administration without significant modifications. They did make some administrative changes during 1946 and 1947, but these were relatively modest. The Education Bureau was renamed the more American-sounding Department of Education, which was subdivided into eight bureaus.[11] The most important innovation was the restructuring of the Bureau of School Affairs into separate divisions for common schools, higher schools, and adult education, the last two reflecting a greater emphasis in these areas. In October 1946, the provincial education sections were transferred from the Interior Department to newly created provincial education bureaus, a move intended to weaken the general administration's control over education. It remained, however, a highly centralized system, still with central control over textbooks and teachers.

The U.S. military government also failed to implement a system of local school boards. Most American educators in Korea believed that the creation of such boards (on the American model) was necessary for democratic education and for building a grassroots democracy. Creating school boards was also seen as a way of solving the problem of financing education by shifting responsibility to local communities. A survey of schools for the 1946–1947 school year showed that 61.7 percent of the funding for elementary schools came from the central government and 38.3 percent from local government sources. For secondary schools the figures were 53.6 and 46.4 percent respectively. Subsequent reports showed that the proportion of central funding was declining and public finance was increasingly coming from local sources. The USAMGIK made no major change in the local tax structure, and the inherited Japanese structure was proving to be inadequate.[12] Furthermore, tax collecting amid the confusion that followed the collapse of the Japanese empire and the relocation of several million Koreans was becoming less effective, and local revenues were declining. Increasingly, education was being supported by an informal system of contributions and fees levied at the initiative of individual schools. To remedy this, a group of Korean representatives met in May 1947 and called for the introduction of a local education tax. This suggestion was supported by the Department of Education and provincial educational advisers, who argued for both the local control of schools and the creation of a local education tax.[13] In January 1948, an Educational Objectives Committee was set up with the purpose of formulating "the broad objectives of democratic education in Korea and to suggest ways and means of accomplishing these objectives."[14] At the recommendation of this committee, three ordinances were issued in May 1948. Ordinance No. 216 established school districts in each county *(kun)*.[15] Ordinance No. 217 established a number of school boards, one for each county and city *(si)*, with sole jurisdiction over local administrative matters and policymaking. Each school board was to employ a superintendent of schools responsible to the board. Ordinance No. 218 established a new system of fiscal support by requiring that the residents of each school district tax themselves, and this tax, it was hoped, would be the major source of funding for public schools.

If the Americans had vigorously implemented these ordinances, they would have created a system of local community control of education. The central government would have still supervised teaching credentials, teaching materials, and teacher training, but these decisions would have been subject to review and modification by the local school boards, which were to function as instruments of local control, support, and participation. This, the Americans believed, would foster democratic values and habits of popular participation in public affairs and fine-tune the system to local needs. The USAMGIK declared in 1947 that "the key note of [the] Korean education program is democratic education at the local level."[16] The Americans, however, never set these ordinances in motion, and when the U.S. occupation ended in August 1948, the administrative structure of South Korean education was little changed.

The question remains why the Americans, in view of the support they enjoyed from a number of highly influential educators, did not do more to reorganize Korean education along American lines. Partly this was due to the brevity of the U.S. occupation; there simply was not time to implement proposed changes, and much of the military government's energy was devoted to merely coping with a wealth of other problems. For example, there was a severe shortage of teachers while at the same time there was a great surge in student enrollment beginning in the fall of 1945. Out of expediency, the Americans simply continued using the existing schools during 1946 and 1947 without any major changes in the inherited system. But it was important also that the U.S. government failed to provide the kind of support that the occupation government had expected.

In Japan, the U.S. Educational Mission to Japan brought together a variety of American educational specialists and Japan experts to compile a systematic and detailed survey of what needed to be done to reform Japanese education. Similar efforts were less successful in Korea. Early in 1946, Lockard organized a Korean Council on Educational Aid from America, drawn from American officials in the Education Bureau, U.S. Army personnel, and Korean educators. The council sent a report, "Program of Educational Aid from America," to the War and State Departments. The report requested that American education specialists be sent as consultants, that 100 American teachers be sent to Korea for teacher training, and that 100 Korean educators and 300 Korean students be sent to the United States for study and teacher training. In March 1946, the Korean Educational Commission, a six-member body, spent three months meeting with American educators and government officials. On 17 June 1946, the U.S. Office of Education recommended sending a mission to Korea to help reorganize education in Korea, but this was opposed by General Douglas MacArthur, Hodge's superior, who suggested that such a mission was premature and that it should be delayed until the basic problem of unity was resolved. For fear of appearing to form a separate government while negotiations over the status of Korea were continuing through the American–Soviet Joint Commission, the United States failed to give the massive support to educational reorganization that the American military government felt was needed.[17]

Not until a year later was the mission finally approved. It proved to be a modest affair; only eight officials were to be sent to spend nine months in Korea. This group, known as the Arndt Commission, was reduced at the last moment to four members and stayed in Korea for only eighteen days. During their brief stay the members talked with USAMGIK officials and with Korean educators about the needs of Korean education. On 20 June 1947, after its return to the United States, the commission issued a fifty-five page "Report of the Educational and Informational Survey Mission to Korea." Unlike the report of the mission to Japan, which gave a detailed outline of educational reforms, this report limited itself to such minor points as standardizing the romanization of Korean, the completion of the School of Engineering at Seoul National University, and greater social contact between USAMGIK officials and Korean educators. There was one important recommendation: the establishment of the Teacher Training Center at Seoul National University; it was implemented the following year. But in general, the Arndt Commission offered little assistance to the American military government, which continued to rely on English-speaking Koreans and which lacked the resources to train the new generation of progressive educators needed to successfully bring about educational reforms.[18] For the Americans in Washington and Tokyo, South Korea was a sideshow, an unexpected, largely unwanted responsibility, and the uncertainty about its future and the desire to pull out as soon as possible meant that the United States was unwilling to commit itself to a sustained and concerted effort.

The failure of the Americans to carry out sweeping educational reform can also be attributed to the USAMGIK's concern with maintaining political stability and its fear of Communist subversion, which made it difficult to give up the centralized system it had inherited from imperial Japan. The U.S. military occupation was a troubled affair from the beginning. With the surrender of Japan on 15 August 1945, a network of popular committees sprang up. Within a few weeks people's committees *(inmin wiwŏnhoe)* were formed in every province and in over half of South Korea's 115 counties, and a Korean People's Republic had been declared in Seoul. Though these self-proclaimed organs of government contained people of diverse backgrounds, Communists and leftists who were suspected of being pro-Communist played a major, if not a leading, role in them. The alarmed U.S. forces refused to recognize the Korean People's Republic or the local people's committees and created a conservative Representative Democratic Council in February 1946. In May 1947, the USAMGIK created a South Korean Interim Government. Both of these bodies were staffed largely by conservatives with uncontested anti-Communist credentials. Most were Korean landowners and bureaucrats who had served or at least prospered under the Japanese. Thus, the South Korean state being created by USAMGIK was tarred with the label of "collaborationist," a government of those who had cooperated with Japan and who lacked bona fide patriotic credentials. Most of the Koreans who manned the occupation bureaucracy had served as lower-ranking officials under their colonial rulers; therefore, their nationalist credentials were also questionable. The Communists, on the other hand, had suffered arrest or had been driven underground. When they emerged in 1945, they did so with their reputation for resisting foreign oppression intact, enabling them to enjoy a good measure of popular support or sympathy, especially among students and teachers. In the face of popular discontent and leftist strength, the American military authorities relied increasingly on the highly centralized national police force inherited from the

Japanese, which they enlarged and trained. Korean security forces were used to put down strikes by the National Council of Labor Unions (Chŏnp'yŏng). This group was formed in the autumn of 1945 and grew to nearly six hundred thousand members by August 1946. The police then crushed the labor movement by arresting its leaders.[19] In the autumn of 1946, insurrections in the southern part of the country, in which an estimated sixty thousand participated, were suppressed by Korean security forces and U.S. troops, and in March 1947 the Korean Communist Party was banned and its leaders arrested.

Education became entangled in this political struggle between leftists and rightists that characterized this period. Strikes and protests by high school and college students were a major problem. Almost immediately after the start of the occupation many student organizations and groups showed sympathy with Communist or other radical groups and maintained an attitude of suspicion, if not open hostility, toward the American military government. Students directed many of their protests at their school administrators, often charging them with being Japanese collaborators or, less often, American puppets. Other strikes and demonstrations were aimed directly at the USAMGIK and its policies. The first wave of student unrest took place in January and February 1946. Most Koreans had expected immediate independence but were dismayed to learn during the winter of 1945–1946 that under U.S. policy Korea would remain a UN Trusteeship for an undefined period while the Americans, with cooperation from the Soviet Union, prepared the country for independence. There was also suspicion that the United States would use this period to create a separate state in its occupation zone. Students were especially active in the protests against a prolonged period of tutelage, and their demonstrations against U.S. policy disrupted most colleges and high schools. In May 1946, the military government reacted to campus disturbances by banning student political demonstrations but was unable to enforce this measure.[20] Student activism, especially demonstrations against authority, which had appeared sporadically under the Japanese, became chronic under the American occupation. This began an adversarial relationship between successive governments in South Korea, which feared student radicalism, and students, who opposed what they often saw as immoral, corrupt, and unpatriotic authorities. This tension characterized the country's education for the next half century. The USAMGIK responded to these protests by expelling students and closing down schools. By early 1947, fifty-seven of the nation's high schools and colleges had been closed due to campus unrest.[21]

The trouble at Seoul National University illustrates the political unrest that plagued the U.S. occupation. In 1946, students protested the appointment of Chang I-uk, a man labeled by many as *"ch'inil-p'a"* (pro-Japanese), as university president. As with most of the prominent educators appointed to posts by the American military government, Chang had an unheroic record; he had worked as a manager of a Japanese automobile factory during the war. After his appointment, he added to his unpopularity by rejecting student demands for participation in the admittance process.[22] The students forced an effective shutdown of the campus following protests over the announcement in August 1946 that the campus was to be a "national university." This meant it would be directly under the supervision of the central government's Department of Education. Many students and some professors feared this would lead to a loss of autonomy and the institution's subordination to a conservative central bureaucracy.[23] As a result, what had been Korea's only university, and after 1945 remained South Korea's most prestigious institute of higher learning, was in almost constant turmoil during the three-year American military rule.

While the Americans struggled with student unrest, they also sought to root out subversive elements among the nation's educators. Korean teachers were quick to organize after the end of colonial rule. As early as September 1945, some four hundred secondary teachers met to form an association for the promotion of democratic education. This and other groups combined to form the Korean Teachers' Federation *(Chosŏn Kyoyukcha Hyŏphoe)* in February 1946.[24] This, the first grassroots teachers' organization in Korean history, became affiliated with the outlawed National Council of Labor Unions and the Korean People's Republic. Worried about Communist influence in the schools, the Americans encouraged the creation of the Korean Federation of Educators' Associations (KFEA) in 1947.[25] Ostensibly an independent professional association, it became a vehicle for the government control and indoctrination of teachers; teachers were automatically enrolled in it, with the dues deducted from their salaries. The authorities closed all other teacher groups. In a further crackdown on dissident educators, the USAMGIK in September 1947 arrested 100 teachers for being political subversives and eventually purged about 1,100 "leftist teachers" from the schools.[26] The U.S. endeavor to "democratize" schooling ran into conflict with the efforts to create an anti-Communist political order in South Korea.

Nonetheless, the USAMGIK for all its limitations presided over the expansion and Koreanization of South Korean education. The Koreanization of education was carried out with great zeal, largely at the initiative of Korean educators. Perhaps the most important effort was the promotion of the twenty-four-letter Korean alphabet, *han'gŭl*. Members of the Korean Language Academy (Han'gŭl Hakhoe, the former Chosŏnŏ Hakhoe), many emerging from prison, where they had been sent following the outlawing of their organization in October 1942, held an emergency meeting on 25 August 1945. Two months later they published the first textbook on the Korean language and the use of *han'gŭl*. Despite disagreements on the standardization of *han'gŭl* that would remain unresolved for a number of years, academy members helped organize the National Language Purification Committee (Kugŏ Chŏnghwa Wiwŏnhoe) in June 1946, setting guidelines for the publication of textbooks and for written Korean materials in general. The Korean alphabet, a unique indigenous system of writing, became a great source of Korean pride and a symbol of national identity and distinctiveness. It greatly facilitated literacy since it was relatively easy to master, certainly far easier than learning several thousand Chinese characters *(hanmun)*, which had been previously necessary to read a newspaper. Yet mastery of *hanmun* had long been a mark of the educated man and a source of pride for the *yangban* elite, and many Koreans were reluctant to abandon it. The enthusiastic promotion of the Korean alphabet helps to account for the sharp rise in adult literacy rates in the late 1940s and 1950s. At the same time, Japanese-language instruction was replaced by Korean; textbooks and materials were all in Korean; and Korean history, geography, and literature assumed a central role in the curriculum.

The most striking feature of the three-year U.S. military occupation was the enormous expansion of schooling that began at this time. Although the USAMGIK did not receive the support it regarded as necessary to promote democratic education, it nonetheless presided over impressive progress in providing educational opportunity for millions of Koreans. The portals of learning opened wide at all levels. The percentage of children attending primary school may have doubled, from less than 40 percent to more than 70 percent.[27] Secondary education expanded at an even more explosive rate. Only a privileged few received a secondary education before 1945. Within two years, the number of secondary schools grew from 62 to over 250, and total enrollment increased six times.[28] In May 1945, there were 3,039 Koreans attending 1 of 19 institutions of higher learning south of the thirty-eighth parallel, but by November 1947 there were 20,545 students enrolled at 29 colleges and universities.[29] Adult education grew from virtually nonexistent to thousands of schools and programs.[30] The literacy rate rose from an estimated 20 percent for women and 25 percent for men to an official (no doubt inflated) combined rate of 71 percent by the end of 1947.[31]

This achievement is even more striking since there was a severe shortage of teachers and teaching materials. Providing enough teachers to cope with an enlarged educational system on this scale would have been an enormous problem in any case, but the shortage of teachers was further aggravated by the fact that 40 percent of the 13,782 elementary teachers in Korea before 1945 were Japanese and had to be replaced.[32] In addition, many Korean primary school teachers were promoted to secondary schools or placed in administrative posts. To deal with these shortages the occupation government launched crash teacher-training programs; in 1945–1946 about seventy-five hundred untrained teachers participated in in-service training programs. The occupation government also expanded the number of teacher-training (normal) schools during the same period from seven to twelve, and the number of their students increased fourfold.[33]

Providing textbooks was no less a herculean labor. Since most of the existing books were in Japanese, they had to be replaced. Books had to be translated, a suitable national history had to be determined, texts that would teach democratic values had to be written, and a decision had to be made on the extent to which to use *han'gǔl* rather than *hanmun* as a medium of instruction. These challenges were compounded by a paper shortage brought about by the fact that almost all the pulp mills were located north of the thirty-eighth parallel. Nonetheless, under Ch'oe Hyŏn-bae, an impressive array of textbooks was written. Naturally, many of these were hastily done or were merely translations from Japanese and American texts, but at least they served provisionally. With American aid thirteen million of these textbooks were printed and distributed between September 1945 and February 1948.[34]

These achievements cannot be credited to the policies and activities of the U.S. military government alone; they were part of an exuberant rush to literacy that took place once the restrictions on educational opportunities had been removed. As part of this burst of enthusiasm, hundreds of private primary, middle, and secondary schools, as well as institutes of higher learning, were established. Most were poorly equipped and understaffed; some were little more than efforts by unscrupulous operators to take advantage of this educational ardor by collecting tuition for minimum services; others, however, were the work of sincere and patriotic individuals.[35] Literacy campaigns, most organized by individual Koreans, were another testament to the national enthusiasm for learning. During their breaks thousands of students from all sorts of schools went to the cities and the countryside, usually to their hometowns, and set up informal schools to teach adults basic literacy.[36] College students set up "folk schools" (minsok hakkyo) to teach illiterate adults. In May 1947, 8,703 folk schools with 16,095 teachers and 773,677 students were reported. To give adult literacy campaigns some organizational structure and establish minimum standards, the USAMGIK's Department of Education in the spring of 1946 oversaw the creation of Adult Education Boards at local administrative levels. These were supervised through a national headquarters in Seoul made up of local representatives who then oversaw the efforts by millions of Korean adults to achieve literacy.

Where it could, the U.S. military government encouraged and assisted a movement toward mass education that was largely spontaneous. But the Department of Education could hardly keep up with the new schools and educational programs, ranging from informal night schools to private educational foundations (chaedan), that sprang up everywhere. As a result, educational statistics for these years are filled with discrepancies and inconsistencies that make it difficult to gauge the magnitude of educational expansion. In addition, many records were destroyed during the Korean War.

As noted, the years immediately after liberation were characterized by enormous dislocation: vast numbers of Koreans were returning home; many colonial industrial concerns were closing down or operating at reduced capacity because the Japanese war machine they were designed to serve had collapsed; and essential Japanese technicians and managers had left. Out of a population of twenty million, one and a half million were returnees, mostly laborers from Japan, Manchuria, and parts of the former Japanese empire. These included hundreds of thousands who had been forcibly conscripted to work in Japan during the war. An additional one million were returnees from North Korea, where many had gone after Japan invaded China to work in the newly created industrial centers.[37] Thus in 1947 one out of every eight South Koreans, and at least one of every six adults, had recently returned from abroad to a nation that was in economic chaos and marked by leftist agitation and anti-leftist suppression. The dislocations and strains caused by this chaos and the hardships and anxieties it created should not be underestimated. Indeed, the period of social upheaval that had begun in the late 1930s with Japan's wartime mobilization continued with the postwar influx of people, exacerbated by political tensions and violence. Despite these troubles, the post-liberation years were also an era of optimism, patriotism, and hope for the future; there was a feeling that anything was possible. The rush to obtain schooling was part of this optimism.

In some ways the educational policies of the American military in South Korea were highly successful. The USAMGIK Koreanized educational content and promoted new educational concepts that were received with enthusiasm by many Korean educators. Also important for the future development of Korean education was the pattern of close cooperation between Korean and American educators. By far the most dramatic achievement was the growth of formal education. School enrollments increased more rapidly during the three years of U.S. military rule than during any other period. The idea of universal, compulsory education as a basic right was proclaimed and incorporated into the constitution of the new republic. Vigorous literacy campaigns brought at least the first steps of literacy to millions. But the explosive surge in education was due more to the release of pent-up social demand than to any specific official policy or action. The USAMGIK can be said to have contributed to this development only in the sense that it encouraged education, placed no major impediments to its growth, and sought to accommodate the burgeoning population of students.

Many other features of Korean education, such as the emphasis on entrance examinations and the inadequate system of financial support for schooling, were left basically unchanged. Most significant, for all their talk of decentralizing and democratizing schooling, the Americans perpetuated the highly centralized, bureaucratic system of educational administration. The Department of Education (after 1948 the Ministry of Education) in Seoul still controlled curriculum and teacher certification and compiled and approved textbooks. It continued to closely supervise training, and it certified and appointed teachers; it spelled out detailed regulations for all schools, public and private. Virtually all significant decision making was done by the department with little local input. The educational bureaucracy itself was largely staffed by Japanese-trained civil servants schooled in administrative routines of the highly authoritarian and autonomous state created by the colonial rulers. Furthermore, with its preoccupation with political stability and its systematic repression of political opposition, the USAMGIK preserved the coercive habits of the colonial regime. There was a wide discrepancy between the democratic ideals promoted by the state and the often brutal methods of dealing with dissent and removing teachers and others whom the state regarded as destabilizing to the political and social order. This contradiction between democratic ideals and authoritarian practice continued to characterize the South Korean state after its independence.

Despite these discrepancies between democratic theory and authoritarian practice, the USAMGIK had a great impact on South Korean society through its introduction of new ideas on education at a time when the training that most Koreans had received seemed suddenly discredited and irrelevant. American educators were generally well liked by Korean teachers and well received. There was a tremendous surge of enthusiasm and idealism and a great deal of interest in and debate about the American model of education. Progressive educators emphasized child-centered learning and more flexible classrooms that encouraged a questioning attitude among children, in contrast to the authoritative, teacher-centered schooling and the emphasis on rote memorization and choral repetition that had characterized traditional and colonial Korean classrooms. More important, such a system, its advocates argued, would create a more democratic society by avoiding elitism and early tracking and would provide equal opportunity for all students to compete for entry into the uppermost levels of the system. It would also establish local school districts and elected school boards that would both break the vertical lines of control and make the school system less subject to manipulation from the top, as well as provide greater parental and community involvement in the schools.

For several reasons the American influence on Korean education went far beyond the limited efforts to reshape it during the brief three-year military occupation. The USAMGIK efforts were part of a larger pattern of American influence on Korean educational development that had begun with the first American missionaries. Furthermore, the Americans brought with them their optimism concerning the power of education to build a strong, prosperous, democratic society. Koreans responded readily to this optimism because it corresponded to their traditional beliefs in the transformational value of formal learning. When the Americans expressed the belief that education could produce democratic citizens for a democratic society, Koreans could easily agree, for they felt that education could create an ethical and superior man and an ethical, superior society. American beliefs reinforced this pattern of thought, adding a new element—the concept of democratic education. In addition, Americans, whose power had defeated the mighty Japanese empire, offered an example of a successful society that could serve Koreans as a model. In their eagerness to acquire superior knowledge, many Koreans readily accepted the American ideology of politics and education as a source of the wisdom they could draw upon to rebuild their society.

As a result, South Korea in 1948 had two basic models for modern education from which to select: the prewar Japanese colonial model and the American model. It remained for the new Republic of Korea to draw up a fundamental education law that would adopt, reject, or modify these models and to spell out the structure for the new South Korean educational system.

THE DEBATE OVER THE EDUCATIONAL SYSTEM: EDUCATORS AND EDUCATIONAL IDEAS

When South Korea became independent in the summer of 1948, it inherited the old Japanese educational structure slightly modified by the U.S. military government. It also inherited the plans that had been drawn up prior to independence for reforming schooling along the lines of the American system. One of the first tasks of the South Korean government was to decide on the type of educational system that was to serve the nation for the next decades.

The debate centered around two main issues. One was whether to maintain the multitrack, elitist path or to adopt the more open American system that avoided early tracking and in which no type of primary or secondary schooling was terminal. For some Koreans, the American system was a dangerous innovation that would erode standards and hinder the development of a structure suitable for Korean needs. They adhered to specialized, multitracked schooling that would maintain the best of pre-liberation education.

The second major issue was the decentralization of educational authority. Many advocates of the American system also aimed at instituting a system of local school boards. While accepting the need for a strong Ministry of Education (MOE), they hoped to fulfill the ideals of democratic and progressive education by giving some authority to elected school boards. Opponents of decentralized education sought to either limit the role of the education boards as much as possible or not carry out the experiment at all. They argued that the need for a strong, centralized, coherent administration outweighed the need for local authority, and they were unwilling to risk the disorder and incompetency of autonomous local bodies. Moreover, could uniformity of content and standards be guaranteed without central control and supervision? Accompanying this concern was the question of educational autonomy. This meant freeing the MOE and the proposed school boards from the general administrative and coercive organs of the state, in particular the Ministry of the Interior (Naemubu), which controlled both the administration of local government and the police. It also meant creating an educational system in which professional educators would enjoy autonomy in decision making and job security, free from the arbitrary intervention of the noneducational organs of government.

Educators were also concerned about whether and how to adopt American instructional methodology. Would it be suitable for Korea? Would it promote a democratic and prosperous society and moral citizens? And they discussed the type of curriculum that should be implemented. In the public debate on education, however, attention was mainly focused on how much access there should be to higher levels of education and how centralized and uniform the system should be.

Much of the debate occurred in the framework of educational organizations. In 1948, there were three main organizations for the promotion of educational ideas in South Korea: the New Education Research Society (Sae Kyoyuk Yŏn'guhoe), the Korean Education Research Society (Chosŏn Kyoyuk Yŏn'guhoe), and the Culture and Education Association (Munhwa Kyoyuk Hyŏphoe). The first, the largest of these, was organized by advocates of *sae kyŏyuk* (new education). Among its leaders were O Ch'ŏn-sŏk and Yun Chaech'ŏn, who had actively promoted progressive educational reforms during the American military government. Their views were disseminated through *Sae kyoyuk* (New education), the main journal of education after 1948; in workshops for teachers; and in pamphlets, textbooks, and newspaper articles. The leaders felt they were introducing a truly new education, which, with its ideas of child-centered classrooms and individualistic learning, broke with traditional Korean Confucian education. Almost all were concerned with both classroom instruction and democratizing society and felt there was a direct link between the structure of the classroom and society. Virtually every article they wrote on education linked the principle or method that was being discussed with the construction of a democratic society.

The chief secretary of the New Education Research Society was Chu Ki-yong, who also sat in the first National Assembly. Chu was educated in Japan and served as principal of the prestigious Osan Middle School in northern Korea during the colonial period. Chu was not atypical of many Korean educators who had been educated under the prewar Japanese system and had served that system yet who found it easy to cooperate with the Americans. During the military government he served in the Department of Education and championed its educational reform efforts.[38] Shortly after assuming his post as chief secretary of the research society, he summed up its aims as carrying out "educational reconstruction." He contrasted the rigid seating arrangements of the Korean schools in the past, in which each seat obediently faced the teacher, with the flexible seating arrangement of the new Korean classroom, where students moved their seats to face each other, form small groups, work alone, or face the teacher according to situation and need. The classroom was flexible and could be adjusted to individual student needs, just as the new Korean society was to be flexible and based on mutual cooperation while each individual pursued his or her own needs. Although guided by the teacher, students sought solutions to problems, and like citizens of a democratic society, were ultimately responsible for decisions.

While it is clear that the American ideals of progressive education had taken firm root in Korean pedagogical thought, there was a significant difference in educational philosophy between the Korean advocates of progressive education and their American counterparts. Korean educators were almost uniformly concerned with the moral component of education. Chu wrote that "life-centered" education was only one of the two basic principles of *sae kyoyuk*; the other was "morally centered" education. Education must teach democratic values and pragmatic problem solving, but it must also have a moral or ethical basis. The teacher must be an exemplar of moral rectitude, and students must be encouraged to develop their ethical consciousness. A democratic education and a democratic society must be rooted in ethical principles.[39] Chu's position is representative of many Korean educators; new and exciting ideas of education are juxtaposed to more traditional concepts of education as a process of moral cultivation. A progressive's concern for the individual is paralleled by the Confucianist's aim of personal ethical enlightenment.

This blend of Deweyism and Confucianism is also found in the thought of O Ch'ŏn-sŏk, the dominant figure in the New Education Movement. He was typical of the small but influential band of educators who truly understood and wholeheartedly advocated the adoption of American progressive education. O was born in P'yŏngan Province in 1901, the son of a Protestant minister. He spent quite a number of years studying in the United States, attending Cornell and Northwestern universities before completing his doctorate in education at Teachers College, Columbia University.[40] After returning to Korea in 1932, he taught at Posŏng College until his forced transfer to Shanghai in 1941. His background is common to that of many progressive educators: he was from northern Korea, where the hold of tradition weakened most; he was Christian; and he had studied in the West. A pro-Western educational reformer, he was conservative by temperament, a gradualist in his approach to reform, and politically anti-Communist.

O Ch'ŏn-sŏk advocated a single-track, coeducational system of education that would be available to everyone and that would delegate authority to local school boards. Progressive teachers would use their autonomy to provide ample opportunity for individual children to solve problems and make decisions. Since the purpose of education was to create a democratic society, O Ch'ŏn-sŏk argued that "Educators should be crusaders of democratization in our country and secure purification against corruption. . . . Democracy is not a problem of form, but of the mind," and the democratization process must begin with "reform of teachers' consciousness."[41] Teachers must develop democratic ways of thinking, apply these to democratic ways of teaching, and then train a generation of Korean youth in "democratic behavior, values, ideas." Education, as the basis for a democratic, progressive, prosperous society, "cannot be accomplished by law and institutions," but only by developing a "democratic mind" through democratic education.[42] O Ch'ŏn-sŏk was also a supporter of educational autonomy and remained throughout the Rhee regime a strong opponent of central bureaucratic control of education. He thus typified the progressive view of educational policy: egalitarianism, autonomy of teaching personnel, decentralized control, and Deweyism.

O Ch'ŏn-sŏk's concept of "democratic mind" reflected a deeply imbedded idea of education as a form of personal cultivation. Careful not to use Confucian vocabulary since he saw Confucianism as an obstacle to progress, he nonetheless maintained that a democratic education was inseparable from an ethical education, and the "democratic mind" was one attuned to moral principles. His ideal of an educated citizen, like that of most educators, came close to the *yangban* ideal of a learned gentlemen for whom education was also a moral cultivation that would prepare him for leadership in society and earn him the right to be respected.

Not surprisingly, members of the New Education Research Society were usually pro-American. Americans were the liberators of Korean education from the rigidity, formalism, and authoritarianism of Japanese education. Americans had been victorious in the war, and this triumph was considered by many a product of a superior society based on superior educational principles. Kang Kil-su, an active supporter of *sae kyoyuk,* wrote that the "Americans listened to educators' opinions." He introduced the idea of an educational system run by professional educators. American education was free from bureaucratic control; it respected the autonomy of teachers and their professional expertise, and it favored decentralized control. If stiffness *(kyŏngjiksŏng)* was the legacy of colonial education, Kang wrote, flexibility *(yunt'ongsŏng)* was the American alternative. This flexibility would allow for individual freedom and a practical, problem-solving approach to South Korea's reconstruction.[43] All agreed that educational reform was part of the reform of society. Kim Pŏm-nin, a Buddhist scholar who served as the third minister of education, echoed the views of most society members when he wrote that "the basic principle of *sae kyoyuk* . . . is to apply education to the needs of society" and that "education must seek to reform society."[44] Members advocated a democratic reform of society through the new, American-inspired education.

A more nationalist tone was characteristic of the Korean Education Research Society, founded in August 1946 by An Ho-sang, who served as President Rhee's first education minister. An and the other core members—Sim T'ae-jin, Son Chin-t'ae, and Sa-gong Hwan—have been regarded as opponents of *sae kyoyuk,* and their organization during its short existence from 1946 to 1949 promoted more traditional views on education. The society's journal, *Chosŏn kyoyuk* (Korean education), and its editor, Kim Ki-o, emphasized education for national revival.[45] The members were critical of those who borrowed too freely from the United States. Articles in the society's journal frequently expressed resentment at Korea's involvement in the Cold War. Sim T'ae-jin, for instance, urged that Korea develop its own educational system based on its own unique culture and different from either an American or a Soviet system. An Ho-sang argued that *sae kyoyuk* was "simply not appropriate" for Korea.[46] Members of this society put greater emphasis on the ethical content of education and often expressed fears that the new educational reforms would lead to a breakdown of discipline and morality. Han Ch'un-sŏp felt that the rapid elimination of the Japanese language and Japan-centered courses was desirable but that many reforms were being carried out too quickly, causing many problems. He expressed a need for a more cautious approach to educational reform.[47] Too rapid an introduction of liberal, American educational ideals, Sa-gong Hwan felt, was resulting in a lack of discipline. Therefore, moral education needed reinstatement, and education needed restructuring to give teachers greater authority.[48] Sa-gong and others were alarmed by student radicalism, especially at Seoul National University, and by the activities of leftist personnel in Korean schools. Their concern about the breakdown of morals and discipline must be seen in the context of the political tensions of this period. Many openly felt that the tight controls of the Japanese system had to be reinstated in some form to maintain stability. Fear of Communist activity, suspicion of American liberalism, and a concept of education centered on nationalist ideology characterized many of these educators.

An Ho-sang was the main force behind this group and the most prominent of the ultranationalist educators. An is noted for his strain of mystical nationalism, leading one student of this period to label him the "closest thing to a Korean fascist" among the leaders of South Korea.[49] He had spent a good many years studying in Japan, China, Germany, and Britain. His main interest was philosophy; he received a Ph.D. in philosophy from the University of Jena (Germany), which he attended from 1924 to 1929. Before liberation, he taught at Posŏng College and at Hyehwa, the Buddhist college, as well as serving for several years as president of the Korean Philosophical Society.[50] From 1946 he also taught at Seoul National University and worked with Yi Pŏm-sŏk's National Youth Corps *(Taehan Minjok Ch'ŏngnyŏndan)*, the largest of the many youth corps that sprang up in Korea after 1945. He continued as the head of the Korean Education Research Society for about a year after he was named minister of education by President Rhee.

A prolific writer, An Ho-sang sought to create a unique Korean style of political, ethical, and pedagogical thought. Disassociating himself from both the United States and the Soviet Union, he advocated what he called *"hanbaeksŏng-juŭi"* (Korean common peoplism). A kind of democracy with Korean characteristics, it differed from "Soviet democracy," which was focused on social class and advocated violence, and "American democracy," which was designed to provide for each person's self-interest. "American-style democracy is intended to help a person make money," he declared; "it is excessively selfish and shares with Communism a materialistic outlook."[51] *Hanbaekṣŏngjuŭi*, on the other hand, was based on the moral development of the individual in order to benefit the *minjok* (nation or race). Korea must develop its own style of democracy rooted in its history, which, according to An, was based on unanimity, consensus, and the subordination of the individual to the needs of the race. The roots of Korean democracy lie in the ancient Hwabaek aristocratic council of the Silla period (traditionally 57 B.C. to A.D. 935) and the Hwarangdo, the Sillan warrior youth code. Korean education must be aimed at teaching racial and national pride and creating Korean democracy. Korean students must be taught that they are of the same blood *(tongil hyŏlt'ong)*, and each individual must work for the welfare of the race to develop a people's livelihood economy *(minsaeng kyŏngje)* that will transcend social class.[52] To do this, Korean education must free itself from foreign influences:

> After the time of our great ancestor Tan'gun [mythical founder of the Korean people], our history and culture was clear; however, after the mid-Koryŏ, foreign religion and ideas obscured our culture. This became more severe during the Chosŏn period and under Japanese colonialism, and under the American and Soviet military governments our national identity has been divided and eradicated. Since we have our own government, we have to seek out our original national identity, make it the basis of our unification and independence; our education should make us search for our national identity and recover our humanity. Our education should be in accordance with general education [principles] suited for all humanity all over the world.[53]

American education, An felt, was inappropriate for Korea. It was developed for a society that was a "carnival of races" *(injong chŏnsijang)* and therefore not suitable for a racially homogenous society like Korea.[54] Furthermore, American education was devoid of spiritual and moral content. Korean education must "develop the mind and spirit" so that "both the individual and society will be democratic" and true to the Korean identity.[55] An disparaged the advocates of American education, calling them *"mich'in nom,"* a play on words that could mean pro-Americans or crazy guys, while leftists were called *"sogyŏng nom,"* another pun meaning pro-Soviets or blind guys.[56]

An's philosophy is a hodgepodge of national socialism, mystical nationalism reminiscent of that of prewar Japanese ideologues, and Confucian didacticism, with a little of the internationalism that was popular among postwar Korean writers. Although An was a bit eccentric, especially in regard to some of his later flights of ultranationalist fantasy, he shared with many Koreans the desperate search for a clear national identity and purpose and the fear that the unstemmed flow of new and foreign ideas might undermine this search.

Some Korean Education Research Society members were more cautious in their use of the past. Son Chin-t'ae, who was also a member of the Korean Historical Society (Chindan Hakhoe), argued that "we have excessive respect for our predecessors." Koreans had to overcome legacies of class distinction, inequality of women, and disregard for work in order to develop an education and a national history that were free from these legacies of the feudal past.[57] Yet he pointed with pride to Korea's history and rejected the uncritical borrowing from foreigners, which he, along with other members, felt was characteristic of both leftists and "pro-Americans." Most nationalist educators shared this concern of excessive foreign influence, contempt for *sadaejuŭi* (uncritical acceptance of foreign ways), and a search for an ethnically based education that would serve to unify the Korean people.

Paek Nak-chun, a major figure in Korean education, founded the Culture and Education Association, which also championed and popularized *sae kyoyuk*. Paek, although the son of a farmer, had a background similar to O Ch'ŏnsŏk's. A northerner from P'yŏngan Province and a Christian, Paek spent twelve years studying in the United States. He graduated from Princeton Theological Seminary and earned a Ph.D. from Yale University in 1928.[58] After his return to Korea, he served as the head of Sinsŏng Hakkyo, a mission school. During the U.S. occupation, Paek enthusiastically served the Americans and later was full of praise for their efforts in education. The Department of Education, where he served, was, he remarked with pride, "the best organized" branch of the military government. He advocated education to "promote social change" and to create a more democratic society. "The idea of democracy was not systematic or formal." It was a matter of practices and values that began in the classroom, he declared.[59] In the years immediately after the war, Paek's efforts were fully absorbed in promoting the expansion of education and the dissemination of new educational theories and practices, and during the Korean War he served as education minister. While he is considered a progressive and was on comfortable terms with American educators, he also advocated ideas of a nationalist and Korean-centered education that at times resembled those of An Ho-sang. Korean education, he argued, should be based on Korea's own cultural traditions, which, like An, he traced to the Hwarangdo ideal of ancient Silla.[60] "We must practice whole personality education [in'kyŏk kyoyuk]"—that is, ethically based education, where the individual student develops his moral sense in order to serve the nation.[61] Paek advocated a "unification of thought" (sasang t'ongil) that would enable the Korean people to develop their "basic spirit and to teach it to their children." This also meant that education must be uniform in content and quality, a point stressed by most educators.[62] Vague and sometimes mystical, Paek reflected the same fundamentally conservative character and the same desire as An and his supporters to look to tradition in order to find a usable past to combat Communism. Unlike An, however, he was less concerned about the American influence, which he regarded as essentially benign. Throughout the late 1940s and 1950s, Paek was regarded as a progressive force in education, a supporter of sae kyoyuk and liberal democratic ideas. Yet he is a good example of how the divisions between liberal and conservative educators were often blurred.

The tendency of Korean educators to mix progressive education with nationalist concerns and more traditional, Confucian-influenced educational values is illustrated in the thought and activity of Yu Sŏk-ch'ang. Yu, like so many educational reformers, was a northerner from Hamgyŏng Province. He was a member of the first class of the Keijō University Medical School and was later active promoting rural, agricultural, and technical education; a theme of his writings was the need for Korea to develop practical scientific and technical skills in its educational system. This, however, did not prevent Kŏn'guk University, which he founded to promote scientific education, from becoming a predominantly liberal arts institute.

Yu's discussion of education reveals a very strong traditionalist tone. Korean education, he wrote, must develop will (ipchi) in the individual student. This will, which can transform Korea into a strong, prosperous state, is possible only when the student has cultivated "sincerity" (sŏng) and "trust" (in), which make up the two principles of education. In order to develop the spiritual basis for a technically competent, good citizen, education must be 70 percent humanistic and 30 percent practical.[63] Yu's philosophy of education on close examination is less progressive than Confucian. He expresses Confucian confidence in education as a means of individual perfection and faith in the power of that individual perfection to transform society. Despite abandoning his *yangban* ancestors' disdain for the specialist and his pursuit of a medical career, Yu held ideas on education that were more humanistic and generalist than technical or vocational. Indeed, Yu was very much the *yangban*, a generalist whose social status was based as much on his prestigious degree and learning as on his family origins.

South Korean educators had much in common. Part of this was due to the suppression of leftist opposition, which placed limits on the range of views that could be expressed. But more important, almost all Korean educators shared the view that education could produce a prosperous and strong nation. This tremendous faith in education was heavily influenced by the traditional Confucian belief in the role of education in transforming the individual and society; the belief was amplified by the Japanese idea of using education to create a rich and powerful state and American ideals of education for all. In addition, all South Korean writers on education appear to have shared the traditional view of the intellectual and educator as the conscience of the nation and saw education as the legitimate means of selecting the leadership of society. At the same time, they sought to achieve uniformity in educational content. As subsequent events demonstrated, these beliefs were not confined to the elite. At all levels of Korean society there was a faith in education as the basis for creating a new nation and conferring moral, political, and social leadership on those who had studied hardest. This placed the issue of education not on the periphery but at the center of public discourse in the new South Korean state.

CREATING AN EDUCATIONAL SYSTEM

Crucial to the course of educational development was the system of education created in the first three years of the new republic, for it was this structure that provided and promoted the framework for the social demand for schooling in subsequent decades. One of the first tasks of independent South Korea was the creation of a national education law that would lay out the educational system. President Rhee appointed An Ho-sang minister of education in 1948, and one of his ministry's first tasks was to get the new educational system in place by the start of the school year in autumn 1949. A number of preliminary meetings were held by the MOE in late 1948 and early 1949 to discuss the establishment of an education law. An Ho-sang formed a committee of the nation's leading educators, including Paek Nak-chun and O Ch'ŏn-sŏk, in May 1949 to draw up the Basic Education Law (Kyoyuk Kibon-bŏp), which defined the educational system.[64] After a number of revisions, the educators came to an agreement on the basic structure to adopt.[65] The law retained essential features of the American system: the 6-3-3-4-year system; the one-track system, in which students pursued a single curriculum path well into secondary school; and the September to June school year. It also called for the implementation of local school boards, which the military government had proposed the previous year. There was, in fact, little change to the educational structure that had been proposed by the American military government.

Initially, most of the prominent educators embraced the American-style, open system of education. Later, in the late 1950s and 1960s, some, such as O Ch'ŏn-sŏk, would modify their enthusiasm for the educational structure they had helped to create, but few wanted to go back to the Japanese-style system of early and inflexible tracking. Furthermore, almost all supported an institutional structure that would safeguard the independence of teachers and allow some measure of decentralization. Yet when appointed to office, many of these educators loyally served their authoritarian presidents and supervised the highly centralized, often highly politicized educational system.

Enacting the Basic Education Law proved to be more difficult than drawing it up. When the minister of education submitted the proposed law to the National Assembly for discussion and approval on 28 September 1949, he set off a national debate that lasted for one and a half years. Instead of adopting this proposal, the National Assembly's Education and Social Affairs Committee (Mun'gyo Sahoe Wiwŏnhoe) drafted its own law. The committee's draft law maintained the six-year elementary school but established a two-track secondary school system. Three to four years of middle school (chunghakkyo) would be followed by a two-year college preparatory or a four-year higher vocational school (kodŭng sirŏp hakkyo). The latter was seen as terminal, but the preparatory school students could continue on to four years of university or college.[66] This draft proposal was submitted to the main Assembly for debate on 26 October, while the MOE draft was rejected by the Education and Social Affairs Committee for consideration on the main floor. MOE officials and supporters then fought for nineteen months to restore their version of the law, a struggle that was ultimately successful.

The first National Assembly debate over the education law continued for five weeks, from 27 October to 30 November. Conferences were held every morning starting in early November to work out an acceptable bill, but by mid-November the education law had become the main issue in the Assembly, delaying other bills. To expedite matters, afternoon conferences were added.[67] No other single issue occupied so much time in debate during that year. The debate centered on fundamental differences in educational policies. The National Assembly draft essentially resembled the prewar Japanese system, with its early sorting of students into specialized tracks. The MOE version maintained the essential features of the American system, with its single track. There was general agreement on universal, compulsory, six-year elementary schooling but little agreement on any other specifics.

Nationalist feeling ran strong, and proponents of both models were careful in arguing that they were creating a Korean educational system and not implementing a purely borrowed one. Supporters of each version attacked the other for uncritical foreign borrowing. Ironically the stigma of being "Japanese" was attached to both versions. The MOE version was defended as "proper for Korea and because every other country has adopted this system,"[68] while supporters of the National Assembly version attacked the current system as too American and unsuitable for Korea's needs. Framers of the MOE version were accused of merely translating the American-inspired 1947 Fundamental Education Law of Japan. What was needed, critics charged, was a truly Korean educational law, not a copy from another country. Responding to these charges, An Ho-sang, in a newspaper interview, replied that "whether it is American or Japanese, we will adopt whatever is best." The MOE proposal, he added, was "far from being Japanese."[69] In turn, opponents lambasted the National Assembly draft as adhering to the prewar imperial Japanese system. Beneath the nationalist rhetoric, the debate centered on two main issues: whether to maintain the multitrack system or to adopt the more open American system and whether to create a decentralized system with local school boards.

SINGLE VS. MULTITRACK SYSTEM

The most significant difference between the American-model/MOE draft and the Japanese-model/National Assembly draft was the greater emphasis on access to upper levels of education in the former and the more elitist approach to education in the latter. The question of how open the educational system should be at the higher levels became the central issue in the formulation of the education law. Politicians, officials, and educators who argued for separate vocational and academic middle schools asserted that a common, general, three-year middle school was a luxury that Korea could not afford. They further maintained that greater emphasis should be placed on career training. These arguments carried considerable weight in the National Assembly, and by November, there was a strong push for a four-year academic or vocational middle school, followed by a two-year college preparatory school for university-bound students and higher technical schools for vocational middle school graduates.[70] However, practical as these arguments may have been, they ran counter to the broad-based push for access to education now occurring throughout Korea.

A related problem was separated middle and high schools. In the MOE draft, secondary education was divided, American-style, into a three-year middle school and a three-year high school, and any separate channel of education would come only at the high school level. This, however, posed a problem since it would mean that existing secondary schools would have to be separated, leading to a multiplicity of administration. Furthermore, in major cities such as Seoul opposition to separate middle and high schools came from parents who, having succeeded in gaining entry for their children into one of the prestigious middle schools, viewed with dismay the prospect of competing again for entry into an academic high school.

During the subsequent debate no clear agreement could be reached, and a bewildering variety of modifications was proposed. Some suggested maintaining a single-track system but reducing secondary school to four years.[71] Most Assemblymen wanted a single institution of secondary education that would be of two types, academic or vocational; others argued that this would force students to decide upon a career while they were still in elementary school.[72] Supporters of vocational secondary education maintained that there was a need to begin vocational education early and that academic students needed a long, rigorous preparation for college.[73] Many also strongly opposed efforts to eliminate separate middle and high schools. According to American educational theory, the middle school gave children a longer time to develop their abilities and determine where their aptitude and interests were, while in high school adolescents began to select courses suitable for preparation for their life's work. Eliminating the separate stages of middle and higher secondary school for a more career-oriented, single middle school seemed to some a regressive step—especially at a time when Japan was adopting the American system and rejecting the very system that many Assemblymen sought to reimpose in a modified form.

Opposition to the MOE plan was strengthened by the argument that a single, multitrack secondary school system would be far more practical. Led by Yi Yŏng-jun, chairman of the National Assembly Education and Social Affairs Committee, proponents of the National Assembly draft felt that they were building an educational system that would serve the nation's need for high professional standards. Korea required an educational system that would both produce qualified specialists with needed technical skills and ensure that the command posts of the new nation would be guided by only the brightest, most talented, and rigorously trained. Yi expressed fear that educational standards were falling as a result of the rapid expansion of education after 1945. American reformers had reformed too fast, without regard to Korea's situation, ultimately endangering not only intellectual and technical skills, but also the morality and the spirit of the nation.[74]

For the opponents of a multitrack system—principally professional educators such as O Ch'ŏn-sŏk, Paek Nak-chun, Kang Kil-su, and their supporters in the National Assembly and the press—the establishment of a single secondary school instead of separate middle and high schools and the division of post-elementary schooling into vocational and academic tracks would be a painful setback to the creation of a new, democratic, egalitarian society. They feared that this would destroy the principle of equal opportunity, lead to class consciousness, and benefit the rich. "The 4-2 system will aggravate class consciousness. . . . Its enactment will be a mistake," the *Chosŏn ilbo,* the leading morning newspaper, editorialized.[75] Defenders of the two-track system countered that in reality most Korean children, especially those in rural areas, could not afford to attend school, so the "principle of uniform education is only an ideal." In practice, the argument went, Korean education was two-tracked: basic education for the poor and advanced education for the rich. The most rural students could expect beyond primary school was some practical training.[76]

Despite the vocal opposition of most leading Korean educators, such as O Ch'ŏn-sŏk, Kang Kil-su, and Hyŏn Sang-yun (president of Koryŏ University), who all wrote and gave speeches against it, a multitrack, single secondary school system won out. Several factors may help to explain this setback to the more American-style system. Principals and owners of secondary schools did not want to see their institutions divided, especially if this meant placing them under separate administrators. Furthermore, parents and educators disliked the idea of children sitting for two sets of entrance exams.[77] Another factor may be the composition of the National Assembly, which had been elected on 10 May 1948 and consisted primarily of independents and members of minor political organizations. Assemblymen tended to be well educated; more than half were college or university educated, although a tenth of them were without any formal education. Many of the older members had been educated during the late Yi dynasty, but most had received their higher education in Japan or in Korea under Japanese rule. Only one in fourteen had received education in the West, although some had attended Western mission schools. By profession, the largest number came from backgrounds in government service; more than a third had served as civil servants in the Japanese bureaucracy. In the second largest occupational category were educators, who made up about 18 percent of the membership in the Assembly.[78] While most of these educators supported the 6-3-3-4 system, the majority of the other Assemblymen supported a system closer to the one in which they had been educated or that they had administered. Consequently, on 26 November 1949, the National Assembly by a comfortable margin voted for the 6-4-2(4)-4 system: six years of elementary school followed by either a four-year academic middle school or a four-year vocational middle school.[79] Those attending the academic middle schools could attend a two-year college preparatory school and continue on to four years of university. Vocational middle school students could continue on to a two- or four-year technical school, which would be the terminus of their education. Specialized normal secondary schools, under strict national supervision, would serve as still another specialized track for teachers. This system was almost identical to the Japanese colonial system, although middle school had been shortened from five to four years. This was seen by its supporters as a sound practical decision. As one of the authors of this change, Assemblyman Yi Chae-ik explained, "For a poor country like Korea . . . trained persons are needed who can finish education in a very short time."[80]

Further details of the education law debate reveal the centrality of the issue of egalitarian, mass education versus elitist education. For example, many felt that technical education was the key to Korea's modernization; they conceived of a system of practical education that would be flexible enough to accommodate to the needs of different areas and sectors of the economy. The Education and Social Affairs Committee plan envisioned a two-to-four-year higher voca-tional school that would be as practical as possible, even to the extent of using factories and working with private companies.[81] This plan was adopted, but only after fears were expressed that this practical instruction would make it im-possible for vocational students to enter college or university. Yi Yŏng-jun in-troduced one-to-three-year agricultural middle schools, arguing that these would be practical and a move to "improve the problems of previous education, which had been [inappropriately] focused on academic matters."[82] This too was unsuccessfully opposed, in this case by Assemblyman Yi Hang-bal, who argued for a uniform national education that would not place rural students at a disad-vantage if they pursued advanced schooling.[83] Further stressing the need for practical training, the legislators also voted to set up junior colleges (ch'ogŭp tae-hakkyo) to teach advanced technical courses, although there was considerable confusion over how these were to differ from higher technical schools.[84]

Thus, a complex system of technical and vocational training was included in the education law, much to the dissatisfaction of many educators and MOE officials. Not only was the principle of equality being violated, but also voca-tional education itself would suffer, MOE officials insisted. They felt that since students would have to decide at an early age on either a vocational or an aca-demic course and since changing from one course to another would in practice be difficult, few would willingly select a vocational education. Instead the ef-fect would be to reinforce the tendency to hold academic education in high es-teem. As a result, most parents would try to push their children into the academic track, where the potential rewards were greater. Only by integrating vocational and academic education could this be avoided.[85] There was already a problem of the educated unemployed, while basic technical skills were in short supply.[86] Yu Chin-o, one of the authors of the MOE draft, charged that the Assembly version would make it difficult to make education of practical value to the nation and would aggravate the problem of nominalism (kanp'an-chuŭi)—that is, the tendency to enroll in a school for the prestige of its name rather than to receive a useful education.[87] This would encourage elitism and work against the move to democratize Korean society.

Teacher training became another issue of elitist versus mass education. Proponents of the former wanted to maintain the separate teacher-training secondary schools and colleges and set high standards of qualification. Others wanted to integrate the higher normal schools with the universities to create a more liberal atmosphere for teacher training and lower the standards in order to counteract teacher shortages. On this issue, the Basic Education Law of 1949 compromised, creating two-year teacher-training schools *(sabŏm hakkyo)* for middle school graduates and college-level schools that would be open to all secondary school graduates. Instead of highly professional training that would have required six years of post–middle school education (and would have restricted the number of teachers available), primary school teachers needed only two years of specialized training. The college-level training was available for secondary school teachers.

The issue of using *han'gŭl* versus *hanmun* was never resolved. Initially Chinese characters were taught along with the Korean alphabet. In the 1960s and 1970s the state moved toward exclusive use and instruction in *han'gŭl,* but the MOE reversed itself in the 1980s and 1990s, when Chinese characters were again taught along with the Korean alphabet.

EDUCATIONAL DECENTRALIZATION

The American military government had, out of expedience and fear of disorder, run education with the apparatus of centralized control that it had found in place in 1945. Yet, as noted, American educators saw local community control over education as an essential feature of a democratic society. They believed a highly centralized system was vulnerable to authoritarian subversion or manipulation, and they regarded such a system as a major factor in the formation of authoritarian regimes in prewar Germany and Japan. Local school boards would break the vertical lines of control that led to authoritarian societies and would stimulate and democratize education by generating alternative viewpoints on educational policy and implementation. For Koreans excited by the new American ideas on education the introduction of local school boards was a high priority.

The issue of decentralized education was closely linked with the broader issue of local administrative autonomy. These two issues were more than a matter of administration; they were direct attacks on the centralized bureaucratic state that had been inherited from colonial times. Since local autonomy had never been part of Korean political policy or practice, it challenged the nation's traditions. The Local Autonomy Law was first submitted to the National Assembly on 20 August 1948, just five days after independence. On 31 January 1949 a draft law prepared by the Legal and Interior Affairs Committee of the Assembly was submitted to the main floor for debate.[88] The basic proposal of creating local elective bodies that would share some decision making at the local level was generally accepted. The points of conflict over the draft were whether the director of each administrative unit should be appointed or elected, whether elections should be direct or indirect, the extent to which local organs would supervise police, whether local officials could be dismissed by the provincial governors (tojisa) or by the president or members of his cabinet, the exact units of local autonomy, the qualifications of officeholders and voters, and the date of implementation.

The law passed on 15 August 1949 was a limited victory for those who sought to restrict central control. Virtually all local administrative officials were to be elected by the provincial and city councils, including the provincial governors and the mayor of Seoul. The councils were to be directly elected, with few restrictions on officeholders. South Korea's 13 provinces are divided into 115 counties (kun), and these in turn are subdivided into townships (myŏn) and towns (ŭp). The smallest units of local autonomy, at the township and town levels, were to have elected councils, although the administrative heads would be appointed by the Ministry of the Interior. Rhee vetoed the law, and after long debates and negotiations a revised law was passed on 19 August 1949 by which the provincial governor and the county administrator would be appointed by the minister of the interior. The power of local councils to supervise the police was also restricted.[89] Thus under the new system the central bureaucracy through the Ministry of the Interior, which also controlled the police, was still a powerful instrument of local control.

The American-initiated plan based on county-level elected school boards to supervise elementary education and nine provincial boards to supervise secondary education was submitted to the National Assembly on 20 August 1948, the same day that the local autonomy law was proposed. It was incorporated in both the MOE and National Assembly drafts of the education law in 1949. The MOE gave three reasons to the National Assembly for the need for local educational autonomy: to avoid bureaucratic "strict control," to ensure that education was suitable for the community, and to develop a sense of national consciousness in educational policy through popular participation in the administrative process.[90] In the following weeks, during which the local autonomy provisions of the education law were being discussed, supporters of educational autonomy defended the need for local school boards along similar lines. Supporters included An Ho-sang and the staff of the MOE, who argued vigorously for educational autonomy; Yi Yŏng-jun, who led the fight against the MOE draft of the education law; and Yi's successors, Yi Kyu-gap and Kim Sang-han. Educators such as O Ch'ŏn-sŏk, Kang Kil-su, Paek Nak-chun, and Yu Chin-o spoke of the need for democratic education, community involvement in schools (reflecting the influence of Deweyism in the discussions of child-centered, community-centered education), and a school system that was a model of democratic values.[91] Legislators and educators spoke of the need to limit bureaucratic authority and to raise local support for the financing of education.

There was little quarrel with the need for local financial support, as it was generally accepted that the national government did not have the means to fully fund education. Assemblyman Kwŏn T'ae-hŭi spoke of the need to distribute the responsibility of educational administration by creating local organs that "would participate in financial policy making."[92] One of the strongest criticisms of Korean education at that time was directed at the role of the school supporters' associations *(huwŏnhoe),* which had begun under the American military government as a means for raising funds by collecting contributions from parents of school children. The fees of these school-based organizations *(huwŏnhoebi)* had become burdensome and controversial. In June 1949 An Ho-sang had expressed the hope that the creation of local school boards would enable local communities to raise alternative funds and lessen the burden of the *huwŏnhoebi.*[93] The need to find local sources of revenue was highlighted by newspaper reports of a fifteen-year-old girl who committed suicide because her parents could not pay the school supporters' association fees. Local educational autonomy, it was argued, was the most practical means of lessening dependence on the *huwŏnhoebi* for the support of education.[94]

The main argument for local educational autonomy, however, was the need to limit the role of the general bureaucracy in controlling education. Yi Yŏng-jun explained that the creation of local school boards and local educational districts *(kyoyukku)* was "the best means of securing educational administration."[95] The issue was to maintain the administration of the schools in the hands of teachers, educators, and parents and prevent them from becoming instruments for authoritarian control. Only with educational districts could the "general administration"—that is, noneducators—be prevented from "impeding genuine educational administration," future Education and Social Affairs Committee chairman Kwŏn T'ae-hŭi declared; "[we must] ensure a consistency of education that is not subject to change in administration." Germany, Italy, and Japan were cited as examples of the political manipulation of education by a strict central bureaucracy unimpeded by the control of schools by educational personnel and local communities.[96] Furthermore, the creation of local educational districts would, it was argued, promote the security of teachers by protecting them from the political pressures exerted by a central bureaucracy.[97]

The education law implemented county and provincial school boards, with county boards administering primary schools and provincial boards, secondary schools. South Korea's educational system, nonetheless, was still highly centralized. Elections were held in 1952 for county and provincial legislative councils, and these in turn appointed members to the county and provincial school broads.[98] These boards wielded little real influence in the schools and were seen primarily as a means of helping to raise local revenues. Local schools boards were attacked by members of the bureaucracy, who saw them as a wasteful duplication of administration, and they were abolished in 1961. In part, the centralized and somewhat authoritarian traditions of the state worked against a localized system. The lack of commitment to effective local educational autonomy was also the result of what was called the "uniformity of administration."[99] There was a consensus that education should be uniform and standardized in the interest of creating an egalitarian society in which all children would have an equal and fair chance of advancement. Local educational autonomy brought with it fears of discrepancies in educational content and standard. Many Koreans were not enthusiastic about local school boards because they believed that only a uniform, centrally controlled system could ensure equal opportunity for all.

THE EDUCATION LAWS AND THEIR REVISIONS

Three laws—the Basic Education Law, the Basic School Law, and the Social Education Law—were passed at the end of November and promulgated on 31 December 1949. A majority in the National Assembly supported Yi Yŏng-jun and his fellow Education and Social Affairs Committee members, who essentially revised the American-inspired system to one closely resembling the Japanese system before 1945. University was four years and six years for medical students—no change from the American proposal. Regulations for a system of adult schools were established basically along the lines of the MOE draft. More important, the principle of local educational autonomy, somewhat compromised by the indirect method of election and the use of county administrators and provincial governors as chairmen of school boards, prevailed. However, the egalitarian ideal and the 6-3-3-4 system associated with it had been lost. The resultant law disappointed An Ho-sang, the staff of the MOE, the leaders of the KFEA, and the professional educators who had supported the MOE draft. Hyŏn Sang-yun, one of the compilers of the MOE draft, expressed "surprise at the changes from [our] proposal."[100] They had lost to a National Assembly majority that was less responsive to the appeal for radical educational reform than MOE education officials.

Contributing to this setback was the fact that the National Assembly was on increasingly bad terms with President Rhee and his administration. Although neither Rhee nor his prime minister, Yi Pŏm-sŏk, actively promoted the bill, tensions between the administration and the National Assembly certainly did not make passage of the education law easier. Elements of the bureaucracy were also opposed to the MOE draft. During the debate over the education law, the MOE draft was discussed before the State Council, the forum for meetings between the prime minister and other cabinet members; the MOE draft was supported only after heated discussion. The Ministry of the Interior objected to the local school boards and argued that these would interfere with the "uniformity of administration." Resistance came also from the minister of finance, who regarded the system as too ambitious and costly.[101] In fact, the most serious problem not addressed by the framers of the Basic Education Law was how an impoverished nation could finance an ambitious system of public education. There was a wide acceptance of the financial limitations of the national and local governments and the need for tuition at post-elementary schools and voluntary contributions at all levels. Although some critics complained of the lack of adequate measures for educational finance, the problem of financial support was not taken up.[102]

Unhappy with the rejection of its original plan, the MOE almost immediately set out to revise the education law. With the support of the KFEA, a series of meetings was held in each province. These meetings organized special committees to lobby for the revision of the law (hakche sujŏng simŭi-hoe), urging the restoration of the 6-3-3-4 system.[103] On 9 February 1950, proposed revisions—

that is, the original MOE draft—were resubmitted to the National Assembly. At that time, Kwŏn T'ae-hŭi, the new chairman of the Education and Social Affairs Committee, came out in support of most of the revisions, suggesting that high school be made uniformly three years, that entrance to high school be limited to those who had completed a three-year middle school, and that the opening day of school be changed to 1 September. An Ho-sang then elaborated on the need to create a uniform educational system.[104] In the ensuing debate, supporters of the proposed revisions argued that the overriding principle had to be equal opportunity for educational advancement. Even though the three-year high schools would be divided into academic, technical, agricultural, and fishery schools, students enrolled at any high school should be allowed to sit for the university entrance exams. All should take a common core of courses that would prepare them for that exam. Supporters of multitrack secondary schooling cited Germany, with its bifurcation of secondary education into *real-schule* and *gymnasium,* as an example of professional excellence and a realistic approach to schooling. They also spoke of the need to limit university enroll-ment to the numbers the economy could absorb. They feared that there was already a surplus of college graduates.[105] In the end, attacked as elitist and un-progressive and as harking back to the discredited system that Japan itself had repudiated, the multitrack system was rejected, and the upper-level secondary school system was revised. In place of the two-year college preparatory school and the two-to-four-year higher technical school, the MOE proposal for a uni-form three-year high school *(kodŭng hakkyo)* was approved on 9 February 1950. The new system was 6-4-3-4: six years of primary school, four years of middle school, three years of vocational or academic high school, and four years of college or university. Consistent with the emphasis on equal opportu-nity, legislators dismissed a suggestion by Kwŏn that the high school entrance exam be limited to middle school students.[106]

But the MOE was not totally successful. It failed to reduce the four-year middle school to an American-style three-year middle school, and it also failed to retain the 1 September school year opening introduced by the Americans. Consequently, efforts to further revise the education law were carried on after the outbreak of the Korean War (25 June 1950). When in February 1951 the Na-tional Assembly met in Pusan, the temporary capital, debate on the education law briefly resumed. On 19 February three revisions were suggested: a reduc-tion of the four-year middle school to three years, a reduction of junior college from four to two years, and the return to a 1 September opening day. This time, only the last and least important part failed, with the school year continuing to start on 1 April (later this was changed to 1 March). Supporters of the 6-3-3-4 system prevailed. Now every major aspect of the MOE draft had been put into law except for the September to June school year.[107] In short, professional educators in the MOE and in the KFEA and other supporters of the American model had succeeded in incorporating most elements of that model into the formal structure of the South Korean school system.

The final outcome reflected the fact that most leading educators supported the concept that education should be uniform and broadly accessible. Even An Ho-sang, a strong opponent of what he felt was an uncritical acceptance of American ideology, believed in as much access to the higher levels of education as possible, and he was willing to support other "American" features of the education draft for this purpose. He accused the adversaries of the MOE draft of seeking to perpetuate the evils of the restrictive Japanese system, which had kept Koreans backward, and he was suspicious of vocational tracking that assigned children to an intellectually inferior education. The uniformity of the American system, he declared, was conducive to national unity and the "unification of the Korean spirit and mind." He remained, however, an opponent of American educational methods and the excessive reliance on translated American textbooks and materials.[108] The MOE version of the education law was also promoted by rallies organized by the KFEA. The prestige of these professional educators and their persistent efforts after their initial setback may have been instrumental in convincing enough Assemblymen to support the MOE's proposal. Conspicuous in the debate was the lack of any clear direction from either Rhee or Prime Minister Yi Pŏm-sŏk, neither of whom appeared to have held a clear and consistent vision of education for the nation. Considering Rhee's weak support in the Assembly, his lack of support for the new educational system probably did little to hamper its acceptance. Furthermore, the adoption of the American system was at least partly accounted for by the prestige of the United States at this time in Korea and by the fact that the Japanese were instituting similar reforms themselves.

Most important, the MOE's call for a single-track system and broad access to education reflected the general desire of most of the articulate Korean public. All the major papers, including the *Tonga ilbo*, the leading evening paper, and the *Chosŏn ilbo*, supported the MOE's proposed educational system. The press in turn reflected its urban, middle-class readers, who placed high priority on educational opportunities for their children. With all seats in the National Assembly up for election in the spring of 1950, this popular demand could not be entirely ignored. Later the broad support for the open educational system reasserted itself when attempts by successive governments to limit access to higher education and reintroduce tracking ran into intense public opposition.

Although much of the bureaucracy and the National Assembly were sympathetic with the more elitist approach, open access to higher education won out because it seemed progressive and in tune with the popular aspirations for educational opportunity. Moreover, the arguments for restricting access to higher education and limiting schooling to suit Korea's economically backward condition were generally rejected as compromising the goal of establishing a fully modern and advanced educational system. Above all, attempts to create a more elitist system ran counter to the Korean people's desire for educational opportunity. Whatever the immediate prospects for most Koreans were, the hope of advancement up the ladder of success was not to be denied.

3 Expanding the Educational System

The restructuring of education that took place in the years immediately after the end of colonial rule facilitated and shaped an explosive growth of schooling. No feature of South Korea in the decades after 1945 is more striking than the rapid expansion of education at all levels. Hundreds of elementary and secondary schools and scores of colleges and universities were established within a decade, and schooling continued to grow impressively thereafter. A country in which fewer than one in twenty adults had a secondary education, the majority had no formal schooling at all, and relatively few trained teachers and virtually no research facilities existed, became one of the world's most literate nations, with universal primary and middle school education, highly trained teachers, and enrollments at the tertiary level approaching most advanced industrial nations. Educational development was interrupted by the Korean War but continued through the corruption and economic stagnation of the Rhee regime, the revolution that overthrew him, and the military regimes that governed the country from 1961 to 1987.

The pattern of educational development remained fairly consistent as well, despite the change of governments and external and internal crises. Public policies concentrated on achieving universal and uniform standards first at the primary and then at the middle school levels before actively promoting the expansion of higher tiers of schooling. Thus, education was developed sequentially. Fairly high standards of professionalism among the teaching corps that had been characteristic during colonial times were maintained and enhanced, even though the demand for teachers strained the capacity of the nation's pedagogical institutions. A rigorous and uniform national curriculum was created in the mid-1950s and adhered to thereafter. South Korean education was also characterized by a high degree of internal efficiency. Once students enrolled in school, they stayed in school, progressed through the grade levels, and graduated on schedule. Constant efforts were made to make access to schooling equally available and the schools themselves equal in standard.

EMPHASIS ON PRIMARY EDUCATION

Among developing nations, few have placed more emphasis on sequential development than South Korea. First devoting its limited resources to the primary level, the state then shifted its focus in the 1960s and 1970s to establishing universal middle schools and then to making high school education available to all. This devotion to sequential development was accompanied by a policy of making schooling at the basic levels not only universal, but also uniform in standard and content. This had important consequences for the national preoccupation with schooling, for it meant that the opportunity for advancement to higher levels of education was fairly open to all children.

The policy of sequential development began in 1948. While the U.S. military government promoted education at all levels, the Rhee administration (1948–1960) gave priority to establishing universal primary education. Unlike secondary or higher education, it was to be exclusively public; from 1948 South Korean law prohibited private elementary schools. The state's commitment to providing basic education began at the inception of the Republic of Korea. Article 16 of the Korean Constitution declared elementary education universal and compulsory, and a few weeks after independence the administration informed the National Assembly that it was devising a program to bring about universal primary education.[1] In 1949 the administration announced a six-year plan for universal primary education. Under this plan, the state was to undertake an ambitious program of classroom construction, teacher recruitment and training, and enrollment campaigns that would expand primary school enrollment until it reached around 95 percent of the elementary-school-age population in 1956. The outbreak of the Korean War derailed the plan just as it was getting under way, but the commitment to primary education remained.

The number of students entering primary school grew rapidly during the republic's first two years. Parents were eager to send their children to school, but parents and officials confronted a shortage of teachers, facilities, and funds. To alleviate the lack of trained teachers, the MOE conducted massive teacher-training programs, which, along with the work done under the supervision of American advisers at the Seoul National University Teacher Training Center, made some headway toward solving the problem. Meanwhile, the shortage of classrooms and teachers resulted in double and even triple class shifts. As a result, teachers at some schools taught from early in the morning until well into the evening. Classes were often huge, with as many as one hundred or more, so that a single teacher conducting more than one class a day was responsible for an enormous number of students. Any available space could serve as a classroom. For example, schools were authorized to use factories and buildings of the many former Japanese properties that were now under government care.[2] As for the problem of funds, the government counted on the help of the school supporters' associations. Individual schools also relied on a variety of other fees and "contributions." This meant that parents were largely responsible for financing their children's education. Passing the cost of education on to the families was from the beginning a basic feature of South Korean education.

Despite the setback of the Korean War, considerable progress was made toward the goal of universal primary education. At the start of the 1950 academic year, 2,426,000 boys and girls were enrolled in elementary schools. There was a drop in enrollment during the Korean War, although it is difficult to determine how much. Figures for the war are not reliable because students were scattered and displaced, and many schools operated on a makeshift basis, making accurate compilation of attendance difficult. But it is clear that the rapid expansion of primary education that began in 1945 continued up to the eve of the war.

While the state took the initiative in implementing universal basic education by declaring it compulsory in the Basic Education Law of 1 December 1949, the success of the Rhee government toward achieving this goal was due as much to public pressure as to state initiative. There was a general consensus for the need to achieve universal primary education and universal literacy as soon as possible. Urban Koreans of all social classes were anxious to place their children in school, while residents in even the remotest rural areas embraced educational opportunities for their children with considerable enthusiasm. Strikingly, among a still largely rural, illiterate, or semiliterate population there was an absence of any resistance to sending children to school. School officials seldom had a problem recruiting students; even the idea that daughters were entitled to some basic education was generally accepted. The main problem was expanding educational facilities and training sufficient teachers to meet demand.[3]

As early as 1949, there were complaints that Rhee was not working hard enough on implementing universal education, and throughout the 1950s a persistent theme of the press was that the administration was not doing enough to construct primary schools. The classroom shortage was greatly aggravated by the Korean War. With the help of the UN Korea Reconstruction Agency (UNKRA), which began operations in late 1952, and a host of U.S. military and civilian agencies, the rebuilding and repairing of schools proceeded rapidly from 1952 through 1955, and a number of new school buildings were constructed. The pace of recovery, however, was widely criticized at the time by the Korean press as too slow, and the problems of overcrowding were horrendous. An impatient press in late 1953 also criticized the MOE for being slow in reviving the Six-Year Compulsory Education Plan. "Koreans need elementary schools," and they need a "new compulsory education plan," the *Tonga ilbo* editorialized in October 1953.[4] In response, the minister of education drew up a new six-year compulsory education plan and submitted it to the National Assembly in early 1954. It was quickly approved. Under the plan, enrollment would reach 88.84 percent of all students of primary school age in 1954, increasing to 91.76 percent in 1955 and 96.13 percent by 1959. The plan called for classrooms to be expanded at the rate of four thousand a year and educational personnel to increase at a faster rate than enrollment so that there could be a reduction in class size. In preparation for the plan, campaigns to register children were launched throughout the country under the supervision of the local school boards. Teachers were asked to go around the neighborhoods to make sure that parents registered their children. Stands were set up in marketplaces to publicize the registration procedures, and in some cases volunteers were asked to make surveys of neighborhoods and report the names of children missing from the registration lists.[5]

Compulsory education largely adhered to the six-year plan, and elementary enrollment increased at an annual rate of about 6 percent from 1954 to 1959, from 2,678,374 in 1954 to 3,549,510 in 1959 (see table 1). The earlier figures include students somewhat older than seven years of age who had missed earlier opportunities to enroll. But by 1960, the overwhelming majority of students who were enrolling were seven-year-olds, the proper age. In terms of meeting its goal of enrolling 96 percent of primary-school-age children by 1959, the Six-

Table 1. School Enrollments in Korea, 1945–1960 (in 1,000s)

Year	Primary Schools	Middle Schools	Academic High Schools	Vocational High Schools	Higher Education
1945	1,366	53	16	12	8
1946	2,159	81	25	19	10
1947	2,183	129	40	29	14
1948	2,426	181	56	41	—
1949	2,771	210	64	48	—
1950	2,658	249	76	57	—
1951	2,073	174	53	40	—
1952	2,369	312	59	74	31
1953	2,259	324	86	93	38
1954	2,679	420	113	111	63
1955	2,947	475	142	123	78
1956	2,997	459	154	135	90
1957	3,171	440	156	128	84
1958	3,316	398	159	120	74
1959	3,358	472	161	110	76
1960	3,662	529	164	99	93

Source: Republic of Korea, MOE, *Mun'gyo t'onggye yoram,* 336–339.

Note: As middle and high schools were combined between 1945 and 1951, enrollments were not reported separately. The figures shown here are estimates given by McGinn et al., 132.

Year Compulsory Education Plan was largely successful at the first-year level. When all six grades are taken into consideration, the figure is closer to 87 percent. The figure was higher for boys and lower for girls. Yet enrollments of girls increased even faster than those for boys. In 1953, 1,385,376 boys and 873,937 girls were enrolled in primary school, but by 1960, this gap had narrowed to 1,976,881 and 1,644,386 respectively. The rate of dropouts was extremely low. By 1960 over 90 percent of students enrolled in primary school would progress orderly through the six grades.[6]

In the early 1960s, the government of President Park Chung Hee sought to make that figure 100 percent. The First Five-Year Educational Development Plan (1962–1966) had as a major objective the completion of universal education. Primary school enrollments went from 3,855,000 in 1961 to 5,749,000 in 1970, by which time enrollment in all six years was virtually universal (see table

Table 2. GDPs and School Enrollment Ratios in Selected Countries, 1960

Country	GDP/ Capita ($)	Primary Schools	Secondary Schools	Higher Education
Korea	155	96	29	4.7
Ecuador	216	81	11	2.6
Egypt	129	58	16	4.7
India	—	61	17	1.2
Iran	—	39	11	.9
Iraq	216	51	19	2.0
Morocco	164	39	5	.5
Pakistan	68	34	9	1.4
Paraguay	164	62	10	2.6
Peru	208	81	18	4.1
Philippines	175	91	29	10.8
Thailand	—	84	13	1.9
Turkey	190	67	14	2.9
Venezuela	1,043	100	23	4.0

Sources: McGinn et al., 64, 150–151; International Monetary Fund, *International Financial Statistics* 14 (January 1961).

Note: Enrollment ratios are based on the percentage of school-age population enrolled in the first grade of each level. The validity of comparisons is limited by differences in school systems. For example, in Thailand primary school is generally four years. Also, the above does not factor in the unusually low dropout rate among Korean pupils.

2 for a comparison of Korean GDP and enrollments with other selected countries). Thereafter, a new demographic trend alleviated the problem of providing primary education. In the 1960s, the regime pursued a vigorous and successful family planning policy, and birthrates dropped sharply, resulting in smaller numbers of children of primary school age after 1970 and declining enrollments.

The problems in bringing about universal primary education were considerable. The situation in Suwŏn, a city thirty kilometers south of Seoul, in 1953 provides one example. Many schools had been closed during the fighting that raged around the city during the Korean War; these were all reopened by 31 December 1952, although in many cases without functioning buildings. Not only had many educational facilities been damaged or destroyed, but also the

number of students in the schools had doubled, partly due to the large number
of people who had moved into the city during the war. For instance, in one
school, Sinch'ung Hakkyo, the enrollment was three times the prewar number
even though some of its classrooms were unusable. Classes here, as elsewhere,
were conducted in the streets. Students met wherever they could; in one case a
match factory was serving double duty as an elementary school. Since the
number of students in a single class could be over one hundred, teachers frequently preferred to hold instruction outdoors if the weather permitted. Textbooks and materials were in short supply, and most classrooms lacked
blackboards. Some classrooms consisted simply of *kamani* (straw bags used for
rice) spread on the ground. Some students could not attend full time, as they
were needed to help their parents financially, earning income by such means as
selling tobacco in the streets. But schoolteachers reported that parents could
usually be persuaded to send their children to school often enough so that they
would not fall behind in their studies. Children were also asked by their teachers to report any friends not attending school. This procedure was successful in
locating and registering such children. A reporter interviewing children at
some of Suwŏn's schools in late 1953 found them taking their studies seriously
and said that most of them expressed hopes of pursuing further education.[7]
Conditions improved somewhat in the late 1950s, but well through the 1960s
South Korean elementary classes remained among the largest in the world.

In part, the Rhee administration's emphasis on primary education was for
economic reasons: primary education was less expensive to implement, needing
simpler facilities and less highly trained teachers. In arguing the need for limiting compulsory and free education to the primary level and devoting the major
portion of the educational budget to elementary schooling, officials both within
and outside of the MOE repeatedly made the case that in a nation as poor as
South Korea, with among the lowest per capita incomes of any independent state
and with a population that was still mostly rural and agricultural, the state could
not afford to do otherwise. Indeed, an argument that had been raised against the
adoption of the American system of education was that it would encourage the
unbridled expansion of costly and unneeded higher levels of schooling.

The state policy prioritizing primary education was also justified with the
slogan "uniformity of education." This, in part, meant that the principle of
equal opportunity necessitated that all young Koreans have access to at least the
first rung of the educational ladder. Political factors also played a part. The

South Korean state presided over a turbulent society and a divided peninsula, where its legitimacy was challenged by a rival regime to the north. The Rhee regime was determined that the national educational system encompass the entire school-age population as soon as possible in order to instill loyalty to the new state and to extend the state's authority into every village and neighborhood. The state needed a broad-based educational system that would embrace all young people, socializing them into good citizens of the Republic of Korea. Universal primary education, seen in this light, was useful for state control over society. Furthermore, the drive toward universal primary education had a momentum of its own, reaching back to the state initiatives of the late 1930s, when the colonial regime committed itself to a systematic expansion of basic education. From 1938 to 1948, primary schooling was expanding continuously, and already by 1948, the framers of the new state had made the goal of universal primary education a promise incorporated into the constitution. The tensions that created instability in South Korea in the first two years of its independence and the Korean War only underlined the need of the state to legitimize itself by fulfilling that promise while strengthening the state in the process.

SECONDARY AND HIGHER EDUCATION

Secondary education expanded at a rapid rate, but unlike the case of primary education, this was as much the result of private as state initiative, especially during the first years of the new state. Half of all new secondary schools opened at this time were private. Indeed, the task of the Rhee administration was as much to control the growth of secondary and higher education as it was to promote it. Overall middle school enrollment grew nearly fivefold between 1945 and 1950, from 53,000 to 249,000. After the Korean War it grew rapidly again, although not at quite the same explosive rate. Middle school enrollment rose from 293,286 in 1952 to 480,295 in 1955 and then slowed as the number of older students who flooded into middle school at the end of the Korean War declined. Enrollment increased again in the late 1950s, reaching 528,593 in 1960 (see table 1).[8] By this time, most of the students entering middle school were entering directly from elementary school. This meant that students in each grade were of the same age, an important factor for consolidating class bonds in a society with strong age-based deference levels.

Middle school enrollment grew by about 8 percent a year from 1952 to 1960. High school enrollment followed the same pattern. After an initial four-fold increase in the five years between liberation from Japan and the Korean War, the rate of growth slowed but still doubled: from 133,000 in 1952 to 263,000 in 1960. Still more rapid after the Korean War was the expansion of higher education, where enrollment grew from 31,000 in 1952 to 93,000 in 1960.[9] When school enrollment as a percentage of the corresponding age group is taken into account, the figure for middle schools is 21.4 percent in 1953 and 33.3 percent in 1960; for high schools, 12.4 percent in 1953 and 19.9 percent in 1960; and for higher education, 3.1 percent in 1953 and 6.4 percent in 1960.[10] Even though the administration gave priority to primary education, the enrollments at the secondary and higher educational levels were in 1960 quite high for a nation at South Korea's level of economic development.

While government policy concentrated on primary education, secondary and especially tertiary education were to a great extent privately funded and organized. Private foundations established many schools at the post-primary level. Throughout the history of South Korea privately owned schools have accounted for 40 to 50 percent of all secondary schools. In general, the higher and more prestigious the level of schooling, the greater the share of enrollment in private institutions. For example, in 1945, 37,000 students were enrolled at public academic schools in grades nine through twelve, while 12,000 were enrolled at private schools. But by 1960 public and private academic high schools each had about 80,000 students. In contrast, in the fall of 1945 only 14,000 boys and 11,000 girls were attending privately owned elementary schools, compared with 904,000 boys and 429,000 girls in public institutions at that level. Under Rhee, the modest role of private primary education diminished further until 1960, when only 3,000 boys and 4,000 girls were enrolled in private elementary schools, accounting for less than 1 percent of total enrollment (see table 3).

Under the Park regime the process of universal primary education was nearly completed, and government efforts to promote education gradually shifted to the secondary level. In 1961, the government announced its plan to extend universal compulsory education to nine years. As a first step in this direction, the MOE announced that it would abolish the middle school entrance examinations in 1963. This, however, was abandoned during the first year of the First Five-Year Educational Development Plan as it was obvious that the number of middle schools would be inadequate. In fact, compulsory education

Table 3. Private and Public School Enrollments in Korea,
1945 and 1960 (in 1,000s)

School Enrollment Category	Male/Female Enrollments	
	1945	1960
Public elementary	904/429	1,966/1,633
Private elementary	14/11	3/4
Public middle	—	262/62
Private middle	—	137/66
Public academic high school	19/18	51/30
Private academic high school	7/5	54/26
Public vocational high school	20/NA	64/3
Private vocational high school	4/1	23/5

Source: Sŏul Kyoyuk T'ukpyŏlsi Wiwŏnhoe, Taehan kyoyuk yŏn'gam 4294 [1961], 348.

remained limited to six years, but middle schools expanded rapidly after the abolition of the middle school entrance examination in 1968. Within a decade middle school enrollment was virtually universal, and the state began shifting its efforts at expanding high school education.

The number of middle school students swelled four times between 1961 and 1980. The proportion of students of middle school age in middle school grew from 33 percent in 1960 to 95 percent in 1980, with the sharpest increase in the 1970s. By 1995, it had reached 99 percent. Secondary enrollment increased five and a half times between 1960 and 1980. In 1961, only one in five adolescents of high school age was attending school, but by 1980, nearly two-thirds were; again the steepest increase in enrollment was in the 1970s. High school enrollments grew steadily, if less dramatically, thereafter, reaching 90 percent by the late 1990s (see table 4).

Colleges and universities mushroomed in South Korea in the two decades after liberation due to public demand, not government policy. In 1948 private schools accounted for about two-thirds of the total higher education enrollments; this figure held in the 1950s despite the establishment of the national university system in the years immediately after the Korean War. By 1958, thirty-eight private colleges and universities had been established.[11] In 1960, 50,000 men and 14,000 women were attending these private institutions, while 30,000 men and 2,000 women were attending the public institutions.[12] In keeping

Table 4. School Enrollments in Korea, 1961–1995 (in 1,000s)

Year	Primary Schools	Middle Schools	Academic High Schools	Vocational High Schools	Higher Education
1961	3,855	621	180	102	134
1965	4,941	751	254	172	106
1970	5,749	1,318	315	275	201
1975	5,749	2,026	648	474	297
1980	5,599	2,471	932	764	615
1985	4,856	2,782	1,266	885	1,277
1990	4,868	2,275	1,490	810	1,490
1995	3,905	2,481	1,246	911	1,756

Sources: Republic of Korea, MOE, *Kyoyuk t'onggye yŏnbo* [Statistical yearbook of education], 1971, 1981, 1996 (Seoul: Mun'gyobu).

with the state policy of sequential development, South Korean policymakers sought to control enrollments. Nonetheless, by the 1990s two out of five South Korean youths were entering college from high school, and this figure was still rising at the end of that decade.

In the long run, the state emphasis on basic education eliminated the sharp disparities among regions and social classes that often characterize developing nations. It contributed to social cohesion and provided a literate workforce with the skills needed for a newly industrializing economy. It generated strains between the demand for higher education and the state's efforts to prevent an oversupply of advanced degree holders. Coupled with an educational system in which no point was terminal, it meant that the possiblity for educational advancement was open to a wide spectrum of the nation's youth. However, it made competition fiercer for the restricted entry into the higher educational tiers, adding to the intensity of South Korea's "education fever."

TEACHER TRAINING

South Korean education not only expanded rapidly, but also improved qualitatively due to the efforts to improve teacher standards. Foreign observers in the late 1940s and early 1950s were very critical of the qualifications of Korean teachers since most had little or no teacher training. Few elementary school teachers had more than a secondary education, and teacher education reflected the inevitable compromise with standards that had to be made as a result of the accelerated growth of post-liberation Korea and the loss of a sizable portion of experienced teachers when the Japanese returned to their homeland.[13] In 1952, only 1.5 percent of secondary teachers had a college education, and only 0.1 percent of primary school teachers were graduates of a college or university. Though typical of developing nations, these figures fell far short of the training levels found in industrialized countries. The UNESCO–UNKRA Educational Planning Mission to Korea, for instance, felt that all teachers should have at least a high school education and a minimum of one year of college.[14]

With assistance from the United States, the South Korean government began a sustained effort at upgrading teacher standards immediately after the Korean War. In 1953, a U.S. educational mission worked with the MOE to launch a three-year project for in-service teacher training; by the end of 1955, 18,300 out of 59,365 teachers had participated.[15] In January 1954, the MOE announced a plan to upgrade all teachers' schools to two-year colleges.[16] Two months later, the MOE announced that all graduates of teachers' colleges would be required to serve as teachers.[17]

Under regulations set up by the MOE in the early 1950s, teachers were licensed as first-class qualified or quasi-qualified. First-class qualification required three years' experience plus a degree from a teachers' high school or college. From 1951 elementary teachers had to have a degree from a teachers' high school; middle school teachers, from a two-year teachers' college; and high school teachers, from a four-year teachers' college. Teachers who lacked these qualifications were quasi-qualified and could earn first-class qualification if they took 180 hours of teacher training and passed an examination. Assistant principals needed to be qualified teachers and in addition had to take 120 hours of administrative workshops or have at least five years' teaching experience. But the rule was flexible, and any administrative experience could be substituted. A principal was expected to have served as a vice-principal first. Principals and vice-principals who lacked these qualifications could be appointed with the approval of the MOE and the recommendation of the Central Board of Education if they possessed "profound knowledge and high character."[18] Though this opened the way to political appointees, for the most part a high degree of professionalism was maintained in educational administration at these levels.

Initially, the MOE exertions centered on gradually enforcing these rules and graduating teachers into the first-class category. By 1957, there was an increasing correspondence between the technical qualification of teachers and reality. Earlier, for the sake of expediency, teachers were appointed without the proper qualifications. For most of the older educational staff, who were trained under the exacting standards of the Japanese imperial system (in which surprisingly high standards were maintained—that is, relative to the level of development of Korea at that time), this was a matter of serious concern. Older teachers constantly bemoaned the lowering of teacher standards. Yet by the late 1950s, standards were being raised at impressive rates as the schools were closely adhering to qualifications regulations.[19] For example, before 1957, about three hundred teachers a year were being certified as first class through the examination, but after 1957, there was a sharp drop in the number passing the exam. The exam itself became increasingly competitive; in 1951, 15 percent who sat for it passed, but in 1957 only about 4 percent of the candidates were successful. Most teachers entering the schools were holding the proper degrees for their job.[20]

The improvement in teacher qualification can be seen in a comparison of statistics from 1952 and 1964 (see table 5). The proportion of elementary teachers with at least a two-year college degree increased from 1.6 to 15.8 percent. Of particular note is that all primary school teachers were required to be at least high school graduates, a standard that many nations at South Korea's economic level failed to maintain. At the secondary level in 1952 only 20.6 percent of middle school teachers and 23.7 percent of high school teachers had four-year university degrees, but by 1964 this had increased to 53.0 and 79.3 percent respectively.[21] These figures represent a substantial accomplishment, especially when the enormous expansion of schools is taken into consideration.

It was possible to improve teacher standards in part because teaching remained a profession that attracted many of the nation's educated young people. This was true in spite of low wages. In 1956, salaries for primary and secondary teachers averaged about 21,000 to 22,500 hwan (1950s currency) a month (about $42 to $45 at the artificially high official rate) and a weekly rice allowance of about one-fifth of a liter per member of the teacher's family.[22] This was less than enough to provide basic subsistence, and even though PTA fees and "gifts" from parents supplemented their incomes, most teachers found it necessary to take outside jobs, most often private teaching.[23] Yet teaching was a highly respected profession. The prestige of the teacher was part of Korea's cultural heri-

Table 5. Educational Attainment Levels of Korean Teachers: Percentages with Two Years/Four Years of College, 1952–1995

Teaching Category and Attainment	1952	1964	1970	1975	1980	1985	1990	1995
Elementary school								
Two years	1.6	15.8	31	44	50	67	79	—
Four years	.1	3.7	8.3	5	6	8	30	48
Middle school								
Two years	63	90	90	93	94	98	99	99
Four years	20	53	66	78	82	88	92	94
Academic high school								
Two years	74*	93*	99	90*	96	96	99	99
Four years	23*	79*	80	85*	90	92	95	98
Vocational high school								
Two years	—	—	82	—	96	95	99	—
Four years	—	—	75	—	81	88	90	—

Sources: 1952 and 1964 from McGinn et al., 52; other years from Republic of Korea, MOE, *Kyoyuk t'onggye yŏnbo,* 1970, 1975, 1980, 1985, 1990, 1995.

* Includes combined percentages from academic and vocational high schools.

tage and was reinforced by the Japanese. Many Koreans found it a source of pride to have teachers in the family and encouraged their children to pursue teaching as a career. Long held ideas on the honorable role of teachers in society contributed to the attraction of teaching and aided in the development of Korean education in much the same way that the historically rooted belief in education as a marker of status contributed to the enlargement of the school system. Two additional factors in the late 1950s also aided in attracting young, college-educated people into teaching. One was the diminishing job prospects for the increasing numbers of college students graduating into a stagnant economy; the other was the decision by the administration in 1958 to postpone military service for students entering teacher-training colleges. (They were then required to teach upon graduation.)[24] In spite of low wages, poor treatment by administration officials, problems of security, and the continued discrimination against women, teaching was a popular career choice.[25]

Extensive in-service training programs brought less well-educated teachers up to the new standards and enabled most teachers to keep up with educational trends. From 1967 in-service training became greatly systematized, with regular centers offering 132 hours of training during winter and summer breaks.[26] As a result of these programs and the new standards, South Korean teachers were extremely well qualified in comparison to other nations at a similar level of development. This held true even as the nation quickly rose in the ranks of economic development. High professional standards among teachers in turn reinforced the importance and respect for education in South Korean society, important components of its zeal for education.

ACCOMMODATING STUDENTS

Physical facilities, which could not keep up with the rush to accommodate students, suffered a horrendous setback when many were destroyed during the Korean War. As a result, classrooms in South Korea before 1975 were appallingly overcrowded, and facilities were crude, even by the standards of a developing nation. Few among the poorest nations had such unfavorable teacher/student ratios (see table 6). There was a severe shortage of classrooms. Although 65 percent of the MOE budget went to primary education, most went to salaries rather than facilities. The Park regime declared the expansion and improvement of facilities a high priority. About 18,000 classrooms were built under the First Five-Year Educational Development Plan and 35,000 under the Second Five-Year Educational Development Plan (1967–1971), but these still proved inadequate.[27] Classroom shortages, already serious, got worse, and by 1966 the number of classrooms was 28,000 fewer than the minimum needed. Even though the state sought to maximize usage by calling for an average of more than sixty pupils in a class, the shortage of classrooms grew by 5,000 a year.[28] When a nine-year plan to end the classroom shortage was inaugurated in 1965, its modest goals were a commentary on the gravity of the problem. Class size for all schools was to be limited to eighty students, and two-shift classes were to be confined to the lower grades. (At that time some Seoul elementary schools operated on three shifts a day.)[29]

Private primary schools were legalized in 1962 to promote the expansion of primary school facilities, but their number was modest and they conflicted with another aim—the equalization of basic education. From their start, the private

Table 6. Comparisons of Primary School Teacher/Student Ratios in Selected Countries, 1961 (in 1,000s)

Country	Teacher/Student Ratio	Country	Teacher/Student Ratio
Korea	61/3,550	Venezuela	30/1,074
Iraq	20/642	India	716/24,101
Ecuador	13/566	Iran	38/1,311
Paraguay	10/301	Indonesia	205/8,220
Morocco	18/375	Pakistan	121/4,469
Turkey	51/2,569	Philippines	102/3,970
Peru	38/1,391	Thailand	100/3,432

Source: United Nations Statistical Office, *United Nations Statistical Yearbook 1961* (New York: United Nations, 1962), 178–179.

primary schools were attacked as "aristocratic" since they charged high fees in return for special preparation for the middle school entrance exams.[30] Since only a small number of private primary schools opened, there was little improvement in the overcrowded conditions of South Korean primary schools. In fact, as noted, conditions worsened in the 1960s. In 1960, the average elementary classroom had fifty-seven children; in 1970 it had sixty-two (see table 7). Double-shift and even triple-shift classes remained common, especially in Seoul. Part of the problem was the continual expansion in enrollment during that decade, largely due to the growth in the school-age population. This was aggravated by rapid urbanization, which resulted from industrialization. Enrollments in rural schools often declined while those in cities swelled. Only after 1975 did class size and double-shift classes diminish, and even then only slightly. This was due less to the growth of facilities or the increase in teachers than to the decline in the numbers of primary school children, beginning in the late 1970s as a result of the state's very effective family planning program.

But middle school enrollment grew faster than facilities, and classrooms at middle schools became progressively more crowded during the two decades of the Park regime, improving somewhat only in the early 1980s. Officials in the 1970s generally attributed this to the no-entrance-exam policy, carried out in stages between 1969 and 1971, which made middle school education virtually universal. While this certainly aggravated the situation, middle school classroom

Table 7. Korean Classroom Size, 1960–1995

Year	Elementary Schools	Middle Schools	High Schools
1960	57 (NA)*	48	46
1965	65 (14%)	61	60
1970	62 (8%)	61	60
1975	57 (NA)	64	58
1980	52 (10%)	66	59
1985	47 (5%)	56	59
1990	41 (3%)	49	53
1995	38 (2%)	48	49

Source: Republic of Korea, MOE, *Kyoyuk t'onggye yŏnbo*, 1995.

*Figures in parentheses represent percent of double-shift classrooms.

construction and the training of middle school teachers had fallen behind increases in enrollment in the early 1960s. High schools also became more overcrowded in the 1970s since there too building construction and teacher training fell behind enrollment increases. Although the nation's wealth increased severalfold between 1961 and 1979, improvements in the quality of primary and secondary education were hindered by the system's failure to keep pace with the growth in enrollment. Conditions improved slightly for middle schools in the 1980s, but high schools became only more crowded. Only when the absolute numbers of middle school students declined (as a result of the lower birthrate) was there an appreciable alleviation of this problem. South Korea's often intolerably packed classrooms, however, did little to dampen the general enthusiasm for schooling. However, it limited the effectiveness of classroom instruction and made out-of-class study all the more important, with serious economic consequences on educational development.

ADULT LITERACY

Massive adult literacy campaigns took place under the U.S. military government and under both the Rhee and Park regimes. However, in contrast to the ever greater popular desire for educating youth, the demand for adult education peaked in the years immediately following liberation. In 1945, it was estimated that two out of three adult Koreans were illiterate. Reducing these illiteracy rates was publicly stated as a high priority of both the U.S. military government and the Rhee administration, and a number of adult literacy programs were started in the late 1940s by the state. The chief initiative for adult literacy, however, came from volunteers such as the People's Enlightenment Movement. People's or folk schools were organized by teachers, students, and educated housewives in the countryside, and evening classes were taught by volunteers in urban areas. But soon this first great burst of enthusiasm for promoting adult education began to wane. Partly this was because the People's Enlightenment Movement fell victim to leftist purges carried out by the U.S. occupation and Rhee governments; the Korean War further disrupted volunteer efforts.[31] With the decline of volunteer movements and as part of the effort to regulate all educational activities, in the spring of 1950 the MOE placed the administration of adult schools under the Korean Adult Education Boards, Inc., a private, nonprofit organization to promote adult literacy. The organization was assigned to manage adult schools, which were of two kinds: civic schools *(kongmin hakkyo)* and senior civic schools *(kodŭng kongmin hakkyo)*. The first dealt with children from about the age of fourteen who were beyond elementary school age, and the second was for adults over eighteen. These schools were frequently attached to regular elementary schools. The elementary school facilities were used in the evenings, and the teachers who conducted the civic classes were frequently the regular elementary teachers. Volunteers such as high school and college students and other educated citizens also conducted classes. Participants recall with fondness the zeal and idealism of teachers and students.[32]

When the school year began in April 1950, the MOE reported that 13,072 civic schools with an enrollment of 1,039,631 students were functioning under this system. There were also 689 senior civic schools with 83,066 students.[33] Many of the civic school operations were erratic. At times students simply participated in the classroom with the younger children; one teacher recalls the attendance of women with babies strapped to their backs in his elementary class.[34] Such scenes were especially common in rural areas. But enrollment in the civic schools was modest, especially in those aimed at people over twenty, despite the fact that after 1950 the state required all adults born after 1910 to take at least 200 hours of basic instruction at these schools or wherever adult classes were held. Attendance at these schools peaked at nearly 70,000 in the early 1950s and fell to 33,665 in 1959.[35]

The first of the annual, state-sponsored adult literacy campaigns was the forty-day "Abolish Illiteracy" *(munmaeng t'oech'i)* campaign launched jointly in the spring of 1954 by the MOE, the Interior Ministry, and the Defense Ministry. From 18 March to 31 May, thousands of teachers, college and high school students, police, soldiers, and government officials were mobilized to conduct crash courses in basic literacy, which was defined as mastery of the Korean alphabet, *han'gŭl.*[36] At the end of the campaign the MOE claimed that 72.1 percent of illiterate adult men and 73.8 percent of illiterate adult women had taken part in literacy classes and that the proportion of illiterate adults had fallen from 18.2 to 5.1 percent for men and from 39.1 to 10 percent for women. In total, illiteracy among adults fell from 27.7 to 7.9 percent.[37] This pattern was followed for the rest of the decade. Each spring the jointly sponsored Abolish Illiteracy campaigns were conducted, and every one claimed equally spectacular results. For example, the 1957 Abolish Illiteracy campaign was reported to have reduced adult illiteracy to only 6.6 percent by the end of May.[38] The following year, another anti-illiteracy campaign was conducted from 21 January to 31 March, and it also provided "refresher" courses for more than half a million functional illiterates.[39]

Another literacy campaign was the Student Rural Enlightenment Movement, in which students were to return home during the vacation and conduct lectures and basic literacy classes. In the first year of the program, the MOE reported that 17,404 students participated: 1,730 university students, 4,824 teachers' school students, and 10,850 high school students. Records state that 54,000 men and 46,000 women attended these classes.[40] Most of the efforts were directed by local school districts, which also undertook adult education programs.[41] The student campaigns were expanded by Park from 1962 to include basic information on health care, farming, and other aspects of modern life. The results of these programs were generally inflated and their goals modest—i.e., mastery of the Korean alphabet.[42] Nonetheless, the entire period from 1945 to 1965 saw great increases in adult literacy. In 1945, by all reckoning the majority of adult Koreans were completely illiterate; by 1965, probably no more than a fifth were functionally illiterate.[43]

Although the achievements in adult literacy were impressive enough, they did not reach the level of success that the state had hoped because the public demand for adult education was less than urgent. Most rural Koreans, while not adverse to learning to read, gave priority to placing their youth in school. Educating their children might bring a better life for sons and daughters and might even result in one or more family members achieving a coveted higher degree, with the status and benefits that this would bring to the family. Investing time or money on education for those already too old to have a chance to advance socially was less practical. Although many adults willingly cooperated in the literacy programs, many did not. Consequently, the Ministry of the Interior instructed police to have the word "literate" stamped on identification cards "so that the illiterate might be ashamed and seek education voluntarily."[44] It is not surprising that the programs that met with the greatest success were those aimed at children beyond the normal years for their grades and young adults, since these students could reasonably hope to advance to some higher level of education and thus make a successful if belated start up the academic ladder. Nor is it surprising that civic schools, especially senior civic schools, contained a disproportionate number of male students since economic opportunities for adult women were far fewer. Even though illiteracy was higher among women, in 1955 fewer than one in seven senior civic students were female. This figure was more pronounced in rural areas; while a third of senior civic students in Seoul were women, in South Chŏlla Province, one of the most rural and impoverished areas of the country, females accounted for only 5 percent of enrollment.[45]

U.S. SUPPORT

U.S. assistance aided South Korea's educational expansion, especially in the decade after the Korean War. Direct financial support to education was modest in the years prior to the peninsular conflict. However, following the Agreement on Economic Co-ordination, signed by the United States and the Republic of Korea in May 1952, direct U.S. aid contributed considerably to the construction of educational facilities. Under this agreement a Combined Economic Board with an American and a Korean representative worked out details for allocating American aid. For the next decade, South Korea received a massive infusion of American aid that became one of the main sources of government revenue. From 1953 to 1962 about $2 billion in nonmilitary aid was distributed, an amount that accounted for about 8 percent of the nation's GNP and financed 70 percent of its imports.[46] But the direct impact of this aid on education was more modest than one would have expected. Only about $100 million of this amount (about 3 percent of the total, including military aid) went to education.[47]

Most U.S. assistance was in the form of program aid, chiefly providing financing for specific categories of imports: agricultural commodities, fertilizers, petroleum, cement, lumber, and equipment. Part of it was project aid, directed toward providing commodities and technical assistance for specific projects. It was this latter type of assistance that was important for classroom construction. From 1953 to 1957, the United States provided the lumber, glass, and other materials for the construction of over 8,700 classrooms. One specific project involved sending technical advisers to provide advice on construction and to survey needs.[48] After 1961, direct financial aid was quite limited, but a steady stream of U.S. educational advisers assisted in educational planning, vocational training, and, most important, teacher training. By the 1970s the MOE and the Korean Educational Development Institute (KEDI), a research institute designed to advise the MOE, were virtually dominated by U.S.-trained educational experts. Such training greatly helped in providing South Korea with professional competence.

Just how important the role of American aid was in the development of Korean education has been subject to various interpretations. One major study on Korean education finds that the role of American aid was modest except for the classroom reconstruction program, which would have proceeded at a much slower pace without it.[49] Another study, however, concludes that the rapid expansion of Korean education during the first two decades after liberation was more profoundly affected by American assistance than most Korean writers have admitted. The technical and teacher-training programs, this author feels, were not only extensive, but also acted as stimuli to the whole enterprise of educational development. American support, for example, encouraged Koreans to achieve high standards in the teaching profession.[50]

The American advisers themselves were often discouraged by the limited impact they were having on Korean education. Few stayed long enough to acquire more than a rudimentary knowledge of the language or to understand a culture very different from their own. As a result, they frequently found Korean behavior confusing, if not perverse. Communication was often restricted to the very tiny number of Korean educators fluent in English. Elizabeth Wilson, herself an American educational adviser in Korea in the early 1950s, made a study of the attitudes of Western educational advisers and found that their views of Korean education were overwhelmingly negative.[51] This was not limited to education; Westerners in Korea, mostly Americans, generally held rather low opinions of Korean culture and were pessimistic about the nation's prospects for the future. Writing in 1990, one former educational adviser admitted that he and most of his colleagues simply were unable to appreciate the nature and strengths of Korean culture and thus badly underestimated the Koreans.[52] Gradually these attitudes changed with the rapid transformation of the country and as Americans became more critical of their own educational shortcomings.

As we have seen, the ideals of American education were strong influences on educational thinking, but the South Korean educational system also seemed resistant to some outside ideas. Perhaps the most glaring example of the limitation of American concepts on Korean education was found in the classroom. American teaching methodology had little impact on Korean teaching, as almost every American noted in discouragement. Korean classes remained teacher-centered and textbook-centered, with lecturing, choral recitation, and rote memorization the norm. This may have been due in part to the fact that American pedagogical ideas were difficult to understand, and the time and means to disseminate them were too restricted. Nonetheless, most Korean teachers felt comfortable in a way of teaching that predated the modern era and that served to enhance the authority of the teacher to prepare the students for exams and to manage huge, overcrowded classrooms. Furthermore, Koreans, even those attracted to democratic progressive education, were more concerned with uniformity and standardization than their American counterparts. While some Korean educators were enthusiastic about introducing American progressive methods, actual pedagogy and administration showed little American influence. Korean teachers, for instance, were less concerned with cultivating individual expression than promoting equal opportunity so that any child could obtain the level of education that corresponded to his or her ability.

Coeducation provides another example of the limitation of American influence on Korean education when it ran counter to cultural patterns. Although the American military government had in one of its early initiatives made all education coeducational, shortly after independence the MOE ordered that education for boys and girls be maintained in separate schools when possible or at least in separate classes at the middle and high school levels.[53] There was little objection to this, and no major battle occurred to restore coeducation in secondary schools. In September 1953, the MOE announced plans to limit coeducation to the first four years of elementary school.[54] By the late 1950s in the larger city schools this had become the practice.[55] This and similar failures at influencing education often discouraged American educators, but most agreed that the desire to acquire education (or degrees) was the most singular and promising feature of Korean education.

As far as promoting educational expansion, the American influence was important in two indirect ways. American aid to South Korea in the 1950s and early 1960s was critical to the functioning of the South Korean government. Even though only a small percentage of this money went directly to education, the task of educational development would have been much more difficult without a financially solvent state. Foreign aid greatly tapered off after 1962, but a number of aid projects that provided technical assistance to education—especially higher education—remained important for another decade. Additionally, scholarships to Koreans to study in the United States started a steady stream of young scholars to American universities that continued long after aid tapered off. In fact, the numbers grew in the 1970s and 1980s. Hundreds received advanced degrees in education from American universities. These American-trained scholars staffed the research institutes and education departments at Korean universities and served in the MOE. They often pushed for more American-style reforms and were sometimes impatient with their Korean-trained colleagues.

The American influence was significant to South Korean educational development in another intangible way. The ideal in America of universal and equal opportunity in education gave confirmation and intellectual support to the mass movement toward schooling in South Korea.

SOCIAL DEMAND AND EDUCATIONAL DEVELOPMENT

The single greatest factor in accounting for the impressive achievements in educational expansion was the social demand for education. From the 1940s through the 1980s, the educational system embraced an ever greater proportion of the nation's youth, and its administrative efficiency improved. Some of the credit should be given to the continuous efforts of the Rhee, Park, and Chun (1980–1988) regimes in building a comprehensive and efficient network of schools. As discussed above, U.S. aid assisted in school construction and teacher training. But the expansion of the Korean educational system was less the product of a systematic and coherent drive by the central government than a mass social movement for educational opportunity. In short, South Korea's obsession with education was the great engine that spurred the rapid growth of the educational system.

A pervasive desire for educational advancement was manifested from the early post-liberation years. As reflected in the debate over the Basic Education Law, the great concern of many Koreans was access to education at all levels. Nor was this concern limited to urban elites. The desire for education appeared throughout the country, in small villages as well as city slums. Persuading parents to send and keep their children in school was seldom a problem. There were problems of students lacking the basic tuition fees, but there was only enthusiasm for the idea of sending children to school. Even farmers would sacrifice the loss of labor for the long-term benefit of having educated children.[56] A lack of classrooms, teachers, and textbooks proved the chief bottleneck to educational growth. The extraordinarily large classrooms and underdeveloped facilities, however, did little to limit the teacher's control over the class or reduce the unusually high rate of internal efficiency (rate of dropouts or repeaters) in Korean elementary and secondary classrooms. All this was a testimony to the strength of parental pressure on Korean children to attend class, stay in school, and keep up with other members of the class.

Foreign observers agreed that the desire for personal advancement through education was nearly universal. Elaine Barnes, an American educational adviser in Taegu in the early 1950s, reported that the "determination of [the mass of people] to get an education is almost frightening."[57] Elizabeth Wilson described what she termed "the impatient popular movement" for education:[58] "It was common in 1953 and 1954 to find elementary and high school students who had spent the night in the cold, dimly lighted shacks committing to memory the day's lessons and preparing for the inevitable given-back [classroom] examinations."[59] A British observer noted that "their love of education" is such that "even the poorest will struggle to send their children to school."[60] In all rural areas, there was a pervasive hope of advancing family fortunes by schooling the children. Anthropologist Cornelius Osborne, working in the village of Samguri in Kanghwa Island, Kyŏnggi Province, in 1947, reported, "The farmers themselves speak of nothing so consistently as the desirability of improving educational facilities." Although a four-year primary school was available in this village, many farmers still hired teachers on their own to teach basic literacy to their sons and daughters.[61]

At the close of 1952, the UNESCO–UNKRA Educational Planning Mission to Korea surveyed the needs and problems of education in preparation for the massive reconstruction efforts that were being planned. It found much to fault. In fact, overall it was highly critical, perhaps unfairly, considering the turmoil of the nation. It reported that there was an "extremely low level of professional preparation" on the part of teachers and educational administrators.[62] Salaries for teachers were low and insufficient to cover basic living costs.[63] There was an "utter inadequacy of school facilities."[64] There was an extensive reliance on textbooks, but the textbooks were inadequate and teaching materials ineffective.[65] Civic and senior civic schools "functioned sporadically," and technical education was also termed inadequate.[66] The report disparaged educational administration, which was "often poor," and it found that there was "little trace of supervision of instruction."[67] It also charged the Rhee administration with political interference in education. Yet despite its critical tone, the UNESCO–UNKRA report expressed admiration for the zeal of Koreans for education. As a result, "Korean education is in a dynamic condition."[68]

South Korea is very mountainous and in the 1950s was almost totally lacking in paved roads, but the enthusiasm for education was felt even in the isolated villages hidden in small, intermontane valleys. For example, the remote and impoverished village of Naejongja in Hamp'yŏng County, South Chŏlla Province, had no elementary school in the late 1950s, but one existed in another village two kilometers away. The fees were about 1,000 hwan a month, more than most could afford, yet virtually all families made the sacrifice for their boys; although girls had a lower priority, most of them also attended school. Still five families sent their boys to a traditional *sŏdang* rather than to the elementary school since at one *mal* (eighteen liters) of rice and one *mal* of barley a month it cost much less than (about one-sixth as much as) the modern school. But the *sŏdang,* even if cheaper, was no longer seen as a suitable alternative by most rural Koreans. Only by attending modern schools did one have a chance at obtaining a prestigious higher degree. And it is clear from most accounts that the hope of seeing their children enter post-elementary education was a major motive for the sacrifices of most rural families. In Naejongja, village parents sending their children to elementary school were unanimous in hoping their boys would advance to the higher levels.[69]

In Hwasin, a village in Kongju County in South Ch'ungch'ong Province that was described as "average," twenty-one of twenty-six boys of school age in

1958 walked to the local elementary school five kilometers away; one stayed with relatives to attend a more desirable school in the city of Kongju; two boys, along with six of the school-age girls, did not go to school due to poverty. The desire to improve their fortunes by sending their children to school, universally expressed, required entry into a good primary school. Most villagers expressed dissatisfaction with the local school and regarded the primary school in the nearest city, Kongju, as offering a better chance for the children to advance their education.[70]

At another village, Napunto, in Yŏngdong County, North Ch'ungch'ong Province, also described as "average," almost all boys and most girls hiked three kilometers to a primary school in 1958. Some parents had been unable to afford the school supporters' association fee, but with the abolition that year of this particularly onerous fee, virtually all were able to save or borrow enough money to educate their children. Several families had children in the nearest middle schools, which were twenty-five and thirty-two kilometers away, and one had a son in high school in Seoul and two other sons in college. It was a great asset to have relatives in Seoul or another city where children could stay and study.[71]

The zeal for education continued to be the driving force behind educational expansion in subsequent decades. Most striking about this fervor was the degree to which it penetrated all levels of society. While peasants in the late 1940s had been eager to educate themselves and their children, many poor families were willing, if reluctant, to forego the education of younger sons and daughters. But as South Korea entered the 1960s, foregoing an education became rarer. Partly this was due to rising incomes, but it was also due to the ever strengthening belief in social mobility through education. Still, while almost every young person sought educational opportunity, Korean families approached education as a collective effort that often required some members to sacrifice for others. Making education a combined family enterprise enabled families of even modest means to support one member's attempts to achieve more advanced schooling.

The willingness of Koreans to sacrifice for the sake of a family member's education is attested by Robert Spencer's study of girls working in factories between 1972 and 1978. Spencer found that earning money for their siblings' education was the primary reason that young, single women sought factory jobs.[72] These young women were under great pressure to earn money so that their siblings, usually but not always brothers, could pay for school. Spencer found that the "issue of education is paramount" in family problems. Nor did the young factory girls abandon plans for their own education. Most found time to study at *hagwŏn*s or at least listen to educational programs on the radio with the hope of resuming their own schooling someday.[73] Nearly all Koreans kept open the possibility of obtaining further education until they became too burdened with supporting their own children's schooling.

Anthropologist Clark Sorensen, studying a village in 1977 and again in 1983, found that the drive for education played a central role in the plans of rural families.[74] The families he observed considered education a good investment since it improved the prospects of getting an urban job and escaping farm work. An important strategy was to have one member move to the city for a job or for schooling. This member would then set up a family branch in the city that could be used as a base by other family members to move to the city to gain an education or to get a job.[75] Korean families often mentioned better job opportunities and disatisfaction with rural life as reasons for migrating to Seoul. The most commonly given reason, however, was to obtain better educational opportunities for their children or siblings.[76]

How rational was this drive for education? Studies of earnings differentials based on education in the first two decades after liberation show a substantial difference in the incomes of secondary school and college-educated workers, although these differentials are less than in most other low-income nations.[77] In rank-conscious Korea, the prestige of having an education and holding a high-status position that was open to the educated was equally important. The alternative to education seemed to be the endless drudgery of farming or manual labor and the low social status attaching to these. No parent wanted that. Furthermore, in the Korean corporate family, all shared to some degree in the success of a family member.

The Woo brothers typify this effort to rise in social rank. The older Woo was born in 1938, a farmer's son from a village near Chŏngŭp in southeast Korea. His father, who briefly worked in a factory near the Manchurian border in the early 1940s, told him to "be anything but a farmer!" Just after liberation, an elementary school opened in his village, and after six years he attended a newly opened middle school just one hour's walk away; he went on to become an elementary teacher in a nearby school. Woo urged his younger siblings to study and if possible to go to college, an opportunity that had been denied to him. His younger brother and sister would stay with him on the weekends so he could tutor them—especially important as there was no *hagwŏn* in the area. Woo's younger brother later recalled how hard he studied, especially from the fourth grade: "After the fourth grade I don't remember playing, just studying. My mother and father would worry if I wasn't studying at home." Summer was best because he could study outside: "Our house was small and crowded, and we, of course, had no electric lights, so studying in winter was more difficult." With his brother's help he passed the middle school entrance exam, and in 1966 he passed the college entrance exam and left to attend a university in Seoul. "All my life I dreamed of entering college in Seoul," the younger brother recalls. His sister soon joined him and cooked for him in a tiny room in the capital, while his father and brother sent money whenever possible.[78]

"Don't be a farmer!" "Don't be a poor laborer!" These became the slogans of millions of Koreans. Fundamental to educational development was the belief of many Koreans, from the middle classes down to the rural poor, that the chance for rising to the upper reaches of the social hierarchy was there for them or their children if only they could succeed in climbing the educational ladder.

FACTORS IN UNDERSTANDING
THE DEMAND FOR EDUCATION

Years of Japanese restrictions on educational opportunity had led to the great pent-up demand for education so commented on by foreign observers. For the middle class of wealthier farmers and larger landowners, government functionaries, businessmen, professionals, and skilled workers, the narrow aperture that the Japanese had imposed on higher education was especially frustrating since it meant condemnation to the lower ranks of status and privilege. Since Confucian values had always equated education with rank and prestige, barriers placed by the colonial state were a cruel reminder of Korean powerlessness. After the fall of the Japanese empire, these middle-class Koreans sought to achieve for their sons and daughters what had been denied to them, creating the great spurt in the growth in education in the late 1940s and 1950s. Though this public pressure for access was strongest among the urban middle class, it was shared by Koreans at all social strata; the farmer who sold his only ox or his best paddy to raise tuition for his children became a stereotype based on the reality of rural aspirations. Indeed, in part because the ambition to achieve social mobility through schooling pervaded all social classes, the discrepancies between urban and rural rates of educational attainment became low compared to other developing nations.[79]

Working in the remote coastal village of Sŏkp'o in 1966, anthropologist Vincent Brandt found education a major concern. "If asked what contributes most to high prestige and social rank, most villagers without hesitation will cite education."[80] He found that people of all age groups attached high status to education. Education alone, they believed, qualified one "to direct others." The desire to obtain education was striking and sad in view of the obstacles presented the impoverished and isolated youth: "When asked about ultimate goals if the village became really prosperous, most people gave priority to higher education for their children. The reverse of this obsessive or mystical attitude toward education is that boys, faced with the realization that they will never study beyond the sixth grade, and that nearly all their ambitions must be renounced, feel stifled *(taptap hada)* in the village environment." Brandt found that it was "difficult to shake this faith in education."[81]

In 1958, the South Korean government sent Lee Man-gap, one of the country's first American-trained sociologists, to survey rural communities. As he studied village attitudes and values, he found everywhere a hope for social advancement through education and frequent complaints of the shortage of facilities and the expense of schooling. Although hope for improving a family's fortune rested on seeing one of its sons rise to a prestigious position in society, Lee found that most parents regarded the education of their daughters to be important as well.[82] It made sense for even the poorest Koreans to invest in the higher reaches of schooling for their oldest or ablest children because of the corporate structure of the Korean family. Status was based as much on the family as a whole as on the attainments of an individual. The success of a student brought social benefits for the entire family. Furthermore, the Confucian emphasis on filial piety strengthened the parental pressure on the pupil, whose education was not simply an individual, but also a corporate concern. This helps to account for the enormous sacrifices families made to educate their children, as Lee Man-gap and others observed.

Traditionally social barriers had restricted access to education, in practice if not in theory. Members of the *yangban* held a monopoly over the higher civil examinations, which were the gateway to coveted government posts that were needed to secure status and privilege in Korean society. For the majority of Koreans, basic instruction in the Confucian classics for their boys was all that could

be expected. This changed with the breakdown of the old order in Korea during the first half of the twentieth century. Under the Japanese, higher education
was no longer the exclusive right of the *yangban* but was in practice open to the
lucky few who possessed the money or connections. After 1945, with the colonial restrictions on education removed and with the old social order crumbling,
a belief that educational chances were there for everyone became the reigning
concept. This was further encouraged by the ideology of equality of opportunity
and "democratic education" open to everyone, which was encouraged by the
American example and which became part of public as well as intellectual discourse. Moreover, as noted, South Korea was an uprooted, turbulent society in
which one in six adults had left home in the 1930s and early 1940s to work in
northern Korea, Japan, Manchuria, and elsewhere. A restless society emerged
in which traditional social distinctions were breaking down, anything seemed
possible, and every family sought a chance for improvement. South Korea's
drive toward education and the agitation of the public for educational opportunities need to be seen in this light.

There was also a great leveling process at work. The landowning class of
mainly *yangban* background lost much of its prestige as it came to be tarred with
a collaborationist brush. Many lost their jobs and the privileged positions they
had held with the collapse of colonial authority. Another major factor in changing the old social order was land reform. Before 1945, income from medium to
large agricultural estates was the single most important source of wealth in Korea. Studies have shown that even with the growth of industrialization under
colonial rule and the participation of some Koreans in commerce, banking, and
industry, agricultural estates remained the main basis of wealth among the Korean elite. More than two-thirds of the farming in Korea was done by tenants,
who paid 50 percent or more of their crops in rent.[83] The most lucrative estates
were in the south. After 1945, the American military government redistributed
Japanese-owned lands to tenant farmers, significantly reducing tenancy. Redistribution of lands held by Korean landlords, in contrast, did not take place until
after 1948, and only after considerable delay. If judged by public statements,
land reform was a high priority of the new government; however, the Rhee regime was slow in carrying out a measure that would undermine the economic
basis of many of the regime's supporters. Minister of Agriculture Cho Pong-am
drew up a plan in November 1948 that would limit all holdings to about three
hectares, with only very modest compensation to the owners.

The Cho plan was too radical and was modified. Yet the principle of radical land reform was accepted and regarded as inevitable in the face of strong rural demands; the example of North Korea, which carried out a comprehensive redistribution of land after 1945; and the need of the government for rural support. Conservatives, often landowners who made up a sizable portion of government and National Assembly members, sought either to delay the reform or at least make the terms of sale as profitable as possible. A long debate over the length and terms of the repayment period delayed passage of the act until March 1950. The law, when it finally passed, stipulated that the owners should be paid 150 percent of the annual value of the harvest over a five-year period and could be paid in government certificates. The reform was implemented only during the Korean War. A Farmland Committee was set up to supervise the land, but many landlords opted to settle the terms of compensation with tenants privately.[84] These were exchanged for monetary payments, which were reduced to insignificance by inflation in the early 1950s. Thus, the land reform further undermined class differences and reduced discrepancies in the distribution of wealth.

If Korea had not become a classless society, it had become one in which attitudes and ideas, especially those pertaining to education, crossed social boundaries. Researcher Song Chick Hong, in surveys conducted in 1959 and 1965, found that there was little difference among rural farmers, middle-class businessmen, and professionals in their views concerning the purpose and importance of education.[85] The chaos and turmoil, abetted by the ethnic and cultural homogeneity of Korean society, had resulted in both broadly shared values and broadly shared aspirations.

THE KOREAN WAR AND ITS IMPACT ON EDUCATIONAL DEVELOPMENT

The Korean War contributed further to the leveling process by wiping out homes, rental properties, and factories owned by the wealthier Koreans. Korea had escaped World War II without serious damage. But five years after liberation and two years after independence, the two Koreas were engaged in a calamitous internecine conflict, its scale of devastation enlarged by the intervention of the major powers. South Korea saw less destruction than North Korea, yet the years of conflict were horribly destructive: cities in ruin; millions of citizens dispersed to wherever they could find refuge; and hundreds of thousands killed, wounded, or missing. It was a rare family that did not lose a member or a home to the war.

The conflict that broke out on 25 June 1950, referred to by South Koreans as the June 25 Incident, brought most of its destruction on South Korea during its first year. The North Koreans initially advanced rapidly. Within two days the South Korean government was forced to flee south to Taejŏn and then to Pusan, where the American forces were able to defend the extreme southeast corner of the nation. Except for the modest territory within the so-called Naktong Parameter, almost all of South Korea had become a battleground. It was a war of rapid movement and sudden turns of fate. Seoul was retaken by the United Nations in late September, fell into Chinese and North Korean hands in early January 1951, and was retaken by allied forces in mid-March. By the time truce talks began on 10 July 1951, the battle lines had stabilized.

Fighting continued for two more years, and American bombers continued to bring destruction upon North Korea during that time, but the zone of conflict on the ground was confined to a ten-mile-wide band that roughly approximated the thirty-eighth parallel, leaving most of South Korea out of the direct path of war. As a result, the task of reconstruction in education was well under way by 1952, although the final truce agreement was signed only on 27 July 1953.

For education, the war was an enormous blow that resulted in the destruction of facilities, the loss of personnel, the dispersal of students, and the disruption of everyday routines so that administration often was a desperate affair. About 80 percent of all educational facilities were damaged or destroyed. According to an official survey, out of nearly 32,000 classrooms, 7,544 were completely destroyed, 3,316 suffered at least 50 percent damage, 12,157 were partially damaged, and only 8,880 were left undamaged. One-third of all schools were damaged beyond repair.[86] In December 1950, the MOE had allowed the use of schools as refugee camps, and both the ROK army and the UN forces occupied school facilities whenever it was convenient.[87] As a result of casualties, conscription, and abduction to North Korea, the number of teachers fell from 42,000 in 1950 to 37,000 in 1952. Of these, a large number were recruited on the spot and had no qualifications so that the percentage of teachers that had received some professional training declined.[88]

The Korean War gave testimony to the zeal for education and contributed to the great social upheaval that helps account for the scramble for social advancement through schooling. The destruction of the war in its first months led to the disruption of almost all schooling, but the start of 1951 was marked by efforts to resume classes. On 7 January 1951, a temporary MOE office was established in Pusan. From this office, on 26 February, the Outline of Special Measures for Education in Wartime was issued to prepare for the commencement of the school year in April. The outline declared that all refugee students should register at their place of refuge so that classes could continue. Classes would be conducted using whatever facilities were available. To deal with the thousands of secondary school students who had fled Seoul with their families, all Seoul secondary schools were ordered to combine and create temporary schools in the major southern cities away from the fighting: Pusan, Taegu, and Taejŏn. Schools were to be set up in refugee camps, and all students at the camps who had been previously enrolled in school were to resume attendance at these "special schools for refugees." In June 1951, the MOE formed a Building Committee to organize and supervise efforts by local groups to construct classrooms; high school and college students were enlisted in this effort.[89]

American relief aid was crucial to this effort. Paek Nak-chun, the education minister with English fluency and many American connections, served the ministry well in its efforts to solicit American help. In July 1951, Paek went to the United States and conducted a campaign to enlist American aid in the reconstruction of Korean education.[90] The U.S. government eventually supplied a large amount of aid for reconstruction, including educational facilities, some through the U.S. Armed Forces and more through the UNKRA.

Much of the recovery of education had a spontaneous quality to it. South Korean parents were quick to send their children to whatever school was available. In tents, ruined buildings, or in the open, students met, exams were administered, and the competition for entry into secondary schools and colleges resumed even under the most unlikely circumstances.[91] A severe shortage of paper and textbooks meant that students and teachers had to make do with whatever materials were available.[92] It became difficult to adhere to regular school terms, and the state simply recommended that local officials and parents set their own schedules and do whatever was necessary to ensure that some instruction was carried on.[93] To accommodate the demand for college education, the MOE created the United Wartime College (Chŏnsi Yŏnhap Taehak) in

May 1951. Almost all higher education had been concentrated in Seoul, a city destroyed in heavy fighting. To resume higher education, all colleges and universities were asked to combine faculty and to set up joint classes in several cities in the south. About 6,500 students were enrolled in the United Wartime College: 4,268 in Pusan, 377 in Taejŏn, 1,283 in Chŏnju, and 527 in Kwangju.[94]

The continuation of education under adverse conditions was primarily the result of the determination of Koreans not to have their children's education disrupted. Because of the confused situation, there are no reliable statistics on enrollments for this period, but foreign observers were impressed at the continuation of schooling under the most difficult of situations. A British UN refugee official, Edgar S. Kennedy, observed in early 1951 that more than anything else, education was the area in which an effort to return to normalcy in Korean life had begun to succeed.[95]

The Korean War can be seen as a part of the process of social turbulence and change that spurred the public demand for educational advancement. It was not an isolated event but part of two decades of upheaval that shook Korean society to its foundations. The Japanese colonial government did not displace the land-based aristocratic elite of Korea but removed it from political power. While the growth of cities and the introduction of modern institutions such as banks and railroads created new opportunities and new social categories, Korean society remained for the most part rural, agricultural, and highly stratified along inherited family lines. Industrial growth, the need for laborers to build the newly expanding Japanese empire, and the mass mobilization campaigns of the late 1930s broke this ancient social pattern. By 1945, a large proportion of the adult population was working away from home. The greatest number came from the populous and overwhelmingly agricultural provinces of southern Korea, but everyone was affected by the war effort. After 1945, when several million returned home, they did not do so unchanged. And the society to which they returned was unsettled and chaotic. Mass movements of people returning home, fleeing the Communists, dislocated by guerrilla warfare and political disturbances, or just trying to find work kept South Korean society unsettled. Then came the Korean War and the destruction and confusion it brought.

Although South Korea did not experience death and destruction on the scale of North Korea, the figures are still appalling. About 280,000 South Korean soldiers were killed or missing. An estimated 400,000 civilians were killed and 80,000 were taken to the North. Two million South Koreans officially were listed as refugees, but when every Korean who fled home to live with a relative or friend is counted, the figure is probably much higher. The scale of this dislocation is revealed in the census figures. In June 1949 Seoul had a population of 1,437,670; on the eve of the war it was a little higher. On 31 March 1952 only 676,121 inhabitants were counted. In contrast to Seoul, the population of South Kyŏngsang, near Pusan, swelled in the first year of the war by almost a quarter.[96] About 600,000 homes were destroyed, a majority of the nation's factories severely damaged, and many family fortunes consequently lost. One quarter of the population was reported in 1952–1953 to be suffering chronic hunger.[97]

The effect of this turbulent period on ordinary Koreans can perhaps be illustrated in the case of Mr. Min. Born the son of an illiterate farmer in a village near Ch'ŏnan in Ch'ungch'ŏng Province, Min was already about ten when he gained the opportunity to attend a newly opened elementary school in a neighboring village in 1933. After a couple of years of schooling he worked on his family's farm but was conscripted by the Japanese to work in Japan in 1942. After three years at an airplane factory in central Japan, he returned home in 1945; restless, he drifted into Taejŏn to work as a laborer. There he attended night school to learn to read Korean, and he got married. His family farm escaped the ravages of the Korean War, but he lost both his brothers and struggled to raise their children. Children in Mr. Min's family had, as far as he knew, never gone to school, and they knew their place in the village. They lived separately from some outcast families and also apart from the *yangban* homes. But Mr. Min was determined that his two sons not be farmers, get an education, and live in town. He eventually sent them to live with a relation in Ch'ŏnan, where they could receive a secondary education, paying for their upkeep with rice and fruit. Echoing so many other Korean parents, he exhorted his sons, "Go to school" and "Never be a farmer."[98] South Korea is full of variations of Mr. Min's story. The Korean War was the last of the great series of convulsions that shook Korean society from the late 1930s to 1953 and pried Koreans from their traditional routines; provided them with a vision of a wider world; and made them restless, ambitious, and hopeful for their children.

The Korean War had another important impact on South Korea: it enhanced the power of the South Korean state. As noted, massive U.S. aid provided an invaluable economic prop to the Rhee government since it gave the state access to foreign currency, which it was able to use to reward or discipline businesses, industries, and other potential supporters and opponents. It created a huge military force, which grew from one hundred thousand troops on the eve of the conflict to six hundred thousand at the end. After the war, the military forces were kept at this level; well equipped by the United States and increasingly well trained, they were one of the ten largest armed forces in the world. South Korean society, to some extent, was also militarized. A huge reserve corps absorbed much of the male population with regular training exercises. Air raid drills, night curfews, and a later requirement that all citizens stand at rigid attention every day at five in the afternoon while the national anthem was played—all became part of South Korean life. The influence of this militarization of society was felt in education as well. Several years of military service was required of all students, and military drill became part of education. Equally important for educational development was the fact that the Korean War provided the state a means of legitimizing itself through the ideology of anti-Communism. Anti-Communism provided a rationale for state power and gave a raison d'être for the South Korean state. South Korea was on the front line of Communism, a member of the free world that had to be ever vigilant against Communist aggression and subversion. Education was a key to promoting this ideology, giving the state a greater concern for enlarging and controlling educational development.

4 Coordinating Education with Economic Planning

The aspirations of millions of rich and poor families for social advancement drove South Korea's remarkable educational expansion, but it did not always drive it in the directions sought by the state. South Korean schools provided an increasingly literate workforce that was of enormous value in the nation's economic development. The state, however, had difficulty harnassing the demand for education toward the needs of an industrializing economy. This accounts for one of the paradoxes of South Korean educational development: in a nation noted for its successful, state-directed economic development policies, there appeared to be a lack of emphasis on vocational and technical education. Instead, educational development had a momentum of its own, independent of economic strategies or needs. This was not because South Korean governments maintained a laissez-faire attitude toward the growth of formal schooling; successive administrations made repeated efforts to coordinate educational development with economic planning. They had, however, only mixed success because attempts to encourage vocational and technical education conflicted with the public's perceptions about the purpose and nature of schooling.

Koreans sought education to gain status for themselves and their families (as noted), and prevailing attitudes were such that this meant being a scholar, not a technician. The South Korean state—especially after 1961, when it became increasingly focused on pursuing economic development objectives—attempted to mesh educational development with economic plans, creating at times a tug-of-war with the public over educational policy. This tug-of-war became important in shaping educational development. It also points to the strengths and limits of the South Korean "developmental state."

EDUCATIONAL AND ECONOMIC PLANNING BEFORE 1961

Before 1961, efforts to coordinate education with economic development were not very systematic. From 1945 Korean officials, many educators, the press, and American advisers called for greater stress on vocational education and less on the humanities, and the Rhee administration made various pronouncements on the importance of promoting technical and vocational training. But vocational education policy in the early years of the republic was largely a failure. This failure illustrates the limitation of formal policy making in constructing the kind of educational system that informed opinion both within and outside the administration thought the state needed. The importance of technical and vocational education was recognized by all administration officials and educators, as well as the knowledgeable public. During the American occupation, emphasis was given to technical education at the secondary level, and most of the new secondary schools opened in the years immediately after 1945 were vocational in orientation. The Korean War further highlighted the need for citizens with practical skills in reconstruction. Korean educators and officials spoke of the need to break with the Confucian tradition of disdain for manual labor. They also worried about the problem of the educated unemployed. Koreans remembered the Japanese emphasis on technical proficiency in education and admired American "know-how." All education ministers, as well as bureaucrats in the ministries of the Interior, Finance, Reconstruction, and Defense, called for greater emphasis on vocational education, as did leaders of the opposition.

Yet vocational education languished. Upon liberation, some 50,000 students enrolled in academic secondary schools and about 30,000 in vocational schools. By 1952, when secondary education was divided into middle schools that all provided general education and high schools with either academic or vocational training, there were 74,463 students attending vocational high schools and 59,431 attending academic high schools (see table 1). There was a sharp rise in high school enrollment immediately after the Korean War. Vocational high schools, however, expanded at a much slower rate than academic ones, and in 1955, the ratio was reversed, with 122,991 in vocational schools and 141,702 in academic schools. As the wave of post–Korean War students subsided and high school enrollment slowed down, the trend away from vocational education continued. By 1960, the number of students in vocational schools had declined to 99,071 while academic school enrollment had increased to 164,492. Vocational secondary school enrollment had increased only 30 percent in eight years and was declining, whereas enrollment in academic secondary schools had increased almost two and a half times.[1]

The MOE under Rhee launched a number of programs to promote vocational education. In 1952, it announced that the promotion of vocational education was one of its main priorities, and during the next six years 2,900 vocational teachers participated in in-service training programs. In 1953, industries began to receive government subsidies for short-term, in-factory training programs. That same year the UNKRA established a training center for technical education, and the United States also conducted a vocational education program.[2] The MOE also attempted to check the tendency of vocational schools to became de facto academic schools by requiring in the curriculum reform of 1955 that all vocational schools devote 60 percent of the class hours to vocational courses. It also required all academic schools to give 20 percent or more of classroom instruction hours to practical subjects.[3]

In 1956, the education minister, Ch'oe Kyu-nam, announced "productivity education," a program for the promotion of vocational education that was to receive the highest priority in educational development. The following year, a five-year plan for technical education (Ogaenyŏn Sirŏp Kyoyuk Kyehoek) was launched. This was to be carried out from 1958 to 1962 with funds from national and local governments, while 50 percent of the funding was to come from foreign aid. As part of the plan, two-thirds of the departments of existing vocational schools were targeted for upgrading—an improvement of facilities, the supply of equipment, and the training of teachers.[4] In 1959, an ambitious twenty-year plan was announced that called for the training of one million qualified, intermediate-level technicians and engineers by 1980.[5] The MOE also inaugurated an on-the-job training program for technical school students, requiring them to spend a few months at an industrial plant.[6] Yet none of these efforts did much to change the trends in Korean education away from vocational schooling and toward academic schooling. Public pressure continued for students to pursue higher education that would lead to a prestigious career in government or business or simply confer the high status of a scholar.

Ideas about education were to some extent shared by educators, who, while supporting vocational education, held contradictory concepts of education that conformed to the popular ideal of a well-rounded generalist. This is reflected in the first national curriculum. So busy was the state in coping with the basic problems of creating an educational system that until 1955 there was no national curriculum or overall effort to systematically determine the content of schooling, let alone a policy of coordinating education with economic development. Since liberation textbooks, teaching materials, and syllabi were not standardized and were haphazardly determined. Texts were often merely translations of Japanese or sometimes American books. Every school more or less independently drew up its curriculum, with the preparation of students for entrance exams being the main force for imposing a certain standardization of materials. Korean educators virtually unanimously agreed that teachers, schools, and pupils would benefit by a single national curriculum. Delays were due to the war, controversies over selecting materials and texts, and a lack of agreement over course content, especially between those who wanted to follow the American model of schooling and those who sought to maintain more of the pre-1945 curriculum or wanted to develop a more specifically Korean one.

The need for a national curriculum was discussed from the onset of the republic, and the administration created a Curriculum Study Council on 2 June 1950. Delayed by the war, a Central Educational Research Institute (Chungang Kyoyuk Yŏn'guso) was created on 9 March 1953. This organization held its first meeting that same month in Pusan, still the wartime capital, and created a committee to work out a national curriculum. It was a major effort involving more than six hundred educators who participated for three years.[7] By the summer of 1955, the committee had finished its recommendations, on the basis of which the MOE on 1 September 1955 issued an order establishing the National Curriculum, which was implemented from 1955 and 1957.[8] American advisers worked closely with Koreans on this project; the Third American Education Mission to Korea, 1954–1955, was concerned primarily with the development of the curriculum. During the drawing up of the curriculum there was talk of stressing subjects that were best suited for the nation's economic development. The American advisers urged stressing vocational and technical subjects in the secondary schools. At their recommendation, the number of hours of nonvocational subjects taught at vocational schools was limited.[9]

The final curriculum was not oriented toward practical skills, as the

American advisers had thought wise. In general, the principle was a well-rounded education rather than specialized skills. While the Americans recommended concentrating on five or six subjects, the Korean educators opted for a plan to include as many as a dozen subjects each week. The Americans complained that too many subjects were being taught at each level and that such a fragmentation of the weekly schedule would make it too difficult to give adequate attention to any one area. They also felt that too many nontechnical subjects were included and that the curriculum was not drawn up with the practical needs of a developing society in mind. Most Korean educators, however, felt that it was best to include as many subjects as possible at each grade level in order to develop "whole person" education.[10] They argued for the need for moral and ethical content, as well as a good grounding in history, literacy, and general math and science.[11] South Koreans were at this point far less committed to the technical or specialized education than their foreign advisers thought appropriate.

Yet the South Korean government before 1961 did make serious moves to coordinate educational development with economic needs. This is seen in its commitment to basic education and its attempts to restrict the expansion of higher education. Following the somewhat chaotic period of educational expansion immediately after 1945, the Rhee administration gradually asserted tighter control over the educational system. Educational policy aimed at adhering more consistently to sequential educational development and at maintaining uniform and higher standards of instruction at all levels. To accomplish these aims, the MOE set up programs to improve teacher training and standards, created a national curriculum for all schools, placed restrictions on the growth of private secondary and tertiary schools, and established a quota system for higher education. The state also made progress toward improving bureaucratic efficiency, including educational administration, and moved toward a greater degree of educational planning.

One of the most significant measures of the Rhee administration to coordinate educational development with economic needs was to reign in the zeal for academic education in order to prevent an oversupply of high school and university graduates. Private foundations had sprung up after 1945 to meet the public demand for schooling by setting up private secondary schools and colleges. The majority of the secondary schools were academic, not vocational. Most of the private colleges also emphasized arts and humanities, which were popular and less expensive to offer. The Rhee government, arguing that the number of such schools exceeded the ability of the economy to absorb their graduates, took measures to restrict the opening of private academic high schools and colleges. The tougher line toward privately owned schools began in 1954, when Education Minister Yi Sŏn-gŭn called for a crackdown on private educational institutions that were run as businesses and instructed his staff to review the funds, facilities, and staff of proposed schools before granting them accreditation.[12] He also gave orders to punish schools that had excessive recruitment and ordered that private foundations with no revenue be denied tax-free status.[13] Periodically announced crackdowns on private foundations that catered to the public demand for more academic institutions became a regular feature of MOE policy for the remainder of the Rhee administration.[14] For example, a thorough investigation of private foundations was launched in April 1957.[15] Few foundations seem to have actually been penalized as a result of such investigations, but it became more difficult for new educational foundations to obtain legal recognition. Subsequently, few new ones were established after 1957.

To control excessive enrollment and lack of standards at private colleges and universities, a twelve-member Committee on Higher Education (Taehakkyo Kyoyuk Simŭi Wiwŏnhoe) was organized at the initiative of the MOE. The committee, whose membership increased as representatives from the new colleges and universities were added, agreed to coordinate university regulation. Previously each college or university had had its own curriculum and its own school and teacher regulations.[16] In February 1955, the committee proposed a set of regulations regarding the length of terms, faculty qualifications, university governance, student evaluations, and entrance qualifications. The MOE urged all schools to voluntarily follow these regulations but soon mandated their adherence. Several months latter at the recommendation of the MOE, President Rhee issued the Presidential Decree on the Establishment of College and University Standards, which sought to check the expansion of higher education by setting quotas for schools and departments. It also authorized the MOE to merge or rearrange the departments at all institutes of higher learning. In 1957 under this decree, thirty-two of fifty-two colleges were required to limit students and merge departments. In 1958, quotas were set for all fifty-six schools of higher education, and significantly their total enrollment was reduced by one thousand to seventy-seven thousand.[17] The state also abolished military deferment for college students to slow down the explosion of enrollment in higher education.

Sound economic arguments existed for these measures. South Korea's secondary and higher education explosion was not the product of economic demand. Economic growth, while real in the late 1950s, was modest, and there were few jobs in the still predominantly agricultural society to absorb the vastly increasing numbers of high school and especially university graduates. On average, only two out of five college graduates found jobs requiring university degrees. This made little real difference for the aspirations of young Koreans and their families. It did, however, provide a rational basis for the implementation of the restrictive measures on higher education.

Since the Rhee administration came to an end shortly after it began to impose restrictions on the growth of higher education, the effectiveness of these measures cannot be assessed. Even in 1960, the number of students who entered college considerably exceeded the official quota, and there were signs of widespread lack of compliance. Events of the 1960s revealed the difficulty that the state had in imposing curbs on education.

Dealing with multiple crises, the Rhee administration did not have a well-thought-out economic development plan that could guide educational need. While some economic planning had existed since the birth of the republic in 1948, neither the Office of Planning (established under the prime minister in 1948) nor the Ministry of Reconstruction (set up in 1955) had the staff or authority to draw up comprehensive economic plans. Only in 1958, with the creation of a Council for Economic Development, was the first comprehensive five-year plan devised, but this was approved in the spring of 1960 as the Rhee regime was collapsing.

Following the overthrow of the Rhee government in a student-led uprising in April 1960, South Korea experimented with a brief period of democratic, parliamentary government known as the Second Republic (1960–1961). After a parliamentary election, a government was formed by Prime Minister Chang Myŏn that formulated a more comprehensive plan for active government intervention into the economy to direct efforts toward economic and social development. Chang Myŏn early in his administration pledged to expand vocational education at all levels. In December, the minister of education announced a comprehensive reorganization of the MOE that enlarged the bureaus and sections dealing with technical, commercial, and physical education.[18] The next month, a new educational plan was issued that included substantial increases in the allocations for vocational training and called for enlarging the technical departments of colleges and universities at the expense of the social sciences and humanities. Furthermore, the plan called for the organization of a committee to consider merging commercial, technical, and academic secondary schools into comprehensive middle and high schools. This idea, long advocated by American educational advisers, was aimed at removing the stigma of attending vocational schools and avoiding the situation in which vocational schools were allotted inferior facilities and teachers.[19]

These efforts to invigorate vocational education were still only in the planning stage when a military coup under General Park Chung Hee (Pak Chŏnghŭi) in May 1961 prevented their implementation. The new military government then launched South Korea on a path of rapid economic growth and carried out a more comprehensive effort to channel the drive for education toward economic objectives.

EDUCATION AND THE DEVELOPMENTAL STATE

Educational development after 1961 occurred in a radically altered political and economic environment. South Korea entered a three-decade period of military-dominated governments and an era of rapid economic growth. Under the leadership of Park Chung Hee, the government in the 1960s launched a concerted and successful effort to industrialize the nation. Committed to economic development, the Park government, after several years of mixed results, oversaw an economic boom in which the nation's GNP grew about 9 percent annually from 1965 to 1978, a rate matched only by Taiwan and Japan. Economic expansion continued until 1997 at a slightly more modest average annual rate of 8 percent. In 1961, Korea was still predominantly rural, had few exports, and was dependent on foreign aid for survival. Under Park Chung Hee and the military-dominated governments that followed, South Korea was transformed into an industrial, urban society that was one of the world's major exporters of manufactured goods.

The military rulers—in particular Park Chung Hee and his chief lieutenant, Colonel Kim Jong Pil (Kim Chong-p'il)—sought to strengthen South Korea by ridding it of corrupt and unwholesome elements, accelerating the modernization of society, and creating a viable economy with a strong industrial base. They were motivated by a sense of being in competition with North Korea, whose recovery from the devastation of war appeared to be faster, its economy more robust and self-reliant, and its claims to represent a more viable model of Korean nationhood increasingly more convincing. Thus, from the beginning, the Park government was motivated by the need to strengthen the state by disciplining and unifying the population and expanding the national economy. These goals led the regime to pursue what has since been described as a developmental economy—one in which the state directed policy toward industrial development and subordinated other concerns to the achievement of rapid economic and industrial growth. While most economic activity remained in the private sector, the central government to a large extent intervened in the economy, aiding or discouraging activity in accordance with overall state plans. In other areas, such as social development or foreign relations, policy was formulated to complement economic objectives, or the areas were relegated to secondary importance. Park's developmental policies were not entirely new. The overall trend toward greater economic planning and emphasis on industrialization had already begun in the late 1950s and had been pursued by the Chang Myŏn administration. The Park administration, however, pursued these policies with a consistency and vigor that was markedly different from those of its predecessors. After a few uncertain years, the administration succeeded in launching the country on a path of sustained economic growth.

Education became part of this developmental strategy. From its first year in power, the new government sought to coordinate educational policy with its economic strategy. To direct educational development toward economic development, the state in the 1960s and 1970s sought to shift the emphasis from academic to vocational and technical education so that skills taught in schools would match economic needs; it also established and maintained quotas on higher education. To implement these policies, the Park government drew up the First Five-Year Educational Development Plan, for 1962–1966, to operate in conjunction with the First Five-Year Economic Development Plan, the first of a series of five-year plans that would serve as basic outlines of the state's developmental policies and objectives. Furthermore, the government pursued a number of more limited, long-term education plans.

It would be wrong to conclude that educational policy was as effective and oriented toward development as was industrial policy. In fact, educational expansion continued to be propelled by public demand, and the state's educational policy was always constrained by public pressure. While policy planners were able to utilize the popular pursuit of education to transfer the financial burden

to the students and their families and thus free themselves of heavy public investment in schooling, the same zeal for education that made this possible also
made it difficult to coordinate education with economic objectives. The Park
government and that of his successor, Chun Doo Hwan (1980–1988), while authoritarian, were not totally free from the need to maintain popular support,
nor was the state totally insulated from pressures by interest groups such as
middle- and upper-class Korean families who sought to bend educational policy to their aspirations for social advancement and status. The result was more
of a compromise between economic rationality and the public demand for
schooling.

The military rulers picked up the economic development plan that was
being drafted by the Chang Myŏn administration and made it the basis for
what became the First Five-Year Economic Development Plan. One important innovation was the establishment of a powerful administrative organ, the
Economic Planning Board (EPB), which could override budget allocation decisions and veto policy decisions of individual ministries. The EPB thus had
considerable authority to pressure or constrain the MOE's policy planning. It
also took charge of all statistics. The EPB members were chiefly technocrats,
often with Ph.D.s in economics from the United States, and were less subject to
political pressures or vested interests. They came to acquire enormous prestige,
and the plan they directed was successful beyond most expectations. The First
Five-Year Economic Development Plan targeted a GNP growth rate of 7.1
percent a year, with a 15 percent annual increase in industrial production and
a drop in the unemployment rate from 24 to 15 percent. New industries such
as iron and steel were to be created, and exports, chiefly textiles, were to be
greatly expanded. The plan exceeded most of its targets.[20]

In conjunction with these ambitious plans, the military government
launched a five-year plan for educational reconstruction that began on 1 January
1962. Drawn up by the Central Educational Research Institute at the request of
the minister of education and adopted by Park's military junta, this was the first
of a series of five educational plans that were to run concurrently with the five
economic plans.[21] Its objectives remained the basic educational policy for the
next two decades. First, as discussed in chapter 3, it sought to widen the number
of Korean children receiving basic education and reduce the numbers at the
higher levels. The educational system would be a clearly defined pyramid, broad
at the base and progressively narrower at the top. This meant normalizing

compulsory education by achieving an enrollment rate of 100 percent for boys and girls of primary school age. Middle schools would be expanded at a much greater rate than high schools, and college and university enrollment would be reduced. Second, there was to be a shift in emphasis from academic to vocational and technical education. This meant that secondary education would be reoriented toward developing the technical skills needed by the new industries. By these means, schooling would be fine-tuned to match economic needs.

PROMOTING VOCATIONAL EDUCATION

The Park government, when it came to power, pledged to reverse the trend toward academic schooling and reorient education toward technical training. It was encouraged in this by U.S. advisers, who were skeptical of the value of the burgeoning academic secondary schools and liberal arts colleges in a country with only a modest industrial infrastructure and a per capita income that placed it among the poorest nations.[22] Consequently, the First Five-Year Educational Development Plan laid out a comprehensive program for transforming the direction of Korean formal instruction. The plan called for radically changing the 5:3 ratio of academic to vocational enrollment in secondary schools to a 7:3 vocational to academic ratio by 1966. At the higher levels, drastic cuts would be made in humanities, arts, social science, law, and journalism departments, while science and technical fields would be strengthened.

In the summer of 1962, three pilot vocational schools were started, and the MOE sent a delegation to Japan to observe vocational education in that country. It set up vocational teacher-training centers attached to schools of science and engineering to solve the shortage of trained instructors in technical and scientific subjects.[23] MOE officials issued directives for greater emphasis on technical and scientific education in the curriculum and required all vocational schools to spend half their class time on vocational subjects. The latter was especially important as vocational schools, especially vocational high schools, were often little more than second-class college preparatory institutes with students and teachers spending more time on the academic subjects needed to pass the entrance exams than on technical subjects. To further reverse this trend, scientific and technical subjects were sometimes added to high school and college preparatory exams so that schools would give attention to them in the classroom.

In 1963, the Park administration launched, as part of the five-year plan, the Vocational Education Promotion Policy, which aimed to coordinate vocational education with economic needs. It called for retraining teachers, increasing the number of vocational high schools, and increasing the number of hours spent on vocational subjects at all levels of schooling. As part of this effort the government-controlled National Assembly passed the Industrial Education Promotion Law, which created guidelines for carrying out technical education in secondary schools, with the curriculum to be adjusted according to industrial needs.[24] (For further aspects of the law; see below.) But the state fell far short of the ambitious goals set in the First Five-Year Educational Development Plan. In 1962, there were 338 academic high schools with 199,000 students and 283 agricultural, technical, commercial, and fisheries high schools with 124,000 students—a substantial increase over the previous year in favor of vocational education. But this improvement was not maintained. At the end of the First Five-Year Educational Development Plan in 1966 there were 397 academic high schools with 259,000 students and 337 vocational high schools with 174,000 students; there was only a slightly higher percentage of enrollment in vocational secondary schools than at the start of the plan.[25] The plan was not successful because vocational and technical schools were unpopular; in practice officials conceded to pressure by not carrying out plans to convert academic schools to vocational ones. Nor were they enthusiastic about constructing new nonacademic institutions. The MOE made hundreds of small concessions to individual academic schools, allowing them to increase their enrollments; in some cases enrollment guidelines were simply ignored.

The problems in developing a more practical, skills-based schooling added weight to the arguments of those within the Park administration who argued that in order to implement this policy, the 6-3-3-4 structure of the educational system would have to change. As noted above, the existing system placed all students in general, six-year primary schools, from which they could go on to general, three-year middle schools, which then led to either an academic or vocational three-year high school, both of which qualified students to compete for admission to any form of higher education—a two- or four-year technical or teacher-training college or university. In November 1962, the Educational Committee of the Supreme Council for National Reconstruction (SCNR), as the military junta called itself, and the MOE worked out a plan to switch to a 6-3-5-4 system that would convert 50-60 percent of all high schools and some colleges to five-year vocational schools that would be terminal institutions. All existing middle schools would also provide a large amount of technical instruction.[26] The following month, President Park formed an Educational Policy Council, which was to report directly to the SCNR on progress in drawing up and implementing the planned restructuring. The current system was, according to the MOE, not suitable because it "merely imitated foreign countries' systems . . . and was inadequate for promoting vocational education, which is essential for developing the nation."[27] The Educational Policy Council announced it would make a final decision on restructuring in June 1963, but when newspapers, education circles, and opposition politicians called for postponing such a momentous change until after a return to civilian rule, President Park agreed to delay any decision until after the presidential and National Assembly elections that were to be held in the fall.[28]

During the course of 1964, the Educational Policy Council, under the chairmanship of Yi Sŏn-gŭn (who had served as education minister under Syngman Rhee), met ten times and finally endorsed the conversion to five-year technical schools. However, the plan was modified so that this level would not be terminal but could lead to a four-year technical college. In this way the technical schools would be a more appealing alternative since they would still serve as a route to social advancement. The plan was immediately opposed by educators, the press, parents, and private secondary schools and colleges, all of whom regarded it as a threat to the principle of equal opportunity. Most of the educated Korean public feared any attempt to restrict access to the prestigious academic track, and most remained committed to the 6-3-3-4 educational system. Consequently the plan was temporarily shelved.[29]

In January 1965, President Park made restructuring the educational system one of the major points in his State of the Nation address. It was Park's most emphatic call to transform education so that it would be directed toward economic development. "The current excessive liberal arts and science education . . . will gradually transform into advance[d] technology and vocational education." To achieve this, "the government will push ahead with [the] reform of the present school system."[30] Subsequently, Park took a personal interest in the plan, meeting with Educational Policy Council members and holding private talks with educators and politicians on the subject. But the proposed change was opposed by the KFEA and the press.[31] Within the administration, a number of alternative plans were proposed, the most radical by the Party Policy Committee of the ruling Democratic Republican Party. It called for the creation of a two-track, four-year middle school that would lead to a three-year academic or vocational high school and would drastically reduce the number of students in the arts and humanities. It also included job placement for all technical graduates.[32] In preparation for this change the MOE announced that all high schools would be merged with middle schools to create a single secondary school.[33] No agreement could be reached, however, because many Korean educators, parents, and bureaucrats objected to changes that might restrict access to higher education. Consequently, the reform of the school system was still in the planning and debate stage when, during the Second Five-Year Economic Development Plan (1967–1971), it was indefinitely shelved.

With the abandonment of plans to restructure the education system, the state was faced with the problem of vocational education becoming merely another means of entry into academic colleges. To prevent this, in December 1968, the government added a requirement that a student would have to select one technical or vocational subject on the college entrance examination along with the standard requirements in Korean language, social science, natural science, and English.[34] But the effect was often to concentrate only on the one vocational test topic in vocational schools and spend much of the rest of the time on the standard test requirements, so vocational secondary schools continued to resemble the academic in the content of instruction. And vocational schools were often in a sad state. In 1966, only about 1,800 out of the 8,000 teachers needed for the 174,000 students in the 337 vocational high schools were available. Most schools were poorly equipped, often lacking even basic texts. Furthermore, only 106 of the estimated 266 textbooks required to cover all the basic subjects in the vocational schools were available.[35] This situation later improved, but only slowly.

The MOE attempted to convert academic schools to vocational institutions but without much success. Private secondary schools through the Private Secondary School Association resisted interference in their administration and fought to preserve their status as academic, college preparatory institutions amid attempts to transform many into vocational schools. Another point of contention between these schools and the administration was over the separation of middle and high schools. Most of the first-rate private schools had both middle and high schools on the same campus, usually under the same principal. They also, in practice, showed a preference for their own middle school students, despite regulations that all students compete equally for entry into high school. Officials felt that separation of middle and high schools would make it easier to convert some of the high schools to vocational ones. Efforts to force the separation met with only mixed success, and this was true even in many public secondary schools as well.[36] Parents whose son or daughter got into a middle school with a good reputation preferred to have the middle and high schools under the same administration. Less prestigious schools sought to retain their middle school students by having them enter their high school. Consequently, there was strong resistance to the separation of middle and high schools from both parents and school officials.

During the Second Five-Year Economic Development Plan, there were modest increases in the expenditures on vocational education, in enrollments at vocational education classes, and in the number of hours in the curriculum devoted to technical subjects. The MOE budget allotted to technical and vocational education increased 2 percent in the late 1960s.[37] The number of vocational high schools increased and the enrollment ratio of vocational to academic students narrowed, although it still fell far short of the plan's goal of having at least two vocational students for every academic one. In 1970, there were 315,000 students in academic high schools and still only 275,000 students in the nation's vocational schools (see table 4).

Overall in its first decade the Park administration, despite the rhetoric, made no radical change in the content of Korean education, only a modest move toward more technical schooling. In general, the emphasis on academic education continued, and the administration encountered resistance from parents, teachers, and school administrators with each effort to limit its expansion. The MOE and the EPB would announce plans for building more vocational schools, training more vocational teachers, and converting some academic schools to technical ones, only to modify these plans in the weeks that followed. While the promotion of technical education brought applause from technocrats, it created tension within much of South Korean society. In fact, few aspects of educational policy produced more frustration for the state's planners.

State efforts at promoting vocational education clashed with Confucian values (as noted above). As studies have shown, the traditional attitudes toward learning were prevalent in the early 1960s, as they still are today.[38] As a result of the social and political upheavals that had taken place since the last decade of colonial rule, South Korea had become a fairly fluid society, and for most a rise to high or elite status via education seemed a reasonable goal. Large segments of the public felt their children's climb up the ranks toward status and power was being threatened by restricting academic education. Income and promotion policies both reflected and added economic rationality to decisions to eschew vocational education. Few Koreans wanted to be mere technicians.

EDUCATION AND THE PUSH FOR
HEAVY AND CHEMICAL INDUSTRY

In 1970–1971, a team from the University of Florida working with the Central Educational Research Institute was highly critical of vocational education. Vocational high schools should "cease to operate in their present form" but should be made part of the job training programs.[39] Vocational training should be exclusively related to specific jobs.[40] (A study by the Central Educational Research Institute had found that less than a third of vocational high school graduates were employed in areas related to their studies.)[41] In the early 1970s economic planners were seriously worried that the training of skilled workers was not keeping pace with the country's new industrial takeoff and that this would result in critical technical manpower shortages that could hamper further economic growth in the coming years. As a result, the Park administration launched what was the nation's most comprehensive effort to coordinate educational development with economic planning during the so-called Yushin (revitalization or restoration) phase of the regime (established in 1972).

From 1971, the Park regime took a more authoritarian turn, declaring a state of national emergency, arresting opponents, and issuing a new Yushin constitution that gave Park Chung Hee near dictatorial powers. With less need to be held accountable, the regime could push forward on vocational education. South Korea's drive toward industrialization took a major turn when Park announced a program to develop heavy and chemical industries at the start of 1973. The campaign, launched just weeks after the Yushin constitution was in place, was to reorient the nation's exports away from textiles and light industry and into automobiles, heavy equipment, steel, ships, and petrochemicals. A massive effort produced impressive results, with great new industrial centers created in the southeastern part of the country. The symbols of this shift toward heavy industry were the huge, ultramodern P'ohang Iron and Steel Company (POSCO) complex in the port of P'ohang and the enormous shipbuilding yards in the nearby port of Ulsan. At the same time, the Park administration made a renewed call for retooling the educational system to serve the needs of this stage in the nation's industrialization.

The state strengthened vocational education in several ways. Annual exams were conducted at vocational secondary schools to enforce national standards. Night schools were encouraged so that industrial workers could earn a middle school or high school degree emphasizing technical skills, and a special curriculum was designed for this purpose. The proportion of the budget allocated for vocational education doubled between 1970 and 1979, with the biggest increases in the years immediately following the announcement of the heavy and chemical industries program.[42]

A major innovation occurred in 1973, when the state issued the Industrial Education Promotion Law, which attempted to reorient vocational high schools toward industrial needs by systematizing on-the-job training programs. Eventually vocational schools were required to devote 70 percent of their class time to vocational subjects. Students were required to spend two to six months of their first two years training at an industrial site and at least four months of their third year on the shop floor. Technical high schools were singled out for development and encouraged to specialize in machinery, electronics, mechanical engineering, and other areas matching the skills demanded by targeted industries. At the urging of the EPB, government officials selected eighty-two vocational high schools for such specialized training and appropriated extra funds to equip them for this purpose.[43] To see to it that vocational secondary schools taught vocational subjects (rather than preparing students for the college entrance examination), a national technical qualification exam was instituted from 1978, and all those expecting to graduate had to demonstrate their competency in the technical areas they studied before receiving a degree.[44]

A few weeks after launching the heavy and chemical industries program, the Park regime organized a cooperative system between vocational education and industries.[45] An Employment Training Centers Law set up a system of licenses for industrial instructors, and in 1974, the Vocational Training Regulation Law expanded the scale of industrial training programs. The Ministry of Defense, the national railroads, the Ministry of Construction, the Ministry of Communication, and the MOE all operated on-the-job training centers. A few private companies such as Kŭmsŏng (Lucky-Goldstar) had had such programs from the 1960s. Now all major industrial concerns were mandated to provide

Table 8. Junior and Four-Year Colleges and Enrollments in Korea, 1961–1995

Year	Junior Colleges		Four-Year Colleges	
	Number of Schools	Enrollment (in 1,000s)	Number of Schools	Enrollment (in 1,000s)
1965	48	23	70	105
1970	65	53	71	146
1975	101	63	72	208
1980	128	165	85	402
1985	120	242	100	932
1990	117	324	107	1,040
1995	145	570	131	1,188

Source: Republic of Korea, MOE , *Kyoyuk t'onggye yŏnbo,* 1971, 1981, 1996.

systematic training programs. The government also encouraged the growth of junior vocational and technical colleges, and the MOE ordered the conversion of some vocational high schools into two-year colleges.

Even this new drive for technical and vocational education, however, met with mixed results since public attitudes toward education did not change. For example, enrollment at the new junior colleges fell far short of that planned (see table 8). To enhance their appeal, the government in 1970 began providing a disproportional share of scholarships to students attending them: about 40 percent of all state scholarships to higher education were allocated to junior vocational and technical college students. But since only a very small amount of the budget was set aside for scholarships, the allocation was not enough to overcome the general aversion of most Koreans for technical and vocational schooling.[46]

The plan to revitalize technical education met with other disappointing results. Korean businesses were not very enthusiastic about the training centers, so during the Fourth Five-Year Economic Development Plan (1977–1981) penalties were imposed on firms that employed more than three hundred workers but did not have in-plant training programs.[47] Many firms, however, preferred paying the fines to setting up the training programs. And the programs that were functioning were often inadequate.[48] A further problem was that many experts began to have doubts about the effectiveness of vocational education, finding it hard to match in-school training with the rapidly shifting needs of industry. (Enrollments in training programs are shown in table 9.)

Table 9. Employees Enrolled in Vocational Training
Programs in Korea, 1967–1988

Type of Program	1967–1971	1977–1981	1982–1986	1987–1988
Government	63,000	81,000	120,000	121,000
Private	36,000	177,000	337,000	114,000

Source: Kim Yŏng-hwa et al., 181.

The biggest single problem facing vocational education, however, re-mained public resistance. It was also reflected by employers, who showed a pref-erence in hiring nonvocational graduates, feeling that technical skills could be picked up on the job. Pupils continued to hope they could reenter the academic track and pass the university entrance examination even when enrolled in voca-tional schools. In the early 1970s, despite the state programs for technical train-ing, academic high school enrollment grew faster than vocational school enrollment. In 1975, there were 648,000 youths at academic high schools and 474,000 at vocational institutes—about the same ratio as in 1961. At the urging of the EPB and technocrats in the administration, the state in the late 1970s launched the construction of new technical and vocational high schools, but this too fell far short of the goal of significantly reversing the preference for academic schools. In 1980, there were still only 764,000 students attending vocational high schools, compared to 932,000 attending academic schools. Government regula-tions forcing technical schools to carry out intensive practical training made them more vocational in fact as well as in name, but this only made them less popular; young people and their parents did what they could to avoid them.

The situation did not improve substantially. Each of the five-year economic development plans was filled with calls for the "improvement of manpower re-sources" by promoting scientific and technical education. Government reports continually warned that the educational system was not producing the techni-cally trained workers needed to maintain the pace of industrial growth. There was a greater enrollment in engineering and science programs because the pres-tige of engineers and scientists and the financial rewards in these professions in-creased their popularity, which resulted in less resistance to higher quotas for these programs. But this quickly led to a glut in highly trained scientists and en-gineers while shortages of medium-level technicians persisted (see table 10). In

Table 10. Majors of Entering Korean University Students, 1962–1978

Year	Humanities and Social Sciences	Education	Science and Engineering	Agriculture
1962	7,010	580	7,685	1,020
1967	10,430	2,070	13,110	825
1972	13,020	5,010	19,300	3,100
1977	17,975	12,285	27,350	4,610
1978	20,915	11,835	33,035	4,610

Source: Yi Hae-yŏng, "Taehak iphak chŏngwŏn kyŏlchŏng ŭi sahoejŏk tongan e kwanhan yŏn'gu" [An analytic study of the social dynamics determining the higher education enrollment quota] (Ph.D. diss., Seoul National University, 1992), 68.

general, neither the content nor the structure of education was ever comprehensively coordinated with the needs perceived by state economic planners and industrial managers, although the quality and numbers of engineering students improved and some of the industrial training programs were useful.

Vocational education fared even more poorly in the 1980s. Under President Chun Doo Hwan, enrollment in academic high schools grew by nearly two-thirds while that in vocational schools stagnated (see table 4). Government support for various vocational training programs also fell, and private spending fell faster.[49] A Presidential Commission for Education Reform in 1985 came to the same conclusion Park had reached twenty years earlier: for technical and vocational education to flourish, the educational system created in 1949–1951 had to be changed. The commission suggested that the 6-3-3-4 school system be replaced by a 5-3-4-4 structure. Under such a new structure, high school would be four years, and after two years students would take a pretest to see if they were suited for vocational or university education.[50] This proposed system was more flexible and could be easily adjusted to encourage more vocational education, but there were technical problems in implementing it— for example, enabling the already overcrowded secondary schools to absorb the extra students that a switch to this system would necessitate. But the main problem, as in the past, was that tampering with the open access system encountered popular resistance, and the initial negative public reaction discouraged the Chun government from promoting this plan further.[51]

Another problem in coordinating educational development with economic planning was the lack of long-term, consistent educational planning. While overall educational policy maintained consistent features—for example, sequential development, emphasis on universal basic education, a uniform national curriculum, and continual upgrading of teacher training—in practice, the details of educational policy tended to be made ad hoc and were subsequently often modified or abandoned. Much of this was due to the conflicting public versus state objectives, which resulted in vacillation and confusing shifts in policies. These were aggravated by the short tenures of education ministers, which in the thirty years from 1948 to 1978 averaged about fifteen months, with each new appointee enunciating his own policy goals.

South Koreans were urged by American advisers to institutionalize long-term planning. In December 1967, the director of the U.S. operations mission in Korea advised educational authorities on the need for an overall reform of education. He was especially concerned about establishing a long-range plan to coordinate educational policies to manpower needs. In January 1968, President Park met with advisers to discuss a major reform of education, including a greater stress on vocational education. In September 1968, in a congressional policy address, he stated three needs: attaining consistency in educational policies, improving manpower development, and maximizing the cost-effectiveness of educational investment. In October, a task force was created.[52] Out of this the Council for Long-Term Educational Planning (CLEP) was created in January 1969. In the summer of 1970, CLEP drew up a medium-range educational development plan concerned with coordinating education to manpower needs, but this plan, as with all long-range educational plans in South Korea, was abortive. Soon after the plans were drawn up, CLEP was dissolved. In 1971, it was replaced by a more informal educational policy council, the first of a series of such councils that were called into being every few years to advise the president and his cabinet on educational reforms. As one contemporary observer remarked, "Most key policymakers did not realize the need for the institutionalization of the Council for Long-Term Educational Planning."[53]

Some measure of assistance to long-range educational planning was provided by the creation of the KEDI, an educational think tank. While the KEDI provided a valuable resource to educational policymakers, the pattern of ad hoc and constantly changing educational policies continued. Educational policy was, in practice, driven more by accommodating the popular pursuit of academic degrees than by rational planning. To remedy this, a number of Presidential Commissions for Education Reform were inaugurated in the 1980s that issued grand reports on the state of education and spelled out often detailed recommendations that drew from a large number of educational experts. Few of the recommendations were ever implemented.

QUOTAS ON HIGHER EDUCATION

The problems of the South Korean government after 1961 in coordinating education with development strategies are most clearly seen in the attempts at establishing quotas on higher education. A major task of the First Five-Year Educational Development Plan was to not only end the explosive growth in higher education, but also reduce the numbers of students in post-secondary institutions. The planned reduction of university enrollment was dramatic; in 1961 there were 125,000 students in higher education; this number was to be slashed to 64,164 in the next three years. To accomplish this, the aperture to higher education was so reduced that only 16,691 students would be admitted in the new academic year beginning 1 March 1962.[54] Ideally only 20 percent of high school graduates would gain entry into college or university. As a first step in these plans, many departments in universities were merged or eliminated, and twelve private universities and colleges were ordered closed in December 1961.[55] Economic planners in the Bureau of International Cooperation, which directed U.S. aid money, and later in the EPB attempted to deny foreign aid funds to higher education except for engineering and some other technical fields. They likened university education to an empty shell or a facade: on the outside a number of schools had built imposing buildings, but inside these buildings were poorly lit; unheated; lacked libraries, resources, and equipment; and were understaffed with faculty members who were poorly paid and underqualified.

Details of the plan to streamline higher education were announced by the minister of education, Colonel Mun Hŭi-sik, at a meeting of the presidents and deans of the nation's forty institutions of higher learning in November 1961. Ten colleges were to be reduced to two-year vocational schools; several universities were to be closed completely; and a number of departments, especially arts and humanities, would be closed or merged. Total enrollment in higher education (as noted above) was to be reduced by half. The remaining private institutions would be subjected to rigid controls. Previously ignored guidelines on the provision of faculty and facilities would be strictly enforced, and school expenditures would be carefully regulated to "restore public confidence in school management."[56] Greater stress would be placed on physical education, and foreign expertise would be sought to improve the quality of physical education and athletic programs and the health of the nation's youth. Supervision of overseas students would intensify in order to avoid a "brain drain" and ensure that Korean students acquired skills that were needed by the national economy and that they returned home after graduation to help in national reconstruction.[57]

In conjunction with the plan, the MOE announced changes in the entrance examination system. It directly took over the examination process from the schools. The middle school, high school, and college exams scheduled for December were to be drawn up by a committee of educators under the supervision of the MOE and administered as uniform national tests. Individual schools would then make selections based on the results of these tests. State officials defended the new state examination system by declaring that its main purpose was to ensure fairness in the competitive entry process. It also enabled the central government to exert stricter control over what was taught in the classroom by determining the subject matter of the tests. Furthermore, irregularities in admissions—including the often reported practice of admission through bribery and family connections—could be more rigorously controlled by the direct involvement of the MOE in the examination process.

From the beginning, the plan was poorly conceived and executed. Details of which schools and departments were to be closed, merged, or demoted changed from week to week, with the final number much smaller than originally announced. Educators greeted the drastic reduction in higher education with dismay. They were joined by C. W. Wood of the University of Minnesota, head of an advisory group assisting higher education in South Korea who warned that such a reduction would greatly impair the country's long-range development.[58] Such protests were initially ignored. However, within weeks, the regime began wavering in its commitment to cut enrollments. Ten colleges were closed, but nine of them were eventually reopened. College quotas were also continually increased from the originally proposed sixteen thousand new entrants for 1962 until the figure reached twenty-six thousand—about the same number as in the previous year.[59] Yet even this number represented less than a third of college aspirants since virtually every high school graduate sought entry into a university.

In the spring of 1963, Park Chung Hee had agreed, under U.S. pressure, to honor a pledge to return the country to civilian rule, and he became a candidate for president under the military-sponsored Democratic Republican Party. As a result, the regime became even more responsive to the public pressure for open access to higher education. Against the counsel of his economic advisers, Park promised in 1963 to raise the quota to thirty-two thousand.[60] At the end of 1963, eight junior colleges were promoted to four-year colleges to deal with the expanded enrollment.[61] In each subsequent year of the First Five-Year Educational Development Plan, the same drama was played out. The government announced little or no increase in the number of students allowed to enter higher education; then, following pressure on administration officials from parents, these figures would be revised upward—never as high as the public wanted, but more than economic planners thought wise.

Furthermore, the government had difficulty enforcing the quotas. One experiment was to limit the number of college graduates by instituting a national qualifying exam for baccalaureate degrees. The baccalaureate examination was designed to screen out students who were incompetent. While there was fierce competition to enter college, once admitted, students seldom failed since attendance was generally not required for classes; colleges and universities that depended on tuition payments had no interest in expelling or failing students. Lacking incentives to study, many college students idled away their time. The baccalaureate exam, the administration declared, would address these problems by holding students accountable, place pressure on universities to provide adequate training, and reduce the excessive number of degree holders. It had the added advantage of directing potentially politically active students toward a preoccupation with their studies.

The exam held on 22 December 1961 created immediate difficulties for the administration. It was greeted with great skepticism by the press, with opposition from college administrators, and with sporadic demonstrations and calls for a boycott from students. Out of a total of nearly 25,700 graduates, 7,242 boycotted it. The administration at first took a hard line against those students, but later almost all were allowed to graduate. Of the 18,448 that sat for it, all but 2,749 were successful. In November 1962, turnout for the exam was better when it became clear that few students would be denied degrees because of the test results.[62] Nonetheless, the baccalaureate exam was immensely unpopular and was continually attacked by the schools, most educators, the press, and students. In 1963 the administration abolished it.

To control the number of students entering college, the MOE instituted a
national preliminary examination, which was also designed to ensure fairness,
disqualify incompetent students, and allow the MOE more say in the selection
process. It allowed 50 percent over the entrance quota to pass the exam. Individual colleges and universities would then make their selection from among
those who passed. This met with less open opposition than the baccalaureate
exam. It proved, however, difficult to prevent schools from accepting more
students than they were allotted. This created a contention that continued during the First Five-Year Educational Development Plan. When the MOE introduced a registration system to keep track of the number of students enrolled
and the number graduating, it ran into resistance from school authorities. A
number of attempts to deny degrees to students who were enrolled beyond the
quotas were also abandoned. As a result, efforts to eliminate what were regarded as excessive numbers of college graduates were not successful. A measure of this failure is the fact that at the end of 1966 there were ninety-eight
colleges and universities and an estimated 164,205 students—48,238 over the
government quota of 115,967, which itself had been doubled from the original
plan to limit the number of students in higher education to 62,000 by 1966.[63]

Although state measures were by 1966 having some effect in tightening
control over enrollments, the initial plan failed because it ran counter to the social demand for higher education. Schools as well were under financial pressure
to increase enrollments since 80 percent of all revenue for private colleges and
universities came from tuition. In addition, school officials were subject to enormous pressure and large bribes from anxious parents. Government officials,
too, used influence and bribery to get their children into desired schools.

These failures are at least partly attributable to the difficulty of the military
government in resisting the demands of interest groups. Among the formidable
interests blocking educational reforms were the private schools and institutes.
In the early 1960s, these formed one of the biggest segments of South Korea's
modest economy. Private schools accounted for a third of the middle school and
vocational high school enrollment, half that of academic high schools, and about
three-quarters of that in higher education. In 1962, 36 of the nation's 48 colleges
and universities were private.[64] The relative power of these institutions was accentuated by the fact that they were concentrated in the cities. In 1966, 89 of
Seoul's 116 middle schools and 34 of the 50 middle schools in Pusan were private, and they accounted for three-quarters and two-thirds of the correspond-

ing enrollment respectively. Similarly, private academic high schools accounted for three-quarters of the high schools and their pupils in Seoul and two-thirds of all high school students in Pusan. Furthermore, nearly 70 percent of all college and university students were concentrated in Seoul, and of these, 90 percent attended private schools.[65] Public institutes of higher learning were concentrated more in provincial areas and suffered in prestige by being "provincial." Only Seoul National University, at the pinnacle of Korean academia, stood out as an exception. Private schools had their own organizations, which lobbied for their interests. Although less well organized, private institutes, especially cram schools, which flourished in great numbers and employed thousands of full- and part-time teachers, formed another huge industry committed to the perpetuation of the existing educational system.[66] The amount of money involved in schooling was enormous and made education the largest single sector of the Korean economy in the early 1960s after agriculture.[67]

South Koreans universally decried the resulting commercialization of education. Both the Chang Myŏn and Park Chung Hee governments pledged to reform the costly and inefficient educational system, and early efforts to more tightly oversee the operation of private educational foundations and private cram schools were well received. The government in 1963 promulgated the Private School Law. This gave the MOE, as well as provincial governors and county chief administrators, extensive power to regulate private schools and made appointment of school officials subject to MOE approval. Mandatory imprisonment was imposed on violators of the numerous regulations governing the appropriation of school funds and the administration of schools.[68] Although principals of secondary schools and presidents of universities were still nominally independent, the minister of education could request their resignation (but could not dismiss them himself). Overall, the act greatly enhanced the state's authority over private schools.

This did not make private schools powerless. The private colleges and universities campaigned for revision of the Private School Law. Calling for "government support, not government control," they supported a proposed revision to the law that was introduced in the National Assembly in 1965.[69] They also waged a battle against the quotas, arguing that since 80 percent of their revenues came from tuition, without adequate numbers of students they could not make ends meet. Meanwhile, the MOE issued continuous directives to improve school facilities and hire more faculty, both of which were far below the legal minimum requirements in almost all universities, private and national. The MOE, other branches of the Park administration, and later the ruling Democratic Republican Party accused the schools of investing in real estate, businesses, and various unrelated enterprises but failing to recycle profits back into the schools. Periodic investigations were launched in school financial accounts.

The private schools frequently ignored the MOE guidelines. Conflicts between the administration and the two leading women's universities illustrate the war of nerves. Ewha Women's University president Kim Ok-kil openly defied the quota and in 1965 enrolled 40 percent more students than allotted, stating that the decision was made in accordance with the "belief and conscience of educators that it was necessary to go against the laws." The minister of education, Yun Ch'ŏn-ju, who had just inaugurated a ten-year plan for university education in another attempt to control the growth of higher education, realized that this new effort would fail in its first year if the quotas were not enforced. Consequently, he threatened to close the university if the extra students were not eliminated. The school remained uncooperative. When inspectors came to check registration lists, all the staff had gone. Eventually Kim was pressured to resign, but the extra students, many from prominent homes, were allowed to stay. After more than a year of acrimonious confrontation, the dispute ended with a compromise in which Ewha submitted student registration lists and no student or staff member was penalized for having violating the quota.[70] The nation's other prestigious higher institution for women, Sukmyong (Sungmyŏng) Women's University, was also challenged by the MOE and filed a civil suit against the ministry for unreasonable interference in its affairs.[71]

Although the MOE made a number of attempts to curtail extra admissions, private schools found ways to ignore or circumvent them. In the spring of 1966, an investigation into seventeen private colleges and universities turned up 76,631 students; the quotas allowed for 38,576. One of these, Hanyang University, had 13,875 students although its quota was only 3,421; the Buddhist Tongguk and the Confucian Sŏnggyun'gwan universities each had over 6,000 enrolled despite respective quotas of 3,130 and 2,494.[72]

In the late 1960s, the state began to manage enrollment in higher education more effectively. The Park regime had hoped to reduce the number of college students by one half but instead saw a 25 percent increase during its first five years in power. After 1967, however, increases were very modest and strictly enforced. A plan in 1967 to create a grading system that would flunk out students was less successful. Partly this was due to the tradition of automatic progression from one grade to another that was characteristic of all the nation's schooling. But it also reflected the undemanding academic standards and the need for schools to maintain their tuition revenue. University presidents opposed the new grading system with virtual unanimity. During the course of 1967 the universities largely ignored it, and it died a quiet death. But the administration proved more adamant in enforcing strict limits on the growth of higher education. During the presidential election campaign in the summer of 1967, the ruling Democratic Republican Party promised only a modest augmentation of four thousand students a year for the next five years and called for this increase to come entirely in the areas of science and technology. As a concession to parents, the party pledged greater government support to higher education in order to lessen the financial burden on students and their families.[73]

The following year, with elections out of the way, the Park government enforced the university quotas with renewed vigor. Much of the push came from technocrats, who pressed for tighter restrictions on the number of college students. EPB officials suggested that the quotas for 1968 were too high and should be cut 5 percent.[74] Park then issued the Presidential Decree for Regulating College Student Quotas and the Decree for Registration of Degree Grantees. The Higher Education Bureau of the MOE was reorganized with personnel designated for implementing these decrees. The MOE announced that it would seek the cooperation of police and prosecutors in enforcing the 1968 quotas.[75] In July, President Park issued a statement that he was ordering his minister of education, Kwŏn O-byŏng, to crack down on all violations of the regulations; a week later the MOE began conducting a series of frequent inspections of institutions of higher learning to check on illegally admitted students. As a result, four schools were found to have admitted 821 undergraduates in excess of their quotas.[76] The National Assembly then began an investigation into quota violations. President Kim Yŏn-jun of Hanyang University, testifying before the legislators, admitted that most colleges and universities continued to violate the limits on new students. But the investigation also made clear that the numbers were small, often involving students from rich or influential families.[77] It was becoming apparent that the quota system inaugurated in 1966 was now being enforced and that the days of uncontrolled growth of higher education were over.

Still colleges and universities continued to overenroll students, if less blatantly than before. It was a practice, Kyŏnghŭi University president Cho

Yŏng-sik argued, that was "a matter of reality" in view of the enormous pressure from parents to send their children to college and the financial needs of schools.[78] Schools sometimes continued to be openly defiant. In 1970, for example, the MOE ordered all colleges and universities to submit lists of alumni to check on recent violations, but not one of the nation's forty-eight institutes of higher learning complied.[79] Even under the more authoritarian Yushin phase the pattern continued in which the government issued modest increases in quotas, universities and parent groups protested, and then the government enlarged the quotas. In a compromise, the government in the spring of 1973 allowed the universities to exceed their official quotas by 10 percent and then levied severe penalties on schools that went beyond this figure.[80].

While the Park government faced enormous problems in controlling the expansion of higher education, it at least checked the growth in the 1970s and established the principle that education should meet the needs of economic development. Many of the regime's efforts, however, were undone after 1980, when the state gave in to public demand and allowed enrollments to soar. In contrast to efforts to limit university enrollments, the policy to expand secondary education met with public enthusiasm. In 1972, as the state began to prepare to rapidly develop heavy industry, it was decided that the need for high school graduates would increase. While this was a continuation of the policy of sequential development, it differed in that it was a serious effort to expand the number of high school students at a pace that would match the needs of the marketplace. Subsequently, secondary education grew from the early 1970s. Nor did the state have to spend much on these new schools since much of the cost of secondary education was financed through a complex system of tuition, fees, and "voluntary" contributions.

In part, the extreme difficulties of the South Korean state in channeling schooling to meet economic objectives suggest that it was not the "strong state" insulated from pressure and vested interests that is often portrayed.[81] Still, the state was strong enough to maintain a sequential, pyramid structure for the nation's education, even if it was often a distorted pyramid. But the effort to prevent an oversupply of higher degree holders contributed to one of the central features of South Korean education: the preoccupation with entrance examinations.

The state was able to direct education toward developmental needs only at great political costs. The problem created by the increasing numbers competing for university entry, along with the state's attempts to bully students and teachers and to impose educational policies from above, contributed to the anger and discontent in the nation that bubbled over in late 1979, leading to Park's assassination. The new government of Chun Doo Hwan, less sure of its legitimacy, was more reluctant to challenge public demand.

South Korea's push for rapid industrialization after 1962 created another, if less traumatic, social upheaval: the countryside became depopulated as hundreds of thousands of young and not so young men and women left the farms to work in the factories of Seoul and the newly established industrial centers such as P'ohang, Ulsan, and Ch'angwŏn. The *saemaŭl* movement, a vigorous campaign to mobilize agricultural villages for modernization and self-improvement projects carried out by President Park in the 1970s, brought further disruption in rural routines. Even the most isolated villages were brought into the vortex of aspiring social climbers seeking to acquire middle-class status. Meanwhile, an expanding educational system and a booming economy created a much larger and more articulate middle class, whose values pervaded society. This great transformation further contributed to the restless quality of Korean society and its pursuit of social advancement through education.

5 The Entrance Examination System

Perhaps the most vivid illustration of South Korea's obsession with education has been what the Koreans term "examination hell" *(sihŏm chiok)* or "examination mania." Soon after 1945, an intense competition emerged for advancement into prestigious, upper-level institutions by obtaining high scores on secondary school and university entrance examinations. Since entrance to any university has been largely determined by the scores on these annual entrance examinations, students have spent most of their waking time preparing for them. This preparation has included evenings and weekends at cram schools and costly private tutoring, which have greatly added to the financial burden for many families. If the main purpose of South Korean education has been status, then it has been these entrance examinations that have been the key mechanism in that process.

The examination system is central to understanding the dynamics of the Korean educational system. It created a high-pressured, narrowly directed educational system and contributed to the role of education as a fundamental mechanism for social advancement. The dominant role of the examination system illustrates the importance of education as a determiner of social status, the Korean concern with rank and status, and the universal desire for and belief in the possibility of upward mobility. The failure to establish a clear, consistent examination policy also reflects the extent to which the educational system was shaped by social pressures, the weight of tradition, and the contradictions between an authoritarian state and public pressure that set limits on its effective control over education.

THE EMERGENCE OF EXAMINATION MANIA

South Korea's national preoccupation with entrance examinations has a long, historical tradition behind it. Success in the civil examinations *(kwagŏ)* was the ambition of almost every upper-class male in Yi dynasty Korea. The modern school entrance examination system, however, was the creation of the Japanese and was retained with only minor modifications by South Korea after independence. After 1945 written examinations for middle and high school entry were prepared by the teaching staff of each school. This was similar to Japanese practice except that Japanese examinations had been divided into verbal and math sections, while after liberation Korean educators chose to switch to subject exams based on what was taught in elementary schools. In 1949, as a result of widespread criticisms of the exams, the MOE ordered that the entrance exams be replaced by intellectual and physical tests and that admittance to higher-level schools be also based on *naesin*, reports by the teacher of a child's achievement and character.[1] This proved difficult to implement. Criteria for intellectual tests could not be agreed upon, and the teachers' reports, while enhancing the authority of teachers and appearing to conform to the ideas of progressive education by deemphasizing exams and stressing a child's classroom performance, also seemed arbitrary and confusing. Examinations appeared simpler to carry out and objective. In fact, few educators were willing to follow the suggestion of American educators and American educational theory in abandoning the central role of the entrance exam as the determiner of a student's future course.

In 1951, the MOE instituted a national comprehensive examination system *(kukka yŏn'hap kosaje)* to provide a uniform entrance exam for all secondary schools. This proved unpopular with public and private school officials. Although they were allowed to pass 150 percent of the quota of students and select students from among these, secondary school principals and teachers saw the national examinations as an erosion of their authority. Due to widespread protests by school principals and educators, the MOE abandoned the procedure after only two years. There was further experimentation with *naesin,* but in general, entrance into secondary schools in the late 1940s and 1950s was determined by written subject tests prepared by a school staff or a provincial education board.[2] At the university level written entrance exams based on subject areas were given by each university. As in the case of the secondary schools, a brief experiment with a national exam in 1954 proved so unpopular that it was discontinued the following year.[3]

The test-taking ordeal for South Korean students began with the middle school entrance examination for twelve-year-olds. Although examinations were held at both the middle school and high school level, it was the middle school exam that was critical. Many middle and high schools were under the same principal, shared staff, or had the same owner (if private); in most cases, once a student entered a middle school, he or she was likely to advance into the related high school, although this was not automatic. When students sought advancement into a more prestigious high school, competition could become fierce. This was especially true in the years 1952–1955, when the shortage of places in high schools was the most severe. Since the middle school exam was generally the more crucial one, the pressure on elementary school students could be considerable, for entrance into a prestigious middle school virtually ensured success in life. Those who had been successful in advancing into middle school would sit for the high school entrance examination three years later, and most high school seniors would compete in the university entrance examination for a coveted place in a prestigious school or in any school at all.

Parents, newspapers, and provincial boards of education all acted as watchdogs to ensure that there was no tampering with the results, and consequently the examinations were generally fairly conducted.[4] Yet despite this general fairness, there was widespread criticism of the examination system. Educators, journalists, and MOE officials widely felt that the system was psychologically damaging and put excessive pressure on children and that it led to a situation in which teachers too often saw their role as preparing students for the exams. Both charges were valid. Some schools offered special classes in the evenings or on weekends and collected tuition for them. This was especially common in Seoul and Pusan, which had the greatest concentration of students, money, and socially ambitious parents. After-school cram sessions became important sources of supplementary income for both schools and teachers.[5]

The practice of extracurricular preparation was criticized as putting too much stress on youngsters, causing an excessive financial burden on parents, and placing poor parents who could not afford such lessons at a disadvantage while benefiting the rich, who could afford private tutoring. Every education minister deplored the practice, and endless MOE directives ordered it be stopped. As early as November 1955, President Rhee issued a public statement ordering all schools to end the extra classes. In the same statement he urged all schools and officials to "make a maximum effort to combat the evil practice" of teachers and schools accepting bribes from parents to ensure that their children received extra preparation in class to perform well on the exams. Accusations were also common that rich parents used influence to gain their children's entry into schools by circumventing the examinations or their results.[6] Cash-starved private schools often accepted students who scored below the cutoff point in exchange for generous payments. Rhee declared that "by taking advantage of the ill balance between the number of applicants and the schools' capacity," many schools and teachers had profited but that in the future such practices, including extracurricular classes, would be strictly prohibited and those guilty of the practice "would receive the full penalty of the law." Since teachers and school officials were legally civil servants, the president warned, they would be punished under the laws covering bribery among government officials.[7] This began a pattern of periodically banning extra classes and then lifting the bans after admitting their ineffectiveness. This pattern characterized educational policy for the next four decades.

Educators also complained that the examinations were not conducive to creativity. They distorted the teaching process since learning, especially in the upper grades, was geared to preparing for exam questions. The questions themselves were multiple choice, based on memorizing factual information. This was made worse by the selection of facts, which often seemed whimsical, and by answers that were sometimes arbitrary.[8]

So widespread was criticism of the exam system that the MOE made constant efforts to reform it. For many educators the best solution for student placement appeared to be a combination of teacher evaluations and the results of entrance tests. But efforts to impose such a system constantly failed. School principals and teachers felt this system would be difficult to implement, many parents were concerned that it would be subject to greater abuse, and there was general disagreement on how school evaluations could be standardized. There was also a concern that standards, which were generally assumed to be declining, would erode further without "objective" exams.[9]

Examination pressure was made more intense by the informal school ranking system. At the top, the most prestigious of the secondary schools (all of which were in Seoul) was Kyŏnggi Middle/High School, second was Seoul Middle/High School, and third was Kyŏngbok High School. This ranking was inherited unchanged from the Japanese period, except that Seoul Middle/High School had previously been a secondary school for Japanese students. For girls, there was Kyŏnggi Girls' School, followed by Ewha Girls' School. All except Ewha were public schools, which in general had higher prestige than private institutions. All schools outside of Seoul were strictly second rank, but each region had its own hierarchy: Kyŏngnam and then Pusan Middle/High Schools in Pusan, Kyŏngbuk Middle/High School in Taegu, Chŏnbuk Middle/High School in Chŏnju, and Chemulp'o Middle/High School in Inch'ŏn. The pressure to enter these schools became greater as the number of primary school graduates increased. In the 1960s and 1970s, the popular expression *samdang sarak* (pass with three [hours' sleep], fail with four) summed up the intense preparation required of children.

Universities were similarly ranked. The top school was Seoul National University (SNU), the former Keijō Imperial University, established by the Japanese in 1925. No other institution could compare in prestige; entry into SNU was the dream of millions of Korean youths and their families. Next was Yonsei University and then Korea University, both private and both in Seoul. The rankings for other universities varied somewhat over time, but the first three institutions were securely at the pinnacle of the prestige hierarchy. In general, universities outside of Seoul were lower in prestige. Although the best of the provincial schools outranked the worst of the capital institutions, the path to a prestigious degree led to Seoul.

EXAMINATIONS AND UNIFORMITY OF EDUCATION

One of the great contradictions of South Korean culture was the concern for assigning rank and status in a society where egalitarian ideals were strong. Educational development reflected this contradiction: the hierarchy of schools ran counter to the strong egalitarian strain. In public policy the egalitarian ideal was expressed by the term "uniformity of education." It took two forms. One was the idea that educational opportunity should be open to all. As the debates over the Basic Education Law illustrate, there was a strong belief in universal educational opportunity. Egalitarian and democratic ideas rejected the rigid and largely hereditary class structure that had characterized the country to the end of the nineteenth century. The American missionaries, Japanese rulers, and Korean intellectuals exposed to modern ideas all preached a sort of democratic ideal of a society based on merit. The concept of equal opportunity had some basis in the nation's traditions as well. Confucianism had always stressed merit as the only valid criterion for judging an individual and awarding status to him. Within the Confucian school of thought was another powerful idea: that each person had the capability to be a moral exemplar who could provide leadership in society. Since education was a key to moral perfection, by implication any person could utilize it in order to manifest his virtue. In practice, as noted above, access to higher education had been restricted, but with the breakdown of the old order in Korea, a popular belief emerged that education should be open to all.

A related concept, uniformity—that is, a sort of equality of condition— was the second form of expressing the egalitarian ideal. It came in part from the socialist conceptions of a mass society that greatly influenced Korean intellectuals and writers in the 1920s and 1930s and from the ethnic–racial nationalism derived from Europe and Japan. It colored the Korean concept of nationalism, which emphasized a uniform, homogeneous nation. Korean nationalists of all political stripes were proud of the long unity and ethnic homogeneity that gave their nation a uniqueness and a clearly defined identity. Nationalist rhetoric and even textbooks proudly proclaimed Korea to be "*t'ong-il minjok*" (united race/nation), a nation of one people, "a single blood," even a "single mind." The two concepts of an egalitarian society and the ultranationalist ideal for ethnic–racial and ideological unity together resulted in an intolerance of glaring social inequalities.

Uniformity of education meant that the school system had to be not just open to all, but also fairly open to all and uniform in content and standard. For post-1945 South Korea it meant, at the very least, that the entrance examination system had to be fair. In official policy this was often termed the "equalization of education." The MOE made ritual vows to end inequities by regularly rotating teachers so that no school acquired a reputation for having the best instruction, by upgrading the facilities of the poorer schools, and by simplifying the examinations so that extra tutoring brought only marginal advantages. Both the Rhee and Park governments sought to limit the disparity in standards between urban and rural schools, between Seoul and the provinces, and between rich and poor neighborhoods. The MOE launched various programs to establish uniform standards. (There were contrary moves in which some officials urged that education conform to the differences in rural and urban life, but these were rejected in favor of the principle of uniformity in education and the elimination of regional disparities.)

Typically schools in downtown urban areas were regarded as superior to those in the outlying sections of a city, and their pupils had a greater chance of entering a prestigious university or getting a good job. In the late 1960s, a study in Taegu, the nation's third largest city, found that there was heated competition to get into the best primary and middle schools.[10] In Taegu, schools could be divided by reputation into downtown, other built-up district, and fringe area establishments. Test scores reflected this division, becoming lower as the schools were further from the city center. Well-to-do parents generally got their children into the coveted downtown schools, either by examination or by "informal means"—that is, using personal connections or bribing school officials.[11] Some of the choice primary schools even gave entrance exams, although this was strictly prohibited by MOE regulations. There were one hundred dred *hagwŏn* in Taegu in 1969 to prepare pupils for middle school and college.[12] Still, even the best schools in Taegu were considered inferior to those in Seoul. The study found that most high school students preferred attending even a second- or third-rank school in the capital to one in Taegu.[13]

There was a rational basis for the widespread belief that schools in Seoul were better than elsewhere. Most studies indicate that schools in Seoul were more likely to produce successful entrants into higher education. The attrition rate was higher in provincial schools. In 1967, the Central Education Research Institute (CERI) found that the national attrition rate in primary school was 2.3 percent—0.8 percent in Seoul and 2.7 percent in the provinces.[14] The same study found that 41.2 percent of those who dropped out in the first grade and 66.8 percent of those who dropped out in the sixth grade did so out of poverty.[15] Absentee rates too were higher outside of Seoul—3.76 percent, compared to 1.05 percent in the capital.[16] Both dropout and absentee rates were low, a testimony to the efficiency of Korea's basic education, yet it is significant that absentee rates were more than three times higher in provincial schools than in the capital, an indicator of regional disparity in educational opportunity. Although the real differences in overall quality between the two groups of students were rather modest, the perception of difference had a profound impact on the rank-conscious public mind.

The Park administration attempted a number of solutions to close the gap in school standards. One was to ensure that all schools received the same amount of government investment. On 24 April 1962, the SCNR enacted the Financial Grant for Compulsory Education Law, providing all school districts with equal expenditures per student.[17] Other measures were promulgated giving greater state financial support to rural and provincial schools, but these measures were of limited effectiveness since most of the support for education came from the parents rather than from the state. Moreover, the primary and secondary school facilities were modest even at the best of schools. Most Koreans regarded teachers to be more important than the physical plant in determining the quality of the school. Accordingly, the Park regime sought to ensure uniformity in the quality of teaching staff.

A key feature of the efforts to establish uniformity of teachers was the practice of rotating teachers among schools. This practice began in the late 1950s, with the goal of carrying out a routine, regular transfer of teachers from one school to another. While the purpose was to prevent the concentration of better-qualified teachers in certain schools and districts, educational officials under Rhee used rotation as a means of disciplining teachers by threatening them with "exile" to remote school districts or rewarding them with assignment to choice schools. The practice was universally disliked by teachers and principals, who feared being sent away from family and friends and who resented the power it gave to ministry and provincial officials. Parents, too, disliked having a favored teacher or principal, or one in whom they had "invested" through gifts and contacts, arbitrarily assigned to another school, and it was primarily parents who resisted rotation.

An early confrontation between parents and officials occurred when Yi Kyu-baek, the principal of Tŏksu Elementary School in downtown Seoul, was transferred to a school on the outskirts of the city in early 1957. Mothers of pupils reacted by storming the Seoul school board in protest. During Yi's eight years as principal, Tŏksu had earned a reputation for getting its pupils into good middle schools and was called the "dream of parents."[18] Yi, with the support of the school PTA, youngsters, and parents, defiantly announced that he would not accept the transfer. Threatened with dismissal, he eventually apologized and accepted the transfer. This led to a protest demonstration by parents and to the occupation of Seoul City Hall by a group of mothers.[19] In this incident, the school board stood by its decision, but this was not always the case. Threatened transfers of principals and teachers often brought protests or simply bribery from parents, and as a result the transfers were frequently not carried out. In Seoul, where the guidelines were for a rotation of teachers every two or three years, implementation was reported in 1959 to have been only nominal.[20]

Under the Park regime, government rotation of teachers began to take place on a fairly regular five-year cycle—but not without problems. Bribery and connections often determined assignments.[21] The Board of Education admitted in 1967 that it was having difficulty transferring teachers from downtown schools. Parents were able to block the transfer of teachers with good reputations by giving generous presents to school administrators and MOE officials.[22] Admitting a spotty record, the MOE in 1968 again announced measures to equalize instructional standards by strictly rotating teachers from urban to rural and from richer to poorer districts.[23] In later years rotation was carried out more regularly, but since teachers were rotated only within a province or metropolitan city district (which functioned as the equivalent of a province), the practice did not mitigate the perceived disparities between teaching staff in the cities and the poorer, more rural provinces.

Efforts at equalizing schools were given a new urgency by the nation's accelerating industrial growth, which some feared would bring a return to sharp class divisions. From the Korean War to the mid-1960s most Koreans had lived a humble economic existence, but economic growth, which in the late 1960s was in the double digits, created vast wealth for those who could best benefit from it. Since most of the new industry was concentrated in Seoul and in the Taegu–Pusan region, marked differences in regional development quickly emerged. Public attitudes toward education were influenced by a strong belief that a small group of industrialists and bureaucrats was amassing great wealth while the poor were falling behind. This spurred efforts to create an equitable educational system. One manifestation of the public concern over creeping inequality was the furor over the decision by the Park regime to allow the creation of private primary schools in order to relieve severe overcrowding. Since the tuition charged at these schools was roughly comparable to a private college, they would be beyond the means of the average Korean family. The press consequently dubbed them "aristocratic schools." As one daily expressed it, "The advent of private elementary schools, it is feared, would lead to social stratification in conjunction with an increasing economic distance between rich and poor."[24] In January 1966, the Korean Mothers' Association issued a report condemning the MOE for both encouraging and not regulating private elementary schools, which "have been showing strong aristocratic tendencies."[25] Interestingly enough, this group contained a number of well-to-do women who might be expected to send their children to the new private schools. No doubt they devoted considerable sums on tutoring their children, but they saw the private elementary schools as another unwanted expense. While their objections may have been based partly on the fear of further escalations in the cost of schooling, they also could appeal to the popular sentiment for uniformity and equality in national education.

In face of the campaign by the press and the Mothers' Association, the MOE decided to assign all students to primary schools by lottery. This would break down the distinction between elite and poor schools. Private primary schools would be included; since the students would be assigned by lottery, these schools would no longer be elitist. Strict regulations would limit tuition fees, and all teachers would be regularly rotated. Poor students, of course, would still not be able to attend, and if the lottery assigned them to a private school, they would have to draw again for a public school. In response to this plan and to public criticism, thirty-eight private primary school principals issued a four-point "self-reflection" pledge to discourage their pupils from developing elitist attitudes and a "superiority complex" and to curb such attitudes among parents.[26]

Although administration officials frequently called for the creation of more private primary schools as an inexpensive way of alleviating the classroom shortage, the resentment they caused discouraged their active promotion. Officials began to vacillate in their support, and as a result only a small number were ever approved. Furthermore, the regulations controlling tuition, limiting recruitment to certain districts, and periodically reassigning their teachers made them less attractive.

Before the lottery system, education officials had proposed a strict school district system in the hope that this would lead to the equalization of schools. At first this proved to be largely unworkable; when it was intermittently implemented, it was largely ignored. One effort to enforce the system in the spring of 1957 led to sit-down strikes in which Education Minister Ch'oe Kyu-nam was trapped in his home.[27] But implementation in the 1960s was a bit stricter, and with the abolition of the middle school entrance examination after 1968 middle school places were also assigned by lottery. The lottery system, however, was criticized as creating a "gambling mentality."[28] Further, critics argued, it would not equalize schools because the districts themselves were uneven in their standards. In 1969, one year after the lottery system was introduced into the middle schools, a massive transfer of middle school teachers took place in Seoul in which 80 percent were reassigned. In the same year school buses were acquired to bus students to schools beyond walking distance.[29]

Still, there were many problems with the school districts, especially in Seoul and Pusan, where the size of the cities made the lottery system difficult. In Seoul there were only four districts in a city that had a population of three million. Although this was expanded to six in 1970 and later to eight, it still meant long rides in crowded public buses, with enormous traffic jams in the mornings and late afternoons, as well as in the evenings, when students returned home from cram schools, rented study rooms, and study sessions. Students were reported to have to wake up at 5:30 in the morning to get to school by 8:30. The commutes were condemned as a waste of time, and the MOE was accused of "experimenting with children."[30] Some asserted that if districts were made smaller, it would nullify the effects of the program.[31] And even after the school district system was enforced, surveys showed that downtown Seoul students still got better grades.[32]

Even more controversial was the issue of equalizing secondary schools. In the early 1970s, as the nation began to expand the middle school level with the intention of making it universal, attention focused on equalizing middle schools. The MOE went so far as to announce the closure of three prestigious middle schools in 1971—Kyŏnggi Girls', Kyŏnggi Boys', and Ewha Girls'. However, plans to shut down these venerable institutions were greeted with outrage by alumni, parents, and educators and were dropped.[33] Critics dubbed such attempts "backward standardization."[34] These efforts at equalization point to the extent to which the problem of creating uniform educational standards was linked with the problem of school entrance exams.

CONTROLLING THE EXAMINATION MANIA

When the military government came to power, the MOE sought to control school entrance exams, or what the press dubbed the "examination mania," by restricting applicants to middle schools and high schools to their resident city or province.[35] The purpose was to halt the tendency of rural families to move into the cities before examination time in order for their children to take exams for better-rated urban schools. Registers were checked to see that families were in fact residents of the city or province where their children were applying to school and to verify a sufficient period of residence to prevent them from moving to desired districts just prior to examination. Nonetheless, the usual efforts to get into the most prestigious schools occurred in December 1961, with competition ratios for desirable secondary schools in Seoul around 2:1, while lesser-ranked institutions failed to meet their quota.[36] As a partial remedy, the examinations were simplified, supposedly reducing the need for private instruction. Greater weight was also given to the physical portion of the test. Yet there was no lessening of competition nor a decline in extracurricular exam preparation.

Park and his education ministers, however, maintained a commitment to reform the college entrance examination system. To remedy the problems, the MOE continuously tinkered with the system.[37] For example, in 1962, it issued the Government Qualifying Examination, which all students would take and which colleges and universities would have to use as the basis of acceptance. The exam consisted of six subjects: Korean language, social studies, math, science, a vocational education subject or home economics, and one optional subject. The examination was used as a means of promoting female education by establishing a quota for women students and of encouraging more students to study science, engineering, and technical subjects by placing quotas for students going into other fields. The number of students allowed to pass was based on 110 percent of the total quota of college students. But this exam was highly unpopular since it was seen as throttling educational opportunity.

In 1964, the Government Qualifying Examination was replaced by individual college entrance examinations that also had problems. The chief criticisms were that universities managed the examinations in inconsistent ways and abused their independence by admitting excessive numbers of students. Moreover, the qualitative gap among schools widened since poorer schools had much lower admission standards; in addition, the whole system was subject to "entering college through the back door"—that is, using bribery and influence.[38] So in 1969, the MOE issued the Ordinance for Preliminary College Entrance Examinations, which again required all aspiring college entrants to take a government-administered examination before taking the tests given by individual institutions. In order that colleges and universities could have some freedom in screening applicants, 150 percent of the quota were allowed to pass. No student could apply at a university unless first successful in the preliminary examination. The press hailed this effort as a move toward greater fairness and a way of checking what was believed to be widespread abuse of the system.[39]

Starting in 1970, the MOE increased the proportion of those who passed to

180 percent of the quota, and in 1972, to 200 percent. With the expansion of junior colleges in the late 1970s, the pass rate was widened until by 1979 at least 90 percent of those taking the preliminary examination passed it, making it nearly useless as a screening device. The MOE also played with the subject matter of the examination. Initially the subjects were the same as in the 1962 examination except that there was no optional topic. In 1972, Korean history was added. After 1972, additional optional subjects were added, such as agricultural science and the arts, in accordance with a student's intended area of study. The MOE also experimented with varying examinations for different cities or provinces to create a regional quota system and to prevent an overwhelming preponderance of passers from urban schools. But since the great majority of students in any case passed, all these efforts were ineffectual.[40]

Another problem that plagued the nation was the legion of repeaters *(chaesusaeng)*. After 1970, the government limited the number of times one could take entrance examinations to three. But each year the number of repeaters increased, some becoming *samsusaeng*, third-time-around exam takers. Many of these were students who could have been admitted to a less competitive university but preferred to try again for a better-ranked school, spending one or two extra years of preparation to get a higher score. Although repeaters remained about the same, 30 to 38 percent of all applicants, concern for their plight grew.[41] This concern was a major factor in the decision in 1976 to increase the number of junior colleges.[42] No solution to this problem was found, and repeaters still plagued education and were a source of public concern at the end of the twentieth century.

MIDDLE SCHOOL EXAM REFORM

The most significant reform of the examination system under Park Chung Hee was the abolition of the middle school entrance examination, carried out in stages between 1969 and 1971. Few issues caused more hand wringing than the intense competition for entry into middle school. As noted, much of primary school, especially the fifth and sixth grades, was directed at preparation for the middle school entrance examination. Since there were more students seeking admission into middle school than places available, failure meant a termination of education at the primary school level and no chance to acquire a well-paying or prestigious job or to be married to someone who had one. In the spring of 1967, educational planners in the MOE began drafting a plan to end these problems by extending compulsory education to nine years in 1972. Under the Second Five-Year Educational Development Plan (1967–1971), enough teachers were to be trained and enough classrooms were to be built to ensure that all Korean children would be adequately accommodated and that they would receive a full day's instruction as middle school was expanded to embrace all students. However, from the first, officials in the EPB, the Ministry of Finance, and some in the MOE expressed skepticism because the funding was not available to build the facilities and train the teachers needed to enroll the entire elementary school class of 1971 into middle school.[43]

Nonetheless, the plan had popular support. In the summer and fall of 1967, parents and educators launched campaigns in Pusan and Seoul calling for the end of examination pressure on primary school teachers. Ad hoc parent groups held several public rallies in Seoul calling for the abolition of the middle school examinations.[44] The press began reporting stories of young children who suffered as a result of overzealous middle school exam preparation—for example, the case of a twelve-year-old Pusan boy killed in a motor accident returning very late at night from a cram school.[45] The government published statistics showing that the average Korean boy at the age of six was 111.7 cm tall and weighed 18.4 kgs, while the figures for Japanese six-year-olds were 117.6 cm and 19.3 kg respectively. By age eleven, the gap had widened, with a Korean boy standing at 130.4 cm and weighing 27.9 kg, while his Japanese counterpart stood 140 cm and weighed 33.1 kg.[46] Examination pressure, many felt, was undermining the health of South Korea's young manhood.

As an expedience measure, the MOE announced that it would begin double shifts in middle schools in 1968. The Chosŏn ilbo attacked this as a "makeshift, no-plan policy" while money was spent on highways, underpasses, and other "flashy projects."[47] But the idea of abolishing the middle school entrance exam and making middle school compulsory was popular. In the fall of 1967, parent groups and teachers, soon joined by college students, launched a petition drive to request President Park to support it.[48] This took place in conjuction with a new campaign organized by the KFEA and the MOE against private tutoring. Parent groups sometimes called for the end of all private tutoring, but attention was focused on the special classes that elementary students were required to attend. Both MOE officials and the press pointed out that the surest way to end the stress and financial burden of extra classes was to make middle school entry automatic and available for all.[49]

In March 1968, the KFEA set up a committee to tackle the problem of how to accommodate all students if the middle school exam was abolished. Although the double shift idea was still pursued by the MOE, it was accepted that initially some selection process would have to be set up, and for this a lottery was proposed.[50] Another problem was the lack of separation between middle and high schools, which, it was felt, would hamper the system. Despite these difficulties, the KFEA in 1968 called for the prompt abolition of the exams and was joined by several major dailies. As one paper declared, "The government and educators should no longer hesitate to take a drastic step" and end the exams immediately.[51] Education minister O Pyŏng-kwŏn then issued what became known as the "July 15 Declaration," announcing the abolition of the middle school examinations. Upon hearing the announcement, primary school pupils were reported to have broken out with cheers. A pupil in Kwanghee Elementary School in Seoul remarked, "I am glad because now I can sleep as much as I want to."[52]

A key to the plan was the equalization of schools—that is, the avoidance of overheated competition into the best middle schools. To accomplish this, fourteen of the most prestigious middle schools would be converted into high schools. In turn, some primary schools would be converted into middle schools. A lottery system would be used to select which students would be allowed into middle school and which of several schools in their districts they would attend. In drawing up the districts, planners attempted to cut across socioeconomic boundaries so that each district would represent a cross section of educational and economic classes. In theory at least, each classroom would be a social microcosm of society, depriving students from affluent or influential backgrounds of a decided advantage in the competition for high school and college entry. In reality, this could not be achieved. As with primary schools, downtown Seoul had the best schools, and the cost of housing automatically rose in whatever district was thought to have superior schools, making it difficult for poorer families to reside there.

Since the perceived quality of middle schools varied greatly, there was much anxiety over which school a child would enter. In February 1969, parents crowded the tea shops in Seoul to watch the lottery numbers drawn on television (television was new to Korea, and most people did not own a set) as ninety thousand children were selected for middle school entry. Not all were pleased with the results, of course, and the inherent unfairness to those not selected caused much ill feeling. The MOE then declared that students who did not come up in the lottery were ineligible for future lotteries, which resulted in angry protests by parents and charges of despotic MOE behavior.[53] Furthermore, students who were assigned to what were deemed less desirable institutions were also disappointed, and many stopped attending classes but spent most of their time at cram schools hoping to get into a high school with a good reputation.[54]

The district system did not eliminate class boundaries but it kept them from being too sharp, and it reflected the deep concern of most South Koreans to avoid class barriers to equality of opportunity. An example of this concern was the lottery fee, which was set at 14,000 won. Many parents complained that this greatly burdened poor parents, and stories circulated about children not participating in the lottery because their families could not afford the fee. But the number of parents too poor to participate in the lottery was small. When the first lottery was held in 1969, the overwhelming majority of sixth-grade boys and girls participated.[55] In 1969, the lottery system applied only to the capital; in 1970, it was extended to ten other cities; and in 1971, it was implemented throughout the nation. In 1968, 55 percent of all students entered middle school upon completion of primary school; in 1969, 58 percent did; in 1970, 62 percent did; and in 1971, 68 percent did. During the 1970s, middle school became nearly universal; nearly 97 percent of all primary school graduates went on to middle school in 1980. The rate of increase was even faster than anticipated and caused a severe shortage of classrooms. During the first three years, 386 new middle schools were established (292 of them public), and 3,349 classrooms were added.[56] As noted, however, construction did not keep up with enrollment so that schools became more overcrowded and understaffed in the late 1970s.

HIGH SCHOOL EQUALIZATION POLICY

The abolition of the middle school entrance examination and the decision to accelerate the expansion of middle school education immediately drew attention to the high school entrance exam. With greater numbers of students entering middle school, competition for high school grew keener, while the lottery system shifted objectives from entry into an elite middle school to entry into an elite high school. In 1972, the MOE formed a committee headed by Seoul National University professor Sŏ Myŏng-wŏn to consider a plan to equalize the high schools. The committee recommended that students be assigned to high school by lottery in much the same way they were assigned to middle school, and this suggestion was implemented by the MOE the following year. The resultant 1973 High School Equalization Plan had several aims: to avoid overheated examination competition, to end an emerging tendency of making middle school education center around preparation for the high school entrance exam, to prevent the practice of private tutoring, to eliminate the disparities in instruction in high schools, and to promote the equality of educational opportunity. The government also hoped that the new system could be used to promote vocational education since there would be no difference in the academic standards of academic and vocational high schools. Worried about the swelling city populations, the government thought that the policy would also slow down the move into the cities by families seeking better educational opportunities.[57]

In face of the controversy the plan aroused, the administration sought to implement it fairly and gradually. The state appointed educators, lawyers, businessmen, and journalists to a Council of School Equalization, which was entrusted with seeing that the policy was carried out equitably. The government executed the plan first in Seoul and Pusan in 1974, and in the next two years it extended equalization to Taejŏn, Inch'ŏn, and Kwangju. By 1980, the government was enforcing the policy in twenty cities but still not in rural areas, where assignment by lottery was not practical since there was often only one high school in the area.

But the plan remained controversial. A survey conducted by the Korean Federation of Private School Foundations Association in the mid-1980s found that 47.1 percent of parents were against it and 40.6 percent in favor. Parents cited the fact that children did not study hard, that the plan denied the children and their parents freedom of choice of schools, and that children were not assigned to the school they wanted.[58] State planners hoped that the measure would at least delay the enormous pressure on pupils and the great expenses of tutoring and private lessons until students were in high school. To some degree this was so—at least temporarily. The burden on parents and children did not appreciably diminish, however, since with a flood of students entering secondary schools in the 1970s, the numbers of potential college aspirants grew proportionately.

With the abolition of the middle school entrance exam and the creation of the high school equalization policy, the full weight of examination pressure was directed at the college entrance examination. The starting point for college preparation began to move to lower and lower levels until most children began their private lessons and after-school classes in primary school, if not earlier. The abolition of the secondary school entrance exams also meant that it was more important than ever to reside in the right school district.

The measures to abolish secondary school entrance examinations, while applauded by the press and many parents, created problems for families who sought to transfer their children to better school districts. When the lottery system for middle schools began, the Seoul Board of Education announced that only those students who could prove that their families had been resident in the city for one year could participate in the lottery. Parents from provincial towns with children in Seoul protested, picketing the board's office. The board then relented and allowed all students residing in the city to participate.[59] But the problem continued, and many parents continued to send children to Seoul or to other major cities.

A survey in 1976 found middle school transfers to Seoul a widespread problem; 60 percent of the transfer students were from areas adjacent to Seoul, but the rest came from all parts of the country. The majority stayed with relatives; 41 percent were not with any family members. The study found that administrative regulations were not vigorously enforced, and a majority of the students paid fees to transfer into a school. A large percentage came from wealthy families, but the majority were lower-middle-class and poor families, often farmers and unskilled laborers who sought to improve their children's chances for a better education and a better position.[60] To alleviate the problem, a special lottery was held in Seoul in 1975 for students illegally residing in the capital. Four thousand of the five thousand who applied were placed in middle schools.[61]

Another problem arose in the 1970s with the practice of grouping students according to ability. This, of course, undermined the entire intent of the middle and high school equalization measures and brought about fears of class divisions since it was assumed students from better-educated and wealthier families would be predominant in the superior groupings. This was especially true since ability grouping was often determined by how well students did in school-administered tests. In the schools that began this practice, it was reported that many parents had to hire tutors to give special lessons so that students could be placed in the superior classes.[62] In a public hearing sponsored by the KFEA, many parents and teachers defended ability grouping, arguing that it prevented the college-bound students from being held back by slow students.[63] Some criticized the entire effort at equalization and the abolition of the secondary school entrance examinations and worried that the mediocre students would set the academic level.[64] But these fears were overridden by the concern to avoid elite schools, and the abolition of the middle school examination and the high school equalization measures were strongly supported by the MOE, the KEDI, and much of the public. They remained policy, and schools were ordered to stop tracking.

As noted, there was no abatement in the heated competition for college entrance and its attendant evils; rather, competition became only more intense. The greatest problem was the varying reputations of school districts. In spite of all the efforts at equalization, certain school districts were known for the success of their students on college entrance exams. In Seoul, the eighth school district, established in the new, upper-middle-class section of Apkujŏng-dong (a sea of newly built high-rise apartments constructed in the 1970s), had the greatest reputation for academic success. It became the most sought-after place of residence, and real estate prices soared. The reputations of course were self-fulfilling: the greater the fame of a school district for placing its graduates in universities, the more it acquired residents who could lavish large sums on private tutoring, which in turn added to the success rate of its students. Residence could be faked, and regular crackdowns had to be held. The removal of illegal transfer students could occasionally result in noisy protests, such as those in the spring of 1974, when a number of pupils refused to move back to their own districts.[65] In Pusan in the summer of 1974, five hundred pupils from rural areas protested their ordered transfer.[66] Families continued to find ways to circumvent regulations.

THE JULY 30 EDUCATIONAL REFORM

When Chun Doo Hwan came to power in 1980, he seized on opportunities to win support by carrying out needed reforms. Not surprisingly, one of the first was to tackle the entrance examination system. During the summer of 1980, MOE, KEDI, EPB, and other government officials held a number of meetings to discuss ways of eliminating the worst of the problems. The EPB estimated that 82 billion won (about $160 million in 1980 dollars) was spent by secondary

school students on private tutoring, and this was only part of the cost of examination preparation.[67] In a public hearing sponsored by the Special Committee
for National Security Measures, educators and officials called upon the government to take extraordinary measures to end out-of-class instruction. Some
argued that by legalizing private tutoring, it could be taxed and controlled.
The administration decided to ban tutoring except in athletics, art, music, tae
kwon do, and *kkotkkoji* (Korean flower arranging), and all extra–high school
classes were prohibited. Along with this measure came the decision to make
major changes in the college entrance system.[68]

The result was the July 30 Educational Reform, named for the date on
which it was publicly announced. Under the measure, the state transferred the
college entrance examinations from the individual schools to the central government. As discussed above, the Government Qualifying Examination used
during the Park regime had not proven to be an effective screening device.[69] As
a result, the Final Selection Test given by individual universities was crucial.
The July 30 Educational Reform abolished both the state-sponsored preliminary test and the Final Selection Test, replacing them with a new College Entrance Achievement Test. This was now the sole entrance examination. While
not differing significantly in content from the state preliminary test, its role was
far more important.[70] In effect, the state was tightening its control over the college entrance system.

The reform contained two other important features. First, a Home School
Records System *(naesin)* was to be gradually implemented until it accounted for
at least 30 percent of the basis for college entrance. The system would be based
on secondary school grades and teachers' evalutions. Second, colleges could
admit students up to 30 percent over their quota, but they could graduate only
their allotted quota. This "admission over quota, graduation by quota" policy, as
it was labeled, meant that institutions of higher learning had to flunk out a substantial number of students by their senior year. This was a new practice since in
South Korea few students dropped out of college and fewer flunked out.

A number of sound educational arguments justified the reforms. The Final
Selection Tests given by the individual colleges had focused on a narrow range
of subjects—chiefly Korean language, mathematics, and English; high school
students would prepare for a wider number of subjects for the state-
administered examination. This would help foster a broader, well-rounded
education, closer to the ideal of "whole person" education. With the elimination

of the second round of examinations, students would be less exhausted psychologically and physically. The Home School Records System would encourage secondary education to be more than just exam preparation, and its gradual introduction would avoid the problems that had been created by the Rhee administration when it had suddenly switched the selection criteria by introducing *naesin*. Education officials also argued that these reforms would reduce the costs of private tutoring since a greater number of students would enter higher education and the inclusion of high school records as part of the selection criteria would diminish the stress on cramming for the entrance examinations.[71] Another supposed benefit was that the quality of higher education would improve because with the fear of flunking out, college students would devote more time to their studies. Minister of Education Yi Kyu-ho admitted (on a television show) that the administration hoped students would concentrate on studying.[72]

The graduation quota had another widely understood but rarely stated goal: to prevent anti-government student demonstrations. University professors and school officials feared that they would be pressured to flunk students who were politically active. School officials, students, and their families could expect that state officials would exert various pressures to see to it that troublesome students failed. But if this were a major purpose of the reform, it failed because student political activism continued.

The July 30 Educational Reform increased the authority of the state over education because the state assumed exclusive control over the college selection process. In some ways this was a logical extension of the role of the central government in its position as the arbiter of the nation's social selection. Perhaps as important, the reform was intended to give the state greater control over students by denying them college entrance if they did not perform well in high school, especially as high school evaluations included a student's extracurricular activities and strict adherence to school discipline. The reform satisfied the public demand for greater access to college entrance while it fortified the state's control over both the selection process and the students themselves.

But the new college entrance system encountered problems from the first year of its implementation. MOE directives required students to take the entrance exam before applying to specific departments at specific universities. This created chaos as most students waited until the deadline to apply because they wanted to know their scores and the number of applicants who had applied to particular schools and departments in order to calculate their chances before applying. This was remedied by changing the requirements in 1986 so that applicants had to submit applications before taking the tests. Other problems were less easily remedied. To encourage a well-rounded education, sixteen or seventeen subjects were placed on the entrance exam. This had the reverse of its intended effect. It added to, rather than reduced, the pressure for extra examination preparation since now even more subjects had to be mastered. The number of subjects was reduced to nine in 1987; however, this had no measurable effect on changing the nature of secondary education as exam preparation or reducing the huge expenditures devoted to extra-class study. Educators also criticized the emphasis on multiple choice questions since this encouraged rote memorization. An essay question was added to the entrance examination in 1986, only to be abolished as impractical in 1988 after parents and educators complained that it was too subjective.[73]

As a result of the reform, quotas for higher education dramatically increased. In the autumn of 1980 a 49.2 percent increase in the freshman enrollment was announced—from 205,000 to 307,000, the largest increase ever. Even the student population of Seoul, frozen since 1978, was enlarged.[74] The increase was a source of alarm for many who feared for the quality of higher education since the greater quota numbers increased the chances of marginal students who may have been previously discouraged from trying for the entrance examinations. The Chun administration countered by suggesting that if the universities had to fail 30 percent of their entrants, the quality of higher education would improve and this threat of failure would act as a deterrent for academically weaker students, who would have to weigh the worth of investing time and resources in trying to enter universities from which they would be unlikely to graduate.[75] Fearing excessive expansion in higher education, the Five-Year Economic Development Plan for 1982–1986, drafted in 1981, called for more modest increases in the number of college graduates: from 144,000 in 1981 (before the plan) to 209,000 in 1986. State planners called the sudden increase in the 1980 freshman enrollment figures a one-time jump and announced that after 1981 the freshmen quota would increase more modestly to accord with economic needs.[76] But higher education expanded faster than called for in the plan because each year the government enlarged the quotas in response to pressure from the public and from tuition-driven private universities.

Higher education enjoyed a boom in the early 1980s as a result of the enlarged quotas. Universities scrambled to hire qualified faculty and to enlarge facilities. The July 30 Educational Reform, however, did not achieve any of its objectives. Competition for university entrance remained fierce, partly driven by the enlarged cohorts of high school graduates and partly by the ranking system that caused many students to retake examinations for prestigious institutions. Nor did the graduation quotas pressure students to study more. Universities were reluctant to fail students for fear of losing tuition, for fear of protests and campus disturbances that would cause the government to intervene, and for fear of the wrath of parents. College and university officials petitioned the MOE to ease up on the requirement that 30 percent of the students fail. In 1983, Yi Kyu-ho responded to these requests by urging the schools to enforce the graduation limits. "The regulations requiring colleges to expel 30 percent of entrants before graduation may be irrational. I think, however, under the current circumstances the system will be effective in making students realize that they cannot graduate if they do not study hard."[77] But seven months later, the MOE ceded to university pressure to be more "flexible" in its graduation quota system, allowing for a number of case-by-case exceptions.[78] Schools and students often circumvented the rules; some students failed only to be readmitted. In 1987, the graduation quota was abandoned. The competition for college entry or the problem of repeaters did not diminish. In 1986, economic planners estimated that of the four hundred thousand high school graduates who failed the university entrance examination, three hundred thousand would not enter the job market, and most of these would devote full time to preparing to retake the exam the following year.[79] To deal with the problems created by the intense competition for college entrance the Chun government in the autumn of 1980 also banned private tutoring, but this too proved ineffective since parents and students found ways to circumvent the ban.

South Korean education under Chun Doo Hwan's "Fifth Republic" continued to make impressive progress in the number of students it embraced. Middle school enrollment went from 95 percent in 1980 to 98 percent in 1989, high school enrollment from 63 percent of the high-school-age population to 86 percent in the same years, and the proportion of college-age people entering higher education grew from 16 to 37 percent. The 1982–1986 Economic Development Plan called for making middle school education compulsory by 1997, starting with islands and remote places in 1985; soon education became universal in these areas, while it had already become virtually universal elsewhere.[80] Middle school was approaching universal enrollment, and four out of five middle school graduates were going on to high school; university enrollment, already high, was increasing. Yet there was a general agreement by the mid-1980s that the educational system was far from satisfactory. Vocational education was not flourishing, classrooms were overcrowded, and the system was regarded as too inflexible. And foremost in the public mind were the problems caused by frantic competition for entrance into prestigious schools; the problems were becoming worse in the 1980s as secondary school education was becoming universal, resulting in unfair advantages for more prosperous families.

EGALITARIANISM AND EXAMINATION REFORMS

The Chun government officially remained committed to the egalitarian concept of the equalization of schools. In line with that policy, the Fifth Five-Year Economic Development Plan (1982–1986) concentrated on investment in schools in remote areas. But the administration took other measures that appeared to be a modest retreat from that policy. In early 1982, Yi Kyu-ho announced a plan to establish special high schools for gifted children, arguing that the lottery system had produced mediocre schooling and that bright students were "bored."[81] Private middle and high schools lobbied to allow each high school to have its own entrance examination. In a further move away from the High School Equalization Plan, the EPB also sought to allow private high schools to set admission standards and fees in order to help them out of their financial difficulties. The Chun government seemed unable to decide, uncertain whether to promote the ideology of equality or of efficiency. The administration was fearful of being charged with contributing to the creation of an elite social class, but it was pressed by wealthy families and some economic planners to allow for private and elite high schools. Nonetheless, public opinion surveys indicated that there was strong support for the High School Equalization Plan.[82] Eventually the government set aside the problem of revising the high school equalization policy for further study, and no change in the policy was made by the Chun administration.[83] Meanwhile, other government policies worked to undermine equal opportunity in at least small ways. For example, fees at the national universities were raised, and the abolition of private tutoring made it harder for many students from low-income families to earn tuition money.[84]

None of these changes represented a fundamental shift in policy. In fact, the egalitarian streak in education was demonstrated among the public in the school uniform policy. The decision in 1981 to end the requirement that secondary students wear a military-style school uniform was welcomed as a progressive move. The uniforms were considered an unlamented Japanese legacy and emphasized the regimented, military style in schooling that most disliked. But not wearing uniforms opened the way for class distinctions because wealthier students could flaunt fancy clothes. Strong pressure emerged from teachers, school officials, and parent groups to encourage students to wear simple clothes and no expensive watches, shoes, or jewelry. These urgings extended to lunch boxes and even their contents: all students were encouraged or required to bring simple foods. Many schools, citing concerns that students would display social distinctions, as well as fears that civilian clothes would lessen discipline, reimposed school uniforms. The concern over this issue and the success of most schools in imposing strict dress and various other egalitarian rules demonstrate just how strongly most felt about the need to view education as egalitarian.

Studies indicate that disparities in educational opportunity were indeed diminishing. As early as the 1960s, there were fewer differences in the educational levels and percentages of entrants into high school and college between urban and rural or metropolitan and provincial areas in South Korea than in most developing and many industrialized nations.[85] A study by Kim Yŏng-hwa, of college students from 1967 to 1984, found that the overall trend was for a greater geographical diversity among university students at all institutions, even the most prestigious.[86]

Still, there was a general feeling that the examinations worked against equal and fair opportunity and needed reform. In the late 1980s, a number of civic groups emerged in the freer and more democratic atmosphere that characterized the nation after 1987 (see chapter 8). The major educational concern for these new groups was the obsession with entrance exams. Cries for reform came from many directions. The Chŏn'kyojo, a technically illegal but openly active dissident teachers' union, called for the end of exam-driven education, as did the KFEA. In the summer of 1988, students in several high schools, most probably encouraged by their teachers, began a hunger strike to demand the end of supplementary classes (poch'ung suŏp) for examination preparation.[87] In the spring of 1991 educators and parents began what they termed the "Movement for True Education." Leaders argued that educational reform needed to be initiated by government but that parents, local government, and various other constituencies needed to join in. In particular, this movement focused on the end of supplementary classes and the abolition of study halls *(chayul hak-sŭp)*, held in many schools from six to nine in the evening. A total of sixty-two associations supported this movement, including the Korean Consumers' League, the Korean University Association, and the Korean Mothers' Association. In face of this pressure, a number of boards of education came out in 1994 in favor of abolishing the after-school classes. The movement ran into opposition from many parents, however, who wanted opportunities for their children to study for the entrance exams, and they placed pressure on the provincial and municipal boards not to abolish the classes.[88] Public opinion remained contradictory and divided on the issue. Civic groups and educators called for "freeing young people from exams" and held seminars on this problem starting in 1988. But since the social demand for educational access remained unabated, efforts at alleviating examination pressures were to no avail.

The administration of President Roh Tae Woo (No T'ae-u) (1988–1993), who succeeded Chun, responded to calls to end "examination mania" by carrying on the tradition of tinkering with the university entrance examination. Looking at the problem, the Presidential Commission for Education Reform proposed a psychometric exam (on the model of the Scholastic Aptitude Test in the United States) that would replace the subject-specific College Entrance Achievement Test; thus, the emphasis would be on the mastery of broader skills rather than facts. The Korean Association for Higher Education then made a study of this proposal, and after a series of public hearings and deliberations, it recommended this change to the MOE. In 1991, the MOE announced that the entrance examination system would undergo another major reform. More autonomy would be given to individual colleges and universities to screen entrants. Each institution would exercise one of four options: (1) it could use the Home School Records as the sole criterion for admission—80 percent of the records would be derived from academic subject grades and 20 percent from Home extracurricular activities; (2) it could use a combination of the Home School Records and the new Higher Education Ability Test (HEAT), based in part on the U.S. Scholastic Aptitude Test; (3) it could give its own college entrance test and use it in combination with the HEAT; or (4) it could use a combination of its own tests, the HEAT, and the Home School Records. In all cases schools had to give the Home School Records at least 40 percent of the total screening score. MOE officials expected most schools to select the last option and use a combination of the HEAT, their own tests, and the Home School Records. The reform was to be implemented in three years so that high school students would have time to prepare for the new entrance criterion.[89]

It was obvious, however, that these changes would do little to alleviate the distortions in education created by the examination system. In fact, responding to public pressure, the Roh administration implemented changes that made education more competitive and costly. The Presidential Commission for Education Reform in 1988 recommended that the high school entrance examinations be revived in order to raise academic standards. MOE officials then proposed that local education boards be allowed to decide whether or not to permit high schools to recruit through competitive exams. In 1989 Roh's administration also partially lifted some of the increasingly unenforceable restrictions on private lessons by allowing high school and college students to earn extra money by tutoring.

If anything, the examination pressure grew more intense, reflected in a number of reports on student suicides. In 1987, a record fifty secondary students took their own lives over failure on the entrance examination.[90] A study released in 1990 stated that 20 percent of all secondary students contemplated suicide and 5 percent attempted it. It also suggested that the examination pressure led to drug addiction and antisocial behavior, although these were low by the standards of many Western countries. It was particularly alarmed at the demoralizing effects of the growing population of repeaters, who devoted several years after finishing high school to studying full time at cram schools.[91]

All of these problems contributed to the pressure on the state to enlarge the college entry quota, a topic of innumerable conferences and discussions. Opposition leader Kim Dae Jung proposed expanding the university enrollment as rapidly as possible, calling for the principle of equal opportunity to let all who wanted to enter but placing strict quotas on graduates. "It is sad to see those unable to enter colleges and universities spend their life as social outcasts," he explained.[92] But the Roh government opted to adhere to strict quotas that would be enlarged only as fast as the market demanded. The administration made only a few minor adjustments in the quota system. One was that universities in Seoul were allowed to admit more students, ending the freeze that had been placed in 1984 on the capital's institutions of higher education. These increases, however, were largely confined to the natural sciences and engineering. Most of the increases in quotas were still in provincial schools. One attempt to prevent a concentration of universities in Seoul was a decision in the late 1970s to allow universities in the capital to establish branch campuses in the countryside. But most universities simply established schools on the outskirts of the capital, adding to the city's growing traffic problems, as students generally resided near the main campus and commuted to the branches. The system of branch campuses on the outskirts of Seoul was recognized as a failure, and the aim became to allow a small number of provincial universities to open, most far from the capital. Three universities, all in Seoul—Sŏnggyun'gwan, Kŏn'guk, and Hansŏng— were punished by having their quotas frozen for illegally admitting students through the back door of bribes and favors.[93]

The most significant change was the growth of junior colleges. Previously junior colleges, despite their encouragement by the Park and Chun administrations, had not flourished. Dismissed as dead-end institutions that provided only vocational training, most students and their families favored renewed attempts at entering a university rather than a junior college. Often they functioned as secretarial schools for women who would work only a few years between graduation and marriage. This began to change in the late 1980s, when many firms began hiring junior college graduates. The high rate of return that a junior college education offered made them more popular. While the number of graduates from four-year institutions who found jobs appropriate for their degrees seldom ranged above 60 percent, for graduates from two-year institutions it was 76 percent in 1987 and 87 percent in 1991—almost twice the rate of the first group during what was a recession year.[94] Indicative of the new trend, some college graduates who were unable to find employment with their four-year degrees entered junior colleges to learn a marketable skill.

Throughout the 1990s, the MOE endlessly tinkered with the examination system, changing the rules almost annually. Entrance examinations remained a national obsession, the subject of newspaper articles, books, a number of popular films, and countless commissions, public hearings, and forums. Universally it was agreed that they distorted education by reducing it to exam preparation, created the need for costly tutoring and private lessons, and put lamentable pressure on young people. In the past, critics had charged that examination pressure resulted in stunted physical development, but by the mid-1990s statistics told of a very healthy young generation who was so much taller than its elders as to appear to be a separate race. Now attention focused on the damage the examinations did to mental health. Frequent reports were given of teenage suicides, with the victims leaving bitter notes complaining of their failure to live up to their parents' expectations. Such incidences became staple fare for popular movies and novels. There were also reports of physical abuse by parents and teachers, who were in part driven by the pressure to see that their charges performed well on exams. One study in 1996 found that 97 percent of all children reported being beaten by parents and/or teachers, many of them frequently. This was attributed primarily to the pressure to do well in school.[95] Parents in a 1992 survey approved corporal punishments in school.[96] Attitudes began to change, however, as private organizations, including the dissident teachers' union, brought the issue of student beatings to public attention, and the MOE announced that corporal punishment in the schools would be abolished in 1998.[97] The practice did not end immediately.

The administration of Roh's successor, Kim Young Sam (1993–1998), made a number of attempts to reform examination policy. None of these was fundamental but rather involved constant fiddling with a system that seemed resistant to any reform. In 1993, the government announced that there would be no separate college entrance tests. Other, mostly minor, changes were unveiled in October 1993, just a few months before the college entrance examination. These infuriated many families since they made it difficult to select the right strategy for preparing for the examination. Moreover, the confusion and inconsistency in policy became worse. In 1994, the Presidential Commission for Education Reform first approved separate examinations from individual colleges, in addition to the state exam, and then it changed its mind. As a result, Seoul National University and other schools defiantly announced that they would go ahead with their own entrance examinations and ignore the new regulations.[98] Plagued by complaints, the commission announced in 1995 that it would allow greater autonomy for colleges. Prestigious Yonsei University then declared that it would abolish the written examination and include Home School Records and the state examination only. The MOE in 1996 decided to replace the school records with a school-life document, which differed from earlier records in that it included outside activities and would be a continual record of personality development. This only added to the confusion and created more paperwork for teachers.[99]

Many were disillusioned with nationally administered tests and with the central government's inconsistent and capricious changes in exam policy, so a growing consensus was emerging in the late 1990s that universities should have more freedom to determine admissions and conduct examinations. Some called for turning the entire selection process over to universities.[100] Upon his election as president in December 1997, Kim Dae Jung promised, as all his successors had before, to reform the exam system. The MOE, meanwhile, moved in the direction of more diversified criteria for university admission.

In 1998, the MOE announced the "Vision for Education beyond 2000." Under this plan college applicants would select five colleges and limit their applications to them. The most radical measure was that university admissions would be based primarily on high school grades and the recommendations of principals. To ensure fairness, a school operations committee of teachers, parents, and leading social figures outside of school would supervise the recommendation process. Student character, "civic mindedness," and participation in extracurricular activities would be included in the recommendation category.[101] The MOE promised the whole process would be transparent and subject to student appeal. In a further reform the number of categories of recommendation would be reduced from twenty-one or twenty-two.[102] This awkward system, most observers felt, was not likely to be a satisfactory substitute for the examination results, which would still be the prime determinants for entrants into prestigious schools.[103]

This was the most radical proposal in the past half century. There was a great deal of skepticism on how well it would work. The plan did not take into consideration the differences in high school standards. In spite of the state's commitment to the uniformity of education, school districts varied, as all Koreans knew. Even if the differences were minor, every competitive edge counted, so the differences mattered a great deal to most families. More fundamentally, many felt the new reform would not liberate students from examination hell, as its authors announced. It would mean, in practice, that high school grades would be the prime determinants of university entrance, which would in turn mean that examination hell would change form, not disappear. The fate of students in South Korea's winner-take-all society would depend on how well they did on a series of high school tests.

Even before this MOE proposal, the Seoul Board of Education declared its intention to eliminate multiple choice exams, a decision that was reported to have sent "shockwaves throughout education."[104] The move was designed to make education more than mere test taking. Critics argued that the college entrance exams were driving the entire educational system, which had been reduced to little more than the constant preparation for and the taking of multiple choice and short-answer exams. This stifled creativity, hindered the development of analytical reasoning, made schooling a process of rote memorization of meaningless facts, and drained all the joy out of learning. Middle and secondary school education would now rely on written tests that would involve problem solving, reasoning, and imagination. But unilateral decisions to overhaul secondary education created more confusion and dismay among children and their parents. If the school and examination policies kept changing, how could they prepare? In addition, teachers were not trained or ready to suddenly change their pedagogical methods. As with the Home Records System, there was a general concern that the new system would be less objective and fair, subject to greater parental influence and other forms of abuse. Doubts about the proposal were highlighted by the fact that its announcement coincided with a new educational scandal. In an anti-corruption investigation, the Board of Audit and Inspection reported a disturbing number of irregularities among teachers. Secondary teachers were accused of accepting payments from parents to give special attention to their children. These, of course, would be the same teachers whose judgments would be relied on to a far greater extent in determining a young person's life chances.[105]

As these and other reform proposals were debated, university entrance examinations went forward as usual. One hundred and eighty college professors, teachers, and officials emerged from a month-long confinement in a secluded hotel under tight security in November 1999 and delivered the examination questions to various testing sites for the examination on 17 November. Nine hundred thousand students competed for three hundred thousand slots. As was customary, parents accompanied their sons and daughters to the exam sites, nervously pacing outside in the cold weather as students went through the nine-hour ordeal that would be so crucial to their future. They had long prepared for the examination, augmenting their chances of success with a variety of strategies that sometimes drew upon supernatural forces. Shamans were consulted. One shaman reported that an average of twenty students and parents came to her per day to find out about their exam prospects.[106] Buddhist temples saw an influx of mothers and grandmothers, some praying hours each day for one hundred days. Some temples reported that the donations given for exam success were their largest single source of revenue.[107] Some hopefuls buried personal items on the campus of the school they sought to enter, and girls wore silver rings given to them by their parents during the admission season. Hundred-won coins with the lucky dates of 1984 and 1994 were valued as talismans, and owners of Hyundai Sonatas reported the "S" in "Sonata" was stolen as the S also stood for student success. Pigs, a traditional symbol of good fortune and the character for fortune on underwear; socks with the characters for "passing"; forks to select the right answers; mirrors to see better; and compasses for the right direction—all were put to use by anxious students and their families.[108]

Some things were new in the examination process. Some freshmen were now being selected through a special screening in which individual universities picked students on a variety of nonexamination criteria. They included those who had demonstrated filial piety, who resided in farming and fishing areas, who had graduated or would graduate from vocational high schools, who were heads of households, and whose parents had rendered distinguished service to the nation. The numbers were very small, but of greater consequence were the seven thousand freshmen selected according to high school principals' recommendations. That number, according to the plan, was to increase to ten thousand in 2000. It was also decided in 1999 that after 2000, about five thousand students who resided in foreign countries and therefore did not have the same opportunity to prepare for the college entrance exams would be accepted on a special quota. Still the main criterion was the College Entrance Achievement Test. Academic performance in high school was a comparatively minor factor: grade point averages accounted for only up to 8.6 percent of the weight in the selection process.[109] For the vast majority of students, the pressure of the entrance examinations remained largely unchanged.

Five decades of experimentation and calls for reforms brought no fundamental change in the use of entrance examinations as the main mechanism for deciding who entered higher education and prestigious institutions. None of the reforms in the 1990s changed the fundamental nature of Korea's examination hell. Even some educational planners felt that there was little that could be done to change the system. The public was committed to it, and until the state lifted all quotas on college freshmen, the feverish competition with all its attendant problems would continue.[110] Even if the state chose to abolish the entrance examination, the competition for entry into the best schools and the best departments would resurface in some other way since the pursuit of education was about status and prestigious degrees were the primary markers of status.

6 The Costs of Educational Zeal

The South Korean drive to get ahead made education not only intensely competitive, but also extremely costly. As noted, education was largely paid for by students and their parents, for one of the most pronounced features of the Korean educational system was the weak fiscal support given to it by the state. And education was not cheap. Some analysts have commented on the cost-effectiveness of South Korean education during its years of most rapid expansion, impressed that a comprehensive national educational system was built with only modest expenditure.[1] This, however, is misleading. If the hidden costs of informal fees, tutoring, gifts to teachers, and supplementary classes and texts are added, it becomes clear that South Korean education in fact absorbed an enormous slice of the nation's financial resources and was a major expenditure for the average family. Measured as a proportion of personal income, it was possibly the world's costliest educational system.

Both the ability of the state to shift the expense of education onto the consumers and the costly nature of schooling were the result of the public's drive for educational attainment. The demand created competition to get into the highest levels of schooling and the most desirable institutions. This led to the additional expenses of out-of-class lessons, private tutoring, and a variety of often financially onerous strategies such as renting rooms in desirable districts. As with the entrance examinations, the high price of schooling and the economic distortions it caused were unfortunate by-products of the zeal for education.

EDUCATIONAL FINANCE UNDER
THE RHEE ADMINISTRATION

South Korea inherited the unsystematic and improvised colonial system of finance that funded schooling through tuition, special school taxes, and school supporters' associations. The U.S. military government, working within financial restrictions, continued this system. Under President Syngman Rhee, an even more bewilderingly complex and unsystematic hodgepodge of private donations, voluntary and mandatory fees, and "gifts," as well as local and national taxes, supported education. National revenues primarily supported the national universities, teachers' colleges, and salaries of elementary teachers and staff. Maintaining school facilities was the responsibility of local government. Public schools, which accounted for about half of all schools, received only modest support, mainly for the construction of classrooms. Most higher education was private and received no direct financial support from the central government. Just how much of the cost of education was covered by the national government is difficult to estimate because of the large proportion of informal contributions and variable and often unreported fees. Some estimates indicate that national funds during the Rhee administration contributed only 10 percent of the cost of education.[2] The funds were distributed through the provincial governments, their allocation largely determined by either the provincial governor or the county chief. School authorities, teachers, and school board members disliked the discretion given to these general administrators, and they frequently complained that money earmarked for education was being diverted for personal or political use by these officials.

Local taxes also accounted for a small share of educational support. Local taxation was a complex system inherited from the Chosŏn and colonial periods. The most important parts were the household assessment tax *(hobyŏlse)*, levied on all households according to their appraised rental values, and the special household tax *(t'ŭkbyŏlse)*, a surtax on households. From 1951, following the land reform, an additional land income tax *(t'oji sodŭkse)* was levied on farm holdings. These taxes accounted for the bulk of local revenue. There were also various taxes on entertainment places, fisheries, and restaurants. These taxes also financed other functions of local government, thus accounting for only a modest percentage of educational expenses.[3] Furthermore, local taxes were collected by local government officials and thus were channeled through the Ministry of the

Interior, which diverted large portions for political purposes, much as it did with the national revenues.[4] Additional funding was provided by a National Education Tax enacted in 1958, but this was modest and also subject to political misuse.[5]

Even if education had received all its allocated funds, these would have represented only a fraction of its needs. The South Korean state in its early years had a weak rate of tax extraction. The effective tax rate of 9.9 percent of the nation's GNP was low even compared to other poor states.[6] Instead, the Rhee administration relied upon a variety of informal revenue-gathering strategies. Fees for education, health services, and police protection were estimated as producing three times as much revenue as local taxes. Voluntary contributions to veterans' groups, police organizations, youth movements, and benevolent associations were impossible to calculate, but such informal methods of paying for public services were common. This practice lent itself to a variety of abuses and was condemned for its arbitrary nature, inequities, and inefficiencies.[7] Nowhere was this more true than in education, for which formal public expenditures accounted for such a small percentage of costs.

Financing education via such informal methods was fairly easy. The high social demand and the resultant willingness of Korean families to make sacrifices to educate their children enabled the Rhee administration to build an educational system on the cheap by transferring the major portion of costs onto students and their families. The most obvious of the user fees was tuition (hak-kyobi), which provided a major share of financial support to all levels of schooling. The MOE set tuition schedules for all schools, public and private, but these were frequently violated by private schools and sometimes by public ones. There also were miscellaneous fees of all kinds such as class fees, entrance fees, and special fees for school activities or repairs. The practice of exacting miscellaneous fees was widely decried, but despite directives theoretically outlawing the practice, these fees continued to be almost universally levied and were a major source of school revenues.

Revenues were generally not sufficient to pay teachers adequate salaries, but many teachers were able to supplement their income through private tutoring. At most schools, teachers held special examination-preparation classes when regular classroom instruction ended. Since teachers often had to teach two and three shifts, after-class instruction could be an onerous economic necessity. There was, however, a way out of this problem: a teacher could give special attention to a student in class in exchange for envelopes of money (ch'ŏnji) from parents.

These were offered by mothers (less often by fathers), who were expected to visit the school at least once a year, and on the annual teachers' day, when students by custom gave gifts to their instructors. Teachers also made home visits to collect fees, raise special funds for the school or the school district, or report on the progress of their pupils; such visits presented another opportunity to receive gifts. Other sources of income might come from the sale of special textbooks and study materials, especially those related to exam preparation.[8] Schools also sold special answer paper for quizzes and tests. The extent to which the informal methods were used to finance education can be seen in primary education, which was by law free. A survey of Seoul's ninety-two primary schools in late 1959 found that all charged extra fees and that most sold extra materials, collected money for unscheduled events, and charged fees connected with classroom tests.[9]

The informal financing of education placed a serious hardship on most parents and put rural and low-income communities at a comparative disadvantage. Teachers, too, felt victimized by a system that could underpay them in the expectation that informal contributions would provide most of their real income, that gave parents leverage over their classroom performance, and in which they had to arrive at school two hours early to conduct extracurricular classes and stay after hours to give more cram classes. Nevertheless, the drive for education kept this system going.

Another means of support came from the school supporters' associations and their successor, the teacher and parent society (sach'inhoe), both modeled in part on the American parent–teacher associations and both often referred to as the PTA. The Korean PTA had been encouraged by the Americans as part of their administrative reforms. In the United States, the PTA had a long history of popular participation in education and was seen as a way to gain cooperation between parents and teachers in the educational process, as well as being a democratizing institution and a major support for the concept of community-controlled schools. But the school supporters' associations formed in South Korea in the late 1940s were from the start different from the American idea of parent–teacher associations since their primary purpose was to raise money. Reorganized as the teacher and parent society in 1950, the PTA was a major source of revenue for schools. It is difficult to determine what proportion of the operating costs of public and private schools the PTA provided, but estimates vary from 10 to 50 percent.[10] In 1957, the MOE calculated that national and local government revenues covered 55 percent of the costs of elementary education, 22 percent of secondary education, and 24 percent of higher education; the remainder came from tuition, informal fees, and PTA contributions.[11] In 1959, Yonsei University professor Im Han-yong estimated that the PTA contributions accounted for 24 percent of the cost of all primary and secondary schooling.[12] Due to the difficulty of separating PTA contributions from the various other informal payments, no reliable estimate of the PTA contribution will likely ever be possible. It is clear, however, that it was an important part of teachers' salaries at almost all public and private schools, at both the elementary and secondary levels, and may have accounted for as much as 30 percent of their income. In some cases, it may have been the main source of income for the school administration and the teaching staff.[13]

Voluntary in theory, the PTA fees were universally regarded by school officials as mandatory; students were frequently refused admittance or threatened with expulsion if their parents did not pay the fees. As noted, the press frequently publicized cases of children committing suicide or parents driven to acts of desperation because they could not pay the fees and the children were subsequently denied admission or asked to withdraw.[14] Stories of teachers beating students because they could not pay the fees were reported.[15] One teacher recalls shouting at students who did not pay the fee, "I'm a man; I have to eat."[16] Yet since the government did not have the funds to support compulsory education, it was accepted that parents would have to bear a large share of the burden, and the willingness of Korean parents to spend large portions of their meager incomes on schooling was taken for granted. But many parents believed that teachers and especially principals diverted the fees for their personal use, and this generated bitter complaints. The press demanded that a system be set up to rationalize revenue and expenditures in order to make educational standards uniform throughout the country.[17] Due to its unpopularity, the PTA was abolished in the early 1960s, but it was too useful as a revenue-producing agency, and the Park government revived it in 1970.

THE ROLE OF PRIVATE FOUNDATIONS

Contributing to the cost of education was the fact that half of the secondary schools and three-quarters of colleges and universities were private. To satisfy the need for more secondary schools and colleges, the South Korean govern-

Table 11. Establishment of Private Foundations in Korea, 1948–1958

Year	Number	Year	Number
1948	83	1954	48
1949	17	1955	38
1950	21	1956	15
1951	26	1957	6
1952	51	1958	1
1953	43		

Source: Im Hanyong, 386.

ment relied on the *chaedan* (educational foundations). The *chaedan* were tax-exempt corporate bodies formed to establish degree-granting institutions consisting of a founder or patron and perhaps several (sometimes several dozen) directors *(isa)*. The tradition of founding schools is an ancient one in Korea. Establishing or participating in the management of a private school such as a *sŏwŏn* was a worthy endeavor for a learned member of the *yangban* class. During the late Chosŏn period a vast number of private schools offering modern learning were established by members of the Korean elite, partly out of political frustration resulting in a retreat from public affairs and into education, but also out of a desire to prepare the nation for the future through self-strengthening efforts. For many educational activists the cultivation of the individual was linked with the strengthening of Korea. These efforts continued throughout the colonial period, and many of the leading figures of Korean society served as heads of school foundations. A notable example was Kim Sŏng-su (already mentioned in ch. 2), a wealthy landlord of *yangban* background who was also one of Korea's leading businessmen. Kim headed Posŏng College, which became Korea University, one of the two most prestigious private universities in South Korea.

Chaedan grew rapidly after liberation, peaking in 1948, when eighty-three were established. The fall to seventeen in 1949 can perhaps be partly attributed to the uncertainty over the educational system. Another growth spurt came between 1952 and 1955, and then a sharp decline between 1956 and 1958 (see Table 11).[18] During the second period of rapid growth, the private foundations accounted for most new high schools and colleges.

Most of the founders of the new schools were educated professionals, often with distinguished careers and some experience in politics. Establishing an educational foundation required some cash, although the amounts were sometimes very modest. A *chaedan* founder usually did not have enough money of his own, so he needed financial backers. These were most often landowners and prosperous businessmen who perhaps did not have as distinguished a reputation as the founder. They served on the board of directors and became part owners of the foundation. For example, Chang Hyŏng, the founder of the *chaedan* that established Tan'guk College in 1948 (later Tan'guk University), studied at Posŏng College, went to China, and became involved in the independence movement. Although Chang served as head of the foundation, the principal financial support came not from Chang, but from a wealthy landlord, Cho Hŭi-jae.[19] Yu Sŏk-ch'ang, a respected educator from a wealthy family, founded Kŏn'guk University in 1949.[20] Sin Ik-hŭi, one of the most prominent politicians in Korea and Rhee's chief opponent in the 1956 presidential elections, founded Kungmin College (later Kungmin University) in 1946. Kungmin College's *chaedan* had a distinguished list of forty founding board members, with Syngman Rhee serving as the foundation's honorary president.[21] Im Yŏng-sin (Louise Lim), an American-educated director of a kindergarten before liberation, in a controversial appointment was selected by Rhee as his first minister of commerce and industry. After her brief involvement in politics, she headed the foundation that operated Chungang University. The foundation that supported Hongik University and its affiliated secondary schools was established by businessman Yi To-yŏng, head of the Ilsin Sanŏp company. Yi was from a *yangban* family, married into the powerful Yŏhŭng Min clan, and received a law degree from Keijō University.[22] Some founders of less distinguished backgrounds developed reputations as successful educational entrepreneurs. Cho Myŏng-ji, founder of what became Kyŏnggi University, studied Buddhism at the Central Buddhist College in Seoul during the colonial period and did research on religion at Keijō University. His educational foundation established a number of schools, including Choyang Nursing Junior College in 1954. Cho was typical in many ways— well educated and from a landlord background. The Sinhŭng foundation, which established what became Kyunghee (Kyŏnghŭi) University, as well as Kyunghee Middle and High Schools, was founded by Yi Kyu-hŏn, son of Yi Si-yŏng, the elderly first vice-president of the Republic of Korea. The foundation, however, was soon taken over by the enterprising Cho Yŏng-sik, who built it up to be one of the wealthiest in Korea.[23] Chŏng Chae-han was a Japanese-trained civil servant who served as public prosecutor in Pusan, Taegu, and Taejŏn and later as a member of the National Assembly. In 1948 he established the *chaedan* for Tonga University in Pusan.[24] Kim Yŏn-jun, a musician who graduated from Yŏnhŭi College, founded Hanyang University, and Kim Hŭng-bae, a businessman, founded Han'guk College of Foreign Languages in 1954.[25]

The distinguished backgrounds of the founders of the early *chaedan* lent the foundations prestige and indicated the importance of education in South Korea. Some Koreans have held that the first surge in private educational foundations was motivated primarily by patriotism and a desire to enlighten the nation, but after 1950, educational foundations tended to be strictly a business.[26] Many of the founders before 1950, such as Sin Ik-hŭi, Chang Hyŏn, Yu Sŏk-ch'ang, and Yi Kyu-hŏn, were prominent in either politics or education or both. Later founders had less distinguished backgrounds, but it is not clear that this supports the belief that their motives were more pecuniary. There are, however, several other reasons to support the idea that education was increasingly becoming a business.

Many landowners receiving compensation under the terms of the land reform, or selling land in anticipation of the reform, sought places to invest their funds. Educational foundations were nonprofit and untaxed forms of investment. Since many had little business experience and the turbulent times and poor state of the economy were not conducive to commercial and industrial enterprises, schools were a safe investment, as well as a means of maintaining social status through the tradition of being a patron of scholarship. Furthermore, schools were profitable investments. Since Koreans were willing to make considerable sacrifices to educate their children, considerable funds were channeled into schools, even in economic hard times. Moreover, the initial investment in establishing a *chaedan* was modest, often requiring only a plot of land and a rudimentary building or two.[27] The connection between the land reform and the establishment of *chaedan* also coincides nicely in terms of chronology. In 1948 a number of landowners sold properties in anticipation of radical land reform. Sales slowed down in 1949, but with the implementation of land reform in 1951–1953 there was a boom in new foundations. The link is also suggested in Yi Kwang-ho's study of the *chaedan* of twenty-two secondary schools in Pusan and in Kyŏngsang and Kyŏnggi Provinces. The founders, Yi found, generally came from backgrounds that suggested landed wealth.[28]

Religious institutions also played an important role in educational expansion. Buddhists expanded the small Hyehwa College into Tongguk University in 1953, and the Wŏn Buddhist sect founded Wŏn'gwang College the same year. Catholics founded Sŏngsin (Sacred Heart) College in 1947, and the Seventh Day Adventists established the Samyuk Theological School in 1954. The Presbyterian Church in Korea had always been active in education, and its two schools of higher learning in Seoul, Yŏnhŭi College and Severance Medical School, were merged to form the large, prestigious Yonsei University.[29] But the great majority of private foundations were nonsectarian. Although the national government contributed to the growth of higher education with the establishment of several branches of the national universities in the provinces between 1952 and 1956, it was the private foundations that accounted for most of the new institutes of higher learning, not just in the 1950s, but in later years as well. In fact, a wave of new foundations appeared again in the late 1980s and 1990s as the state allowed more colleges to open.

Government policy toward the establishment of educational foundations before 1961 has been described as "laissez-faire."[30] This was certainly the case under the U.S. military occupation. Yu Ŏk-kyŏm, the Korean adviser in the Department of Education from 1945 to 1947, remarked, "When the people want to invest their clean money in establishing higher education institutes, which the government cannot offer to do, how is it possible to deny them? Once they start the institution, they will apply their conscious efforts for the social development of their institutions."[31] But soon after the Rhee government was established, its officials began criticizing the proliferation of private schools. They were joined by many educators and newspaper editors in expressing concern over the commercialization of education and the lack of effective controls over standards. Some felt that tight controls over private schools should have been included in the Basic Education Law, and others argued for the need for more careful MOE regulations for private foundations.[32] "Education has become a marketplace with more interest in making money. Private schools are taking advantage of the desire for education," the *Tonga ilbo* editorialized in 1953. It accused MOE officials of accepting bribes in exchange for approving schools even though the schools lacked even the minimal facilities.[33] The *chaedan* were accused of not spending any of their money on education. The number of teachers was inadequate, and they failed to meet the minimum requirements. Facilities were substandard. But rather than limitations on new private schools, the solution, according to the *Tonga ilbo,* was more careful government regulation and public financial support for both private and public schools.[34]

For many officials, the problem was more secondary school and college graduates than were needed by the economy and the loss of "uniformity of education"—that is, centralized control of teachers and curricula—that unchecked expansion brought. Private colleges, in particular, expanded so fast that standards were thought to have been lowered. By the mid-1950s, almost every college had become a general university, and admission standards at the less prestigious institutions had fallen to the point that almost any high school graduate could enter. Some schools by 1955 reported a shortage of students despite the swelling number of those entering college, a number inflated as a result of a desire both to seek military exemption and postpone entry into a job market unable to absorb secondary school graduates. This shortage of students, however, did not apply to high schools or middle schools, where a chronic shortage of places continued throughout the 1950s. It was therefore easier to enter college than secondary school, although competition for entry into the prestigious universities, especially Seoul National University and Yonsei, Korea, and Ewha Women's Universities, remained fierce.[35] In fact, by the late 1950s the percentage of South Koreans of college age entering college was rivaling that of some developed nations such as Britain, a testimony to the social demand for higher education. In response, the state made it difficult to establish new foundations after 1957.

EDUCATIONAL FINANCE UNDER PARK CHUNG HEE

The complicated and inadequate system of state financial support of education continued with little substantive change during the three decades of military-dominated governments. Financial reform of schooling was not a high priority for the Park government, although some lip service was given to the problem. In his 1965 State of the Nation address, President Park pledged to "reduce school expenditures for the parents and students," but no measures were taken.[36] The Park administration frequently condemned the unfair burden on families and declared its intention to ensure greater fiscal support from the state. Yet although the Park regime tinkered with the system's finances, the basic pattern persisted of state underfunding and the resultant reliance on Korean families to assume most of the costs. Incomes rose with the economic takeoff that Park's development policies generated; however, the cost of education rose at least as fast so that the financial burden on Korean families remained largely unchanged.

In point of fact, public expenditure on education as a proportion of the national budget remained quite modest by the standards of developing nations, averaging about 17.0 percent of the national budget in 1965–1966—only slightly above the 15.1 percent recorded for the last two full years of civilian rule, 1959–1960.[37] Each year education officials and the press complained about the cuts in spending. For instance, the Second Five-Year Economic Development Plan included an ambitious attempt to build 34,566 classrooms by the end of 1971 and thereby end double-shift classes and accommodate the increases in the student population. In spite of its initial approval of the plan, the National Assembly made drastic cuts in the budget, while the EPB—which tended to give low priority to classroom construction or teacher training—refused to approve loan and aid money to the project so that only 4.6 billion won, or 13 percent of the originally allocated funds, were made available.[38] Again in 1975, a plan to launch nine-year compulsory education in 1981 called for an enormous increase in the state expenditure on education. This was justified as necessary, to improve the quality of education, and as feasible in light of the nation's double-digit economic growth.[39] But no major increases in the state's share of educational support were forthcoming. The proportion of the national budget devoted to education remained in the 15–17 percent range throughout the 1960s and 1970s.

There are several reasons why the state share did not increase. The economic planners simply did not make education, which was already expanding rapidly, a high priority for major public investments. Money poured into education did not pay the political dividends of showy projects such as highways, public buildings, and dams. Most of all, the Park regime knew that the public would continue to sacrifice to educate its children so that educational expenditures could be taken for granted, and money could be concentrated elsewhere. Educators and the press complained that the portion of the budget devoted to education was too small, but the state had no incentive to increase it.

Primary schooling was the only level of education that was tuition free, but most elementary schools levied school support fees. These were reduced by half in 1967 to "relieve parents of excessive burdens," but then the Seoul Board of Education asked all public elementary schools to organize voluntary associations of parents to make up the financial shortage.[40] In theory, if the fees were voluntary, they would not place an undue expense on poor families. But richer families were allowed to contribute more, so such fees ran the risk of encouraging special treatment and undermining equality of opportunity. Furthermore, the pressure to contribute voluntary fees was such that most families would pay them. Schools continued to charge fees of all kinds, ranging from those for exam papers to special reference materials. MOE directives against miscellaneous fees were largely ignored, even though inspection teams were sent to see that schools adhered to the ban on special fees.

One of the few major state changes in educational finance was the abolition of the PTA in 1961. State planners regarded the abolition as a major reform of education since the organization was considered the "greenhouse of educational corruption." But since the state refused to commit itself to an appreciably larger share of financial responsibility, there were discussions on reviving the PTA as early as 1963.[41] In 1966, the MOE announced that it would allow support organizations for schools in some areas to help out financially. The *Han'guk ilbo* editorialized that temporary measures were becoming permanent: "It's quite obvious that the government budget for primary education must be expanded drastically."[42] In the meanwhile, an investigation by the National Assembly revealed that miscellaneous fees cost parents 9 billion won ($18 million in 1969 dollars) a year. But this was probably an underestimate. In 1969, the MOE gave the city and provincial boards of education permission to reinstate the PTA, arguing that it would eliminate up to forty miscellaneous fees. The press welcomed the move as a temporary measure but warned about the need to avoid the corruption of the organization by mothers seeking influence.[43] The Yuksŏnghoe, as the PTA was now called, was reestablished in 1970.[44] It was accompanied by an association for school management in each school under the supervision of the city and provincial boards to see to it that the fees were not used to harm or corrupt education.[45] Regulations were issued to avoid the direct collection of fees by teachers, but these were not always enforced. Unwilling to provide for adequate fiscal support, the best the state could do was to try to consolidate and regulate the collection of fees through the PTA. In reality, there was little way to do so since there was no overall organization to supervise the collections.

The revived PTA was a disappointment in that the amounts collected were less than anticipated. Official estimates were that PTA fees accounted for 15 percent of total expenditures on education, but these did not prove adequate.[46] For one thing the fees, set by the MOE, were too small. (In 1975 they were about

$2 a year per primary school student and $3 per secondary school student.)[47] Five years after the PTA was revived, a study found that most of the miscellaneous fees that it was meant to eliminate were still being collected. Students were still paying for toilet paper, reference books, stationery, uniforms, and other items.[48]

Since the reinstitution of the Yuksŏnghoe did not help to lower tuition, eliminate various fees, or address the burden of private tutoring and cram schools, it only added one more expense to schooling. The Yuksŏnghoe did, however, as had its predecessor, provide a useful vehicle for parental influence in the schools. One researcher in Taegu found that many parents welcomed the revival since through the PTA they could have almost "contractual relations with teachers."[49] About 20 percent of urban and 30 percent of rural pupils were exempted from the fees due to poverty. Some educators feared this would create inferiority complexes among the poor and disproportional influence among the wealthier parents. President Park issued an eight-point memorandum against unauthorized fees and announced stern measures to see that fairness was ensured in the treatment of pupils regardless of income, but he did not make a financial commitment that would have alleviated the need for the PTA.[50]

In 1969, just before the Yuksŏnghoe was reinstated, the Central Educational Research Institute reported that total tuition and fees from primary to high school were 93,000 won for rural families, 135,000 won for urban families other than in Seoul or Pusan, and 263,000 won for Seoul and Pusan—nearly a fifth of a family's income for the relevant period.[51] Korean education was indeed costly. Yet this was not a real measure since much of the cost was based on after-school lessons and private tutoring that the institute did not include in its figures. There were also the various gifts to teachers, sometimes directly collected when teachers visited homes. The latter practice was strictly prohibited; nonetheless, it was prevalent enough that in 1977 MOE issued warnings against teachers who visited the homes of their students.[52] In all, after food, education was probably the greatest single expense for most Korean families. Some estimates placed the cost at as much as 30 percent of total household income.[53]

The Chun regime after 1980 promised to shift more of the financial burden from individual families to the state; however, its reforms did little to change the reality of educational finance. In 1981, the Ministry of Finance introduced a new education tax (kyoyukse). The education minister announced that it would "normalize in-school education," while the government was eliminating "overheated out-of-school lessons."[54] The tax went into effect in 1982 for five years; the administration justified it as a temporary expedient, but it was extended for another five years in 1987, and shortly after, it was made permanent. The new levy, which included taxes on cigarettes and alcohol and property surtaxes, was admittedly inadequate, and in fact the increased government share fell short of projections. Partly this was due to bad timing. The call for the state to assume a greater proportion of the cost of education ran counter to the administration's struggle to achieve greater financial stability. To solve the problem of rampant inflation, the state cut public expenditure drastically in the early 1980s and controlled monetary growth. This proved to be successful; inflation dropped from the double-digit rates of the 1960s and 1970s to about 5 percent annually. The fiscal deficit dropped sharply, and foreign debt declined. As a result, economic growth from 1981 to 1987 averaged 9 percent amid low inflation. Real wages were higher, and the government hoped that the public would, as a consequence, be better able to assume the expense of education.

KWAOE FRENZY AND THE ESCALATING COSTS OF EDUCATION

While the income of most South Koreans rose sharply after 1975, so did educational costs. The percentage of household income spent on basic necessities such as housing, clothing, and food declined, especially after the mid-1980s. Educational expenditures, however, for most Korean families rose faster than the general cost of living. The greatest single factor in the escalating price of schooling was private tutoring and out-of-school lessons, known as *kwaoe*. *Kwaoe* not only placed an enormous burden on Korean families, but it also accentuated the differences in income among sectors of society, undermining the policy of egalitarian access to education. Further, it represented a drain of resources that economic planners would rather have seen in savings and used for capital investment.

To control the rising problem of *kwaoe*, the Chun administration in 1980 banned all private tutoring. Some concessions to private instruction were made. Special summer classes were permitted—and in fact were virtually compulsory—and exceptions were made for extra classes for high school seniors. It is difficult to estimate the cost of private tutoring in the 1980s because it had largely been driven underground; most reports estimate that at first there was a real decline in expenditures on tutoring, perhaps by a quarter, during the first two years of the ban.[55] But enormous amounts were still spent. Moreover, it was an open secret that private tutoring remained the main source of financial support for a large proportion of college students and an important income supplement for many teachers—and even a career for many college graduates. Since the ban simply attacked the symptoms, it became increasingly less effective. The practice of secret lessons and the money spent on education on extra-class instruction grew.

Parents went to great lengths to avoid the regulations against private tutoring. College student tutors sometimes dressed up in high school uniforms in order to enter the apartments of their students without drawing suspicion. Some families rented out apartments to tutors so that they could offer lessons to the children of one or more families without drawing the attention of the apartment watchmen. Resorts and hotels, as well as condos, often housed secret cram schools. The rich sent children abroad for tutoring. Even student radicals supported themselves through illegal tutoring, their political views being less important to parents than their having been accepted into select universities.[56]

In the summer of 1989, the state ended the ban on private tutors. The administration justified this reversal by explaining it was "deferring to the student's right to learn" and the need for college students to earn money. Privately, however, many officials admitted the growing ineffectiveness of the ban on tutoring. Private tutoring could now flourish in the open. And flourish it did, with students from the best universities earning more from tutoring than their professors from their jobs. Some college graduates found the practice so lucrative that they opted to continue it rather than take a drastic salary cut to work for a government agency or business. One could argue that by the early 1990s private tutoring and after-school lessons were the fastest growing of South Korea's many booming industries.

Fears arose that legalizing tutoring would result in a widening opportunity gap between rich and poor students. For this reason many MOE officials considered placing a ban on live-in tutors and enacting a variety of restrictions that would limit the amount of money any one family could spend, but these suggestions were obviously impractical.[57] Private help had been restricted to tutoring by college students, but in 1991 middle and high school students were permitted to take private lessons at government-approved *hagwŏn*s. Many officials in private admitted that the attempts to control *kwaoe* had failed and that as long as competition for entrance examinations remained so acute, any reform would be ineffectual.

Since the feverish competition for entry into the best colleges did not let up in the 1990s and the nation became more affluent, the demand for and expense of after-school instruction only rose. The KEDI in early 1995 estimated that families annually paid 17 trillion won ($21 billion) on direct educational expenditures such as tuition, mandatory fees, extracurricular activities sponsored by schools, transportation, and textbooks. By contrast, total government expenditure on education in 1994 amounted to 16.7 trillion won. That is, the public paid 51 percent of the total direct cost of education. In addition, an estimated 6 trillion won was spent on private tutoring. According to the KEDI study, when tutoring was included, parents and students absorbed 69 percent of the costs of education.[58] State expenditures on education accounted for about 4 percent of the GNP—somewhat less than in most developed countries—but if the total costs were to be calculated, Koreans spent as much as 12 percent of their GNP on education—considerably higher than most other industrialized nations.

In reality, the costs of education are much greater than even these figures suggest. First, the cost of private tutoring is very hard to estimate since a great deal of it lies outside the formal economy. Several surveys conducted in the mid-1990s came up with varying figures of the average expenditure on after-school lessons. One, in mid-1993, estimated that private tutoring for high school students came to 580,000 won a month ($465) per household.[59] Although some officials expressed private doubts on the accuracy of these figures, it was clear that the amounts spent were enormous. Furthermore, the huge industry geared toward cramming students for exams was growing in the 1990s. "*Kwaoe* frenzy" provided lucrative economic opportunities, with well-known private instructors charging as much as 1.5 million won a month ($2,100) for lessons at their institutes, although the average charge was much less. Three-quarters of college students engaged in private tutoring, with their average income in 1995 estimated between 300,000 and 400,000 won a month—enough to pay for living expenses. Wealthier parents began sending children abroad when the restrictions on overseas travel eased after the 1988 Seoul Olympics. Thousands of families sent children to U.S. high schools, and they would pay a Korean family in America an average of $2,000–3,000 a month to watch over them. By 1995, this practice was growing so fast that the government placed restrictions to prevent it, citing the drain on the balance of payments it caused.

These restrictions did not affect the tens of thousands of teenagers who participated each summer in English classes abroad.

Among the hidden costs was the practice of giving gifts to teachers. Although reliable information on the scale of this practice is lacking, one educator
estimated that this amounted to an average of 100,000 won ($125) a year per stu-
dent.[60] A police investigation that accidentally stumbled upon a teacher's note-
book itemizing money and presents received from parents suggested that in
many cases the amount was much higher. Civic groups attacked the practice of
money envelopes, and the government vowed to crack down on it.[61] The emp-
tiness of this vow was indicated in a 1999 survey that found most Korean parents still giving money envelopes—and the amount was increasing.[62] Still, for
all the publicity this practice generated, it was only a minor burden compared to
the rising expense of private lessons.

The sharpest rise in educational costs in the 1990s came from after-school
lessons for elementary students. By the early 1970s the middle school entrance
exams had been abolished, but in the 1990s the burden reappeared in a new
form. Most parents now saw competence at an early age as the key to later academic success and sent their children to *hagwŏn*s for academic study. In fact, the
tendency was to stress education and private lessons at earlier and earlier ages.
A survey in 1994 found that 87 percent of all primary students took private lessons, while another study in the following year estimated that 90 percent did.[63]
Most of these were in areas such as tae kwon do and athletics, but increasingly
parents were spending money on academic lessons, especially English, where an
early start was thought to give a great advantage. (English was always a concern
for parents; it was a major subject in middle and high school, on the college entrance exams, and on the hiring exams given by prestigious companies.) In 1990,
only one in twelve elementary students was taking private lessons for Korean
language, and one in seven for math. In 1997, however, about a quarter were
taking after-school Korean-language lessons, and nearly half had math lessons.
English saw the most dramatic rise. Half of all students of elementary school
age were enrolled in private English-language schools in 1997, although only 4
percent had been in 1990.[64] Inevitably, perhaps, preschool education was emerging as the newest area of concern for parents, and in the late 1990s, it was becoming the fastest growing sector of the private educational market.[65] According to
a 1998 MOE study, the amount spent on private lessons to prepare students for
higher education exams rose 70 percent from 1994 to 1997.[66]

As noted, all indicators suggest that educational expenses were rising faster than the cost of living and at an accelerating rate. A 1999 study found that they had risen 2.5 times from 1988 to 1998, outstripping the cost increases in food, housing, health, transportation, utilities, or any other major category.[67] According to a report of the National Statistics Office in 1997, urban workers spent 9.8 percent of their incomes on education (up from 6.7 percent in 1987), while rural families devoted a smaller proportion. South Korea in 1997 was 85 percent urban. The magnitude of this expenditure can perhaps be understood by comparing it with expenditures in Japan, where a similar obsession with educational achievement had created the same reliance on private lessons and tutoring. In Japan, urban workers spent 5.4 percent of their incomes on education (up from 4.7 percent in 1987).[68] While Japanese commentators regarded this as a major economic and social problem and the *juku* (cram school) was a ubiquitous feature of life, the economic burden was still modest by Korean standards.

The real costs of education involved additional sacrifices by Korean families that do not generally show up in official studies. For one thing, the desire to live in the best school districts resulted in distortions in real estate prices. The best-known case is the Apkujŏng-dong district in southern Seoul (discussed in chapter 5), where the cost of apartments has soared above any logic in terms of quality and special amenities. For another, mothers traditionally had the principal responsibility for supervising the education of their children, a role that may have inhibited the entry of women into the workforce and that required fathers to work long hours to pay for the education of their children and support their nonworking wives. Most South Koreans have accepted much of this burden, but in surveys, they have stated that they feel "greatly burdened" by the costs of education.

Government planners wanted to lessen the growing expenditures and absorb much of the money spent on private tutoring into productive investments in education (such as improving school facilities) and economic development. Certainly the competition for schooling has contributed to the high performance of South Korean middle and high school students in international mathematics and science tests. But in other ways it has been inefficient. For example, math and science, in which South Korean students excel, are among the less stressed areas in the entrance examinations. On the other hand, probably no subject is the object of more extra lessons than English, and yet the results are modest, to say the least. South Korean competence in English or any foreign language has been low enough to be a concern for government and industry, which feared a linguistic handicap that would hurt the international competitiveness of Korean firms. But every effort to cool down *"kwaoe* frenzy" has failed.

In 1995, the Presidential Commission for Education Reform unveiled a new, state-administered entrance examination that would give more or less equal weight to all subjects in the curriculum. Previously the college entrance exams had emphasized English, Korean, and math. The new exam gave greater emphasis to chemistry, biology, geology, physics, geography, politics, economics, national and world history, and ethics. It had the opposite of the intended effect. Now there were even more subjects for which to cram, so most parents felt obligated to pay for more lessons, with private cram schools responding by offering special science and social science preparatory lessons.[69] Giving greater weight to high school records simply made it more important that students score well on the periodic tests that high schools gave, necessitating more extra lessons. A proposed reform was to set up committees of parents, teachers, and community leaders in the schools to oversee extracurricular activities. The idea was to have the schools themselves set up comprehensive programs for after-class lessons that would bring revenue into the schools rather than to private tutors and institutes. Educational reformers also hoped that such programs would stress healthy, unstressful activities that would not require students to devote long hours to cramming for exams.[70] Even in this proposal, education officials made concessions by suggesting such extracurricular activities as English conversation clubs that would, in fact, help students in the skills needed for examinations. It appeared that this would be no more successful in curbing educational expenditures than earlier proposals had been.

The Kim Young Sam administration (1993–1998) pledged to sharply increase public expenditure on education. In 1995, the National Assembly approved a 24.6-percent increase. Even when the generally rapid rise in costs is factored in, this was the highest increase in state spending in three decades. In the same year, the administration announced its goal of increasing public spending on education from 4 percent of the GNP to 5 percent by 1998, making it roughly comparable to that in most developed states. Most of the increase would be used to upgrade facilities to "world-class standards" by the twenty-first century.[71] Part of this new expenditure was to be used to raise teacher salaries. Another plan was to encourage more investment in education by private companies. A trend in this direction had already started as the *chaebŏl*s (conglomerates) began to acquire secondary schools and colleges and upgrade their facilities.[72] However, with the financial difficulties of many large business concerns at the end of the decade, it became uncertain whether this could be a major source of financial assistance.

Kim Young Sam's successor, Kim Dae Jung, upon becoming president in 1998, also vowed to increase expenditure, announcing a new target of 6 percent, but in 1999 the state was still spending only 4.3 percent of the GNP on education. Kim Dae Jung also discussed a total ban on all forms of private tutoring, but there was widespread public skepticism that such a ban could be enforced.[73] Hopes for a government-imposed restriction on tutoring were given an unexpected blow by the nation's Constitutional Court, which in April 2000 ruled that all restictions on private lessons were unconstitutional. The court declared that the restrictions still in place were an unlawful limitation on personal freedom and the right to education. Kim Dae Jung reacted by looking at ways to investigate the tax returns of those who charged "excessive amounts" for private tutoring. The minister of education formed a committee to find ways to curb tutoring despite the court ruling, but committee members started to resign shortly after it was formed, arguing that what was needed was a sweeping reform of education and not patchwork solutions.[74] Despite promises by political leaders to curb costs, it did not appear likely at the start of a new century that the cost of education would come under control soon. Indeed, although the economic crisis of 1997–1998 saw a dip in educational expenditures, with the economy recovering in 1999, spending on schooling rose an estimated 15 percent in real terms.[75]

7 Education and State Control

South Korea's education was not only extraordinarily competitive and expensive, but it also was highly political. Educational systems are integral parts of modern states and play a crucial role in influencing political behavior and maintaining political systems. The Rhee, Park, and Chun administrations used the educational system to enhance their control over the state apparatus and strengthen the power of the South Korean state over society. In pursuit of such objectives, the state made full use of the nation's rapidly growing student population: it organized and mobilized students to demonstrate and display public support for government policies, promote loyalty to the state regime, and disseminate political information. None of this created the country's "education fever," but it provided a degree of regimentation as well as discipline to the nation's schools, which in turn contributed to the pressure-cooker atmosphere of South Korean education. The emphasis on military drills and political indoctrination also generated impatience among students and parents, who wanted to focus on academic pursuits. It also alienated a segment of teachers and students who resented the heavy-handed political manipulation and the hypocrisy and self-serving nature of government propaganda.

MOBILIZING STUDENTS AND MILITARIZING EDUCATION UNDER RHEE

The South Korean government's educational objectives were given urgency by the social and political turmoil that characterized the post-liberation years.

The formation of the educational system after 1948 took place in an unstable political environment in which national security was an all-consuming concern for the new government. The main reason for this instability was the fact that the South Korean state was the product of a divided nation. From the onset, the division of the nation into two rival regimes was almost universally regarded as tragic and unacceptable. Korea was a homogeneous nation with thirteen centuries of national unity; its new division was based on an arbitrary boundary with no geographical or cultural logic to it. Families found themselves divided, and hundreds of thousands of refugees from the north living in the south created a powerful lobby for reunification. Koreans generally conceived of the South Korean state as a temporary unit that would function only as long as it took to reconstitute a united Korea. Meanwhile, the South Korean state found itself in competition with a North Korean political entity that offered an alternative version of national development.

Another serious reason for the South Korean state's instability was the weak nationalist credentials of its leadership. The majority of the officials serving in the Syngman Rhee administration and most of the leaders of the opposition were tainted with collaboration. Although the bureaucrats and politicians were little different from the vast majority of Koreans, who had simply compromised with the Japanese authorities as they tried to maintain their daily lives, the political and moral authority of the state was undermined by the fact that it was commanded and served mainly by those who not only had cooperated, but also had often prospered under colonial rule.

Despite the repression of leftist elements under the U.S. military regime, there were still pro-Communist and pro–North Korea sympathizers in South Korea. The Rhee administration also faced fierce opposition from moderate and rightist political opponents, both within and outside of the National Assembly. Many of these opponents in 1948 favored a parliamentary form of government, while Rhee and his allies favored a presidential system with broad powers concentrated in the chief executive. To undermine the Rhee government, opponents of the administration in the National Assembly secured passage of the National Traitors Act on 7 September 1948 and began setting up separate investigation machinery to eliminate those within the bureaucracy who had collaborated with the Japanese. As the majority of government officials could have fallen into this category, the act was a provocative attack on the administration and a threat to the entire national bureaucracy and police.

Just how unstable the new regime was became apparent only weeks after the Republic of Korea was proclaimed. On 13 September 1948, the American military completed the transfer of administration to the Koreans, and on 13 October the United States began to withdraw its troops. A week later, units of the newly formed Army of the Republic of Korea, assembled in the southern port of Yŏsu on their way to put down a leftist rebellion on the island of Cheju, themselves rebelled. After a few days of heavy fighting, the revolt was quelled, although some soldiers and supporters continued to hold out in nearby mountains. The Yŏsu rebellion, occurring almost immediately after responsibility for national security was transferred from the U.S. military to the republic's forces, was a powerful blow to the confidence of the new government, which reacted with a heightened emphasis on internal security.

Education became part of the effort to promote national security when the National Assembly began an investigation into the "Yŏsu Incident" in late October 1948 and attention was given to the influence of "leftist" ideas on the nation's youth. Prime Minister Yi Pŏm-sŏk noted that middle school students showed widespread support for the rebels and charged that they were often led by their teachers. Speaking before the legislative body, he called for the creation of a national youth corps to encompass all Korean students and to spread "national consciousness." He also called for the rapid expansion of adult education and the linking of that education with some sort of patriotic organization and training.[1] The veteran nationalist leader Yi Ch'ŏng-ch'ŏn also called for "ideological education" to be taught at all levels so that South Korean students could have a clear set of beliefs to counter the arguments of agents and sympathizers of the North Korean regime.[2] On 27 October, a Law for Special Punishments for Rioters was passed, and on 20 November a more sweeping National Security Law was issued; both gave broad authority to the National Police, which had proven itself a reliable instrument of control at Yŏsu, to arrest those who were endangering the security of the state. Subsequently, a staggeringly large number of Koreans fell victim to these measures. More than 700 persons were arrested as subversives in the first week of November alone.[3] American sources estimated that by mid-1949 there were more than 30,000 political prisoners in South Korean jails.[4] Rumors of North Korean infiltrators and conspiratorial activity by subversives became a pervasive part of the South Korean scene. On 1 December 1948, for instance, the Seoul chief of police had posters placed on the city streets proclaiming, "The North Korean People's Army has already begun its invasion of South Korea. . . . Persons inciting civil disturbances will be shot on sight."[5] Many students and teachers were arrested at this time, and pressure was put on principals to report leftists on their staff. In early December, Minister of Education An Ho-sang ordered all schools to provide the MOE with personal histories of all their teachers, clarifying their political positions so that "teachers who are Communist or lean to the left or who do not make their beliefs clear will be excluded from any positions in the educational field."[6] Student committees *(haksaeng wiwŏnhoe)* were organized at each school to report leftists and anti-government students. On 10 January 1949, a conference of elementary and secondary school principals was held to form an association to root out "impure teachers." The Association to Purge Impure Teachers (Puron Kyosa Sukch'ŏng Hyŏphoe) was set up to supervise the efforts by school authorities to "purify" teaching staff.[7] By 15 March 1949, the organization reported that 1,641 teachers and administrative staff had been purged from elementary and secondary schools, and these figures excluded three provinces: Kangwŏn, North Ch'ungch'ŏng, and Cheju, where the bloody civil conflict was continuing.[8] The MOE at this time sternly warned that it would "purify persons who destroy democracy in our schools."[9] A few years later, the MOE was to boast that by 1949, the "thought movement" *(sasang undong)* was under way to "purify thought for a democratic nation" *(minju ŭi minjok).*[10]

Soon after independence, the militarization of education that had characterized the last seven years of Japanese colonial rule reemerged as a result of the tense political atmosphere on the Korean Peninsula. The most significant instrument in this process was the Student Defense Corps (Hakto Hoguktan), created by the MOE and An Ho-sang in 1949. The origins of the Student Defense Corps lie in the wake of the Yŏsu Incident, when, at the suggestion of several members of government, including Yi Pŏm-sŏk and An Ho-sang, a series of meetings was convened to discuss the creation of a nationwide student organization. In December 1948, 2,400 "cadres" *(kanbu)* were organized at various secondary schools. The following month, the MOE ordered that colleges and universities also organize cadres to serve as student leaders. This was carried out on the nation's campuses in March and April, and on 22 April 1949 the Central Student Defense Corps (Chungang Hakto Hoguktan) was formally inaugurated. On 28 September 1949, a presidential order spelled out the regulations of the Student Defense Corps, whose membership was now compulsory for all secondary and higher-education students.[11]

The Student Defense Corps was organized along military lines: the president of the republic was its commander in chief, the minister of education was the corps commander, and the vice-minister was the vice-commander. The provincial governors and the city mayors served as regional commanders, with the provincial or city superintendent of education serving as the regional vice-commander. Each school formed a company headed by the principal and subdivided into brigades (based on grade levels) and further subdivided into classroom-sized platoons, which in turn consisted of two or more squads. Students served as class leaders (for a single grade) and as classroom leaders. All secondary students automatically became members and were supposed to undergo periodic examinations of their thoughts. Military training was compulsory, and each school day began with the students marching in military formation before the principal and the assembled teachers. The teachers themselves were to act as advisers to the students and supervise corps-related activities in their classes. During the colonial period, Korean secondary school students wore Japanese military-style uniforms whose designs derived from Wilhelmian Germany; South Korean students continued this custom after liberation. The uniforms were now to be subjected to daily inspection, and improper attire—along with improper performance of military drills and improper speech and thoughts— could lead to disciplinary action.[12]

According to An Ho-sang, the chief purpose of the Student Defense Corps was to "consolidate anti-Communist thought."[13] The motto of the corps was "Protect students [from subversive ideas] and defend the nation" *(Hagwŏn-ŭl suho hago nara-rŭl chik'iryonŭn)*. Students took an oath: "We students shall put a complete end to all anti-national acts and thoughts. . . . We, the students, shall restore order in schools."[14] Writing in an educational journal, *Chosŏn kyoyuk*, An stated that the corps had three goals: to democratize education, to purify impure persons, and to unite the people.[15] The ideology initially expounded by the corps could be summarized as national unity, a strong sense of national and ethnic identity or "pride of race" (as it was often termed), and, above all, anti-Communism. National unity meant that the division of the peninsula into two states was unacceptable, so students were to work to achieve unification, a task set in rhetoric that implied the use of armed force. The emphasis on ethnic identity or race was part of the Koreanization of education that had been a major objective since liberation in 1945. It was both a reaction to the forced assimilation of Koreans during World War II and a borrowing of prewar Japanese racial nationalism. But the core element of the student organization's ideology was anti-Communism.

To promote correct thinking the MOE set up a Thought Institute, under the direction of the central organization of the corps, to train teachers and student leaders who could then be sent out into the public as well as into the schools to conduct ideological training. The first group of two hundred students began training at the institute in the spring of 1949, and during that summer, programs were intensified. Special student teams were sent to various schools and also to the countryside to "spread enlightenment."[16] In carrying out these activities, the corps was able to draw upon the experience of student mobilization under Japanese rule. After the China Incident (Japan's term for its war with China, 1937–1945) began, military drills were a major part of the secondary school boys' day. Both boys and girls began each school day lining up in military formation; military-like discipline was maintained in each classroom by the student leader; and (as noted) secondary, college, and sometimes primary school children were mobilized for the war effort in such projects as building airstrips, practicing first aid, and even "volunteer" work in defense-related industries. In many ways the political mobilization of students after 1948 was a continuation of these colonial practices.[17]

Continued political tensions only strengthened arguments for the need to provide heavy doses of ideological training in education. From May 1949, the sporadic infiltration of North Korean trained guerrillas helped to create a sense of civil war in South Korea. And the summer of 1949 saw military clashes along the thirty-eighth parallel, which divided the two halves of Korea. It was an unpleasant time for many teachers, who feared being denounced as leftists. Adding to the uncertainty, the MOE reported that many officially approved textbooks were found to have been written by impure elements, and thus teachers and principals had to frequently change the texts they were using or found themselves in trouble.[18] Then the outbreak of the Korean War led to the mobilization of the entire society for the war effort and the organization of students into a great, patriotic enterprise.

The new education minister, Paek Nak-chun, responded to this crisis with what he labeled "defense education," an education that would create "fighting citizens" (ssaunŭn kungmin). He declared a need for "combative education," which would battle for national independence and the national spirit.[19] The MOE made extensive use of the hwarangdo ideal in educational literature. The *hwarangdo* were bands of adolescent aristocratic warriors in ancient Korea; Paek used the term to convey a sense that the training of youth and the defense of the state were an ancient tradition. The MOE established a National Thought Leadership Council, which published books and pamphlets urging patriotism and national unity, and its monthly journal, *Sasang* (Thought), was distributed to school administrators.[20] Perhaps more significant, greater stress was given to military training in the high school and college curricula, and the colonial practice of sending army officers to high schools was resumed. Military training was incorporated into the Student Defense Corps and supervised by military officers.

During the Korean War, Rhee made use of students for mass political rallies. In June 1951, the Student Defense Corps sponsored mass demonstrations against the U.S.-proposed armistice, starting a pattern of displaying official displeasure that continued for the next forty years.[21] After 1953, this practice became more prevalent, with primary school students participating in these rallies as well. Provincial, city, and county officials from the Ministry of the Interior would often give orders, either through local MOE staff or directly to primary school principals, that their pupils participate in demonstrations and bring appropriate signs, banners, and other paraphernalia.

The student rallies were used most often to represent the national will on foreign policy matters. An example was the issue of the Neutral Nations Supervising Committee, a group of six nations that was set up under the United Nations to review the truce agreement that ended armed hostilities on the peninsula in July 1953. Unhappy with the truce and suspicious of the United Nations, Rhee was outraged that the committee included representatives from Poland and Czechoslovakia, Communist nations aligned with North Korea. On 6 August 1954, massive demonstrations were organized to protest the presence of the committee in the observation of the cease-fire. Hundreds of thousands of students participated, and in Taegu, the Student Defense Corps was mobilized for displays of anger that kept the UN observers effectively trapped for days in a U.S. military compound where they were billeted.[22]

In September 1954, several days of nationwide student demonstrations began calling for a million-man ROK army. Rhee, speaking through "spontaneous" rallies of veterans, civil servants, and Student Defense Corps units, demanded that the United States provide military aid to expand the South Korean Army from seven hundred thousand to one million members. The next month, after an announcement by the United States that it planned to reduce its troops in South Korea, the Rhee government launched more than a week of demonstrations in which more than one hundred thousand students paraded for six hours in the streets of Seoul while concurrent marches were carried out throughout the country.[23] Again, on 27–28 November 1954, two days of mass demonstrations were held in which most of the nation's middle and high school students and some primary school children participated. This time it was to protest a British–Canadian proposal at the United Nations to end the tensions on the Korean Peninsula by conducting a UN-supervised, all-Korean election, a plan Rhee quickly denounced as echoing an earlier position of the North Koreans.[24]

In between these huge displays, smaller-scale rallies by secondary and university students were organized by the MOE for such purposes as to protest Japanese violations of Korean fishing zones. Rhee, passionately anti-Japanese, was particularly frustrated at efforts by the United States to encourage economic and political cooperation between South Korea and Japan because he saw it as a threat to the independence of Korea. He was also constantly worried about the strength of the U.S. commitment to the defense of South Korea and maintained hopes of achieving unification of his homeland during his tenure in office. An early example of these concerns occurred in 1952. Attempts at negotiating a treaty that would restore relations between Japan and South Korea broke off when Japanese negotiators rejected Rhee's reparation demands. Rhee then began an unrelenting campaign against the Japanese that lasted for eight years and involved innumerable student rallies. These centered around alleged Japanese violations of Korean fishing zones, Japanese claims to the uninhabited island of Tokto, and the support of North Korea by the Japanese Communist Party. Often the rallies were accompanied by special anti-Japanese lectures given by teachers with materials supplied by the administration.[25]

POLITICAL MOBILIZATION AND SOCIAL DEMAND

Internal and external tensions and war had created what appeared to be an inexorable trend toward a highly regimented, increasingly militaristic education. But in fact this trend often ran counter to the purposes of Korean families, who sought education as a means to reaffirm or acquire social status. The mass mobilization of students, therefore, rather than enhancing political support for the regime, aggravated parents, whose aspirations for educational opportunity conflicted with the state efforts to use the schools as a political instrument. As early as 1949, this militarization and regimentation of the schools drew opposition both from the public and within the government. A number of prominent educators spoke out against "undemocratic tendencies" in education. Much of the criticism was focused on the Student Defense Corps. Opponents of the government in the National Assembly and many leading educators called for a reorganization of the corps along more "democratic" lines, meaning a more decentralized organization in which classroom teachers and principals would be in control.

The most vociferous objections to the corps came from parents. From the corps' beginnings in 1949, parents feared that time spent on military drills was time taken away from exam preparation. Parents of high school students (who normally devoted their last two years primarily to preparing for the college/ university entrance examinations) were especially anxious about this drain on study time. An Ho-sang, in an interview in the *Chosŏn ilbo,* responded by arguing that the corps had restored order in the schools, had ended student strikes, and had kept the students from being distracted by subversive thoughts and activities so that they actually had more time to study.[26] But public criticism of the corps persisted throughout its existence.[27] Responding to complaints about the "undemocratic nature" of the corps and its effect on academic education, the MOE under Paek Nak-chun—who later stated that he had intended to abolish it altogether but had been prevented by the outbreak of war—created a committee in July 1951 to reform the organization.[28] The reforms were intended to change the focus of the Student Defense Corps from state-centered to student-centered.[29] Its goals were now stated as the cultivation of individual student personality, the development of a student's abilities and self-confidence, and service to the state. Essentially this meant the corps would not interfere with the education of the nation's youth. Officials declared that activities were being redesigned so that they would better assist that education.[30]

Throughout the 1950s, parents, educators, and newspapers complained about the student demonstrations, which forced children to march in the rain, disrupted traffic, and detracted from education. Parents were especially concerned when demonstrations took place at times when pressure to study for the entrance examinations was highest. Especially objectionable was the use of fifth- and sixth-grade elementary students, second- and third-year middle school students, and senior high school students because full energies were needed in these grades for examination preparation. Decades later, many teachers, students, and families recalled the demonstrations as a waste of time that could have been better devoted to study.[31]

A celebrated incident that brought the issue of student mobilization to the forefront of public discussion occurred in October 1955, when the pro-opposition newspaper, the *Taegu maeil sinmun,* ran an editorial entitled "Don't Use the Student Corps as an Instrument." The paper declared, "Nowadays street parades of middle school and high school students have become very common. . . . In Taegu students are forced to spend money on flags and to line up along the street and wave them." The paper also complained that students were being mobilized for government ceremonies. It was a common practice, the newspaper charged, for students to line the streets and wave flags to welcome cabinet ministers and presidential emissaries as they arrived in town from Seoul or returned from or went abroad. Following the publication of the editorial, members of the newspaper's staff were attacked by thugs, and the State Council (the cabinet) called for the punishment of the editors, creating what became known as the *Taegu maeil sinmun* Incident. But the controversy brought forth new criticism of the use of the Student Defense Corps for political purposes.[32] Newspapers and opposition members of the National Assembly called for the dismissal of the persons responsible for the attack on the newspaper and joined in a call to end excessive government-sponsored student demonstrations. Several opposition members of the National Assembly criticized the MOE for misusing the students, forcing them to participate in politically motivated demonstrations rather than in their studies.[33]

Ad hoc parental groups led the call to end student mobilization when, from February to August 1959, the government carried out continual demonstrations to protest the repatriation of Korean residents in Japan to North Korea.[34] In the capital, school principals and educational foundation members, responding to parental complaints, urged the Seoul Board of Education and the MOE to limit the demonstrations. School officials reported they were concerned that student demonstrations "hindered work and were detrimental to health," reflecting "a broad appeal to decrease demonstrations."[35] A survey by the Seoul Board of Education showed that from 1 April to 15 May an average of eighteen hundred Seoul secondary students were on the streets each day in officially sponsored demonstrations.[36] In early June 1959, the board issued guidelines limiting the demonstrations to "national events and ceremonies."

But it also added that although it would seek to limit the number of student mobilizations, demonstrations such as those currently under way opposing the repatriation to North Korea were "unavoidable."[37]

Parents also complained of the military drills that had become part of school life. Students were constantly told they were waging a battle against Communism; against the enemies of Korea (such as the Japanese); and for democracy, national independence, and military preparedness. In 1954, a new program of military training was instituted in the universities at the initiative of the minister of defense, Son Wŏn-il. Military exercises had been conducted on campuses, but under the new plan all seniors would receive ten weeks of training at military bases and students would be integrated into the Army Reserve Corps.[38] This training was intended to "build-up the anti-Communist fighting potential" of the nation's youth.[39] The following year, all high school students were required to receive military training at reserve corps centers.[40]

In light of the fact that South Korea had just faced a vicious internecine conflict and that it was still technically at war with North Korea, the emphasis on military training and the use of military terminology in the schools were not surprising. More interesting are the criticism and resistance. Teachers and parents protested what they regarded as excessive time spent in military drills, much as they complained about the mass mobilization campaigns. Furthermore, school officials and members of the MOE carried on a running feud with the Defense Ministry over the amount of time spent on drills. Sending students to military centers for training was especially unpopular, and in 1957, after repeated efforts to change the regulations and after parents had carried out a number of protests badgering ministry officials to stop the off-campus training, the program for high school students was discontinued. The reasons for this change of policy are not clear, but President Rhee seems to have suggested that the military concede on this issue.[41] The Defense Ministry announced a reinstatement of the off-campus training in 1958, only to be again bombarded by MOE protests so that the proposed training was limited to a few select schools.[42]

STUDENT MOBILIZATIONS UNDER PARK CHUNG HEE

Park continued the practice begun by Rhee of organizing students for massive displays of support for government campaigns (although not quite as frequently), despite the resentment it had created. For example, in May 1966, a "purification of education" movement was launched in the secondary schools against excessive private lessons and tutoring. On 10 May, twenty-four hundred students marched in the streets of Seoul demanding that *hagwŏns* be "purified." Two weeks later, another demonstration, by more than ten thousand students, took place calling for an end to overcommercialized education. This soon became a national campaign, with middle and high school students parading on the campus grounds or in local stadiums.[43] As under Rhee, parents often complained about these endless demonstrations. In response, the principals of Kwangju schools met in the summer of 1966 and announced a policy to ban all student mobilizations unless authorized by the provincial superintendent of education. The *Han'guk ilbo* praised the decision, labeling such uses of students "foolish efforts to use student bodies for political purposes."[44] Public pressure to end the practice came to the fore, and provincial officials announced the discontinuance of the practice. But in 1968, following a North Korean commando attack on the presidential mansion and the heightened tensions between the two states that followed, mobilization was resumed. An anti-Communist crusade was launched in which students at all grade levels were mobilized for rallies and fund-raising campaigns for national defense. Students themselves were required to give donations for the purchase of military weaponry.[45]

Park also mobilized students for rural development programs, enlisting high school and college students in rural development and literacy campaigns. This policy was not new, as it had been used by every government in Korea since the Japanese in the 1930s. Park gave it special emphasis in his early years in power. In the summer of 1962, all post–middle school students were required to work under state supervision on national reconstruction projects. These included irrigation, reclamation, road repair, and insecticide distribution. Many carried out such activities in their home villages and neighborhoods, while others were bused to distant parts of the country. The effort would (officials said) teach young people the value of hard work, it would instill discipline, and it would assist rural communities. In general, however, the effort was disorganized and inefficient. It was also unpopular with parents and teachers, who saw it as interference with the task of examination preparation. Many argued that only volunteers should be involved in these activities or that the activities should be confined to those with technical skills, such as engineering or medical students.[46] The MOE then set up the Youth Service Corps to "enlist"—but in reality to order—students to participate as "volunteers." This too was widely unpopular and not carried out regularly but rather on an ad hoc basis each summer. Despite the unpopularity, Park remained committed to the idea, changing the name of the Youth Service Corps to the Hwarang Youth Association, a name taken from the elite military corps of the early Korean state of Silla. For women students, he organized a Women's Association, in which young women were supposed to go to villages and help with rural illiteracy and with the "no gambling movement." Neither organization inspired much public enthusiasm.[47]

Park wanted to use the educational system as a means of creating a disciplined, loyal youth committed to the Korean state and its defense. Most parents, however, were focused almost exclusively on obtaining degrees for their children. As a result, a continual tug-of-war was waged between the public and the state over student mobilization. The greatest public criticism was levied at the endless disruption of classes for students to attend public ceremonies. Even the government's own press was critical of this policy.[48] Responding to these criticisms, the interior minister in August 1971 issued a sixteen-item guide for civil servants "to serve the people." It included the banning of student mobilization for groundbreaking and official welcoming ceremonies. As a result of parent complaints against enforced summer service, Minister of Education Min Kwan-sik said in January 1972 that the MOE would actively encourage but not require students to "volunteer" for social service.[49]

Park's efforts to promote military training in the schools ran into opposition as well. Starting in the late 1960s, administration officials discussed the need to place greater emphasis on the so-called "second economy"—that is, "spiritual" development, as opposed to material development such as industrialization, which they termed the "first economy." As the MOE in its official history defined it, the second economy meant "not material modernization" but "a firm spiritual basis for modernization through a revival of the national [minjok] spiritual education."[50] In practice, it meant more military training in the curriculum and indoctrination in the values of loyalty to the state, anti-Communism, and ultranationalism. Most South Korean men received training from one of three groups: the ROTC, created by Rhee and patterned on the U.S. model; the Homeland Reserve Forces, for students who had completed their military training; and the general military, for all male students in high school and college. It was the last that was the most controversial. Following North Korean provocations in 1968, a military training program for all male high school and college students began in 1969. In February 1969, President Park ordered the MOE to require military drills on high school campuses.[51] In 1971, measures were taken to standardize the military training to make it more comprehensive. A total of 711 hours were now required for college students. This, however, led to an outburst of anger from parents and students, who regarded it as an excessive drain away from academic work. Student demonstrations opposing the measure took place on many campuses, and groups of parents lodged protests with the MOE. In the face of this furor, the minister of education resigned in May 1971, and the government announced that the hours would be reduced to 180 a year.

After his regime took a more authoritarian turn in the early 1970s, Park, less subject to public pressure, renewed his effort to promote more military training in education. In 1974, Min Kwan-sik reversed the pledge he had made two years previously and announced that military training and drilling would be intensified at all levels. He announced that education would emphasize the "national situation" and thus include a greater awareness of duty and service to the nation and above all military preparedness of all kinds. The MOE would even encourage training for biological, chemical, and radioactive warfare.[52] During the next several years military drills expanded to include female students as well. Drill contests were held in Yoido Plaza, a huge square in the newly developed southern part of Seoul especially designed for massive rallies: South Korea's Red Square or Tiananmen Square. One such rally in the summer of 1974 saw half a million high school students perform military drills.[53] The following summer high school students were issued M1 rifles and paraded the streets of Seoul in military uniforms; they were accompanied by women students in white uniforms, many carrying first aid kits. Passersby gave cold water to the students as they marched in the hot weather.[54] On 20 May 1978, the MOE, before the deans of the nation's colleges and universities, revealed the Military Education Strengthening Plan (Taehak Kunsa Kyoyuk Kanghwa Pangan) to further intensify military training.[55] But this new plan was delayed by unenthusiastic universities and education officials, and the Park regime ended before it could be implemented.

Among the most controversial changes in education during this period was the revival of the Student Defense Corps in the spring of 1976. All high school and college students were required to join, and by fall, 1,565,000 students had been organized into twenty-five divisions under the motto "Study while defending the nation." Teachers, who were required to supervise the corps activities, were ordered to "inspire a correct national defense spirit in students."[56] The corps was composed of three major organizations: the Central Student Defense Corps (with the minister of education as its commander), which oversaw the entire organization; the Collegial Defense Corps, also under central control; and the City and Provincial Defense Corps, which supervised high school units. The purpose of the revived organization, the MOE explained, was to inculcate patriotism and nationalism and "to eliminate subversive elements from the schools."[57] The state-controlled daily newspaper, *Sŏul sinmun*, proudly proclaimed that "the campuses are now national military barracks."[58] In addition to marching and drilling, the corps sponsored seminars on anti-Communism and organized visits to national monuments and military cemeteries. Yet much like its predecessor, the corps was disliked by parents, students, teachers, and the general public. Its unpopularity was reflected in the defensive edge to its own propaganda. The MOE contrasted the new Student Defense Corps with the earlier one under Rhee, claiming it was better run and efficient and did not promote militarism (but it did promote a martial spirit, an obscure distinction). Rather, its purpose was to teach students how to be good citizens. Furthermore, the administration defended the corps as aiding students in their academic studies by making them more disciplined and directing them away from harmful extracurricular activities.[59] All of these were arguments that the Rhee administration had used to answer the same parental complaints.

In another change in education during this period, greater importance was given to physical education, considered important for creating disciplined as well as healthy young citizens. Park created a Council of National Physical Education and Sports Deliberation and established a Bureau of Physical Education and Sports in the MOE. More time and money were given to athletics in the secondary schools. This stress on sports continued until the Seoul Olympics in 1988, when national greatness was measured in gold and silver medals. The MOE carried out physical examinations from the fifth grade (about age ten) through high school (age seventeen), and from 1972 physical exams were necessary to enter middle and high school. Students were required to run 100 meters, throw objects, do chin-ups and sit-ups, and participate in relays. These physical exams were made more stringent in 1973.[60]

Even under the harsh repression that characterized the mid- and late 1970s, the public balked at too much stress on nonacademic education. Many educators and parents were unhappy with the attention to athletics. Physical education was not well received by the public, who feared that it took time and energy away from exam preparation. Newspapers, despite heavy censorship, reported stories of children injured in physical education exercises. In 1974, when the government ordered that all workers be given periodic physical examinations, the move was ridiculed in the press. "Do we know that running 100 meters makes a good worker?" the *Han'guk ilbo* asked.[61] Three years later, when three girls died while performing the physical part of the high school entrance exam, the MOE modified the physical education requirements.[62] President Park's policies to promote physical fitness and martial discipline caused both bitterness and cynicism. Education, already an intense experience because of the competitive pressure to score well on exams, became more intense. Education took a more military cast and contributed to the disciplined nature and the militancy of Korean society.

IDEOLOGICAL TRAINING

Along with the rallies and drills the South Korean state carried out extensive political indoctrination. Ideological training found expression in the Student Defense Corps activities, the frequent rallies that took place after 1948, and the introduction of moral education in 1955. In the postwar years the Americans had removed moral education *(shūshin)* from both the Japanese and South Korean curricula. In both countries, this was viewed as part of the democratization process, but in both, moral education was reintroduced in the 1950s, not only to teach ethical conduct, but also to establish an ideology of nationalism and anti-Communism. The emphasis under both Rhee and Park was on teaching values that emphasized authority, loyalty, and patriotism. A survey of secondary textbooks by a Korean researcher found that 50 percent of social science education, which included moral education at the middle-school level, dealt with themes that legitimized government and authority. Social science and moral texts contained frequent discussions of democracy, but textbooks explained democracy as involving a consciousness of order; thus, the duty of citizens of democratic societies was to obey the national laws and rules such as traffic regulations.[63] These texts stressed duty *(ŭimu)*, respect for law *(chunbŏp)*, and order *(chilsŏ)*.[64]

Anti-Communism became a central theme of moral education as well as social science and history texts. Special after-class lectures were often conducted

on the evils of Communism; the lectures were reinforced by frequent demonstrations in which students, especially in urban areas, participated. Teacher-
training classes emphasized the need to ensure domestic stability to bring about
a unified sense of patriotism and loyalty, to combat Communism, and to preserve what was regarded as best in traditional ethical values. Under Rhee, the
school year abounded in commemorative days in the struggle against Communism. Children's Day on 5 May celebrated the free, anti-Communist youth of
Korea.[65] The Day of Anti-Communist Youth, 18 June, commemorated the an-
niversary of Rhee's unilateral freeing of twenty-five thousand anti-Communist
prisoners of war in 1953, a move that nearly sabotaged the truce talks.[66] The date
of the North Korean invasion, 25 June, was another day of anti-Communist
vigilance, and 23 November, which commemorated an anti-Communist uprising in the North Korean city of Sinŭiju in 1945, was usually accompanied by
mass rallies and special lectures. And *myŏlgong* (destroy Communism) posters
became a standard feature of Korean classrooms.

Demonstrations wishing Rhee well on his birthday were customary, but in
the mid-1950s his birthday, 26 March, became a day totally given to celebrating
his achievements.[67] On Rhee's eightieth birthday in 1955, a day-long celebration
lifted the normal midnight curfew, and electricity, which was usually rationed,
was on all day in Seoul so that special radio broadcasts could be aired. A bronze
statue of the leader was unveiled, and special commemorative stamps were issued.[68] Later that year, a contest was held for a new name for Seoul after Rhee
suggested that the current name was "too difficult for foreigners to pronounce."
Schoolchildren, who were asked to propose their ideas for a new name, overwhelmingly chose Unam, the pen name of Syngman Rhee.[69] Illustrative of this
tendency to idolize the president was a poem selected for memorization after it
won a national student competition in 1959 on the topic of "Our President Yi
Sŭng-man":

> This year he is eighty-five
> He suffered in prison when he was young
> What a great contribution to rescue our people
> When we hang his picture on our wall
> Our house seems to grow brighter
> Like Paektusan, the East Sea and the Pine Tree
> Is the picture of our President Yi Sŭng-man
> Who has received white snow on his hair.[70]

Songs in a similar vein, still remembered by Koreans today, were sung by schoolchildren.

While the cult of Rhee did not outlast his ouster in April 1960, anti-Communism remained an ideological anchor for Korean education for decades. The MOE under Park standardized the anti-Communist texts in the early 1960s: *The Road to Achieving Unity through Victory over Communism (Sǔnggong t'ongil ǔi kil)* for middle schools and *The Road to Safeguarding Freedom (Chayu suho ǔi kil)* for high schools.[71] Such heavy-handed anti-Communist indoctrination reached its peak with the third curriculum revision, carried out in 1973–1974 under the Yushin constitution, which stressed even more ethics and national history. A strident tone was set in the government-issued texts for these courses.[72] High school social science texts allotted greater space to anti-Communism and were filled with grim pictures of Communist claws clutching the globe and desperate refugees fleeing the "Red Menace"; they stressed the need for national pride and economic strength.[73] From 1974, history textbooks moved from the officially approved to the MOE-issued category, ensuring a uniform presentation of national history. They gave greater attention to the early modern period from 1864 to 1945, when Korea suffered foreign humiliation and oppression.[74] To reinforce these lessons, businesses, both small and large, were required to include questions on national history in their company entrance examinations.[75]

A decidedly anti-Western tone also entered education. The government often defined the development of "the second economy" as the creation of an educational system that "imbued the nation with an independent spirit" versus the "onslaught of Western culture."[76] Korea was to follow its own path toward disciplined democracy by a responsible citizenry steeped in the traditional virtue of loyalty to the state. Language policy changed as part of this reorientation from Western to "Eastern" values. At first, in the 1960s, Park banned the teaching of Chinese characters, opting for exclusive use of the Korean alphabet, *han'gǔl*. The reversal of Park's policy was part of a greater emphasis on the East Asian and non-Western nature of Korean culture. Japanese was reintroduced as an optional foreign language in the high schools, and *hanmun* was reintroduced in the curriculum. Conversely, the time devoted to English was reduced. Traditional values would be used to inoculate the youth from the seductions of Communism and Western values. This was spelled out in 1977, when the MOE issued policy guidelines calling for a more thorough revision of the curriculum in order to strengthen "spiritual education" at all levels.

"Special attention will be directed [at] developing the willingness to perform duties emanating from the struggle against Communism. An anti-Communist posture will be nurtured with the heightened awareness of democracy."[77] National ethics was to be given greater weight in the curriculum at all levels. This would include the revival of Confucian values, although the term "Confucian" was often replaced by "traditional Korean." These "traditional Korean values" included filial piety, respect for the aged, loyalty, and mutual assistance and co-operation (as opposed to Western individualism). All this was to be embodied in the "Yushin spirit." Democracy itself had to be modified in that "democratic ideals may have potential incompatibility with the national cause in this unique setting of Korea."[78] In a handbook to teachers, *Minjok ŭi sŭsŭng* (The nation's teachers), teachers were instructed to "emphasize and clarify the essence of Confucian morality."[79] There were few Western examples in the textbooks on ethics and many examples drawn from Korean history.

A curious feature of South Korean education became the ceremonies revolving around the National Charter of Education. In January 1968, North Korean commandos attacked the Blue House (residence of the president), in the same month the USS *Pueblo* was seized by North Korea, and in April a U.S. reconnaissance plane was shot down by the North Korean forces. In the wake of these events, Park promulgated the National Charter of Education on 5 December 1968. This document was patterned on the Imperial Rescript on Education, which had been issued by the Japanese government in 1890. This had been recited in daily rituals and memorized by all schoolchildren in Japan and in its Korean colony. The stated purpose of the National Charter of Education was "to promote creativity and a pioneer spirit," "to cultivate a spirit of social cooperation," and to instill patriotism and "love of the Korean people" by creating a regular ritual in which these goals would be recited. The MOE explained the necessity: "During the 1950s Korea's conception of public education was confused and obscure. This was the result of post-liberation conflicts between foreign ideas and Korean traditions, postwar value disorientation, and the unquestioning acceptance of foreign ways of thinking. However, the economic development of the 1960s brought with it an increasing national self-consciousness and new reflection on the educational ideals of the past."[80] In the 1970s students had to memorize and recite the charter at school ceremonies.

Anti-Westernism was not consistently pursued since South Korea still saw itself as part of the free world, with the United States and the Western democratic states as its main allies. Despite comments that suggested Park and his advisers sometimes saw the West as a threat equal to Communism, textbooks still gave long accounts of the rise of democracy and freedom, from ancient Athens and the Magna Carta to the speeches of Abraham Lincoln.[81] Furthermore, educational and business circles opposed the decision to reduce English instruction.[82] The reduction was quietly abandoned.

SCHOOLS AS POLITICAL INSTRUMENTS

Numbering forty thousand by the late 1950s, the nation's teachers and school administrators were important in the Rhee and Park efforts to consolidate state control over society. As noted, traditionally teachers had been accorded a place of honor in Korean society, and in premodern Korea, as Buddhism retreated to a more peripheral position, the teacher–scholar took on the functions of a moral leader and guide to the community. Much of this attitude continued into the post-liberation era, adding prestige to the education profession and making control over teachers essential for any government seeking to secure its command of society. The South Korean government, following the precedent of the Japanese colonial government, used schoolteachers as instruments of state authority.

Teachers were carefully controlled by the South Korean state. The Basic Education Law (1949) preserved the central government's broad powers to regulate the qualifications and the hiring of teachers and school administrators. It also guaranteed teachers status as professionals and set up a system of local educational autonomy, designed in part to ensure a degree of independence for schools and teachers from central bureaucratic and political control. In practice, however, teachers had little autonomy, and education was administered on a top-down basis. Furthermore, the early purges of teachers were a reminder of the power of the state to discipline and punish recalcitrant behavior.

The Rhee administration and its successors upheld the principle of the political neutrality of education. Nonetheless, the legal guarantees were not effective in protecting teachers and their schools from being used by the administration to maintain itself in power and extend its control over society. In 1952, the UNESCO–UNKRA Educational Planning Mission to Korea reported a widespread use of education for partisan interests. It reported cases where "only active members of the ruling Liberal Party were promoted" up the educational ladder.[83] Teachers were frequently victims of the spoils system; transfers to desirable districts and promotions to principal or vice-principal or to higher and more prestigious positions were often determined by party loyalty.[84] Most teachers sought to avoid politics, but pressure to actively participate in political activities was often difficult to resist. Rhee's Liberal Party representatives visited schools and urged teachers to persuade parents to vote for Liberal Party candidates. Since voting was held at schools, teachers were often required to assist in the voting procedure—often by holding practice sessions in which voters were shown how to vote and for whom to vote. It was also reported that teachers formed three- or five-member teams who escorted voters to the polling stations. Supporters of the party would see to it that other team members hinted or instructed the voters for whom to vote. This strategy did not necessarily mean intimidating voters but simply using the prestige of the teacher to influence local people, a strategy that appears to have been effective in rural areas.[85]

The authoritarian style of educational administration contributed to the ease with which teachers and principals could be intimidated. Teachers who openly expressed opposition views outside the classroom were disciplined or dismissed.[86] Anti-leftist purges of the late 1940s and early 1950s and the system of continuous orders and directives led to what became known by critical educators as *myŏngnyŏngwijuŭi changhak haengjŏng* (educational promotion by orders from above).[87] MOE officials, provincial education chiefs, and county chiefs delivered the orders in a constant stream to school principals, who read them to their teaching staff at morning meetings. Teachers adopted a submissive attitude and became accustomed to the high-handed treatment by their superiors. Higher officials in turn expected lower civil servants and teachers to be obedient and loyal, especially to the administration.

Nonetheless, throughout the 1950s, the professional education journals, especially the monthly *Sae kyoyuk,* promoted ideas such as independent school boards, teacher autonomy from political control, and texts and methods to promote democratic values. A group of teachers emerged who believed such democratic education could be created only if teachers were organized into a labor union with the right of collective bargaining. In early 1959, under the leadership of Seoul schoolteacher Kang Ki-ch'ŏl, they made an attempt to organize a teachers' labor union. The Ministry of Justice swiftly ruled that the union violated Article 37 of the Public Service Law, which stipulated that public servants may not engage in any group activity unless for official purposes. The MOE and the Ministry of Health and Social Affairs supported the ruling, and the Seoul Board of Education dismissed several teachers who had participated in the preliminary work for forming the union, including Kang Ki-ch'ŏl's wife, a primary school teacher.[88] Arguing that the KFEA and the Educators' Civil Service Law did not protect the rights and autonomy of teachers, the rebellious educators sought and received support from the Korean Federation of Trade Unions, normally a complacent, government-controlled body.[89] The government, however, dismissed the organizers, and the movement was quickly squashed.

In April 1960, within days of the overthrow of the Rhee government in a student-led uprising, twelve hundred primary and secondary school teachers in Taegu organized a teachers' guild. They adopted a resolution calling for the independence of education from government interference, the establishment of genuine educational autonomy, the enactment of a law guaranteeing the right of teachers to form a labor union and to strike, the end to corruption among private school foundations, the removal of teachers and officials who had acquired wealth while in office, and the general improvement in the economic and social status of teachers.[90] The Taegu teachers further indicated that they intended to create a nationwide teachers' guild to press for their demands.[91]

The movement begun in Taegu quickly spread to Pusan, Seoul, and other cities. On 22 May, two hundred delegates representing teachers across the nation met in the capital to establish the National League of Teachers' Labor Unions (NLTLU, or Kyowŏn Nojo). But the new, more democratic government that followed the overthrow of President Rhee regarded the new teachers' union as a threat to the educational system and to the government, in part because in Japan, the Japan Teachers' Labor Union (Nikkyōso) was affiliated with the Communist Party and was a major source of opposition to the government.[92] South Korean officials and conservative educators, many of whom saw the Japanese Communists as active allies of North Korea and a serious threat to national security, generally regarded the newly organized union as a clone of its Japanese counterpart, a source of intellectual and political subversion. The NLTLU, with a membership of eighteen thousand, called for decentralizing the school system, giving teachers greater voice in decision making, and the end of political interference in the schools. The vehemence of the NLTLU's demonstrations, mass hunger strikes, and sometimes violent protests brought to light the frustrations of teachers. Its activities ended with the military coup of May 1961, when its leaders were arrested.

Park and his military sucessors kept a tight leash on teachers. Hundreds of teachers were removed from their posts in 1961 and 1962, along with 640 staff members of the MOE in an anti-corruption campaign aimed at removing political dissension as much as eliminating corruption.[93] But as in the case of the purification campaigns of 1949 and 1951, most of the dismissed teachers were reinstated, and the reform movement itself subsided during 1962. In January 1971, a new "purification of education" movement was launched. Originally aimed at improving the moral standards of judges, it was soon directed at the nation's teachers. The MOE then expanded this to a "new education movement," in which teachers and students attended rallies and pledged to live frugal lives and to stop collecting irregular fees.[94] These campaigns brought little real change in educational practices but served as a means of intimidating the nation's educators.

There were many other ways of controlling teachers. Teachers with outspoken political beliefs were occasionally removed under Paragraph 2, Article 31, of the Educators' Civil Service Law, which gave the MOE authority to dismiss teachers who were "unable to perform or neglected their duties." A more common means of disciplining teachers was transferring them to undesirable locations. When private tutoring was banned, teachers who ignored the regulation were threatened with reassignment to impoverished rural areas where the people were too poor to afford tutoring.[95] In 1972, the MOE tried to extend the practice of using transfers for discipline as a way of controlling college professors, and it introduced a plan for reassigning university professors to provincial campuses if they were needed there.

One of the most notorious measures of the Park administration was an education law passed in July 1975 that introduced a contract renewal system for college professors *(kyosu chaeimyong chedo)*. The stated purpose was to weed out "incompetent" academics, but it was widely understood that this was a means of removing college instructors considered unfriendly to the regime. The contract renewal policy was a powerful weapon to pressure faculty, especially as the criteria for renewal were vague and therefore subject to political abuse. Six months after the measure was implemented, 376 professors were found "incompetent" and removed. Some universities resisted or attempted to delay the process, but the administration put pressure on them to deal with "problem political professors."[96] Although some argued that it was a quality-control device to prevent the automatic tenure and promotion that character-

ized higher education, its political uses were obvious.[97] As one educator remarked, "Its negative effects could not be understated."[98]

Park and his military successors continued to require teachers to organize
students for endless pro-government and anti-Communist political rallies and
demonstrations, which often involved working late at night or on Sundays.
Compulsory in-service training programs included frequent political seminars,
sometimes referred to as "spiritual education." The Park administration's practice of intense anti-Communist indoctrination and the bullying and political
manipulation of teachers did little to win teacher loyalty and at times were
counterproductive to promoting the regime's stability. Teachers, while seldom
openly defying the regime, remained resentful of government interference. It is
difficult to believe that their cynicism, skepticism of government policies, and
resentment were not, at times, conveyed to their pupils, limiting the effectiveness of state policies. Government policies did, however, contribute to the regimentation of South Korean education. When added to other features of the
educational system, such as the intensely competitive examination system, this
regimentation helped create a highly disciplined, if contentious and often resentful, workforce.

Life for Korean teachers was hard, driven by long hours and few vacations.
A survey of teachers in 1966 found that 28 percent of primary and 38 percent of
secondary teachers wanted to change jobs. The biggest reason was low salaries.
About 41 percent of primary and 23 percent of secondary teachers said they belonged to the lower class. Most feared being sent to a hardship post.[99] A study by
the KFEA in the late 1960s indicated that elementary teachers worked 58.6
hours a week, while middle and high school teachers put in 55.1 and 57 hours a
week respectively.[100] The press frequently issued reports of teacher poverty and
misery, presenting stories of teachers suffering from malnutrition because they
were unable to feed both themselves and their families. Each year reports of
teacher resignations were accompanied by complaints of low pay and mistreat-
ment by both parents and an abusive state insensitive to their needs. However,
considering the enormous economic boom of the late 1960s and 1970s and the
resultant growth in employment opportunities, the number of teachers who resigned was not that high. Partly this was because there was always an overabun-
dance of college graduates, but it was also due to the fact that teaching remained
a respected profession, and for those located in a prosperous urban district, there
were many opportunities to supplement incomes.

While many teachers felt frustrated and held cynical views toward the state and the teachers' federation that supposedly represented them, most were politically quiescent. But a radical fringe of dissident teachers emerged during the 1970s. Some of these, along with other intellectuals, taught in the night school movement. At first, the night schools were set up to prepare those who were unable to attend school during the day for the college entrance examinations, but gradually they became a forum in which to teach workers about their rights, thus earning the nickname of "labor night schools."[101] As a result, dissident teachers became linked with radical labor organizations. But it was only in the 1980s that the dissident teacher movement emerged as a force in politics and in educational reform.

Since administration was highly centralized, there was little local autonomy, even though the Basic Education Law provided for it. In practice, local school boards, created in 1952, had little effective power and were abolished in 1961. Although there were defenders of local autonomy in the 1950s who sought to protect and enhance the power of local boards, bureaucrats saw them as wasteful duplications and joined Interior Ministry officials and some MOE officials who regarded them as obstacles to central control of education. In 1956, the cabinet set up a committee to streamline the government by centralizing local administrative units. This included the abolition of the education districts. The committee, which was chaired by In Tae-sik of the Ministry of Finance and Kim Hyŏn-ch'ŏl, the minister of reconstruction, argued that merging the local education administration with the general local administration would reduce personnel. They also argued that the school boards were failing to collect adequate revenue or control the excesses of the school administrators and local PTA leaders, who were demanding high fees from parents to finance education.[102] The unpopularity of the PTA, which served primarily as a revenue-gathering organization in Korea, was linked with the school boards, and both were cited by many within the government as misguided attempts to introduce inappropriate American educational practices.

The Korean press, reflecting the concerns of many of its middle-class readers, came to the defense of local school boards. The *Han'guk ilbo,* calling educational autonomy the "scaffold of liberal democracy," editorialized, "We adopted the district system not because we were in implicit obedience to the patterns advocated by foreign institutions but because we wanted to usher in the era of democratic education."[103] The KFEA joined the campaign and formed a special committee for the protection of educational autonomy. Between August 1956 and March 1957 the committee met fifteen times to discuss strategy for blocking efforts to undermine school districts. After two reorganizations, the committee became known in September 1958 as the Educational Autonomy Committee (Kyoyuk Chach'i Wiwŏnhoe), and for the next two years it worked with Assemblymen, journalists, government officials, and teachers to promote educational autonomy.[104]

The military coup of 16 May 1961 brought local educational autonomy, as well as local government autonomy, to a sudden end. All school boards were immediately suspended and abolished on 6 October by an executive order of the military junta, which constituted itself as the SCNR.[105] Korean educators continued to urge the formation of a genuine system of local education boards based in part on the U.S. model. Park's administration gave lip service to this idea, but there was no clear agreement within the government on whether some sort of local autonomy should be reinstated and, if so, to what degree or purpose. MOE officials held a range of ideas about how decentralized or autonomous education should be, but they shared a desire to minimize the Interior Ministry's involvement in educational affairs.[106] The reestablishment of local school boards was linked with the reestablishment of local elected provincial and county assemblies, which the military had abolished. Despite promises to reestablish both, the Park regime kept postponing a decision until the December 1972 Yushin constitution declared that local self-government would be established only when the nation was unified. In fact, local units of government were not elected until 1991.

The American ideal of local educational autonomy failed in South Korea for several reasons. One was that it was simply incompatible with the highly centralized system of administration. Another was the government concern for uniformity of education in both content and quality. But there were other reasons as well. The fear that middle-class parents would gain control of the school boards to promote their own educational agenda was felt not only by the state, but also by some parents and teachers. Local education boards might prove to be a vehicle to subvert the objective nature of the educational process, as the most influential families would pressure teachers and education officials to give their children extra advantages. The political needs of the state to exercise control over education, the desire for administrative efficiency by technocrats, the desire of officials and educators to create uniform standards, and the

desire to protect the educational system as a social selection mechanism over-
came the efforts of advocates of U.S.-style democratic education and many
middle-class Koreans who desired greater direct control over the schools.

The government's tight control over the education system and the political
mobilization of students and teachers had the effect of training them as political
opponents. Students used the Student Defense Corps as an organizational base
for their demonstrations against the Rhee government in the spring of 1960,
after what was widely thought to have been a rigged reelection of Rhee and an
unpopular vice-president. Student demonstrations calling for radical political
reforms, the arrest of Rhee administration officials, and the unification of Korea
had unsettled the Chang Myŏn regime and along with the teacher protests provided a justification for the military to restore order by staging the 1961 coup.
Park was troubled by student demonstrations from 1965 to his assassination in
1979. After 1971, the heavy-handed repression of students, including troops on
campus and frequent arrests or expulsions of student activists, added to the atmosphere of oppression and alienation. It also drove the student protesters underground and into increasingly leftist and anti-American positions.

SEOUL SPRING AND CHUN DOO HWAN

The assassination of President Park by his security chief, Kim Chae-kyu, on 26
October 1979 brought hope for democratic reform in politics and in education.
In the brief period between the assassination of Park and the consolidation of
power of the new military strongman, General Chun Doo Hwan, in April and
May 1980, South Korea experienced a period of openness commonly referred to
as "Seoul Spring." In this open atmsophere, educational issues emerged as central to the discussion of reform and change. At the start of 1980, South Korea's
major newspapers called for greater academic freedom, and the MOE pledged
that it would revise its regulations to create a freer atmosphere on university
campuses. In January, the MOE announced it would allow all 750 students who
had been expelled from universities for anti-government acitivities to return.[107]

All sorts of reforms were discussed during these weeks. For instance, a
great deal of public discussion occurred over implementing local government
autonomy and of having the school boards either appointed by independent, locally elected councils or directly elected.[108] In the excitement of Seoul Spring,

educators also discussed reforming the curriculum in order to make education more democratic. Deans from twenty-eight universities met in February for this purpose and called for the rewriting of textbooks, criticizing the current ones as designed to promote the "undemocratic" Yushin constitution. They also called for greater liberalization of college regulations, giving individual schools more freedom to set fees and establish administrative and academic policies.[109]

On campuses throughout the country, college professors held meetings and issued declarations demanding the reform of higher education. In early May, over three hundred professors met in Seoul to discuss the reform of college administration. They demanded that university administrators end such practices as nepotism and that private foundations stop seeing their schools as profit-making ventures. The professors called for the democratization of university administration, greater power to faculty senates, the end of all restrictions on public speech by faculty, and the reform of student military training. Speakers such as the distinguished historian Yi U-sŏng argued that the universities should be the "vanguard of democratization."[110] Many professors called on their school administrations to resign, while the Seoul National University faculty voted overwhelmingly to petition the MOE for direct faculty election of the university president and deans without government interference. Foremost among the proposals was the abolition of the hated faculty contract system, which had become a symbol of the worst aspects of the Park regime's attempts to control the faculty at institutes of higher education.[111]

Meanwhile, secondary and primary school teachers joined many prominent professors in calling for reform of the KFEA, labeling it a corrupt tool of the state and unrepresentative and unresponsive to the needs of the nation's educators. Again, college faculty took the lead and demanded the immediate resignation of the KFEA officers; at the end of May, Kwak Chong-wŏn, the organization's president, submitted his resignation. Following this resignation, a 220-member national delegation of the organization met and for the first time directly elected the new president. Unlike the selection of presidents in the years since the mid-1960s, this was done without the pressure of the MOE.[112]

These moves to free educational institutions from state control were accompanied by a surge of student activism that threatened to get out of hand, as it had after Rhee's ouster. Students held almost daily demonstrations and rallies at universities and at some high schools. At first, most of the demonstrations were directed against faculty and administration. Militant students called for

the ouster of "political professors," by which they meant faculty who were regarded as pro-government under Park. A number of professors resigned under
this pressure. Others were required to issue statements of "self-reflection,"
vaguely echoing the tribulations of professors under the tyranny of the Red
Guards in China a decade earlier. State efforts to contain this zealousness were
confused and ineffective. The MOE pleaded to no avail with students to understand that most professors had no choice but to follow government guidelines.
By April, so many college and university presidents had resigned that the minister of education, Kim Ok-kil, announced she would refuse to recognize any
more such resignations.[113]

Students abolished the hated Student Defense Corps on their own, and on
many campuses they simply refused to attend military drills. In April, the education minister told students that the drills were now voluntary but pleaded
with them to participate.[114] From the state's point of view, the most serious of
the student actions was the refusal to attend the compulsory ten days of drills
held each year on a military base. The penalty for failing to do so was immediate
conscription, and the MOE promised the Defense Ministry it would enforce
this rule. But when thirteen hundred Sŏnggyun'gwan University students refused to go, they were told they would be given another chance to go at a later
time. Students at other universities then vowed they would not go either. The
MOE met with Defense Ministry officials to discuss ways of revamping the military drills. In early May, military drills were reduced from four to two hours a
week, and all on-base student drills were temporarily suspended.[115]

But ending the drills did not end the student challenge to state authority.
The day after the announcement that on-base military drills would be discontinued, the largest student demonstration in fifteen years took place. Student concern, however, had shifted. With the government giving way on the issue of
military drills and the Student Defense Corps ceasing to function, students focused more on national political issues. Twelve thousand students met on Seoul
University's Acropolis Square to rally for the end to martial law and the establishment of a new, democratic government. The two-day meeting, to the great
relief of the government, ended peacefully, with students singing the national anthem and going home.[116] But three days later, student representatives of thirty-
three universities met to form the Struggle Committee for Democratization. In
an open letter, Kim Ok-kil asked the students to refrain from protests, stating
that "the spirit of criticism of the freedom-loving students, motivated by strong

patriotism and a firm sense of national security, is highly appreciated" but that street protests were jeopardizing democratization.[117] The government, she told them, was attentive to the "righteous assertions and demands" of the students.[118] The presidents of the nation's universities, many recently appointed following the resignation of their predecessors, then urged students in a joint appeal to confine their demonstrations to the campuses. Almost immediately the demonstrations spilled out into the streets, with violent clashes with police. On 15 May, tens of thousands of students poured into the streets of Seoul, Pusan, and other cities, paralyzing traffic and briefly occupying major train stations. On 16 May, the prime minister hinted that stern measures would be taken to curtail "reckless behavior destroying the social order."[119] Because few nonstudents joined the rally, student leaders of twenty-six departments meeting at Korea University and representatives of fifty-five universities meeting at Ewha University decided on 18 May to call off the demonstrations and "watch the situation."[120]

The central focus of student wrath was General Chun Doo Hwan, whose assumption of the leadership of the Korean Central Intelligence Agency (KCIA) in April 1980 made it increasingly clear that he was the real power in the government. Faced with student demonstrations and calls by opposition candidates for free elections, Chun declared martial law on 17 May and arrested Kim Young Sam and a number of other opposition leaders, including the popular Kim Dae Jung. Massive and violent protests erupted in Kwangju, the largest city in Kim Dae Jung's home province of South Chŏlla. Chun responded by sending in paratroopers, who brutally suppressed the uprising, killing hundreds in the process. This came to be known as the "Kwangju Incident." Seoul Spring was over.

Chun Doo Hwan then proceeded to assert tight political control over the schools. Except for token steps at creating a more liberal school atmosphere, such as abolishing school uniforms, Chun maintained the authoritarian practices of President Park in education as well as in politics. The ex-general launched another "purification of education" campaign in the summer and fall of 1980 to "weed out student hoodlums and other bad students" and to "stamp out impure student circles."[121] The campaign combined removing politically active students (and a few teachers) and breaking up student political organizations with an effort to end corruption and illegal fee collection in the schools.

Government circles were still concerned over the "second economy." Some in the administration believed that education had overemphasized economic growth at the expense of spiritual education.[122] At the start of 1981, the MOE announced that there would be a government effort to "free young people from ideological contamination."[123] The effort became systemized the following year under what was known as "citizens' spiritual education" (kungmin chŏngsin kyoyuk), intended to promote nationalism through the study of the nation's struggle against foreign aggression and an appreciation of the country's traditions; it included the need for vigilance against North Korea and Communism.

Administration officials stated that education was to give greater emphasis to ethics. In practice, this meant that anti-Communist education was stepped up at all levels, especially in high schools and colleges. Calling for the "strengthening of pure thought in education," the MOE set up departments of national ethics in teachers' colleges; a greater component of teacher education was given to studying "democracy," "anti-Communism," and Korean nationalism. Some of the task of redirecting schools toward spiritual education was given to the Han'guk Chŏngsin Munhwa Yŏn'guwŏn, usually translated as the Academy of Korean Studies but more literally translated as the Korean Spiritual/Cultural Research Institute. Established by President Park in 1978, its purpose was to study Korean history in order to create a "correct historical viewpoint" and to conduct research into the basis of national ethics. In other words, its purpose was to formulate an official national history and ideology to "revive the national spirit."[124] In 1983, the institute was asked to prepare guidebooks for spiritual education. Courses in "ideological criticism training" were compulsory for all college students.[125] In one interesting way the Chun government departed from past practice: it allowed students to read Communist works such as Das Kapital and the Communist Manifesto by including them in the college curriculum. Officials argued that in the past students had failed to appreciate the demerits of Communism since they were introduced to it in a "negative" and "monotonous" way. Others objected that this would stimulate interest in Communist doctrines, so the policy remained controversial within the administration.

The rhetoric of the Chun administration exaggerated the real changes in education. There was little modification of textbooks or curriculum; Chun continued the large dose of ideological content, with its militant nationalism and anti-Communism, that had characterized South Korean education since the 1950s. The practice of mobilizing students for political purposes also persisted, despite the ban declared during Seoul Spring. The time taken up by state-sponsored rallies and assemblies varied considerably, with one school in Seoul reporting forty cases of student mobilization in 1986 alone, most of which had no educational purpose.[126] In addition, the Chun government carried out periodic crackdowns on student dissidents. For three years the government took a hard line on expelling students, announcing as late as November 1983 that there would be no change in policy, but toward the end of 1983 the government began allowing ousted students to return to school.[127] Despite the policy of clemency, student radicalism grew. Many expelled students declined to reenter their universities, refusing to take pledges to avoid political activities. One group of one hundred expelled students from Seoul National University formed a reinstatement committee that listed a set of demands to be met before they would return; these demands were rejected by the school authorities.[128] President Chun nonetheless sought to mollify the students and withdrew the police from the campuses in 1984, stating that it was time for restoring the tradition of campus freedom.[129] Chun's administration, however, continued to be plagued by student political unrest and by the increasing radical, leftist drift of the student movement that had begun in the late 1970s. His continuation of political mobilzation (although less frequent than in the past), the military drills, and propaganda lessons were considered by many citizens as a waste of precious academic time.

The Rhee, Park, and Chun regimes perpetuated the regimented character that had been stamped on Korean schooling since colonial times, and through universal education, they helped to stamp it on the character of an entire nation. No account of South Korea's educational development could be complete without mentioning this aspect of it. It is probably impossible to measure the impact of military drills, political indoctination, and mass student rallies on the nation's development, but certainly the militancy of student radicals and radical teachers may in part be attributed to their training and experience in school. So often told they were the vanguard of the nation, teachers, and especially students, took this literally enough to play a major role in bringing down authoritarian rule in the 1980s. Perhaps, more important, the often harsh military drills and the constant mobilization of students reinforced the discipline so characteristic of Korean students as they competed for educational advancement up the educational ladder.

8

Democratization, Prosperity, and Educational Change

The fever-pitch obsession with education has been a fixed feature of South Korean society. Most of the striking products of this obsession—the enormous costs of education, the sacrifices families were prepared to make to meet them, "examination mania," and the nearly universal drive for high-status degrees—remained unaltered at the end of the twentieth century. But in other ways the nation went through profound changes. In the late 1980s and 1990s South Korea entered an era of democratization and economic prosperity, both of which can at least partly be attributed to the "education fever" that drove educational development. From 1987, South Korea began a bumpy transition to a more democratic political system, with the less authoritarian state more responsive to a greatly enlarged and empowered civil society. At the same time, the sustained economic growth than began in the mid-1960s continued through the 1980s and 1990s, bringing the nation into the ranks of modern industrialized states. Two events symbolized this entry into industrially advanced status: the 1988 Seoul Olympics, in which the nation was able to showcase its development, open its markets, and lift restrictions on travel abroad, and the 1996 admittance of South Korea into the OECD, an organization of industrially advanced nations. South Korea's educational development helped bring about both these achievements and in turn was challenged by the new requirements of a transformed society.

STUDENT AND TEACHER MOVEMENTS

An increasingly literate society resented being shut out of active participation in political affairs. Millions of Koreans saw models to emulate in the advanced nations of Western Europe, the United States, and Japan. A well-informed public was aware of the democratic rights enjoyed by members of these societies and viewed these rights as components of their success. A phrase sometimes heard in the 1980s expressed this perception: "We are becoming economically first world but are still politically third world." In addition to heightening public awareness of democratic alternatives and bringing about a greater public confidence in the right to be involved in the political process, the South Korean educational system produced two groups that acted as a vanguard for political change: students and teachers.

As noted in chapter 7, throughout the 1970s groups of student activists held demonstrations calling for an end to President Park's authoritarian rule and for democratic reform. The government quickly squashed these groups and jailed hundreds of college students. Other such clandestine groups formed. Some teachers, as well, formed underground groups that sought to promote democracy; a few outspoken teachers, mostly college professors, were arrested for voicing their criticisms. This undercurrent of discontent surfaced during Seoul Spring but was driven underground again by the Chun Doo Hwan government. The Chun administration was characterized by a crisis of legitimacy greater than that of his predecessors. Because of Chun's brutal seizure of power, the bloody Kwangju Incident, Chun's lack of personal charm, and the corruption of members of his family, he was highly disliked by the country's growing middle class, despite the impressive economic achievements of his administration. He also became a target of student protests. Although the Chun administration softened its line on expelled students toward the end of 1983, student radicalism grew, and the administration continued to be plagued by it.

Meanwhile, the student movement in the 1980s began to take on an increasingly anti-U.S. and anti-capitalist tone. The Kwangju Incident fed the growing hostility of student radicals toward the United States. Although the United States was not directly responsible for the incident, since the ROK troops were technically under the American Combined Forces Commander, it was held morally accountable. The fact that a few months later Chun was invited by President Ronald Reagan to be the first head of state he hosted at the White House seemed to give tacit U.S. approval to the Chun regime. In any case, the radicals saw the military and industrial elite as instruments of U.S. and Japanese capitalist imperialists. The anti-U.S. tone seemed especially threatening to the South Korean state because it depended on the U.S. commitment to defend it and on U.S. markets to maintain economic growth. The United States absorbed up to half the nation's exports (although this figure declined steadily in the 1980s), and it was, after Japan, South Korea's most important source of foreign investment and technical cooperation.

In the 1980s, politically active college students became influenced by *minjung*, a term that defies translation. The word literally means "masses," but to many Korean thinkers, it meant the Korean people in a broad sense, excluding only the very elite of society but including more than a specific social class. *Minjung* thinkers saw the Korean people as victims exploited by the *yangban* class in premodern times, by the Japanese in colonial times, and by the superpowers and major industrial nations (chiefly the United States and Japan) in the post-1945 era. The state was an alien organ of oppression serving the neocolonialist foreign powers and a small comprador elite of big business and high government officials. Marxism, liberation theology, and even Wallerstein's world systems theory influenced *minjung* thought. There was also a strong nationalistic flavor to *minjung* thought, which looked to elements of Korean folk traditions such as shamanism for inspiration.[1] In part, the *minjung* movement was a nativist reaction to the rapid change brought about by industrialization and the integration of South Korea into the world economy. However, it was a nativist reaction led and directed by educated, middle-class Koreans who were far removed from the folk culture they exalted. *Minjung* thought became, for many dissident groups in the 1980s—including radical labor and teachers' groups—the ideological basis for criticism of the Korean state and society. Students were often able to strike a chord with many Koreans who felt uncomfortable with the rapid changes that the authoritarian state was bringing about. They played to the fear that Korea was in danger of losing its national identity and was too dependent on the United States and Japan for economic and military support. Sometimes in alliance with dissident teacher groups, student groups used *minjung* thought to criticize their schools. In their view, the educational system served to discipline and control the people in order to produce obedient workers for the state and the neocolonial powers that the state served.

The student movement, armed with this new ideology, began a shift to nationally coordinated student activism. This began with the creation of the Samint'u (Struggle Committee for Minjung Democratization) in May 1985. In spring 1986, the Samint'u split into the Minmint'u, formed at Seoul National University, and the Chamint'u, based at Seoul National University and Korea

University; the latter espoused a more radical ideology centered on liberating the "toiling masses." Organized by these groups, students demonstrated with increasing frequency and scale throughout 1985 and 1986, with the unrest culminating in the massive demonstrations that began in the spring of 1987.[2] Student militants stormed the U.S. Information Service library in Seoul in the spring of 1985, and after this and several other attacks and threatened attacks, the U.S. Embassy and other installations took on the appearance of fortresses. Perhaps most shocking to Korean public opinion were several self-immolations by students protesting the Chun regime. The immolations suggested the growing fanaticism of radical youths and tended to appall the public rather than gain its sympathy.

For the most part, the ideology of these student groups was far more radical than that of the general public, but the radical student organizations served as spearheads for the protest movements against the Chun government. A turning point in Korean political development came in 1987. The Chun government's hold on power seemed strengthened in the 1985 National Assembly elections, in which the ruling Democratic Justice Party captured most seats under an election system designed in its favor. But in this election, the opposition gained a majority in urban areas, and soon its leaders were taking a more confrontational stance toward the government. The following year, opposition leaders launched a campaign to revise the constitution to allow for direct election of the president, and they began organizing rallies that called not only for constitutional revisions, but also for the resignation of Chun Doo Hwan. Students demonstrated in support. Then the death of a student from police torture in January 1987 set off a series of increasingly large and vociferous anti-government rallies. As Chun's seven-year term ran out, political tension mounted. On 13 April 1987, Chun rejected the demands for an open presidential election and announced that the government-appointed National Unification Council would select the next president. The designated heir was former general Roh Tae Woo, a leader in the coup that had brought Chun to power and now head of the committee entrusted with preparing for the 1988 Seoul Olympics.

News of the decision set off the largest demonstrations in South Korea's history. Initially these were mainly student demonstrations, but in June hundreds of thousands of middle-class citizens were joining them, and the country was edging toward the brink of chaos. Faced with growing turmoil and the possible relocation of the Olympics, Roh issued a declaration on 29 June 1987 supporting free elections, the release of most political prisoners, and the abolition of press and broadcast censorship. Openly contested elections were then held in December. Thus, students were pivotal in forcing the administration to loosen its authoritarian grip. In the elections, however, the two main opposition leaders, Kim Young Sam and Kim Dae Jung, ran separately, along with a third opposition candidate, Kim Jong Pil, thus splitting the anti-government vote. The split enabled Roh Tae Woo to win with 37 percent of the electoral returns. Roh's government was now more responsive to public opinion; furthermore, the following year the opposition parties won a substantial majority in the National Assembly. Under Roh, the press was freer, labor was able to organize independently of government control and hold strikes, and opposition candidates were able to get broadcast air time.

During Seoul Spring, teachers had publicly discussed autonomy from government control, but the events of May 1980 and the subsequent crackdown by the state on all forms of dissent prevented any organized activity.[3] Still there existed during the Chun regime a small but growing number of activist teachers who belonged to a loosely organized "teachers' movement for democracy in education." The state responded to this nascent movement by turning over teachers known to be involved to city or provincial board of education "disciplinary committees." They were often dismissed from their posts or transferred to undesirable rural locations. Emboldened by the growing unrest, politically active teachers in 1987 began to protest more openly. Several teachers transferred from Pusan to the countryside launched a protest in late February, calling their transfer "unjustified government oppression."[4] Other teachers began giving briefing sessions on the anti-government demonstrations to their middle school and high school students.

In 1981, a group of mainly young teachers formed the YMCA Teachers' Association. Some were Marxist in orientation. Others, less ideologically focused, were simply dissatisfied with the authoritarian nature of the state, disenchanted with its obsessive stress on economic development, and concerned by the lack of a social welfare safety net for the poor and needy. They also sought radical educational reform allowing for greater teacher autonomy, greater decentralization of the educational system, an end to the practice of mobilizing students and teachers for pro-government rallies, and an end to military drills and "spiritual education," all of which they linked with political reform. On 10 May 1986, eight hundred teachers and expelled former teachers met and issued a "Declaration of Educational Democratization" (Kyoyuk Minjuhwa Sŏnŏn).[5] This document was important because it spelled out the basic goals of the so-called "democratic education movement" and significantly influenced the course of Korean education during the next decade. The declaration called for the political neutrality of education; the protection of teachers from arbitrary dismissal, transfer, or demotion; the liberalization of educational administration; and the implementation of local autonomy.[6] These were, for the most part, the same goals that had been advocated by the New Education Movement reformists after liberation, and when the *minjung* phraseology is removed, they are a restatement of the ongoing democratic and progressive critique of Korean education. The movement called for the end of top-down administration of education. Parents, teachers, students, and the public would decide policies and direct education to the needs and wishes of society. The declaration called for protecting the rights of citizens as well as those of teachers; the movement, its leaders made clear, was based on the belief that democratizing education was inseparable from the process of democratizing society.

On the eve of the political turmoil of 1987, the beginnings of an organized dissident teachers' movement were evident. After Roh's 29 June declaration against censorship, its activities came into the open. The YMCA Teachers' Association created an educators' association that contacted teachers in every city and county in the country.[7] On 27 September 1987, amid the presidential elections, the first formal organization was created, the National Teachers' Association (Chŏn'guk Kyosa Hyŏphoe), at the Han'guk Theological College. Police surrounded the building but did not enter as several hundred teachers and former teachers inaugurated the organization, which soon claimed to have twenty thousand members. In 1989, the dissident teachers organized themselves into the Korean Teachers and Education Workers' Union (Chŏn'kyojo). The union set up over 150 branches throughout the country, attracting fifteen thousand members within months, its recruitment slowing down only when the MOE banned it and threatened members with immediate dismissal. Many teachers became affiliated without actually becoming members, participating in various meetings or joining associated clubs, so that about 12 percent of all the country's educators were linked to it.[8] As with the dissident groups, the teachers' union acted as a constant critic of the administration, quickly and loudly protesting any lack of progress toward democracy.

DEMOCRATIZING EDUCATION

After 1987, as a result of the freer political atmosphere South Korean education underwent a gradual process of "democratization": a decentralization of educational administration, the granting of greater autonomy to individual schools in decision making, and a modification of the curriculum so that it conformed to the norms of a democratic society. In the era of democratization, educational policy became more responsive to public pressure. The Roh administration, in one of its first moves, ceased the practice of student mobilization, long hated by parents and teachers. Administrators were told by the MOE not to mobilize students for noneducational purposes even if they had permission from the local boards. The MOE promised to discourage any activity that would interfere with study. As a result, student mobilizations became less frequent; however, they did not come to a complete end until 1993.

Meanwhile, middle-class citizens organized a host of civic groups, many of which lobbied for educational reform. In 1989, a group of parents organized the Parent Association for True Education (Ch'am Kyoyuk ŭl Wihan Chŏn'guk Hakpumohoe), which advocated the greater involvement of parents in educational policy, the end of corruption in the schools, and greater efforts to contain the rising cost of education. This group launched a campaign to abolish the practice of giving money envelopes to teachers and sued the MOE for misusing PTA fees, but it lost the case when the courts ruled in favor of the ministry in 1992. Another group, the Parents for Students League, advocated educational reforms to make education more child-focused and less preoccupied with grades.[9] Many of these new civic groups lobbied for reforms of the examination system and advocated ways to prevent costly private lessons.

Civic groups were joined by the dissident teachers' union. Banned, its leaders dismissed from their posts, the union nonetheless maintained a strong influence on educational policy making. The leaders, supported by membership dues and by working spouses, set up headquarters in southern Seoul and worked as a pressure group. From February 1990, they published *Uri kyoyuk* (Our education), a glossy monthly devoted to critically analyzing the nation's educational system. Most South Korean teachers were ambivalent toward this union. They found its tactics too confrontational and its ideology too radical, but they enjoyed and appreciated the role it played in improving their working conditions.[10] The official KFEA, despite a supposed reorganization and dem ocratic reform after 1987, was still regarded as largely an instrument of the state. The teachers' union's role in shaping education was much greater. As one educator remarked, the KFEA had "ten times the membership but only one tenth the influence" in shaping educational policy.[11] The opposition too was ambivalent about the teachers' union. Kim Young Sam was initially supportive, but after merging his party with the ruling party in 1990, he became less sympathetic; after becoming president in 1993, Kim adopted Roh's hardline stance against recognizing the union or rehiring its dismissed members. Finally in July 1999, the new government of Kim Dae Jung, himself a former political dissident and critic of the authoritarian style of education, legalized the teachers' union, which was now able to openly act as a pressure group for an educational system more responsive to students, teachers, and parents.

The state in this atmosphere of more democratic education took some small steps toward greater educational autonomy. Following the recommendation of the Presidential Commission for Education Reform, the MOE delegated more responsibility for decision making to the national universities and gave the faculty real power in selecting candidates for university president.[12] A series of decrees gave greater administrative authority to the provincial school boards. Meanwhile, the composition and role of the school boards changed with the advent of elected local government. In 1991, South Koreans for the first time in thirty years elected provincial and city councils. These councils in turn selected the members of the provincial and city boards of education for three-year terms. Teachers were barred from serving—a regulation that provided another issue for politically active teachers—but the councils often selected persons with educational backgrounds, such as retired teachers and professors. A second round of local elections was held in 1994, but in contrast to the great controversies over local election boards that had taken place under President Rhee, voter turnout and interest in the elections were low. The apathy reflected the public awareness that these boards of education still had only limited power. MOE officials still issued orders and directives regulating school life in detail.

Change in educational policy making was slow to come. The MOE was staffed in the late 1980s and 1990s by the same bureaucrats who had served under Park and Chun, although less so as the years went on. Educational policy continued to come from the top, albeit more subject to public pressures than previously. The presence of radical student organizations served as a warning of the dangers of loosening state control over education and provided an excuse for maintaining a huge system of security organs. Moreover, the state was still devoted to the concepts of "guidance" and "ethical education." For instance, in 1991, the MOE launched yet another campaign to "guide students." Labeled "democratic citizens' education" *(minju simin kyoyuk)*, it called upon all teachers to develop the spirit of cooperation in a democratic society and a respect for the democratic orderly processes and for administrators to see that teachers' abilities to guide education were strengthened. Each city and province was instructed to develop an "ethical education and democratic promotion plan." The ministry prepared a number of materials to aid teachers and administrators in these tasks.[13] The administration now demonstrated more sophistication in its political indoctrination. For example, it dropped the heavy-handed anti–North Korean propaganda and instead let the North Korean regime speak for itself, both by showing North Korean film clips on television and by issuing factual information and selected materials from its Communist rival.

A marked general trend away from the highly regimented and military nature of education occurred, especially under Kim Young Sam. Kim's administration reduced military drills and abolished on-campus ROTC training in 1995.[14] The practice of mobilizing students for political purposes was finally terminated. The National Charter of Education, President Park's oath of loyalty and obedience, was denounced by the MOE as "fraught with authoritarian descriptions incompatible with the era of democracy." The charter was dropped from 1994 textbooks, and the ceremonies in which the charter was read also ended.[15]

Kim Young Sam, following the pattern of his two predecessors, established a Presidential Commission for Education Reform in February 1994 to provide guidelines for a major overhaul of the educational system, and among its recommendations was the granting of greater autonomy to individual schools. In particular, it called for granting universities the right to determine quotas for freshmen and to decide the size of their departments.[16] This, of course, would have reversed forty years of state policy. The universities, which were agitating for greater freedom in setting quotas and placing students into areas of study, welcomed the recommendations. The administration also discussed giving high schools more leeway in deciding policies. The number of elective subjects in high school was increased, and a less uniform curriculum was created whereby different high schools were allowed a different choice of electives.[17]

In 1994, the Kim Young Sam government began the sixth reform of the curriculum with the aim of rewriting texts to reflect the new era of democracy. In addition, President Kim talked of "globalizing" the curriculum, a part of his broader policy of *segyehwa* (globalization). Precisely what he meant was never clear, but it was generally assumed this entailed making Korean education similar in content and method to those of developed democracies and adding more international content to the curriculum. Following the curriculum revision, the new textbooks issued in 1995 contained less anti-Communist rhetoric and gave greater attention to explanations of liberal democratic ideals. Middle school ethics texts emphasized ethics for a democratic society, respect for fellow citizens, and the need for peaceful unification of the peninsula. High school social studies texts dropped much of the anti-Communist rhetoric and discussed Communist ideas within a broad survey of world societies and cultures.[18] Roh's policy of introducing Communist texts was extended to the high schools, and from 1995, North Korea's *juche* (*chuch'e*, self-reliance) ideology was included. This complemented what was already a frank reporting of North Korea in the broadcast media. Recent history was also revised in the texts. The 19 April 1960 student uprising that toppled Syngman Rhee was redefined as the "April Revolution," while the 16 May 1961 military revolution that brought Park Chung Hee to power was "downgraded to the May 16 military coup."[19] Textbook revisions, while significant, were not radical, partly because many topics were still too sensitive for agreement to emerge on how to deal with them. The committee of nine professors who supervised the history revisions, for instance, could not decide on how to treat the assassination of Park on 26 October 1979 and the 12 December military coup that brought Chun Doo Hwan to power.[20] The limits on revising history were illustrated by the uproar caused when education minister Kim Suk-hee (Kim Suk-hŭi) suggested in a speech to the War College that the Korean War was unnecessary. She was forced to resign.[21]

Discussions of curriculum revision reflected the change in the nation's political and economic situation. Education had been used by the state as a means of establishing its legitimacy, but the new administration did not face this problem since few South Koreans questioned the right of Kim Young Sam to serve as president. South Korea's rapid economic growth, the marked rise in wages for industrial workers that occurred from the late 1980s, and the end of the country's diplomatic isolation gave a pride and credibility to the South Korean political and social order that it had previously lacked. Except for the radical fringe of the student movement, few saw North Korea's system of Communism as an alternative. A popular feeling emerged that the country was entering the ranks of the successful nations exemplified by the United States, Western Europe, and Japan. No longer a pariah nation and moving out from the shadow of the United States, South Korea developed a new nationalism based on a sense of strength and achievement.

The effect of this greater political stability and national self-confidence on educational content was complex. South Koreans eagerly sought to democratize and internationalize their education, the latter illustrated by the fad for promoting English education and the introduction of the English language in the primary schools. English was both the language of democratic nations and the medium of global commerce, science, technology, and culture. At the same time, there was a greater pride in the nation's own cultural inheritance, and many believed that the traditional values were a source of strength. Along with pride came the fear that the nation's rush to modernization would lead to a loss of cultural identity. Conservatives sought to ensure that loyalty to nation and family persisted as central values and that Korea avoided the excesses of materialism and self-serving individualism they saw in Western culture.

Concerns over preserving cultural identity appeared in the KEDI's proposed blueprint for education, "Envisioning Globalized Education in Korea," issued in 1995. The authors urged that traditional culture and values be studied because "a sense of national identity should be internalized by students."[22] While calling for the "globalization" of Korean education, President Kim Young Sam also stressed the importance of filial piety and respect for the elderly among the youth. Educational discussions among KEDI officials and in the media were filled with contradictions in which calls for internationalization were followed by concerns over strengthening the "national spirit" and the need for promoting democracy and individual freedom was coupled with the desire to promote loyalty, discipline, and the subordination of the individual to the needs of family and society. The era of blatant government manipulation of education was over, but no consensus had yet been reached over how to democratize and globalize society and still maintain a distinctive sense of Korean identity.

The election of Kim Dae Jung in December 1997 brought to the presidency a former dissident long critical of the state politicization of education. His election and assumption of office, the first completely peaceful transfer of power in South Korean history, marked another milestone in the nation's transition to democracy. His legalization of the teachers' union, further removal of harsh anti-Communist texts, and verbal commitment to decentralizing schooling suggested that the process of democratization of education was irreversible. It was a process to which the Korean people's zeal for education and the strong egalitarian streak in educational thought and practice had greatly contributed.

EDUCATION IN A NEW ECONOMIC ERA

South Korea's transition into a modern industrial nation brought about several changes in its educational development. For one thing, the demographic transition was nearly complete by the 1990s; not only was the population of school-age children no longer growing, but it was actually declining. With the average number of children in a family falling to slightly below two, the long baby boom was over. As a result, cohorts of elementary students became progressively smaller from the 1980s, and by the 1990s the middle school cohorts were also slowly shrinking. Eventually educators and officials realized that unless there was a dramatic reduction or abolition of the quotas on college students, the university population too might start shrinking in the early twenty-first century. The decline in school enrollment meant an opportunity to end the overcrowded conditions in the nation's classrooms: the average size of an elementary classroom had fallen from fifty-six pupils in 1970 to thirty-five in 1998. The decline also drew further attention to the need to concentrate on the quality of instruction.[23]

Yet teacher–student ratios and physical facilities still lagged behind those in developed nations, a fact highlighted by South Korea's 1996 entry into the OECD. In a study that year the OECD recommended that Seoul set targets and dates for the improvement of both physical facilities and classroom size. In response, the government formulated the Educational Environment Improvement Plan 1996–2000 to deal with the inadequate accommodation of pupils. A second OECD study in 1998 again recommended that the state do more to improve facilities and alleviate overcrowding.[24] The MOE then came out with another, longer-range plan to reduce class size.[25] The average primary school class in 1996 had 36 pupils, while the average secondary school class had 48. The MOE sought to reduce these sizes to 30 for primary schools in 2010 and 24 for secondary schools in 2020, bringing them closer to classroom sizes in Western

Europe. University student–faculty ratios fared the worst in comparisons, averaging 34:1 in four-year universities, in contrast to 8.4 students per faculty member in Britain and 9.9 students per professor in Japan.[26] The university targets, even if met, would still result in much larger classrooms than in the United States, Japan, and Western Europe.

Advanced industrial status meant that the problems of vocational education changed as well. A Presidential Commission for Education Reform report in 1997 found that vocational education was inadequate since the curriculum did not reflect the changing needs of an industrial society. In the fast-paced South Korean economy the skills required changed quickly but changes in education came about more slowly, so instruction seldom matched the demands of the marketplace. The commission urged vocational and technical institutions to work in close partnership and to establish a complex network among schools, between schools and industry, and among the different school levels.[27]

But the main challenge to education was that South Korea's economic base was moving away from heavy industry and into high technology and knowledge-based industry. Furthermore, the nation had, up to the 1990s, relied on technology-transfer strategies but now was less able to base its economy on borrowed technology. Instead, future growth depended on its developing its own technical know-how. Policymakers called for an education that concentrated on promoting research and creativity. Considerable hand wringing took place over the lack of creativity among the nation's young, the lack of innovation, and the shortage and inadequate state of research facilities. Even the best schools, such as Seoul National University, ranked below the major universities of Western Europe and North America in research facilities and (many argued) in the quality of their scientific, engineering, and technical programs as well.

South Korean education was strongest at the bottom and weakest at the top. The great majority of the nation's 186 four-year colleges and universities were private, and private universities at the end of the century were tuition driven. Over 80 percent of private college revenues came from tuition and fees. These were regulated by the government to keep them from being prohibitive for families with modest means. Thus, even prestigious institutions could not charge high tuition to fund well-equipped facilities and adequate faculty. As a result, university libraries and labs were extremely modest and classes large. And yet most institutions struggled financially. A number of mediocre institutions had problems even attracting enough students since most young people preferred making another attempt at the entrance exams than being consigned to a low-prestige school. The worst part of the financial structure was that it did not allow the best schools to establish high-quality programs. Other practices contributed to mediocrity; the most notorious was the tendency of universities to hire their own graduates. At a majority of universities most faculty were alumni. Virtually all professors became tenured once hired, freeing them from the intense pressure to do research and publish. Deference to one's senior colleagues, especially if they were one's former teachers, also stifled initiative. A number of reforms were proposed, and the MOE issued regulations to limit the practice of universities hiring their own graduates and demanded performance-based faculty evaluations. But the basic problem of finance was not seriously addressed.

One often praised center for research and training was the Korean Advanced Institute for Science and Technology (KAIST), established in 1981 as a graduate institute. In 1989 KAIST merged with the Korean Institute of Technology to become a comprehensive teaching and research institute. Another institute devoted to training researchers and carrying out research was POSTECH, established in 1986 by the P'ohang Iron and Steel Company. These two institutions evolved into two of the more highly regarded universities in Asia. Some in South Korea thought they could be models for higher education in general. Universities would be classified into institutions that were primarily for teaching and others that focused on research. One way of effecting this change would be to designate certain universities as research institutions and provide them with financial support to develop their science and technology programs. Another would be to create new institutions that through government funding and scholarships could be centers to draw and train the most talented students.[28]

Korea's financial crisis of 1997–1998 only increased the concerns that the nation was not prepared for the economic and technological challenges ahead. The government response was to create the awkwardly titled "Brain Korea 21" (BK 21). Under this program, initiated by the controversial education minister and former political dissident Yi Hae-chan, the South Korean state would invest considerable sums into engineering, science, and technical programs at universities that established serious graduate programs and carried out serious research. Three-quarters of the funding was earmarked for supporting graduate students. In order to compete for the largesse, 83 universities formed 443 research teams to establish departments and programs that would be eligible for funding. Seoul National University received by far the largest government funding, followed by KAIST and POSTECH.[29]

Universities that did not receive money vigorously protested. Top-ranking private universities—Yonsei and Korea, for example—received only modest amounts, and some aspiring universities received no funds at all. The decision to heavily support a few universities at the expense of others raised concerns that a few elite, high-tech universities would emerge, eclipsing all other institutions, while some schools might not survive at all. Students at a number of universities staged noisy demonstrations against the plan, and fifteen hundred professors, the majority at provincial colleges, held a protest in Myŏngdong Cathedral in downtown Seoul, the traditional center for anti-government protests. The demonstrating professors and students argued that the measure would work against the uniformity of educational standards, further undermine the lower prestige of provincial institutions, and slight the arts and humanities. The plan's defenders pointed to the expense it would eliminate since students who wanted current, state-of-the-art scientific and technical training would not have to go abroad; they also argued that this was the reasonable way to ensure that Korea would be able to catch up to the technological standards of other developed countries. Others argued that universities would be better off forming consortiums to pool resources and attract government and private funding and student and professorial talent. Despite the funding it received, under BK 21 Seoul National University would have to reduce the size of its undergraduate enrollment. In response, the university announced a decline in the number of new freshmen it would admit. Since Seoul National was the apex of the university prestige pyramid, the idea that the bar for admission would be raised angered many families. At the end of 1999, it remained difficult to determine how successful BK 21 would be. Recent history suggested problems. The state was tightfisted when financing education, having long been accustomed to relying on user fees and private industry; it had not developed the habit of giving generously to education. Korean alumni, lacking American-style tax incentives, had not developed a tradition of generous giving either. Furthermore, there was no guarantee that the favored institutions would be able to overcome the timeworn attitudes that favored the humanities over science and technology.

CHALLENGING THE IDEALS OF
EQUALITY AND OPPORTUNITY

The criticism that BK 21 would foster elitism was significant. South Korean educational policy had always been characterized by a desire for uniformity of standards and equality of opportunity. Studies have found that South Korea had a more equitable distribution of wealth and more socially mobile population than most nations, with smaller differentials in income and educational opportunity between socioeconomic classes and between urban and rural areas. Most South Koreans, however, maintained that economic and social inequity was one of the worst features of their society. At times there were good reasons for this conviction; the policy of suppressing labor unions and the greater concentration of development in Seoul and in the southeastern region of the country did create vast economic disparities. But such trends toward inequality were countered by other developments. Park Chung Hee's *saemaul* movement and government agricultural price supports and protection from imports reduced the gap between rural and city incomes, and sharp rises in industrial workers' wages in the late 1980s greatly narrowed the range between blue-collar and white-collar salaries. Some trends, such as a pattern of marriages among the children of *chaebŏl* owners, raised fears that a new, endogamous neo-elite was emerging similar to the old *yangban* class.[30] Yet official statistics at least suggested that there was no substantial change in income distribution in the late 1980s or early 1990s.[31]

In education, as noted, a demand for equality of opportunity had shaped the educational system from the time of the U.S. occupation. South Korea, along with East Asian nations such as Japan, Taiwan, and Singapore, stands out in the way education was expanded sequentially, raising all students to a basic standard before concentrating on higher levels.[32] The Korean public remained ever vigilant for any attempts to create an "elitist" school system. Examples of this focus on equality of education by both the state and the public are the high school equalization policy carried out in the 1970s and measures such as the regular rotation of teachers, the lottery method of middle and high school entrance, a rigidly uniform curriculum, and standardized facilities. The South Korean state was also committed to narrowing the gaps in educational quality and opportunity between Seoul and provincial areas. To upgrade all provincial universities, special aid and scholarships were offered (although these did little to

change public perceptions that all provincial colleges were second rate). The
state also gave advantage to poor rural areas by basing school records on the
overall percentile among students in each individual school, thus, for college-
entrance purposes, weighing the scores as if all secondary schools were of the
same standard. An affirmative action policy set a quota on students from fishing
villages and remote areas that universities were required to fulfill; in 1996 this
was expanded.[33]

Education officials often insisted that the standards in elementary and secondary schools be consistent enough to ensure fairness in educational opportunity.[34] Statistics on the results of college entrance exams were not tabulated by
schools, and the figures were not made public so that rates of success for each
school could not be kept. Still the public knew which high schools produced the
greatest number of entrants into prestigious universities. As the school records
were given more weight in college admissions, the quality of the schools began
to take on greater importance. Students in high schools were graded according
to a 15-notch standing scheme. In order to evaluate students more carefully, the
MOE proposed in the spring of 1996 a 100-notch standing scheme. But the distinctions failed to reflect the generally perceived differences in the standards of
secondary schools. Parents at better schools felt that less emphasis on the examination scores gave students from poorer schools an unfair advantage. The government backed down from the plan and suggested that universities could have
more freedom in evaluating student qualifications.[35]

Some of the state's efforts at reform came into conflict with the long-
standing goals of creating uniformity of standards and equality of opportunity.
By permitting universities to judge the quality of the high school as well as the
grades, for instance, the government was opening the door to institutionaliz-
ing inequality in secondary school standards. Schools, critics charged, would
not only earn a good reputation because of their record of producing a high
rate of college entrants, but would also send more graduates to prestigious universities because of their reputation. In other small ways too the government in
the 1990s was moving away from uniformity of education. For instance, the
MOE decided in 1994 to abolish standard high school tests, giving each school
the opportunity to develop its own tests.[36]

Uniformity and equality were also challenged by the rise of free marketeers
within the bureaucracy, the academy, and the media who questioned the attempts by the state to micromanage education and called for the liberation of

education from government restrictions. Education, these critics argued, should be subject to the laws of economics to create greater competition, and students and parents should be given greater freedom of choice. According to this line of thought, only by allowing high schools to compete for students and giving them a freer hand in setting rates and selecting students could Korean education reach an international standard. These views dominated the Presidential Commission for Education Reform, which pushed the sometimes reluctant MOE into experimenting with modifications in the equalization policy. The MOE gave provincial and city boards of education outside Seoul permission to decide whether to allow high schools to compete for student selections, and some began to do so. Some provincial boards of education then experimented with permitting private high schools to recruit freshmen from within a certain geographical range. In 1995, the Seoul Board of Education followed these initiatives and allowed private high schools from 1998 to select freshmen from within ten educational districts; admission was to be based on middle school records, not on entrance examinations. This was necessary, board members argued, because the uniform system of admission "brought down overall quality of education."[37]

These changes brought protests from various civil groups, including the still technically illegal Chŏn'kyojo, which launched a campaign to prevent high schools from being allowed to recruit students. Opponents of the change argued that it would lead to feverish competition to enter prestigious high schools and make the financial burden of extra lessons even greater at an earlier stage in schooling.[38] Not only would this aggravate the heavy cost of schooling and the pressure on young people to study until late at night, but it would also undermine the principle of equality of opportunity, giving an unfair advantage to those who could afford the preparation and private tutors. At the time of the debates over the Basic Education Law in 1949–1951, early tracking was rejected; then in 1969–1971 the middle school (and later high school) entrance exams were abolished. Each step moved South Korea in the direction of an open system that allowed greater numbers of young people more access to education. Now it was feared that this pattern of creating a more egalitarian educational system was being threatened, even if only in a limited way. The plan was delayed, but the crack in the high school equalization plan had appeared.

To promote diversity and experimentation, the MOE began a shift away from the uniform curriculum. Small steps had begun in 1989 with the Fifth

National Curriculum, which permitted school boards some minor variations in instructional content. The Sixth National Curriculum in 1995 went a little further by allowing the fifteen provincial and city boards of education to "localize" course work. Each province, for example, was to add a unit of its local history in the fourth grade. Provincial boards were allowed to make decisions on nearly half the units in the fifth and sixth grades, and primary school principals could add up to thirty-four hours of additional subjects in grades four to six. Secondary school principals were given some, although less, freedom to add subjects.[39] Still, in the late 1990s, South Korea's schools ran on a fairly tight national curriculum, and high school students had no electives.

The plan to encourage business firms to invest in education was a part of this move away from uniform management to a more market-oriented and competitive system. Advocates for corporate involvement in education hoped that this would result not only in private funds improving educational facilities, but also in a spirit of entrepreneurship that would permeate the schools.

Thus in the late 1990s two competing philosophies of education were emerging: equality and uniformity through active state control over education versus greater freedom of choice and market-driven competition. Freedom of choice also meant making the system more flexible. Under a policy labeled "open education," the MOE sought to encourage life-long learning by permitting universities to admit students at any age. This would create a new phenomenon: the nontraditional student. (It remained unclear, however, how students could enter or go back to school for retraining under the existing entrance examination system.) Flexibility was to extend to teaching methods; under a plan introduced in the mid-1990s in pilot schools, the classroom was restructured to allow for pupils to learn at an individual pace. Problems arose with this experiment, with many principals resisting the changes and teachers confused by them.[40] Another fundamental departure was a reform entitled "Curriculum 2000." Pupils would receive a common basic education for ten years with a limited number of electives. If these electives were not available at their school, they could take them at another. The most radical component of this plan was the introduction of a flexible curriculum in the eleventh and twelfth years of schooling. To create greater flexibility as well as to foster vocational education, a plan was introduced under which graduates of vocational high schools could enter junior colleges at any time and junior college graduates could complete a four-year degree at a university.

Concern for equality and uniformity, in the opinion of some, was stifling individuality and creativity. In the past many American-influenced educators had advocated promoting individuality through education as a way to achieve a more democratic society. Now officials, academics, and some journalists argued for individuality as a way of achieving economic competitiveness. In 1994, the Presidential Commission for Education Reform recommended promoting diversity among schools and giving parents freedom to choose. These steps would make secondary schools more competitive but would enable students to find schools that best served their individual needs. Schools, the commission argued, should be allowed to specialize, as well as set their tuition rates. Eventually, it argued, private secondary schools would be totally self-supporting and offer a meaningful choice.

Equality of opportunity was not abandoned, however, for the government of President Kim Dae Jung, who himself had risen from humble origins, planned to provided assistance to low-income families. A 1999 plan proposed that four hundred thousand secondary and twenty thousand kindergarten students from low-income families be exempted from fees and that the government extend low-interest college loans, already available in limited numbers, to three hundred thousand men and women.[41] The South Korean public still expressed concerns over economic disparities that would hinder equality of opportunity. The 1997–1998 economic crisis, which temporarily threw large numbers out of work in a country that had been enjoying a labor shortage for over a decade, pointed out the precariousness of middle-class or respectable working-class status and the great advantages that the more affluent had in this period. The crisis appeared to increase concerns about an egalitarian society.

Heightened attention to economic disparities arose while the general drift of recommendations by commissions and experts seemed to be challenging the very fundamentals of South Korea education. The educational system, which had been structured to allow for maximum social mobility, had been made possible, in part, by an authoritarian state strong enough to maintain a course of universal and standardized education. But critics charged the education it produced was mediocre. It provided fairly high basic standards of literacy, numeracy, and scientific knowledge, but it stifled true talent. South Korea's education did not produce a Bill Gates or any Nobel Prize winners, and in the twenty-first century, perhaps South Korea itself would cease to be a winner in what most Koreans saw as a tough race for elite status for not only themselves, but also their society.

It is interesting to note that most of the tentative shifts away from uniformity and toward greater flexibility were being proposed and imposed from the top by government bureaucrats. South Korean education during the Kim Young Sam administration and even under his successor, Kim Dae Jung, remained highly centralized and uniform in standard, content, and method. The MOE still issued detailed regulations in the scheduling and conducting of classes, and teachers received a standardized and high level of training. Frequent in-service training programs meant that teachers were being retrained and indoctrinated into state educational policy on a regular basis. From state bureaucrats there was a demonstrated reluctance to relinquish the management and direction of the nation's social and economic development. The South Korean state in the late 1990s was still a powerful, bureaucratic entity, with a pattern of authoritarian paternalism. While the government was more open to public accountability and pressure than ever before, it received from the citizenry two contradictory messages. Teachers, school administrators, and some parent groups clamored for more autonomy in decision making and more flexibility in instruction. But many civic groups—from some teachers to many parents, journalists, and intellectuals—called for equality, fairness, and the imposition of uniform polices so that varying standards would not give any groups in society an unfair advantage. And the South Korean public was still animated by the same concerns for personal advancement, social justice and equality, and the right of families to enhance their material existence and their social position through hard work and education. All of these ideals and concerns made it seem unlikely that there would be any truly radical departures in the educational system.

GENDER AND EQUALITY IN EDUCATION

South Korea's commitment to egalitarianism in education did not fully apply to half the population. Women were not exempted from the national zeal for education; the numbers competing for admission to the best high schools, colleges, and universities began to approach those of men in the late 1990s. The increase in female enrollment occurred even though the employment possibilities for most remained bleak and the cost of education soared. Yet female enrollment in graduate schools lagged far behind that of males, rising from 22 percent of all graduate students in 1990 to a still modest 27 percent in 1995, even though at the undergraduate level the gap was narrowing.[42]

Women were generally viewed as temporary employees who were expected to resign upon marriage and whose duties were more secretarial than managerial. Throughout the industrial world women were pouring into the professions and into virtually every career track, but in Korea they did so far more slowly, even more slowly than in Japan. The fifty top firms hired 2,741 women college graduates in 1994. This was only 8.6 percent of the total number of college graduates they hired that year. The same firms, partly due to government pressure, took on 4,353 women in 1995, but this still amounted to only 11.3 percent of the college graduates hired.[43] In 1995, the median income of female workers was 58 percent of that of male workers. Women professionals fared better than average, earning a median income that was 83 percent of that of their male counterparts in 1996—a considerable improvement from 1985, when women professionals earned only 68 percent as much as their male counterparts. But the number of professionals was small and growing more slowly than the rise in wages. A 1997 survey found that women held only 27 percent of the professional jobs, with the highest percentage in education and the lowest in the legal profession.[44] As the country entered an economic recession brought about by the financial crisis of late 1997, even these modest gains were threatened. Many female graduates looked for jobs that were far from the professional managerial track. The 1994 Expo in Taejŏn, for example, popularized the job of *toumi*, narrator–models used by companies to promote products; it was reported to have become a much sought-after job for young women with college degrees.[45]

Discrimination against women in the educational system and society was still strong. In January 1996, parents of middle-school girls brought to the Women's Council (Yŏhyŏp), an umbrella group of organizations, a complaint that 4,300 Seoul middle-school girls had been denied entry into high school even though they had scored higher on the high school entrance examinations than many of the boys who had been admitted. In this case the MOE ordered the girls to be admitted; nonetheless, that such practices occurred exemplified the lingering attitude that women were not as important as men.[46] Indeed, the cultural bias in Korea that favored boys over girls resulted in the abortion of many female fetuses. As most South Korean families chose to have only one or two children, girls became less welcome, and many pregnant wives had doctors illegally determine the sex of their fetus. As a result, 52 percent of primary school chil-dren were boys in 1995.[47] The problem was less severe in South Korea than in China, but the gender imbalance was great enough to be a cause for alarm.

Education for women was widely linked with marriage. Parents sought higher education for their daughters, despite poor employment opportunities and the less favored position of women, in order to make a good marriage for them. In a nation where marriages were still commonly arranged, a well-educated daughter-in-law made a proper "education mother," or, to use the more popular expression, "skirt wind" *(ch'ima param)*. A survey conducted by the KEDI in 1994 found that parents were three times as likely to give "obtain-ing a good job" as the reason for educating their sons than they gave for edu-cating their daughters. They were four times more likely to mention "advantage in marriage" as a reason for educating their daughters. College-eduated parents were less likely to state "advantage in marriage" as the pur-pose of educating their daughters but still stated marriage more often as a goal of the daughters' education than jobs or careers.[48]

The lack of professional opportunities for women is intertwined with the nation's "education fever" in a complex way. Some observers have argued that the absence of opportunities for women has resulted in a process by which mothers project their ambitions onto their children.[49] At the same time, the role of a "skirt wind," who supervises a child's education, absorbs an enormous amount of time. Mothers get up early to gently wake their children and ready them for school. Children are virtually free from all chores while their mothers wait on them like servants—for example, bringing trays of beverages and snacks to them while they study. Mothers spend a great deal of time checking out information on tutors and private cram schools, meeting with teachers, and (most of all) being available to their young scholars twenty-four hours a day. All this makes a full-time job not only difficult, but also a dereliction of their duty as a mother and wife.

While job opportunities opened up slowly for women, the Kim Dae Jung administration showed a renewed concern for equality in education. To end discrimination the MOE announced in 1998 that all new middle and high schools would be coed. As of 1998 only 50 percent of middle schools and 46 percent of high schools were coed. Furthermore, new guidelines would see that texts would be free from gender bias.[50] The administration also displayed some concern for the fact that the teaching profession was male dominated.

While about 50 percent of all teachers below the tertiary level were women, women made up only 6 percent of the assistant principals and 5 percent of principals. And women were extremely underrepresented in the high grades. The MOE issued new guidelines in 1999 to see that more women were promoted to administrative positions. That South Korea had a long way to go to achieve gender equity was highlighted by the 1997–1998 economic slump, which saw sharper declines among women graduates seeking employment than among men. It was reported that there was a corresponding rise in the number of women applying at matchmaking agencies and in prostitution dating agencies.[51]

THE DRIVE FOR EDUCATION

Since the collapse of the Japanese colonial regime in 1945, an insistent public demand for education has been the main engine driving educational development. The 1990s saw no abatement of this demand—only rising expectations as the numbers of students that reached upper levels of schooling increased. Virtually all parents sought a university education for their children. Nor was this only a vague wish; most parents went to enormous lengths to see to it that their son or daughter attained this goal. Pressure to enter the best schools and advance academically as far as possible failed to diminish, despite the oversupply of college degree holders and the declining wage differentials between college and high school graduates. Employment opportunities in the mid-1990s were much better for nongraduates. In 1995, only about 61 percent of college graduates were able to find jobs within six months of receiving their degrees, despite the booming economy and a labor shortage. Women fared worse than men: only half found jobs, while seven out of ten male graduates did. This differential was better than at many points in the past, but it has to be placed in the context of an expanding economy in which unemployment hit an all-time low of 2 percent. By contrast, for graduates of technical high schools, the employment rate for first-time job seekers was 97 percent. Among unskilled laborers there was a labor shortage, leading to the phenomenon of foreign guest workers for factory and menial labor jobs. As noted, the rate of return for a college education was diminishing. In the mid-1980s college graduates earned 2.3 times as much as high school graduates, but from the late 1980s wages for blue-collar and service

Table 12. Wage Levels by Educational Attainment in Korea, 1976–1994

Year	Middle School Graduates	High School Graduates	Junior College Graduates	University Graduates
1976	59.1	100	145.3	229.7
1979	65.9	100	147.6	230.7
1982	69.9	100	129.8	226.5
1988	74.7	100	128.1	202.7
1991	84.6	100	117.4	179.2
1994	88.9	100	108.0	150.5

Source: 1976–1991: Chon Sun Ihm, "South Korea Education," in Morris and Sweeting, eds., 143; 1994: *Han'guk Kyoyuk Kaebalwŏn, Han'guk ŭi kyoyuk chip'yo*, 133.

jobs rose faster than for white-collar jobs, and in 1994 college graduates earned only 1.6 times as much (see table 12).[52]

Educational demand was not totally unresponsive to the market, as the growing popularity of junior colleges indicated (see table 8). In the early and mid-1990s, between 83 and 85 percent of two-year college graduates found suitable jobs, even as their numbers grew rapidly. As a result, many students who had failed to enter college and a few who had graduated but could not find jobs competed for entry into junior college. In 1995, the competition for junior college was an unexpectedly high 3.8 applicants per admitted student. In response, the government announced plans to build ten more two-year institutions.[53] Junior colleges were not without their problems; many did not have the number of qualified professors and facilities required by the MOE and thereby were in danger of acquiring a reputation for providing a lower level of professional skills than were needed by the expanding industrial and service sector. And they made only a small dent in the pressure to enter four-year schools.

With the rate of return for higher levels of education diminishing, one might expect a slowdown in the competition for college entry, yet this seems not to have made an appreciable difference; if anything, competition for prestigious degrees intensified in the 1990s. In financial terms, the income differentials were still significant enough to justify educational expenditures. However, it was the nonmarket rate of return that was—and probably had always been—more significant in promoting educational demands. The *sŏnbi* (teacher–scholar) tradition still prevailed, which meant that academic degrees themselves brought status and honor to the recipients and their families. South Korea had gone through a radical physical and economic transformation from the 1950s to the 1990s—from a nation where the majority still lived in villages of mud-walled, thatched-roof homes to an overwhelmingly urban society of high-rise apartment dwellers and where per capita income had increased manyfold. Nonetheless, traditional attitudes about family, status, and the purpose of education remained remarkably strong. Parents still wielded considerable authority over adult sons and daughters, and individual family members were economically dependent on and obligated to each other. Education was still a collective family effort, where resources were pooled to help educate the young.[54] The strength of traditional attitudes toward schooling is suggested by a study in 1994 that found that most parents still viewed the purpose of education as promoting superior character (in'gyŏk) and cultivation (kyoyang). Only 36 percent saw obtaining a good job as the top priority. Interestingly, the higher the educational attainment of the parents, the less they viewed schooling as a means of securing a good job.[55] Education was still a primary marker of social status. Marriage was also an important way to obtain status, but it too was linked with education. Most surveys showed that the first or second factor in determining the suitability of a spouse was his or her educational attainment.

Public views of education as the measure of social status had an empirical basis; getting into the right school was still the key to success. Sung Chul Yang, in a study of the nation's top bureaucrats, found that of the 1,708 who had achieved vice-ministerial level or above, hagyŏn (school connections) were of vital importance. Furthermore, the pattern of recruitment and promotion showed an increasing domination of graduates from elite schools, especially Seoul National University. While in 1964–1972, 34 percent of the top bureaucrats were SNU graduates, the proportion rose to 51 percent in 1972–1980, and during the first year of the Kim Young Sam administration, 65 percent were SNU alumni.[56] In business, as well, there remained an emphasis on education over skill level in hiring and promotion.[57] Nonuniversity graduates were less likely to climb very high up the corporate ladder. South Korea was not unique in having a society dominated by members from elite schools; there are parallels with Tokyo University in Japan, Oxford and Cambridge Universities in Britain, and the elitist national écoles in France. But in South Korea this trend was increasing. With the military declining as an alternative route to elite status, South Korea was becoming a meritocracy in which government, business, and other institutions were dominated by the graduates of the highly ranked universities. Therefore, the drive for education was at least in part rational, based on an accurate perception that only educational attainment could ensure social and economic success. Coupled with the traditional Korean concern for status, the persistence of the Confucian ideal of the learned gentleman, and the relative openness of post-liberation society, the scramble to gain degrees from ranked institutions is understandable since the rewards were great.

CONCLUSION

A 1998 OECD study of South Korean education sounded in some respects remarkably like the UNESCO–UNKRA Educational Planning Mission to Korea report in 1954. Both found overcrowded classrooms, too much reliance on rote memorization and a rigid or inflexible manner of instruction, deficiencies in technical education, overcentralization of educational administration, and a pedagogy that hindered creativity and independent thought. There are some major differences in the two reports. Absent in the OECD report was the sharp condemnation of rampant corruption and blatant political interference in the school system and the inadequate training of teachers. In general, the OECD report is clearly viewing a school system with impressive accomplishments, and it does not have the earlier report's patronizing tone, the voice of first-world experts viewing a struggling, impoverished society's dubious efforts at nation building. But it strikingly echoes the UNESCO–UNKRA report when it states, "The strong zeal for education among Koreans cannot be matched anywhere else in the world." The report attributes this zeal to the importance of credentials in South Korean society, with the most important being diplomas, "which are frequently the most important criterion for evaluation in employment, marriage and informal interpersonal relations."[58]

How can we explain the zeal for education? Denise Lett, in a study of South Korean society in the 1990s, explained it by what she termed the "yangbanization" of South Korean society. The country's growing middle class, she found, had acquired the traditional concepts of elite status once held by the *yangban,* except that with the decline of hereditary privilege, ancestry no longer was important. The markers of status had become material goods, good marriages, and—above all—impressive educational degrees.[59] Korean parents do seem to have emulated the *yangban* attitude of regarding education as conferring moral authority and the right to privilege, as well as the *yangban* disdain for manual labor. The OECD report agrees that traditional values continue to influence education; Koreans have inherited a worldview that is hierarchical and rank-conscious so that education is a means of firmly establishing one's position in society. Indeed, attitudes toward education that give primacy to the importance of enhancing one's status and acquiring moral authority while also recognizing education's practical economic value have remained surprisingly consistent in surveys in the 1950s, 1960s, and 1990s.[60]

Although it is often difficult to untangle cultural factors from economic ones, South Korea's recent history suggests just how strong the nation's premodern and recent cultural heritage is in shaping the social demand for education. Researchers in the late 1950s and 1960s found that South Koreans still saw the purpose of education as moral cultivation and the development of character and virtue. They also asssociated these values with social and political leadership. Interestingly, these attitudes were shared by all sectors of society.[61] A generation later a survey by the KEDI found more frankness from respondents about the need to get education in order to get a good job, but the cultivation of character was still the leading reason for obtaining an education. Furthermore, college-educated parents were more likely to give moral development or character building as the primary purpose of education than were noncollege-educated parents.[62]

Studies examining South Korea's transition to democracy indicate just how strong these traditional cultural values were at the end of the twentieth century.[63] Doh C. Shin in six surveys taken between 1988 and 1997 found that while most Koreans had become committed to the ideals of democracy and political equality, Confucian authoritarian values were still strong. A majority polled in a 1997 survey agreed with statements suggesting that they placed greater importance on the judgments of morally upright leaders than on democratic processes and attached greater importance to social harmony than to political and social pluralism.[64] Similarly, in 1990 and 1995 surveys Geir Helgesen found that attitudes toward politics were still strongly shaped by Confucian concepts. For example, she found that Koreans, while distrustful of leaders, thought of good leaders in traditional terms as those who were "honest, have moral integrity, and [are] benevolent, knowledgeable, humble-minded, compassionate and virtuous."[65]

What is perhaps most fascinating about the Korean experience is the extent to which social demand for schooling has pervaded every sector of society. If South Korea was becoming "yangbanized," that process was not confined to a small middle class but permeated the entire society. This phenomenon, in turn, was linked to a contradiction in South Korean society—its emphasis on hierarchy and rank and its equally significant commitment to egalitarianism. The dynamic tension between the two is key to understanding modern Korean society. The universality of educational demand is reflected in surveys in the 1990s. In one study 98 percent of parents responded that university education for their children was a prime goal, a figure that was considerably higher than in the United States or Western Europe.[66]

As a result of the relentless pursuit of education South Korea had "caught up" with most developed nations in terms of secondary and college enrollments (see table 13). Literacy was virtually universal, as was secondary school education (see table 14). In international tests conducted by various educational organizations, South Korean secondary students scored close to the top in math and science, usually in overall averages outperforming students from the United States and virtually all developing countries and sometimes Japan.[67] South Korean schools had among the lowest dropout ratios in the world (see table 15) and low incidents of absenteeism, tardiness, and school violence. South Korean teachers were well trained and maintained a high level of professionalism. Primary and secondary school facilities such as labs, libraries, and computers lagged behind most advanced industrial countries, but these were being upgraded at the end of the century. University education was generally of a lower standard academically than in the United States, Western Europe, and Japan; research facilities were especially inadequate. Teacher–student ratios were also higher than in most developed societies. In terms of quality, Korean education was most effective at the lower levels but less impressive at the tertiary level, a fact recognized by government and industry. It seemed likely that improving the standards of higher education would loom larger as the country entered the information age and as the nation's economy could no longer depend on borrowed licensed technology.

Yet for all its achievements, the national obsession with education has created many problems. The linking of education with traditional Confucian, or more properly *yangban*, notions of social status has made implementing technical and vocational education difficult and has produced a constant oversupply of

Table 13. Comparative Enrollment Ratios, 1990

Country	Primary	Secondary	Higher Education
South Korea	**100**	**88**	**38.7**
United States	99	80	69.5
Japan	100	98	31.3
Singapore	100	70	—
France	100	88	39.6
Netherlands	95	76	37.6
Thailand	90	33	16.3
Turkey	100	40	13.2
Mexico	100	46	15.2
Egypt	101	81	19.2
Morocco	57	28	10.2
Brazil	88	16	11.6
Indonesia	98	38	8.7
Philippines	111	54	26.4

Source: UNESCO Statistical Yearbook 1993 (Paris: UNESCO, 1993).

Table 14. Entrance Rates in Korea, 1965–1989

Year	Middle School	High School	Higher Education
1965	48.8 (40.8)*	81.1 (71.6)	25.9
1970	63.8 (53.4)	70.9 (70.3)	34.5
1975	76.9 (69.0)	75.6 (70.1)	33.1
1980	96.8 (95.0)	84.8 (80.1)	47.1
1985	99.1 (98.7)	88.8 (84.9)	59.1 (40.6)
1989	99.5 (99.3)	90.1 (85.2)	50.2 (40.7)

Source: Republic of Korea, MOE, *Kyoyuk t'onggye yŏnbo,* 1990.

* Figures are percentages of graduates of the previous level of schooling directly entering the next level. Figures in parentheses are for females.

Table 15. Dropout Rates in Korea, 1970–1995 (in percent)

Year	Middle School	High School	Junior College	University
1970	2.5	3.7	16.8	14.1
1975	2.2	2.3	16.2	11.2
1980	1.2	2.1	5.2	9.7
1985	1.2	3.0	14.9	13.4
1990	1.0	2.3	16.1	15.5
1995	0.8	2.1	15.9	16.8

Source: Han'guk Kyoyuk Kaebalwŏn, Han'guk ŭi kyoyuk chip'yo 1996, 128.

graduates in the humanities and social sciences. The intense pressure for educational attainment created the competitive entrance examination system that has reduced much of schooling to test preparation, placed enormous pressure on young people, and stifled attempts at educational innovation. It has also created an enormously expensive and arguably inefficient system. In their ceaseless efforts to gain a competitive edge, families have spent huge portions of their incomes on tutoring, private lessons, and various other expenditures. This has not only placed a great burden on most families, but has also caused various distortions in the economy and has generated tension between egalitarian ideals and the reality of discrepancies in wealth and financial resources. The competitive nature of education, the focus on prestigious degrees, and lavish financial expenditures have helped to perpetuate traditional methods of rote memorization and have, in the opinion of many, stifled creativity. How to make schooling more conducive for developing creative skills was one of the major problems vexing educators—a problem that they shared with Japan, whose educational system had so influenced their own.[68]

A host of other problems continued to plague the national education system so that rather than congratulate themselves on their achievements, Koreans complained about the inadequacy of the nation's schooling. All the old problems and dilemmas of the last half century continued to haunt them: the costly nature of the educational system; how to prevent the emergence of sharply defined social classes by ensuring equality of educational opportunity; the unreasonable obsession with entrance examinations and the undue pressure this created on the nation's youth; the difficulty of coordinating education and training with economic needs; how to channel the zeal for education in the

most productive way; and—not the least—how to create an educational system that would not be subject to political abuse by a state with authoritarian
traditions, but rather would serve as a foundation for a democratic society.

But solving these problems would not be a matter of government decree. At
all times educational policy making reflected the demands of a turbulent, restless, and ambitious society, as well as a development-oriented state. Education in
South Korea was influenced by inherited cultural values and shaped by the experience of recent history. The evolution of the system had been a process
marked by confrontation of parents, students, and teachers with an authoritarian, bureaucratic state. The 1990s saw the emergence of independent labor
unions and a number of viable citizen groups advocating environmental and
other issues.[69] In fact, a University of Michigan study in 1996 found that between
1981 and 1995 South Korea had the greatest rate of increase in membership in
voluntary social, religious, cultural, and political groups of any of forty-three
surveyed nations.[70] Education too began to reflect this trend with a proliferation
of parent and civic groups concerned with schooling. It also seemed increasingly
likely that with the legalization of teachers' unions in 1999 teachers would become more important in educational policy making and that the political system
would become more responsive to public opinion, so it appeared that the state
would have less control over education that it had in the past. As the nation entered the twenty-first century, as the state became more democratic, and as civil
society became more complex with competing centers of power, the need for a
more consensual style of policy making became apparent. Apparent too was the
need for a consensus on what kind of education was required to prepare the nation as it moved from a struggling developing nation with an authoritarian government to a first-world economy and a democratic society.

A popular film in 1998, *Shadow of Acacia,* which may have created a new
genre of educational horror movies, aroused the ire of the Korean Teachers'
Federation for depicting teachers as cruel, corrupt bullies who beat and sexu-
ally harassed students. While undoubtedly a distorted picture of the nation's
teachers, the film did portray one of the genuine horrors of Korean schooling:
its reduction to high-pressured examination preparation. In one scene a
teacher beats a student, yelling, "You are lowering the average score of the
class."[71] Truly, the costs, high pressure, and inflexibility of the system were
troubling. The search for a competitive edge and the inadequacies of the educational system resulted in a huge exodus of students, with an estimated

133,000 young men and women studying abroad in 1998, about half of them in the United States.[72] Many of these students simply sought a second chance abroad that had been denied them at home if they had failed to gain admission to a desirable school or department. Indeed the search for educational opportunity—and at lower cost—was a prime motive for Korean emigration to countries such as the United States and Canada.

Yet a majority of Koreans still maintain their "unshakable faith" in education. A Korea Gallup Poll in early 2000 found that most of those surveyed felt that education was the single most important factor in the nation's future and that they would be willing to pay higher taxes to finance it. Nor did the survey suggest that the feverish pursuit of degrees would diminish soon. An overwhelming 83 percent of respondents felt that "academic credentials will be more important in the future."[73]

South Korea's "education fever" brought about one of the most remarkable social transformations in modern history. A land of illiterate and semiliterate peasants and only a very small urban middle class has become one of the world's most well-schooled nations. At the end of the twentieth century the South Korean state and public discussed various, often bold and innovative, ideas to reform their system of schooling and to contain the obsessive zeal for prestigious degrees. As long as education remains linked to widely held ideas of social status, however, most of these reforms are not likely to succeed. More likely, the mass streaming of Koreans toward the educational ladder of social success will continue. It is also likely that the educational system the South Koreans have fashioned will remain among the most costly and high pressured in the world but will also continue to produce one of the world's most highly literate, competitive, and ambitious citizenries.

Notes

INTRODUCTION

1. *Korea Herald*, 18 November 1999; *Han'guk ilbo*, 18 November 1999.

2. In 1997, the Third International Math and Science Study tested thirteen-year-olds in forty-one countries. South Korean students placed second in math (behind Singapore) and fourth in science. *The Economist*, 20 March 1997, 21–23.

3. John W. Meyer, Francisco O. Ramirez, Richard Robinson, and John Boli-Bennett, "The World Educational Revolution, 1950–1970," in *National Development and the World System*, ed. John W. Meyer and Michael T. Hannan (Chicago: University of Chicago Press, 1979), 37–55.

4. The mean primary school enrollment rate for the fifty-six poorest nations (measured in 1970 GNP per capita and including South Korea) grew from 37 percent in 1950 to 53 percent in 1960 and to 72 percent in 1970. For secondary school enrollments the figures are 5.3, 9.4, and 17 percent respectively. Meyer et al., eds., 40. In South Korea if we start in 1945 (1950 figures are unreliable), we find that primary school enrollment grew from about 37 percent to 96 percent in 1960 and to 100 percent by 1965. At the secondary level enrollment grew from about 4 percent in 1945 to 29 percent in 1960.

5. Paul Morris and Anthony Sweeting, eds., *Education and Development in East Asia* (New York and London: Garland Publishing, 1995).

6. For a comprehensive attempt to link economic development with educational development, see Noel F. McGinn, Donald Snodgrass, Yung Bong Kim, Shin-bok Kim, and Quee-young Kim, *Education and Development in Korea* (Cambridge, Mass.: Harvard University Press, 1980).

7. A partial exception is the important study by McGinn et al., but this focuses primarily on the link between education and economic development and covers only the period to 1975.

CHAPTER I: KOREAN EDUCATION UNTIL 1945

1. Kim Yŏng-il, *Han'guk kyoyuksa* [History of Korean education] (Seoul: Sung-myŏng Yŏja Taehakkyo Ch'ulp'ansa, 1984), 82.

2. James Palais, *Politics and Policy in Traditional Korea* (Cambridge, Mass.: Harvard University Press, 1975), 112, 326 n. 9; Kim Yŏng-il, 102.

3. Palais, 326 n. 9.

4. Son In-su, *Han'guk kyoyuksa* [History of Korean education], 2 vols. (Seoul: Munŭmsa, 1977), 1:276–278, 281–283; Palais, 112; Kim Yŏng-il, 81.

5. Palais, 113–131.

6. See Yong-ho Choe: *The Civil Examinations and the Social Structure in Early Yi Dynasty Korea, 1392–1600* (Seoul: Korean Research Society, 1987), and "Commoners in Early Yi Dynasty Civil Examinations: An Aspect of Korean Social Structure," *Journal of Asian Studies* 33, 4 (August 1974): 611–632; Watanabe Manabu, *Kintai chōsen kyōiku kenkyū* [History of modern Korean education] (Tokyo: Yuzankaku, 1969).

7. Cited in Yong-ho Choe, *Civil Examinations*, 98.

8. Yi Hŭi-gwŏn: "Chosŏn chŏn'gi ŭi konggwan yŏn'gu" [Student protests in early Chosŏn], *Sahak yŏn'gu* 28 (December 1978): 1–30, and "Chosŏn hugi ŭi konggwan kwŏndang yŏn'gu" [Student protests and strikes in early Chosŏn], *Sahak yŏn'gu* 30 (June 1980): 31–64.

9. The concept of a vortex was developed by Gregory Henderson in *Korea: The Politics of the Vortex* (Cambridge, Mass.: Harvard University Press, 1968).

10. Yong-ha Shin [Sin Yong-ha], "The Establishment of the First Modern School in Korea," *Korean Social Science Journal* 5, 1 (1978): 127–141.

11. Son In-su, *Han'guk kaehwa kyoyuk yŏn'gu* [A study of Korean enlightenment education] (Seoul: Ilchogak, 1980), 68–80, 357–382.

12. Harry Bang [Pang Hŭng-gyu], "Japan's Colonial Education Policy in Korea, 1905–1930" (Ph.D. diss., University of Arizona, 1971), 69–73.

13. Son In-su, *Han'guk kaehwa kyoyuk yŏn'gu*, 130, 132.

14. The views and activities of early Korean educational reformers are discussed in Son In-su, *Han'guk kaehwa kyoyuk yŏn'gu,* and in No In-hwa, "Taehan cheguk sigi kwanhan hakkyo, kyoyuk ŭi sŏngyŏn'gu" (Study of the characteristics of education in the schools of the Taehan Empire) (Ph.D. diss., Ewha University, 1989), 18–40.

15. Son In-su, *Han'guk kaehwa kyoyuk yŏn'gu,* 81; Chŏng Chae-ch'ŏl, *Ilche ŭi taehan'guk singminji kyoyuk chŏngch'aeksa* [A history of imperial Japan's colonial education policy toward Korea] (Seoul: Ilchisa, 1985), 206.

16. No In-hwa, 220.

17. Ibid., 54, 60.

18. "The Educational Needs of Korea," *Korea Review* 4, 10 (October 1904): 443–452; No In-hwa, 70.

19. No In-hwa, 52.

20. "The Educational Needs of Korea (continued)," *Korea Review* 4, 11 (November 1904): 484.

21. Ibid., 488. The article stated that Korea was in an educational vacuum, with the old system having collapsed while the new system "fails to interest the people."

22. Kim Ŭn-ju, "Taehan chegugi ŭi kyoyuk kŭndae kwa kwajŏng e kwanhan yŏn'gu" [Study of the process of modernization of education during the Taehan Empire period] (Master's thesis, Yonsei University, 1987), 78; Son In-su, *Han'guk kyoyuksa*, 2:556.

23. Chŏng Chae-ch'ŏl, 225.

24. The Ministry of Education issued detailed regulations on the quality of paper to be used in textbooks. Hyojae Kungmin Hakkyo, *Hyojae kusibinyŏnsa* [Ninety-two-year history of Hyojae Elementary School] (Seoul: Hyojae Kungmin Hakkyo, 1987), 54.

25. In 1939 there were 650,000 Japanese (including dependents) living in Korea. Out of those employed 41 percent were engaged in government service (not counting the military troops station there) in 1937. Andrew Grajdanzev, *Modern Korea* (New York: Institute of Pacific Relations, 1944), 76–79.

26. Government-General of Chosen, *Annual Report on Reforms and Progress in Chosen 1910–1911* (Keijō [Seoul]: Sōtokufu, 1911), 201.

27. Ibid.

28. Son In-su, *Han'guk kaehwa kyoyuk yŏn'gu,* 628–632; Donald K. Adams, "Education in Korea 1945–1955" (Ph.D. diss., University of Connecticut, 1956), 24–41. The "common schools" that were set up often provided only two or three years of instruction instead of the statutory four years.

29. Horace H. Underwood, *Modern Education in Korea* (New York: Columbia University Press, 1926), 195–205; James Ernest Fisher, *Democracy and Mission Education in Korea* (New York: Columbia University Press, 1928), 65–93.

30. Bang, 186.

31. Chŏng Chae-ch'ŏl, 345–347.

32. Patricia Tsurumi, "Colonial Education in Korea and Taiwan," in *The Japanese Colonial Empire: 1895–1945,* ed. Ramon H. Myers and Mark R. Peattie (Princeton, N.J.: Princeton University Press, 1984), 305. The average township *(men)* in 1930 would have had a population of about ten thousand. Since students were expected to walk to school, a township school could serve only those children living in nearby villages. See also Won-mo Dong, "Japanese Colonial Policy and Practice in Korea, 1905–1945" (Ph.D. diss., Georgetown University, 1965), 384.

33. Ibid., 394.

34. Ibid., 395.

35. Hong Ung-sŏn, interview with author, Seoul, September 1991; Kim Yŏng-don, interview with author, Seoul, September 1991; Russell Anthony Vicante, "Japanese Colonial Education in Korea, 1910–1945: An Oral History" (Ph.D. diss., State University of New York at Buffalo, 1987).

36. Chŏng Chae-ch'ŏl, 348–353; Kim Yŏng-il, 149–158.

37. Pae Chŏng-gun, "Ilbon-ha minjok kyoyuk ŭi pyŏngch'ŏn e kwanhan yŏn'gu" [A study of changes in Korean national education under Japan] (Master's thesis, Yonsei University, 1984), 21–30.

38. Hamakichi Takahashi, *Chōsen kyōiku shikō* [Survey of Korean education] (Keijō [Seoul]: Chōsen Sōtokufu 1927), 458–459.

39. Pae, 18–30.

40. This is dealt with at great length in Han Young Rim [Im Han-yŏng], "The Development of Higher Education in Korea during the Japanese Occupation" (Ph.D. diss., Columbia University, 1952).

41. Adams, "Education in Korea," 47. Korean discrimination was admitted and even defended by the Japanese and by some Westerners. See Henry Burgess Drake, *Korea of the Japanese* (London: John Lone and the Badly Head, 1930), 138–139. For comments on the personal experience of a Korean student, see Rim, 183–184, 190, 192.

42. See Dong, passim. After 1922 the provincial governments were responsible for secondary education, but their accomplishments were modest.

43. Ibid., 427–429.

44. Ibid., 164. High-rank officials are defined as those holding the two highest levels in the Japanese bureaucracy, *chokuninkan* and *soninkan,* and middle rank as those with the rank of *hanninkan* or its equivalent. In 1943, only 12 percent of those holding the highest rank, *chokuninkan*, were Korean. Pak Mun-ok, *Han'guk chŏngburon* [Principles of Korean government] (Seoul: Pakyongsa, 1958), 116–117.

45. *Chōsen Nenkan 1941* (Keijō [Seoul]: Keijō Nipposha), 551–552.

46. Bang, 178.

47. Cited in Adams, "Education in Korea," 33. Similar remarks appear in various places; for examples, see Government-General of Chosen, *Annual Report 1912–1913*, 207–208.

48. Government-General of Chosen, *Annual Report 1937–1938*, 86.

49. Chŏng Chae-ch'ŏl, 427–430, 439.

50. Ibid., 430–494.

51. Ibid., 463–496.

52. Ibid., 468–475; Kim Yŏng-il, 164.

53. Kim Kuk-hwan, "Ilche singminji-ha kodŭng kyoyuk chŏngch'aek e kwanhan yŏn'gu" [Study of higher education policy under the imperial Japanese colonial rule] (Master's thesis, Yonsei University, 1977), 85–86.

54. Grajdanzev, 75–79; Bruce Cumings, *The Origins of the Korean War,* vol. 1: *Liberation and the Emergence of Separate Regimes, 1945–1947* (Princeton, N.J.: Princeton University Press, 1981), 12.

55. Hagen Koo, ed., *State and Society in Contemporary Korea* (Ithaca, N.Y.: Cornell University Press, 1993), 231–236.

56. Kim Yŏng-don, interview with author, Seoul, September 1991; Hong Ung-sŏn, interview with author, Seoul, September 1991. For Japanese teacher training, see Benjamin Duke, *Japan's Militant Teachers* (Honolulu: University of Hawai'i Press, 1973), 19.

57. Author interviews with retired teachers, Seoul, summer 1991.

58. Yong-ho Choe, *Civil Examinations,* 32–36.

59. Jong Hae Yoo [Yu Chong-hae], "The System of Korean Local Government," in *Korea under Japanese Colonial Rule: Studies of the Policy and Technique of Japanese Colonialism*, ed. Andrew Nahm (Kalamazoo, Mich.: Western Michigan University, Institute for International and Area Studies, Center for Korean Studies, 1973), 55-59.

60. Dong, 384; Yoo, 62.

61. Only 3,186,000 yen out of a central colonial budget of 184,100,000 yen were spent on education in 1934. Government-General of Chosen, *Annual Report 1933– 1934*, 43-45.

62. Older Koreans in interviews conducted by the author in Seoul and Honolulu in 1991 and 1992 still recall the tremendous family pressure to enter schools during this period. It is clear that the social demand for education was quite intense, at least in urban areas, and that by the 1930s the modern educational system was winning broad recognition as the major vehicle for social and economic advancement.

63. Dong, 162.

64. Chŏng Chae-ch'ŏl, 390-398.

65. Ibid., 417-420.

66. Carter Eckert, "Total War, Industrialization, and Social Change in Late Co- lonial Korea," in *The Japanese Wartime Empire, 1931–1945*, ed. Peter Duus, Ramon H. Myers, and Mark R. Peattie (Princeton, N.J.: Princeton University Press, 1996), 12-37.

67. Cumings, *Origins of the Korean War*, 1:53-61.

68. Bruce Cumings, *Korea's Place in the Sun: A Modern History* (New York: W. W. Norton, 1997), 177.

CHAPTER 2: ESTABLISHING THE EDUCATIONAL SYSTEM, 1945-1951

1. Cumings, *Origins of the Korean War*, 1:101-131.

2. McGinn et al., 36.

3. For Yu Ŏk-kyŏm's involvement in educational, nationalist, and Christian movements during the colonial period, see Kenneth M. Wells, *New God, New Nation: Protestants and Reconstruction Nationalism in Korea, 1896–1937* (Honolulu: University of Hawai'i Press, 1990), 66, 119, 161.

4. O Ch'ŏn-sŏk, *Han'guk sin kyoyuksa* [A history of the new education in Korea] (Seoul: Hyŏndae Kyoyuk Chisa Ch'ulp'ansa, 1964), 104, 108-109.

5. Ibid., 108-109.

6. USAMGIK (United States Army Military Government in Korea), *Summation of the U.S. Army Military Government Activities in Korea* (Seoul: General Headquarters, Commander-in-Chief, U.S. Army Forces, Pacific, March 1946), 19.

7. Eiko Seki, "An Endeavor by Koreans toward the Reestablishment of an Edu- cational System under the U.S. Military Government," *East–West Education* 5, 1 (Spring 1986): 34-43.

8. Adams, "Education in Korea," 65-78; Byung Hun Nam, "Educational Reorga-

nization in South Korea under the United States Army Military Government 1945–1948" (Ph.D. diss., University of Pittsburgh, 1962), 3–97.

9. Seki, 44.

10. Hyojae Kungmin Hakkyo, 78.

11. United States Department of the Army, *Educator's Guide to Korea* (Seoul: Reports and Analysis Branch, Civil Affairs Division, 1 April 1948), 6–7.

12. Hiroshi Abe, "U.S. Educational Policy in Korea," *East–West Education* 6, 1 (Spring 1986).

13. Byung Hun Nam, 98–100; USAMGIK, *Summation,* May 1948, 213.

14. USAMGIK, *Summation*, January 1948, 203.

15. USAMGIK, *Official Gazette*, 29 May 1948.

16. USAMGIK, *Summation,* March 1948, 190.

17. In a letter dated 26 June 1946, MacArthur objected to an educational survey and information mission as the American–Soviet Joint Commission talks had just terminated in May without agreement and he did not want to take any action that could be construed as setting up a separate administration before the talks could be reconvened (Abe, 28). At this time U.S. officials still entertained hopes that the division of Korea into two occupational zones would be temporary.

18. Abe, 28–33. See also United States Department of the Army, *Report of the Staff of the Teacher Training Center* (Seoul: Reports and Analysis Branch, Civil Affairs Division, 1 April 1949).

19. Byung Hun Nam, 147. Yi Chae-o, *Haebang hu han'guk haksaeng undongsa* [A history of the Korean student movement after liberation] (Seoul: Hyŏngsŏngsa, 1984).

20. Byung Hun Nam, 147.

21. Yi Chae-o, 74, 88–92. For an example of U.S. official fears of campus unrest, see USAMGIK, *Summation,* April 1946, 191.

22. Chang I-uk, *Na ŭi hoegorok* [A record of my recollections] (Seoul: Saemt'o, 1975), 217–220.

23. Ibid., 232.

24. Han'guk Kyoyuk Yŏn'guso, *Han'guk kyoyuksa kŭnhyŏndae p'yŏn* [Studies on modern and recent Korean history] (Seoul: Han'guk Kyoyuk Yŏn'guso, 1994), 450–451.

25. Taehan Kyoyuk Yŏnhaphoe (Korean Federation of Educators' Associations), *Taehan kyoryŏn sasipnyŏnsa* [Forty-year history of the Korean Federation of Educators' Associations] (Seoul: Taehan Kyoyuk Yŏnhaphoe, 1987), 4.

26. Han'guk Kyoyuk Yŏn'guso, 441, 454–457.

27. Figures for school attendance in 1945 vary; the figures given are based on McGinn et al., 4.

28. Byung Hun Nam, 129.

29. USAMGIK, *Summation*, March 1948, 191.

30. Ibid., 191–192.

31. Ibid., 190. Adams gives an even higher figure of 77 percent (Adams, "Educa-

tion in Korea," 78). The figures based on USAMGIK reports are too high to be credible; an additional problem is that the standard for determining literacy is unclear.

32. At the beginning of the American occupation there were fifteen thousand Japanese teachers in South Korea. USAMGIK, *Summation*, May 1946, 83.

33. Byung Hun Nam, 117.

34. USAMGIK, *Summation*, February 1948, 200.

35. Monika Kehoe, "Higher Education in Korea," *Far Eastern Quarterly* 7 (February 1949): 184–185.

36. USAMGIK, *Summation*, June 1947, 86.

37. Cumings, *Origins of the Korean War,* 1:54–60.

38. Hwang Sok-chun, ed., *Yoktae kukhoe ŭiwŏn ch'ongnam* [Comprehensive biography of former lawmakers] (Seoul: Ulchisa, 1982), 847.

39. Chu Ki-yong, "Kyoyuk chaegŏn" [Educational reconstruction], *Sae kyoyuk* 2, 2 (March 1949): 26–30.

40. Son In-su, *Han'guk kyoyuksa,* 1:805–806.

41. O Ch'ŏn-sŏk, *Minju kyoyuk ŭl chihyang hayŏ* [Toward a democratic education] (Seoul: Hyŏndae Kyoyuk Ch'ulp'ansa, 1960), 14.

42. O Ch'ŏn-sŏk, "Chŏngyunyŏn kyoyukkye ŭi chŏnmang" [The prospects for the education of the world in 1957], *Sae kyoyuk* 9, 1 (January 1957): 22, and *Minju kyoyuk ŭl chihyang hayŏ,* 14, 302.

43. Kang Kil-su, *Kyoyuk haengchŏng* [Educational administration] (Seoul: P'ungguk Hagwŏn, 1957), 291–311.

44. Sŏul T'ŭkpyŏlsi Kyoyuk Wiwŏnhoe (Seoul Board of Education), *Taehan kyoyuk yŏn'gam 4286* [Yearbook of Korean education, 1953] (Seoul: Sŏul T'ŭkpyŏlsi Kyoyuk Wiwŏnhoe, 1953), 94.

45. The organization was founded under the name Minju Kyoyuk Yŏn'guhoe (Democratic Education Research Society) and changed its name in December 1946. See Hong Ung-sŏn, *Kwangbokhu ŭi sin kyoyuk undong, 1946–1949, chosŏn kyoyuk yŏn'gu rŭl chungsim ŭro* [The New Education Movement after liberation, 1946–1949, centered on the Chosŏn Education Research Society] (Seoul: Taehan Kyogwasŏsa, 1991), 45–63.

46. Ibid., 66–69.

47. Ibid., 202.

48. Sa-gong Hwan in *Sae kyoyuk* 2, 2 (March 1949): 17–22. Sa-gong based his argument on nineteenth-century German pedagogue Johann Friedrich Hebart, who taught that all education begins with moral education.

49. Bruce Cumings, *The Origins of the Korean War,* vol. 2: *The Roaring of the Cataract, 1947–1950* (Princeton, N.J.: Princeton University Press, 1990), 214.

50. An Ho-sang, *Minjujuŭi ŭi yŏksa wa chŏngnyu* [Democracy and its varieties] (Seoul: Ilmin Ch'ulp'ansa, 1953), 59–60.

51. Ibid., 53–54.

52. An Ho-sang: *Uri ŭi purujijŭm* [Our cry] (Seoul: Munhwadang, 1947), 117, and

Minjujŏk minjŏngnon: Hanbaeksŏngjuŭi iron [Democratic nationalism: Hanbaeksŏng theory] (Seoul: Omun'gak, 1961), 239.

53. Cited in Han'guk Kyoyuk Sipnyŏnsa Kanhaenghoe, *Han'guk kyoyuk sipnyŏnsa* [Ten-year history of Korean education] (Seoul: Han'guk Kyoyuk Sipnyŏnsa Kanhaenghoe, 1959), 44–45.

54. An Ho-sang, *Minjujŏk minjŏngnon*, 239.

55. An Ho-sang, *Minjujuŭi ŭi yŏksa wa chŏngnyu*, 54.

56. Cited in Hong Ung-sŏn, 69.

57. Son Chin-t'ae in *Sae kyoyuk* 1, 2 (1948): 47–56.

58. Chŏngmyohoe, *Paek Nak-chun: Hakhoe kirok* [Record of Paek Nak-chun] (Seoul: Chongmyohoe, 1952), 3–9.

59. Paek Nak-chun, *Han'guk kyoyuk kwa minjok chŏngsin* [Korean education and the national spirit] (Seoul: Han'guk Munhwa Hyŏphoe, 1954), 33.

60. Ibid., 62.

61. Ibid., 88.

62. Ibid., 24, 87.

63. Son In-su, *Han'guk kyoyuksa*, 2:795–804; Yu Sŏk-ch'ang, *Choyanghan hyŏng-myŏng ŭi hayŏ* [For a quiet revolution] (Seoul: Tosŏ Ch'ulp'ansa, 1987).

64. Kang Kil-su, 314.

65. Taehan Kyoyuk Yŏnhaphoe, *Taehan kyoyuksa 1947–1973* [History of Korean education 1947–1973] (Seoul: Taehan Kyoyuk Yŏnhaphoe, 1974).

66. Kang Kil-su, 315.

67. *Tonga ilbo*, 24 November 1949.

68. Kukhoe Samuch'ŏ, *Kukhoe sokkirok* [Minutes of the National Assembly] (Seoul: Kukhoe Samuch'ŏ), 31 October 1949, 553.

69. *Chosŏn ilbo*, 21 September 1949.

70. Kukhoe Samuch'ŏ, *Kukhoe sokkirok*, 3 November 1949, 631–648; *Chosŏn ilbo*, 17 November 1949.

71. Ibid., 31 October 1949, 559.

72. Ibid., 25 November 1949, 1181.

73. Ibid., 5 November 1949, 794, and 25 November 1949, 1181.

74. Ibid., 4 November 1949, 746.

75. *Chosŏn ilbo*, 17 November 1949.

76. Kukhoe Samuch'ŏ, *Kukhoe sokkirok*, 31 October 1949, 553–554.

77. Kang Kil-su, 314–324.

78. Chi-young Pak, *Political Opposition in Korea, 1945–1960* (Seoul: Seoul National University Press, 1980), 68–81; Institute of Social Sciences, Korean Studies Series 2.

79. Kukhoe Samuch'ŏ, *Kukhoe sokkirok*, 26 November 1949, 1186.

80. Ibid., 1185.

81. Ibid., 3 November 1949, 643.

82. Ibid., 633.

83. Ibid., 634.

84. Ibid., 31 October 1949, 557.

85. *Tonga ilbo*, 21 September 1949.

86. Ibid., 17 November 1949.

87. Ibid.

88. Kukhoe Samuch'ŏ, *Kukhoesa* [History of the National Assembly], 2 vols. (Seoul: Kukhoe Samuch'ŏ, 1971), 1:138.

89. Ibid., 1:138–140.

90. Ibid.

91. Kukhoe Samuch'ŏ, *Kukhoe sokkirok*, 3 November 1949, 638; O Ch'ŏn-sŏk, *Han'guk sinkyoyuksa*, 432–434; Kang Kil-su, 392–393.

92. Kukhoe Samuch'ŏ, *Kukhoe sokkirok*, 31 October 1949, 552.

93. *Tonga ilbo*, 3 June 1949.

94. Kukhoe Samuch'ŏ, *Kukhoe sokkirok*, 31 October 1949, 558.

95. Ibid., 560.

96. Ibid., 551.

97. Ibid., 3 November 1949, 655.

98. *Tonga ilbo*, 26 April and 10 May 1952.

99. *Chosŏn ilbo*, 11 November 1949.

100. Cited in *Tonga ilbo*, 1 December 1949.

101. *Chosŏn ilbo*, 11 November 1949.

102. Kukhoe Samuch'ŏ, *Kukhoe sokkirok*, 3 November 1949, 642.

103. Taehan Kyoyuk Yŏnhaphoe, *Taehan kyoyuksa 1947–1973*, 59–60; *Chosŏn ilbo*, 10 February 1950.

104. Kukhoe Samuch'ŏ, *Kukhoe sokkirok*, 9 February 1950, 552.

105. Ibid., 554–555; *Chosŏn ilbo*, 12 February 1950.

106. *Chosŏn ilbo*, 10 February 1950.

107. Kukhoe Samuch'ŏ, *Kukhoe sokkirok*, 7 March 1951, no page number; Sŏul Kyoyuk T'ŭkpyŏlsi Wiwŏnhoe, *Taehan kyoyuk yŏn'gam 4288* [1955], 16.

108. See interviews in *Tonga ilbo*, 3 June 1949, and *Chosŏn ilbo*, 21 September 1949.

CHAPTER 3: EXPANDING THE EDUCATIONAL SYSTEM

1. Kukhoe Samuch'ŏ, *Kukhoe sokkirok*, 30 October 1948.

2. Ibid., 27 November 1948, 1106.

3. Former schoolteachers, interviews with author, Seoul, July–November 1991.

4. *Tonga ilbo*, 8 October 1953.

5. Sŏul Kyoyuk T'ŭkpyŏlsi Wiwŏnhoe, *Taehan kyoyuk yŏn'gam 4288* [1955], 93–95.

6. Republic of Korea, MOE, *Mun'gyo t'onggye yoram* [Outline of educational statistics] (Seoul: Mun'gyobu, 1963), 336–337; Sŏul Kyoyuk T'ŭkpyŏlsi Wiwŏnhoe, *Taehan kyoyuk yŏn'gam 4294* [1961], 347–351.

7. *Chosŏn ilbo*, 9 June 1953.

8. Republic of Korea, MOE, *Mun'gyo t'onggye yoram*, 368–369.

9. Ibid., 340–341. A figure of 101,000 is also given for higher education in 1960.

10. For a summary of these figures, based on UNESCO reports, see McGinn et al., 47.

11. Republic of Korea, Office of Information and Research, *Korean Report: Reports from the Cabinet Ministries of the Republic of Korea* (Washington, D.C.: Korea Pacific House, 1952–1959), 6:95–96.

12. Sŏul Kyoyuk T'ŭkpyŏlsi Wiwŏnhoe, *Taehan kyoyuk yŏn'gam 4294* [1961], 349. This figure does not include teachers' colleges.

13. Educational Planning Mission to Korea, *Rebuilding Education in the Republic of Korea: Report of the UNESCO-UNKRA Educational Planning Mission to Korea* (Paris: UNESCO, May 1954), 105; Elaine Milam Barnes, "The Schools of Taegu, Kyongsang Pukto Province, Korea, in 1954–1955: An Investigation into the Interaction between Culture and Education" (Ph.D. diss., University of Maryland, 1960), 95; Elizabeth Cecil Wilson, "The Problem of Value in Technical Assistance in Education: The Case of Korea, 1945–1955" (Ph.D. diss., New York University, 1959).

14. Educational Planning Mission to Korea, 146; McGinn et al., 52.

15. Korean Commission for UNESCO, *Korean Survey* (Seoul: Dong-a Publishing, 1960), 146.

16. *Tonga ilbo*, 17 January 1954.

17. Sŏul Kyoyuk T'ŭkpyŏlsi Wiwŏnhoe, *Taehan kyoyuk yŏn'gam 4288* [1955], 35.

18. Republic of Korea, MOE, *Mun'gyo kaeyo* [Outline of schooling] (Seoul: Mungyobu, 1958), 292; Sung-il Kim, "A Study of Certain Aspects of Educational Policy in Korea" (Ph.D. diss., Syracuse University, 1961). The system of accreditation was finalized on 11 November 1954. Republic of Korea, MOE, *Mun'gyo kaeyo*, 290.

19. Reublic of Korea, MOE, *Mun'gyo kaeyo*, 290–292. This statement is also based on interviews with teachers and officials.

20. Ibid., 293. Only 250 out of 5,901 competitors passed the exam in 1957.

21. McGinn et al., 52.

22. See C. W. Wood, "Post-Liberation Problems in Korean Education," *Phi Delta Kappan* 39 (December 1957): 115–118; Willard E. Goslin, *Han'guk kyoyuk e issŏ ŭi munje wa paljŏn* [Development and problems of current Korean education] (Seoul: Combined Economic Board, 1958), 13.

23. Wood, 116. This statement is also based on interviews with teachers.

24. You Sang Rhee [Yi Yu-sang], "Korean Education, 1956–1965," *Journal of Social Sciences and Humanities* 31 (December 1969): 34–39.

25. Teaching remained a predominantly male profession. In 1957, the male/female ratio among elementary teachers was 4:1. This figure was 1:1 in Seoul but 8:1 in Chŏlla Province. Sung-il Kim, 374.

26. Kim Yŏng-hwa et al., *Kukka paljŏn esŏ ŭi kyoyuk ŭi yŏkhal punsŏk yŏn'gu* [The role of Korean education in national development] (Seoul: Han'guk Kyoyuk Kaebalwŏn, 1996), 157.

27. Ibid., 147.

28. *Korea Times*, 1 January 1966.

29. Taehan Kyoyuk Yŏnhaphoe, *Han'guk kyoyuk yŏn'gam 1967–1968* [Yearbook of Korean education 1967–1968] (Seoul: Taehan Kyoyuk Yŏnhaphoe), 91–92.

30. *Korea Times*, 8 May 1962 and 8 January 1963.

31. Han'guk Kyoyuk Yŏn'guso, 454–457.

32. Former schoolteachers, interviews by author, Seoul, June–November 1991.

33. Chungang Taehakkyo Pusŏl Han'guk Kyoyuk Munje Yŏn'guso, *Mun'gyosa* [History of the Ministry of Education] (Seoul: Chungang Taehakkyo Pusŏl Han'guk Kyoyuk Munje Yŏn'guso, 1974), 253; Korean Commission for UNESCO, *Korean Survey*, 157–158.

34. This and similar stories were related to the author in discussions with schoolteachers active during this period.

35. Chungang Taehakkyo Pusŏl Han'guk Kyoyuk Munje Yŏn'guso, 253; Korean Commission for UNESCO, *Korean Survey*, 143.

36. Sŏul Kyoyuk T'ŭkpyŏlsi Wiwŏnhoe, *Taehan kyoyuk yŏn'gam 4288* [1955], 359.

37. Ibid., 360–361.

38. Korean Commission for UNESCO, *Korean Survey,* 153.

39. Republic of Korea, Office of Information and Research, *Korean Report* 6:98.

40. Sŏul Kyoyuk T'ŭkpyŏlsi Wiwŏnhoe, *Taehan kyoyuk yŏn'gam 4288* [1955], 370.

41. Kang Kil-su, 397; *Tonga ilbo*, 18 May 1953.

42. Kim Chong-sŏ, interview with author, Seoul, September 1991.

43. This estimate is only a rough guess based in part on the contradictory figures cited in MOE annual reports and an unpublished study cited by Kim Chong-sŏ, interview with author, Seoul, September 1991.

44. Korean Commission for UNESCO, *Korean Survey*, 126.

45. Figures from Sŏul Kyoyuk T'ŭkpyŏlsi Wiwŏnhoe: *Taehan kyoyuk yŏn'gam 4288* [1955], 359–361, and *Taehan kyoyuk yŏn'gam 4294* [1961], 347–351; and Republic of Korea, MOE, *Mun'gyo t'onggye yoram*, 336–337.

46. Edward S. Mason, Mahn Je Kim, Dwight H. Perkins, Kwang Suk Kim, and David C. Cole, *The Economic and Social Modernization of the Republic of Korea* (Cambridge, Mass.: Harvard University Press, 1980), 165–205.

47. McGinn, et al., 89–97. The question of American aid to Korea has been the subject of an extensive literature in both Korean and English. Recent Korean writers stress the negative role it had in suppressing farm incomes with cheap food aid and of either inhibiting the growth of indigenous industry or creating economically infeasible plants that were dependent on subsidized imported materials and parts. It also helped to maintain a high level of corruption, for aid profiteering was a major means by which the Liberal Party financed itself.

48. Herbert Wesley Dodge, "A History of U.S. Assistance to Korean Education: 1953–1966" (Ph.D. diss., George Washington University, 1971), 27.

49. McGinn et al., 89–98.

50. Umakoshi Toru, "Dokuritsugo ni okeru kankoku kyoiku no saiken to

amerika no kyoiku enjo" [Rebuilding Korean education after independence and U.S. educational assistance], *Han,* no. 112 (1988): 67–100.

51. Wilson, 166–225.

52. Donald K. Adams, "Educational Change and Korean Development," in G. Lim and W. Chang, eds., 376–377.

53. *Tonga ilbo,* 13 October 1948.

54. *Chosŏn ilbo,* 12 September 1953.

55. Paek Hŏn'gi, *Kyoyuk haengjŏng-hak* [Educational administration] (Seoul: Uryu Munhwasa, 1962), 359.

56. Former schoolteachers, interviews with author, Seoul, July–November 1991.

57. Barnes, 97.

58. Wilson, 198. See also Educational Planning Mission to Korea, 29.

59. Wilson, 77.

60. Cited in *Korea Times,* 20 May 1958.

61. Cornelius Osborne, *The Koreans and Their Culture* (New York: Ronald Press, 1951), 100, 103.

62. Educational Planning Mission to Korea, 105.

63. Ibid., 88.

64. Ibid., 44.

65. Ibid., 45, 128

66. Ibid., 40, 62–72.

67. Ibid., 103.

68. Ibid., 108.

69. Eul Byung Yoon, "Naejongja, Hampyong-gun, Cholla Namdo," in Mills, ed., 6–8.

70. Park Joon, "Hwasin Village," in Mills, ed., 8.

71. Baek Kyu Nam, "Napunto Village," in Mills, ed., 13.

72. Robert F. Spencer, *Yŏgong: Factory Girl* (Seoul: Royal Asiatic Society–Korean Branch, 1988).

73. Ibid., 117.

74. Clark W. Sorenson, *Over the Mountains Are Mountains: Korean Peasant Households and Their Adaptation to Rapid Industrialization* (Seattle: University of Washington Press, 1988).

75. Ibid., 267 n. 19.

76. This statement is based on the author's interviews with Koreans in 1991, 1996, and 1997.

77. McGinn et al., 180.

78. Woo brothers, interview by author, Seoul, July 1997.

79. Kim Hee-don, "The Social Mobility and the Effects of Schooling in Korea" (Ph.D. diss., Korea University, 1988).

80. Vincent Brandt, *A Korean Village, Between Mountain and Sea* (Cambridge, Mass.: Harvard University Press, 1971), 95.

81. Ibid., 95–96.

82. Lee Man-gap, interview by author, Honolulu, July 1992.

83. Ha Woo Lee [Yi Ha-u], "The Korean Polity under Syngman Rhee: An Analysis of the Culture, Structure and Elite" (Ph.D. diss., American University, 1973), 178–200; Jae Hong Cho, "Post-1945 Land Reforms and Their Consequences in South Korea" (Ph.D. diss., Indiana University, 1964).

84. Ha Woo Lee, 195–197.

85. Sung Chick Hong [Hong Sŭng-jik], "Values of Korean Farmers, Businessmen and Professors," in *International Conference on the Problems of Modernization in Asia: Report* (Seoul: Asiatic Research Center, Korea University, 1965).

86. Educational Planning Mission to Korea, 25.

87. Sŏul Kyoyuk T'ŭkpyŏlsi Wiwŏnhoe, *Taehan kyoyuk yŏn'gam 4288* [1955], 243.

88. Sŏul Kyoyuk T'ŭkpyŏlsi Wiwŏnhoe, *Taehan kyoyuk yŏn'gam 4286* [1953], 22.

89. Son In-su, *Han'guk kyoyuksa*, 2:704–705.

90. Ibid., 2:705–709.

91. This was especially the case in Pusan, where the greatest number of refugees was concentrated. In March 1951, the city of Pusan ordered tents to be set up for conducting classes. *Tonga ilbo*, 2 March 1951.

92. *Chosŏn ilbo*, 31 May 1953.

93. Ibid., 30 November 1950.

94. Son In-su, *Han'guk kyoyuksa*, 2:707.

95. Edgar S. Kennedy, *Mission to Korea* (London: Derek Verschoyle, 1952), 140; *New York Times*, 8 June 1951.

96. An Yong-hyŏn, ed., *Han'guk chŏnjaeng pisa* [Critical history of the Korean War] (Seoul: Kyŏngin Munhwasa, 1992), 515–518.

97. Ibid., 348.

98. Mr. Min, interview by author, Seoul, June 1996.

CHAPTER 4: COORDINATING EDUCATION WITH ECONOMIC PLANNING

1. Sŏul Kyoyuk T'ŭkpyŏlsi Wiwŏnhoe, *Taehan kyoyuk yŏn'gam 4294* [1961], 338–339, 342–343.

2. Chungang Taehakkyo Pusŏl Han'guk Kyoyuk Munje Yŏn'guso, 193–194.

3. Korean Commission for UNESCO, *Korean Survey*, 131.

4. Sŏul Kyoyuk T'ŭkpyŏlsi Wiwŏnhoe, *Taehan kyoyuk yŏn'gam 4293* [1960], 102–104.

5. Chungang Taehakkyo Pusŏl Han'guk Kyoyuk Munje Yŏn'guso, 194.

6. Ibid., 210.

7. Im Hanyong, "Korean Private Education," in Korean Commission for UNESCO, 379–381; Taehan Kyoyuk Yŏnhaphoe, *Taehan kyoyuksa 1947–1973,* 94.

8. Chungang Taehakkyo Pusŏl Han'guk Kyoyuk Munje Yŏn'guso, 705–706.

9. Son In-su, *Han'guk kyoyuksa*, 2:719.

10. Im Hanyong, 380–381.

11. "Toŭi kyoyuk ŭi kunbun munje" [The issue of moral education], *Sae kyoyuk* 6, 3 (June 1954): 55–62; Kukhoe Samuch'o, *Kukhoesa*, 1:1231.

12. *Tonga ilbo*, 21 October 1955.

13. Ibid., 20 February 1956 and 1 March 1956.

14. Campaigns to stop the commercialization of schools were announced in September 1956, February 1957, August 1957, and April 1959. *Tonga ilbo*, 9 September 1956, 2 February 1957, 1 August 1957, and 4 April 1959.

15. Ibid., 16 April 1957.

16. Sŏul Kyoyuk T'ŭkpyŏlsi Wiwŏnhoe, *Taehan kyoyuk yŏn'gam 4288* [1955], 120.

17. Sŏul Kyoyuk T'ŭkpyŏlsi Wiwŏnhoe, *Taehan kyoyuk yŏn'gam 4290* [1957], 280–283; Kim Jongchol [Kim Chong-ch'ŏl, *Education and Development: Some Essays and Thoughts on Korean Education*] (Seoul: Seoul National University Press, 1985), 187.

18. *Korea Times*, 13 December 1960.

19. Ibid., 31 January 1961.

20. David C. Cole and Princeton N. Lyman, *Korean Development: The Interplay of Politics and Economics* (Cambridge, Mass: Harvard University Press, 1971).

21. Jin Eun Kim [Kim Chin-ŭn], "An Analysis of the National Planning Process for Educational Development in the Republic of Korea, 1945–1970" (Ph.D. diss., Harvard University, 1975), 129.

22. The per capita income of South Korea in 1960 was only $85 a year—less than in the Philippines or Ghana and on a level with that in Pakistan and Uganda.

23. Kim Yŏng-hwa et al., 153.

24. Ibid., 154–157.

25. Republic of Korea, MOE: *Mun'gyo t'onggye yoram*, 2–5, and *Kyoyuk t'onggye yŏnbo 1966* [Statistical yearbook of education, 1966] (Seoul: Mun'gyobu, 1967), 74, 110.

26. *Korea Times*, 11 November 1962.

27. Cited in ibid., 3 February 1963.

28. Ibid., 3 October 1963.

29. Taehan Kyoyuk Yŏnhaphoe, *Han'guk kyoyuk yŏn'gam 1967–1968*, 56–57.

30. Cited in ibid., 57; *Korea Herald*, 17 January 1965.

31. *Tonga ilbo*, 30 January and 9 March 1965.

32. *Korea Herald*, 13 and 16 January 1965; *Korea Times*, 11 July 1965.

33. *Tonga ilbo*, 19 September 1965; *Korea Times*, 16 September 1965.

34. Yung Dug Lee, *Educational Innovation in the Republic of Korea* (Paris: UNESCO, 1974), 7.

35. *Korea Times*, 20 November 1966.

36. Ibid., 5 February 1964.

37. Kim Yŏng-hwa et al., 154.

38. For example, see Sung Chick Hong.

39. Robert M. Morgan and Clifton B. Chadwick, eds., *Systems Analysis for Educa-*

tional Change: The Republic of Korea (Tallahasee, Fla.: Department of Education Research, Florida State University, 1971), 5.

40. Ibid., 7.

41. Ibid., 73.

42. Kim Yŏng-hwa et al., 175.

43. Ibid., 175–177.

44. Ibid., 178.

45. Republic of Korea, MOE, *Kyoyuk kibon t'onggye* [Basic statistics on education] (Seoul: Mun'gyobu, 1974), 220.

46. Ibid., 28–29.

47. Alice Amsden, *Asia's Next Giant: South Korea and Late Industrialization* (New York: Oxford University Press, 1989), 223.

48. Ibid., 223–224.

49. Kim Yŏng-hwa et al., 231–232.

50. *Korea Times*, 4 March 1987.

51. Kim Yŏng-ch'ŏl, interview by author, Seoul, July 1997.

52. Yung Dug Lee, 14–16.

53. Cited in ibid., 16.

54. *Korea Times*, 5 December 1961. The SCNR decreed that the academic year was to begin on 1 March rather than 1 April so that the winter vacation would be shortened.

55. *Tonga ilbo,* 3 December 1961.

56. Republic of Korea, MOE, *Education in Korea 1962* (Seoul: Mun'gyobu, 1963), 11.

57. Ibid., 11–12.

58. *Korea Times*, 9 November 1961.

59. Republic of Korea, MOE, *Education in Korea 1962*, 27.

60. *Korea Times*, 6 February 1963.

61. Ibid., 18 December 1963.

62. Republic of Korea, MOE, *Education in Korea 1962,* 26.

63. *Korea Times*, 20 October 1966.

64. Republic of Korea, MOE, *Mun'gyo t'onggye yoram*, 2–5.

65. Republic of Korea, MOE, *Kyoyuk t'onggye yŏnbo 1966,* 74, 110, passim.

66. In early 1966, there were 1,136 licensed cram schools—236 in Seoul alone— plus innumerable unlicensed schools. See *Korea Times*, 12 March 1966.

67. Estimates of the size of education as a business vary considerably, but it was probably second only to agriculture in terms of money at this time.

68. Chungang Taehakkyo Pusŏl Han'guk Kyoyuk Munje Yŏn'guso, 323–326; *Tonga ilbo*, 26 June 1963.

69. *Korea Times*, 13 March 1964.

70. *Tonga ilbo*, 9 and 11 March 1965; *Korea Times*, 7 and 9 March 1965.

71. *Tonga ilbo*, 9 August and 1 September 1966.

72. Ibid., 25 May 1966.

73. *Korea Times,* 8 August and 9 September 1967.
74. *Tonga ilbo,* 11 January 1967.
75. Kim Yŏng-hwa et al., 152.
76. *Korea Times,* 18 January 1969.
77. Ibid., 21 January 1969.
78. Ibid., 22 January 1969.
79. Ibid., 11 June 1970.
80. Ibid., 15 April 1973.
81. Among this body of literature emphasizing the ability of the South Korean state to implement developmentalist policies are the following: Amsden; Stephan Haggard and Chung-in Moon, "Institutions and Economic Policy: Theory and a Korean Case Study," *World Politics* 17, 2 (January 1990): 210–237; Chalmers Johnson, "Political Institutions and Economic Performance: The Government–Business Relationship in Japan, South Korea, and Taiwan," in Deyo, ed., 136–164; Mason et al.; Joel S. Migdal, *Strong Societies and Weak States: State–Society Relations and State Capabilities in the Third World* (Princeton, N.J.: Princeton University Press, 1988). For a corrective to this view, see Koo, ed.

CHAPTER 5: THE ENTRANCE EXAMINATION SYSTEM

1. Kim Jongchol, *Education and Development,* 70.
2. Ibid., 71.
3. *Kyŏnghyang sinmun,* 27 December 1954.
4. Kim Chong-sŏ, former education official, interview by author, Seoul, October 1991. At the time, Kim worked for the MOE as an examination expert and often sat on the provincial boards of education that reviewed complaints. He recalled no case of tampering with the examinations.
5. *Tonga ilbo,* 20 November 1949.
6. Sŏul Kyoyuk T'ŭkpyŏlsi Wiwŏnhoe, *Taehan kyoyuk yŏn'gam 4290* [1957], 118.
7. Cited in *Korean Republic,* 14 November 1955.
8. A discussion of the types of exam questions used is given in Yun Tae-yong, "Chunghakkyo ipsi munje" [The problems of the middle school exam system], *Sae kyoyuk* 2, 2 (March 1949): 52–59; summaries of criticism of the exam system are given in "Ipsi munje" [The entrance exam problem], *Sae kyoyuk* 8, 2 (February 1956): 27–43, and in "Musihŏmje" [The no-exam system], *Sae kyoyuk* 11, 5 (May 1959): 8–30.
9. "Musihŏmje," 22–26; *Han'guk ilbo,* 1 October 1954.
10. Si-joung Yu, "Educational Institutions," in Man-gap Lee and Barringer, eds., 423–453.
11. Ibid., 430–431.
12. Ibid., 427.
13. Ibid., 442.

14. Republic of Korea, CERI, "A Study for Solving the Problems of Compulsory Education" (Seoul: CERI, 1967), 34.

15. Ibid., 33.

16. Ibid.

17. Myung Han Kim, "The Educational Policy-Making Process in the Republic of Korea: A Systems Analysis" (Ph.D. diss., North Texas State University, 1974), 89.

18. *Korea Times*, 4 February 1957.

19. Ibid., 5 March 1957.

20. Ibid., 23 April 1959.

21. *Kyŏnghyang sinmun,* 29 January 1967; *Chungang ilbo*, 21 February 1967.

22. *Kyŏnghyang sinmun,* 29 January 1967.

23. *Korea Times*, 15 March 1968.

24. *Han'guk ilbo*, 8 January 1966.

25. *Korea Times*, 14 January 1966.

26. Ibid., 15 June 1966.

27. *Tonga ilbo*, 31 March 1957.

28. *Korea Times*, 6 June 1966.

29. Ibid., 11 February 1969.

30. Ibid., 6 and 9 March 1969.

31. Ibid., 15 July 1969.

32. Ibid., 27 August 1969.

33. Ibid., 15 January 1971.

34. Ibid., 3 February 1972.

35. Ibid., 5 August 1961.

36. Ibid., 23 November 1961.

37. Details of these reforms are given in a National Institute of Educational Evaluation study: Yi Chin-jae et al., *Uri nara sihŏm chedo ŭi p'yŏnch'ŏnsa* [The history of the change in Korean school entrance examination systems] (Seoul: Chungang Kyoyuk P'yŏngkawŏn, 1986).

38. Hwang Ŭn-yuk, "Ipsi-pŏp ŭi chindan kwa haekyŏl ch'ak ŭl wihan mosaek" [The evil influence of the entrance examinations and its solutions], *Sae kʸoyuk* 20, 4 (April 1968): 47–54.

39. *Chosŏn ilbo*, 22 January 1969.

40. Yi Chin-jae et al., 34–38.

41. Information is based on Republic of Korea, MOE, *Kyoyuk t'onggye yŏnbo*, 1970, 1971, 1975, 1976, 1980.

42. *Chosŏn ilbo*, 25 January 1976.

43. Ibid.

44. Ibid., 28 October 1967.

45. Ibid., 30 October 1967.

46. *Korea Times*, 29 October 1967.

47. Ibid., 13 August 1967.

48. Ibid., 12 October 1967.

49. Ibid., 29 and 31 October 1967.

50. Ibid., 17 March 1968.

51. *Han'guk ilbo* in the *Korea Times,* 30 April 1968.

52. Cited in *Korea Times,* 16 July 1968.

53. Ibid., 8 February 1969.

54. Ibid., 14 February 1969.

55. Kim Jongchol, "Impact and Problems of the Middle School No-Examination Admission Policy," *Korea Journal* 11, 10 (May 1971): 4–7.

56. Ibid., 6.

57. Bu Kwon Park, "The State, Class and Educational Policy: A Study of South Korea's High School Equalization Policy" (Ph.D. diss., University of Wisconsin–Madison, 1988), 2–5.

58. Ibid., 6–7.

59. *Korea Times*, 9 September and 2 October 1968.

60. Kim Ch'ong-su, "Chibang chunghaksaeng ŭi sŏul chŏnip e kwanhan yŏn'gu" [Study of middle school transfer students in Seoul] (Master's thesis, Yonsei University, 1976), 86–88.

61. Ibid., 65.

62. *Korea Times*, 6 February 1971.

63. Ibid., 3 April 1971.

64. Ibid., 9 February 1972.

65. Ibid., 29 March 1974.

66. Ibid., 28 June 1974.

67. Yi Chin-jae et al., 223.

68. *Korea Herald*, 23 July 1980.

69. Yi Chin-jae et al., 231.

70. Kwak Byong-sun, "Examination Hell in Korea Revisited: An External Malady in Education?" *Koreana* 5, 2 (1991): 45–55.

71. Yi Chin-jae et al., 223–247; author interviews with educators, Seoul, summer 1997.

72. Cited in Bu Kwon Park, 82.

73. Yi Chin-jae et al., 248–251.

74. Taehan Kyoyuk Yŏnhaphoe, *Han'guk kyoyuk yŏn'gam 1981–1982*, 26.

75. *Sŏul sinmun*, 10 October 1980.

76. *Korea Newsreview*, 21 February 1981, 11.

77. Cited in ibid., 8 January 1983, 15.

78. Ibid., 27 August 1983, 4.

79. *Korea Times*, 15 January 1987.

80. Kim Yŏng-hwa et al., 207.

81. *Korea Newsreview*, 20 February 1982, 20.

82. Kim Yŏng-ch'ŏl et al., *Kodŭng hakkyo p'yŏngjunhwa chŏngch'aek ŭi kaesŏn pangan* [Plans for the reform of the high school equalization policy] (Seoul: Han'guk Kyoyuk Kaebalwŏn, 1996), 71.

83. Bu Kwon Park, 209–210.

84. Ibid., 81–82.

85. McGinn et al., 88–90.

86. Kim Yŏng-hwa, *Han'guk ŭi kyoyuk pul p'yŏngdŭng* [Education and inequality in Korea], (Seoul: Kyoyuk Kwahaksa, 1993), 158–159, 208–209.

87. Yi Chŏng-sik, *Haksaeng undongsa* [History of the student movement] (Seoul: Tosŏ Ch'ulp'ansa, 1993), 318.

88. Kim Yŏng-hwa et al., 259–261.

89. Byong-sun Kwak, 49–50.

90. *Korea Newsreview*, 4 June 1988, 29.

91. Ibid., 13 January 1990, 30.

92. Cited in *Korea Times*, 10 June 1988.

93. *Korea Newsreview*, 26 October 1991, 7.

94. Ibid., 28 December 1991, 34.

95. Ibid., 27 January 1996, 34.

96. Taehan Kyoyuk Yŏnhaphoe, *Han'guk kyoyuk yŏn'gam 1992*, 32.

97. *Korea Times*, 21 July 1996.

98. *Korea Herald*, 29 April and 17 June 1994.

99. Han'guk Kyoyuk Kaebalwŏn, *Research Abstracts 1996* (Seoul: Han'guk Kyoyuk Kaebalwŏn, 1996), 5–6.

100. *Korea Herald,* 26 April 1998.

101. Students volunteered for community service to improve their chances for college entrance, but they spent only about eighteen hours a year on it, much less than planners had anticipated. *Korea Times,* 3 November 1998.

102. *Korea Herald*, 22 October 1998.

103. Ibid.

104. *Korea Newreview*, 29 August 1998, 34.

105. Ibid., 17 October 1998, 32.

106. Ibid., 19 November 1994, 10–11.

107. Author interview with monks, Seoul, August 1997.

108. *Korea Times*, 9 November 1999.

109. *Korea Herald,* 13 November 1999.

110. Belief in the inevitability of examination competition was widely held in the 1990s by educational experts such as Im Hyŏng and Kim Chin-gyu, officials at the MOE, National Institute of Educational Evaluation (Kungnip Kyoyuk P'yŏngkawŏn). Interviews by author, Seoul, May 1996.

CHAPTER 6: THE COSTS OF EDUCATIONAL ZEAL

1. McGinn et al., 15–27.

2. Republic of Korea, MOE, *Mun'gyo t'onggye yoram*, 344–345; Adams, "Educational Change," 375.

3. Republic of Korea, MOE, *Mun'gyo t'onggye yoram*, 344–345.

4. Kun Pyung Kang, "The Role of Local Government in Community Development in Korea" (Ph.D. diss., University of Minnesota, 1966), 206–207.

5. Kukhoe Samuch'o, *Kukhoesa*, 2:91.

6. Jung-en Woo, *Race to the Swift: State and Finance in Korean Industrialization* (New York: Columbia University Press, 1991), 81.

7. W. D. Reeve, *The Republic of Korea: A Political and Economic Study* (London: Oxford University Press, 1963), 78–79; Roy Bahl, Chuk Kyo Kim, and Chong Kee Park, *Public Finances during the Korean Modernization Process* (Cambridge, Mass.: Harvard University Press, 1986), 48–49, 106–107; Kun Pyung Kang, passim.

8. Han'guk Hyŏngmyŏng Chaep'ansa P'yonch'an Wiwŏnhoe, *Han'guk hyŏngmyŏng chaep'ansa* [History of the Korean Revolutionary Tribunal] (Seoul: Han'guk Hyŏngmyŏng Chaep'ansa P'yŏnch'an Wiwŏnhoe, 1962), 3:1078.

9. *Korea Times*, 3 September 1959.

10. These figures are based on contemporary newspaper reports and estimates given by interviewees. For example, one former vice-principal of a middle school in South Chŏlla Province estimated that about 20 percent of his school's budget came from the PTA fees. Ch'oe Myŏng-suk, interview with author, Seoul, September 1991.

11. Republic of Korea, MOE, *Mun'gyo kaeyo*, 305, 310, 318.

12. Im Hanyong, 383.

13. Because of the informal methods of collecting money and the lack of reliable statistics, these figures are a matter of guesswork. The figure of 30 percent is derived from interviews and from contemporary reports in the press, and it seems to be the most generous but still plausible figure.

14. For one example, see *Tonga ilbo*, 3 June 1949.

15. *Han'guk ilbo*, 6 August 1958.

16. Ch'oe Myŏng-suk, interview by author, Seoul, September 1991.

17. *Kyŏnghyang sinmun*, 26 May 1957; *Sŏul sinmun*, 30 May 1957; *Han'guk ilbo*, 6 June 1957.

18. Im Hanyong, 386.

19. Tan'guk Samsipnyŏnsahoe, *Tan'guk samsipnyŏnsa* [Thirty-year history of Tan'guk] (Seoul: Tan'guk Taehakkyo, 1978), 4, 11.

20. Kŏn'guk Taehakkyo Kyoji P'yŏnch'an Wiwŏnhoe, *Kŏn'guk taehakkyo kyoji jeijip* [Collection of school records of Kŏn'guk University] (Seoul: Kŏn'guk Taehakkyo Ch'ulp'anbu, 1971).

21. Kungmin Taehakkyo Samsipnyŏnsa P'yŏnch'an Wiwŏnhoe, *Kungmin taehakkyo samsipnyŏnsa* [Thirty-year history of Kungmin University] (Seoul: Kungmin Taehakkyo Ch'ulp'ansa, 1976), 64–70.

22. Carter Eckert, *Offspring of Empire* (Seattle: University of Washington Press, 1991), 336.

23. Kyŏnghŭi Isipnyŏn P'yŏnch'an Wiwŏnhoe, *Kyŏnghŭi isipnyŏn* [Twenty years of Kyunghee University] (Seoul: Kyŏnghŭi Taehakkyo Ch'ulp'ansa, 1969).

24. Tonga Taehakkyo, *Tonga hakkyo samsipnyŏnsa, 1948–1978* [Thirty-year history of Tonga University, 1948–1978] (Pusan: Tonga Taehakkyo Ch'ulp'ansa, 1976).

25. Hanyang Hagwon P'yŏnch'an Wiwŏnhoe, *Hanyang hagwŏn osipnyŏnsa* [Fifty-year history of the Hanyang Educational Foundation] (Seoul: Hanyang Taehakkyo Ch'ulp'ansa, 1989); Yi Kwang-ho, "Han'guk kyoyuk ch'eje chaep'yŏn ŭi kujojŏk t'ŭksŏng e kwanhan yŏn'gu, 1945–1955" [Study of the special characteristics of the reorganization of Korean education, 1945–1955] (Master's thesis, Yonsei University, 1990).

26. This view is expressed in the press and also by most Koreans active in education and interviewed by author, Seoul, June–November 1991.

27. Estimated amounts invested in the *chaedan* vary considerably, and there does not appear to be any systematic study to confirm any of these figures.

28. Yi Kwang-ho, 124. The founders included Protestant ministers, university professors, lawyers, bureaucrats, businessmen, journalists, and an oriental herb doctor. People from these professions were likely to be landowners.

29. Kim Jongchol, *Education and Development,* 184–186.

30. Ibid., 148–149.

31. Cited in ibid., 181.

32. Kukhoe Samuch'o, *Kukhoe sokkirok,* 25 November 1949, 1163.

33. *Tonga ilbo,* 8 October 1953.

34. Ibid., 9 April 1954.

35. Yi Kwang-ho, 70.

36. Cited in *Korea Times,* 7 January 1965.

37. Republic of Korea, MOE, *Kyoyuk t'onggye yŏnbo 1975.*

38. *Korea Times,* 13 and 15 January 1967.

39. Ibid., 20 December 1975.

40. Ibid., 11 July 1967.

41. Ibid., 22 and 26 October and 25 December 1963.

42. *Han'guk ilbo,* 26 October 1966.

43. *Tonga ilbo,* 6 August 1969; *Chosŏn ilbo,* 8 August 1969; *Han'guk ilbo,* 8 August 1969.

44. The term *yuksŏnghoe* more literally translates as "educational support association" but was generally called PTA in English.

45. Republic of Korea, MOE, *Education in Korea 1972,* 28; *Korea Times,* 17 January 1970.

46. McGinn et al., 71.

47. *Korea Times,* 23 March 1975.

48. Ibid., 4 March 1975.

49. Si-joung Yu, 433.

50. *Korea Times,* 7 February 1970.

51. Ibid., 13 July 1969.

52. Ibid., 14 May 1977.

53. Bae Chong-keun, "Education Top Reason behind Rapid Growth: Schooling

for Economic Takeoff," *Koreana* 5, 2 (July 1991): 58. UNESCO estimated that in 1963 fees alone cost the average household with two children in school between 5 and 30 percent of its income, depending on the level of education. This does not account for private tutoring, educational taxes, and books. UNESCO, *Long-Term Projections for Education in the Republic of Korea* (Bangkok: UNESCO Regional Office for Education in Asia, 1965).

54. Taehan Kyoyuk Yŏnhaphoe, *Han'guk kyoyuk yŏn'gam 1981–1982*, 38.

55. Han'guk Kyoyuk Chaejŏng Kyŏngje Hakhoe, *Kwaoe wa sa kyoyukpi* [Tutoring and private educational fees], April report (Seoul: Han'guk Kyoyuk Chaejŏng Kyŏngje Hakhoe, 1997), 8.

56. *Korea Times*, 2 March 1988.

57. Ibid., 24 and 25 February 1988.

58. *Korea Newsreview*, 4 February 1995, 12; *Korea Herald*, 24 January 1995.

59. *Korea Herald*, 4 June 1993.

60. Author interview with Kim Yŏng-ch'ŏl, Seoul, July 1997.

61. *Korea Herald*, 1 September 1998.

62. *Korea Times* , 2 April and 13 May 1999.

63. *Korea Herald*, 22 July 1994 and 3 May 1995.

64. Han'guk Kyoyuk Chaejŏng Kyŏngje Hakhoe, June report, 8, 35.

65. Ibid., 34.

66. *Korea Newsreview*, 12 September 1998, 14.

67. *Korea Times*, 19 January 1999.

68. Ibid., 6 August 1997.

69. *Korea Newsreview*, 31 August 1996, 10.

70. Ibid., 17 June 1995, 5.

71. Ibid., 30 March 1996, 4.

72. Ibid., 10 June 1995, 5.

73. Ibid.

74. *Korea Times*, 13 June 2000; *Korea Herald*, 29 April and 3 May 2000.

75. *Korea Times*, 22 May 1999.

CHAPTER 7: EDUCATION AND STATE CONTROL

1. Kukhoe Samuch'o, *Kukhoe sokkirok*, 28 October 1948, 669.

2. Ibid., 29 October 1948, 689.

3. George McCune and Arthur L. Grey, Jr., *Korea Today* (Cambridge, Mass.: Harvard University Press, 1950), 243.

4. Cumings, *Origins of the Korean War*, 2:217.

5. Cited in McCune and Grey, 243.

6. *Tonga ilbo*, 8 December 1948; cited in John Kie-chiang Oh, *Korea: Democracy on Trial* (Ithaca, N.Y.: Cornell University Press, 1968), 110.

7. Chŏng Mi-suk, "Han'guk mun'gyo chŏngch'aek ŭi kyoyuk inyŏn kusŏng e kwanhan kyoyuk sahoe hakchŏk punsŏk , 1948–1953" [Educational and social analysis of Korean educational structure and ideology, 1948–1953] (Master's thesis, Yonsei University, 1987).

8. *Tonga ilbo*, 17 March 1949.

9. Ibid.

10. Han'guk Kyoyuk Sipnyŏnsa Kanhaenghoe, 126.

11. Chungang Hakto Hoguktan, *Hakto hoguktan sipnyŏnji* [Ten-year record of the Student Defense Corps] (Seoul: Chungang Hakto Hoguktan, 1959), 89–93.

12. Ibid., 251–254.

13. Ibid., 107.

14. Cited in Korean Commission for UNESCO, *Korean Survey*, 116.

15. Hong Ung-sŏn, 210.

16. Chungang Hakto Hoguktan, 254; Sŏul Kyoyuk T'ŭkpyŏlsi Wiwŏnhoe, *Taehan kyoyuk yŏn'gam 4288* [1955], 370.

17. After 1938 military training and student mobilization drives were universal in colonial Korean schools.

18. Kim Tong-gil, "Minjok minjujuŭi ranŭn inyŏm" [The educational ideology known as democratic nationalism], *Sae kyoyuk* 13, 2 (1964): 12; former schoolteachers, interviews with author, Seoul, June–November 1991.

19. Paek Nak-chun, 57.

20. Chŏng Mi-suk, 39.

21. Chungang Hakto Hoguktan, 254.

22. *Korean Republic*, 10 and 11 August 1954; *Tonga ilbo*, 10 August 1954.

23. *Korean Republic*, 24 September 1954.

24. Ibid., 28 November 1954.

25. Ibid., 11 August and 9 October 1954. During the Korean War Generals Mac-Arthur and Mark Clark issued a maritime demarcation line varying from 60 to 170 miles off the Korean coastline to prevent Communist infiltration. After the July 1953 cease-fire Rhee reimposed this line to protect Korean fisheries and seized many Japanese fishing boats. The dispute was compounded by the Japanese claim to Tokto (Takeshima) Island, which Koreans traditionally regarded as theirs. See Reeve, 54–60.

26. *Chosŏn ilbo*, 17 February 1950.

27. Son In-su, "Yŏktae mun'gyo changgwan ŭi chuyo sich'aek kwa ŏpchŏk" [An outline of achievements and policies of successive ministers of education], *Kyoyuk p'yŏngnon*, no. 2 (1972): 70–75.

28. Ibid., 75.

29. Chungang Hakto Hoguktan, 120.

30. Ibid.

31. Former schoolteachers, interviews with author, Seoul, July–November 1991.

32. Kim Hak-chun, *"Taegu maeil sinmun* p'isŭp sagŏn" [The *Taegu maeil sinmun* attack incident], in Chŏn Tok-kyu et al., 432–436.

33. Kukhoe Samuch'o, *Kukhoe sokkirok*, 27 October 1955, 3–9.

34. Yi Hae-sŏng, T'ongch'i ch'eje ŭi musun gwa hakkyo kyoyuk ŭi chŏngch'i sahoehwa kinŭng" [Contradictions in the political system and the ability to politically socialize school education] (Ph.D. diss., Yonsei University, 1987), 109–110.

35. *Korea Times*, 2 June 1959.

36. *Tonga ilbo*, 2 June 1959.

37. *Korea Times*, 3 June 1959; Kim Yŏng-don, educator, interview by author, Seoul, July and September 1991.

38. *Korean Republic*, 3 July 1954.

39. Ibid., 9 July 1954.

40. Ibid., 2 February 1955.

41. *Tonga ilbo*, 17 December 1957; Ch'oe Myŏng-suk, interview with author, Seoul, September 1991.

42. *Korean Republic*, 12 December 1958.

43. *Chosŏn ilbo*, 10 and 23 May 1966.

44. *Han'guk ilbo*, 31 August 1966; translated in *Korea Times*, same day.

45. *Korea Times*, 2 February 1968; *Korea Herald*, 14 February 1968.

46. *Korea Times*, 7 and 19 July 1962.

47. Ibid., 24 February 1971; author interviews with former teachers and students, Seoul, summer 1991 and summer 1996.

48. *Korea Herald*, 6 August 1971.

49. *Korea Times*, 18 January 1972.

50. Republic of Korea, MOE, *Mun'gyo sasimnyŏnsa* [Forty-year history of the Ministry of Education] (Seoul: Mun'gyobu, 1988), 249.

51. *Chosŏn ilbo*, 9 February 1969.

52. *Korea Times*, 18 January 1972.

53. Ibid., 25 June 1974.

54. Ibid., 3 July 1975.

55. Son In-su, *Han'guk kyoyuk undongsa* [History of the Korean educational movement] (Seoul: Munŭmsa, 1994), 188.

56. *Korea Times*, 3 September 1976.

57. Taehan Kyoyuk Yŏnhaphoe, *Han'guk kyoyuk yŏn'gam 1977*, 63.

58. *Sŏul sinmun*, 4 September 1976.

59. *Korea Times*, 2 and 3 September 1977.

60. Sung Jae Park, "Physical Education and Sport as an Instrument of Nation Building in the Republic of Korea" (Ph.D. diss., Ohio State University, 1974), 114–116.

61. Reprinted in *Korea Times*, 11 May 1974.

62. Son In-su, *Han'guk kyoyuk undongsa*, 172–173.

63. Yi Hae-sŏng, "T'ongch'i ch'eje ŭi musun gwa hakkyo kyoyuk ŭichŏngch'i sahoehwa kinŭng," 74–80.

64. Yi Hae-sŏng, "1950 nyŏndae ŭi kukka kwalyŏk kwa kyoyuk kwa hakkyo kyoyuk: Saeroŭn iron chongnip ŭl wihan nonjaeng koridŭl" [National authority in

the 1950s and education], in *Han'guk kyoyuk-ŭi hyŏndankye* [Current stage of Korean education], ed. Kim Sin-il et al. (Seoul: Kyoyuk Kwahaksa, 1990), 104–105.

65. *Korean Republic*, 6 May 1954.

66. Ibid., 18 June 1955.

67. Chungang Hakto Hoguktan, 268.

68. *Korean Republic*, 26 March 1955.

69. Ibid., 30 November 1955.

70. Published in *Mun'gyo ilbo*, July 1957; cited in Yi Hae-sŏng, "T'ongch'i ch'eje ŭi musun gwa hakkyo kyoyuk ŭichŏngch'i sahoehwa kinŭng," 63. Translated by Yi Che-gyŏng.

71. Chŏng Yŏng-su et al., *Han'guk kyoyuk chŏngch'aek ŭinyŏn yŏn'gu 1960–1979* [An examination of educational ideals in major educational policies in Korea], 3 vols. (Seoul: Han'guk Kyoyuk Kaebalwŏn, 1986), 1:66.

72. Sŏul Taehakkyo Sabŏm Taehale, *Chung hakkyo kyoyuk* [Middle school ethics] (Seoul: Sŏul Taehakkyo Sabŏm Taehale, 1995). The word *chuch'e* (or *juche*, self-reliance) in the textbooks is the same term used to label the ideology of the North Korean state as expounded by Kim Il-sung.

73. Kim Sŏng-jin, *Ch'oesin ilban sahoe* [General social studies] (Seoul: Minju Segwan, 1974); Sŏ Ton'gak, *Chŏngch'i-kyŏngje* [Politics and economics] (Seoul: Pŏpmunsa, 1974).

74. Sŏng Chŏng-a, "Kodŭng hakkyo kuksa kyogwasŏ ŭi ch'eji wa naeyong punsŏk yŏn'gu" [The study and analysis of the content and structure of Korean high school history textbooks (Master's thesis, Ewha University, 1993), 20.

75. *Korea Times*, 19 August 1973.

76. Ibid., 1 January 1973.

77. Republic of Korea, MOE, *Education in Korea 1977*, 31.

78. Republic of Korea, MOE, *Education in Korea 1978*, 32.

79. Taehan Kyoyuk Yŏnhaphoe, *Han'guk kyoyuk yŏn'gam 1974*, 286.

80. Republic of Korea, MOE, *Education in Korea 1971*, 10.

81. Kim Sŏng-jin, 9–30.

82. *Korea Times*, 24 May 1973.

83. Educational Planning Mission to Korea, 102.

84. O Ch'ŏn-sŏk in *Sae kyoyuk* 8, 9 (September 1956): 49.

85. Han'guk Hyŏngmyŏng Chaep'ansa P'yŏnch'an Wiwŏnhoe, 3:1077–1078; former schoolteachers, interviews by author, Seoul, June–November 1991.

86. *Korea Times*, 14 April 1959 and 16 January 1960.

87. Yi Hae-sŏng, "1950 nyŏndae ŭi kukka kwalyŏk kwa kyoyuk kwa hakkyo kyoyuk," 105.

88. *Korea Times*, 19 March 1959.

89. *Tonga ilbo*, 19 March 1959.

90. *Korea Times*, 19 May 1960.

91. Sung-joo Han [Han Sŏng-ju], *The Failure of Democracy in South Korea* (Berkeley: University of California Press, 1974), 191.

92. See Duke.

93. *Tonga ilbo*, 10 June 1961.

94. *Korea Times*, 20 January 1971.

95. Ibid.

96. Ibid., 12 and 17 February and 9 March 1976.

97. Kim Jongchol, "Higher Education Policies in Korea," *Korea Journal* 23, 10 (October 1983): 7.

98. Shin Bok Kim, "Educational Policy Changes in Korea: Ideology and Praxis," in G. Lim and W. Chang, eds., 397.

99. Chung Tai-si, "Problems Facing the Enhancement of the Status of Teachers in Korea," *Korea Journal* 6, 7 (July 1966): 15.

100. *Korea Times*, 16 May 1968.

101. Yu Sang Duk [Yu Sang-dŏk]. "Korean Teachers' Struggle for Education Reform," unpublished paper, March 1996, 5.

102. *Korea Times*, 14 July 1956.

103. *Han'guk ilbo,* 7 July 1956.

104. Taehan Kyoyuk Yŏnhaphoe, *Taehan kyoyuksa 1947–1973,* 137–140.

105. *Korea Times*, 7 October 1961.

106. Kim Kyu-taik, "Decision Making in an Inter-Departmental Conflict: The Case of the Revival of Educational Autonomy in Korea," in *Inter-Group Conflicts and Political Decision Making in Korea* (Seoul: Social Science Research Institute, Yonsei University, 1968), 61–65.

107. *Korea Times,* 5 January 1980.

108. Cho Chang-Hyun, "The Politics of Local Self-Government in South Korea," in *Korean Public Administration and Policy in Transition*, ed. Kwang-woong Kim and Yong-duck Jung (Seoul: Jangwon Publishing, 1993), 1:229–235.

109. Taehan Kyoyuk Yŏnhaphoe, *Han'guk kyoyuk yŏn'gam 1981–1982,* 15; *Korea Times*, 20 February 1980.

110. Cited in *Korea Newsreview*, 3 May 1980, 8.

111. Taehan Kyoyuk Yŏnhaphoe, *Han'guk kyoyuk yŏn'gam 1981–1982,* 16.

112. *Korea Newsreview*, 10 May 1980, 10; educators, interviews by author, Seoul, summer 1997.

113. Educators, interviews by author, Seoul, summer 1997; *Korea Herald*, 4 April 1980.

114. Taehan Kyoyuk Yŏnhaphoe, *Han'guk kyoyuk yŏn'gam 1981–1982*, 18.

115. Ibid., 19; *Korea Herald*, 2 May 1980.

116. Taehan Kyoyuk Yŏnhaphoe, *Han'guk kyoyuk yŏn'gam 1981–1982*, 19; *Korea Times*, 3 and 4 May 1980.

117. Cited in *Tonga ilbo*, 8 May 1980.

118. Ibid., 9 May 1980; *Korea Herald*, 9 May 1980.

119. *Korea Herald*, 16 May 1980.

120. *Korea Times,* 17 and 18 May 1980.

121. *Korea Herald*, 5 August 1980.
122. Chŏng Yŏng-su et al., 3:191–192.
123. *Korea Newsreview*, 10 January 1981, 12.
124. Kim Yŏng-hwa et al., 185.
125. Ibid., 210–212.
126. *Korea Times*, 2 March 1988.
127. *Korea Newsreview*, 5 November 1983, 23, and 31 December 1983, 5.
128. Ibid., 4 February 1984, 5, and 18 February 1984, 5.
129. Ibid., 24 March 1984, 4.

CHAPTER 8: DEMOCRATIZATION, PROSPERITY, AND EDUCATIONAL CHANGE

1. See Kenneth M. Wells, ed., *South Korea's Minjung Movement* (Honolulu: University of Hawai'i Press, 1995), 4–23.
2. Namhee Lee, "The South Korean Student Movement, 1980–1987," *Chicago Occasional Papers on Korea* 6, 6 (1994): 204–225; Seongyi Yun, "Contributions and Limitations of Student Movement in South Korea Democratization, 1980–1987," *Korea Observer* 3, 3 (Autumn 1999): 487–506; Han Yŏng, *80nyŏndae han'guk sahoe wa haksaeng undong* [Korean society and student movements in the 1980s] (Seoul: Chungnyunsa, 1989), 23–29.
3. Kim In-hoe et al., "Han'guk kyoyuk 1980 nyŏndae ŭi kwamok" [Topics for Korean education in the 1980s], *Sae kyoyuk* 32, 1 (January 1980): 24–55.
4. *Korea Times*, 1 March 1987.
5. Yu Sang Duk, 6.
6. Yi Chang-wŏn, "80nyŏndae ŭi kyosa undong" [The 1980s teachers' movement], in *Minjung kyoyuk* [Minjung education], ed. Kim Chin'gyŏng et al., 113–115 (Seoul: P'urŭn Namu, 1988).
7. Ibid., 118–119.
8. This of course is only an estimate; it is based on both union and MOE reports.
9. Kim Yŏng-hwa et al., 259–262
10. This statement is based on author's conversations with teachers and educators, Seoul, May–June 1996 and July 1997.
11. Kim Kyŏng-sŏng, interview with author, Seoul, June 1996.
12. William Boyer and Nancy E. Boyer, "Democratization of South Korea's National Universities," *Korea Studies* 15 (1991): 87–90.
13. Kim Yŏng-hwa et al., 230–231.
14. *Korea Herald*, 23 April 1995.
15. Ibid., 2 December 1995.
16. Ibid., 5 February 1995.
17. Ibid., 15 December 1995.

18. Sŏul Taehakkyo Sabŏm Taehak; Kang Sang-gyun et al., *Kodŭng hakkyo sahoe munhwa* [High school society and culture] (Seoul: Tusan Tonga, 1995); Ch'oe Hyŏn-sŏp et al., *Kodŭng hakkyo sahoe munhwa* [High school society and culture] (Seoul: Hansaem Ch'ulp'an, 1995); Republic of Korea, MOE, *Kodŭng hakkyo kyoryŏn* [High school ethics] (Seoul: Mun'gyubu, 1995).

19. *Korea Herald*, 1 September 1994.

20. *Korea Newsreview*, 10 September 1994, 12.

21. *Korea Herald*, 13 May 1995.

22. Kang Mu-sŏp et al., *Kyoyuk ŭi sekyehwa kusang* [Envisioning globalized education in Korea] (Seoul: Han'guk Kyoyuk Kaebalwŏn, 1995), 12.

23. *Korea Herald*, 26 July 1999.

24. OECD, *Reviews of National Policies for Education: Korea* (Paris: OECD, 1998).

25. *Korea Herald*, 13 April 1998.

26. *Korea Newsreview*, 1 June 1996, 13; Kim Heung-ju, "Korea's Obsession with Private Tutoring," *Korea Focus* 8, 5 (September–October 2000): 76–89.

27. Cited in OECD, 31, 53–61.

28. *Korea Newsreview*, 7 March 1999, 14–15.

29. Ibid., 9 April 1999, 10.

30. Choong Soon Kim, *The Culture of Korean Industry: An Ethnography of Poongsan Corporation* (Tucson: University of Arizona Press, 1992), 77.

31. Republic of Korea, National Statistical Office, *Statistical Indicators in Korea 1995* (Seoul: National Statistical Office, 1995), 50.

32. Paul Morris, "Asia's Four Little Tigers: A Comparison of the Role of Education in Their Development," *Comparative Education* 37, 1 (March 1996): 95–109; for comparisons with other East Asian nations, see World Bank, *The East Asian Miracle: Economic Growth and Public Policy* (Oxford: Oxford University Press, 1993), and Morris and Sweeting, eds., 244–258.

33. *Korea Times*, 12 April 1996.

34. Im Hyŏng and Kim Chin'gyu, MOE examination officials, interviews by author, Seoul, 1996.

35. *Korea Times*, 1 January 1996; author's interviews with education officials, Seoul, summer 1997.

36. *Korea Herald*, 4 October 1994.

37. Ibid., 27 January 1995.

38. Yu Sang-duk, vice-president of Chŏn'kyojo, interview by author, Seoul, June 1996.

39. OECD, 32–33.

40. Han'guk Kyoyuk Kaebalwŏn, *Research Abstracts 1996*, 5–6; author interview with Sŏng Kyŏng-hŭi, Seoul, July 1997.

41. *Korea Herald*, 20 August 1999.

42. Republic of Korea, MOE, *Kyoyuk t'onggye yŏnbo 1996*.

43. *Korea Newsreview*, 5 November 1996, 11.

44. Ibid., 1 November 1997, 32–33.

45. *Korea Herald*, 10 September 1994.

46. *Korea Times*, 21 January 1997.

47. Republic of Korea, MOE, *Kyoyuk t'onggye yŏnbo 1996.*

48. Han'guk Kyoyuk Kaebalwŏn, *Han'guk ŭi kyoyuk chip'yo* [Index of Korean education] (Seoul: Han'guk Kyoyuk Kaebalwŏn, 1996), 20–23.

49. Geir Helgesen, *Democracy and Authority in Korea: The Cultural Dimension in Korean Politics* (New York: St. Martin's Press, 1998), 150.

50. *Korea Newsreview*, 12 September 1998, 13.

51. Ibid., 20 March 1999, 22.

52. Chon Sun Ihm, "South Korean Education," in Morris and Sweeting, eds., 140–143; *Korea Newsreview*, 15 June 1996, 24–25.

53. *Korea Herald*, 2 February and 12 October 1995.

54. This statement is based in part on author interviews with Koreans in 1996 and 1997; their stories of families pooling resources to help each other achieve as prestigious a degree as possible were similar to those of earlier generations.

55. Han'guk Kyoyuk Kaebalwŏn, *Han'guk ŭi kyoyuk chip'yo,* 21–22.

56. Sung Chul Yang, "South Korea's Top Bureaucratic Elites, 1948–1973: Their Recruitment Patterns and Modal Characteristics," *Korea Journal* 34, 4 (Autumn 1994): 8–19.

57. Choong Soon Kim, 88–89, 103–109.

58. OECD, 27.

59. Denise Potrzeba Lett, *In Pursuit of Status* (Cambridge, Mass.: Harvard University Press, 1998), 207–212.

60. See Sung Chick Hong; see also Solomon Rettig and Benjamin Pasamanick, "Moral Codes of American and Korean University Students," *Journal of Social Psychology* 50 (1959): 65–73; Kim Ki-ok, "Kajŏng kyosa wa pumo wa kyosa" [Tutors, parents, and teachers], *Sae kyoyuk* 15, 11 (November 1963): 85–91; Lee Man-gap, interview by author, Honolulu, 1992; Lett, 161.

61. David Ashton, Francis Green, Donna James, and Johnny Sung, *Education and Training for Development in East Asia: The Political Economy of Skill Formation in East Asian Newly Industrialized Economies* (London: Routledge, 1999), 57–58.

62. Han'guk Kyoyuk Kaebalwŏn, *Han'guk ŭi kyoyuk chip'yo*, 20–23.

63. See Helgesen; see also Doh C. Shin, *Mass Politics and Culture in Democratizing Korea* (New York: Cambridge University Press, 1999); Larry Diamond and Byung-Kook Kim, eds., *Consolidating Democracy in South Korea* (Boulder, Colo.: Lynne Rienner, 2000).

64. Shin, 260–261.

65. Helgesen, 248.

66. *Korea Newsreview*, 7 January 1995, 28.

67. See introduction.

68. For a summary of Japan's educational problems and reforms see Christopher P.

Hood, *Japanese Education Reform: Nakasone's Legacy* (London: Routledge, 2001). Japan, which had laid the foundations of South Korea's educational system, shared many of its problems, such as the excessive focus on examinations, the expense of private lessons and tutoring, a lack of flexibility in the centrally regulated education system, concern for prestigious degrees, and an emphasis on memorization instead of independent and creative thinking.

69. These are briefly outlined in Sunhyuk Kim, "Civil Society in South Korea: From Grand Democracy Movements to Petty Interest Groups?" *Journal of Northeast Asian Studies* (Summer 1996): 81–97, and Yong Rae Kim, "Emerging Civil Society in the Development of Interest Group Politics in Korea," *Korea Observer* 30, 2 (Summer 1999): 247–268.

70. Cited in Francis Fukuyama, "Falling Global Trends and U.S. Civil Society," *Harvard International Review,* Winter 1997/1998, 60–64.

71. *Korea Herald,* 17 June 1998.

72. Ibid., 29 October 1998.

73. Ibid., 3 January 2000.

Bibliography

Abe, Hiroshi. "U.S. Educational Policy in Korea." *East–West Education* 6, 1 (Spring 1986).

Adams, Donald K. "Educational Change and Korean Development." In G. Lim and Chang, eds., 370–382.

———. "Education in Korea 1945–1955." Ph.D. diss., University of Connecticut, 1956.

Amsden, Alice. *Asia's Next Giant: South Korea and Late Industrialization*. New York: Oxford University Press, 1989.

An Ho-sang. *Minjujŏk minjŏngnon: Hanbaeksŏngju ŭi iron* [Democratic nationalism: Hanbaeksŏng theory]. Seoul: Omun'gak, 1961.

———. *Minjujuŭi ŭi yŏksa wa chŏngnyu* [Democracy and its varieties]. Seoul: Ilmin Ch'ulp'ansa, 1953.

———. *Uri ŭi purujijŭm* [Our cry]. Seoul: Munhwadang, 1947.

An Yong-hyŏn, ed. *Han'guk chŏnjaeng pisa* [Critical history of the Korean War]. Seoul: Kyŏngin Munhwasa, 1992.

Ashton, David, Francis Green, Donna James, and Johnny Sung. *Education and Training for Development in East Asia: The Political Economy of Skill Formation in East Asian Newly Industrialized Economies* (London: Routledge, 1999).

Bae Chong-keun. "Education Top Reason behind Rapid Growth: Schooling for Economic Takeoff." *Koreana* 5, 2 (July 1991): 58.

Bahl, Roy, Chuk Kyo Kim, and Chang Kee Park. *Public Finances during the Korean Modernization Process*. Cambridge, Mass.: Harvard University Press, 1986.

Bang, Harry [Pang Hŭng-gyu]. "Japan's Colonial Education Policy in Korea, 1905–1930." Ph.D. diss., University of Arizona, 1971.

Barnes, Elaine Milam. "The Schools of Taegu, Kyongsang Pukto Province, Korea, in 1954–1955: An Investigation into the Interaction between Culture and Education." Ph.D. diss., University of Maryland, 1960.

Boyer, William, and Nancy E. Boyer. "Democratization of South Korea's National Universities." *Korea Studies* 15 (1991): 83–98.

Brandt, Vincent. *A Korean Village, Between Mountain and Sea*. Cambridge, Mass.: Harvard University Press, 1971.

Chang I-uk. *Na ŭi hoegorok* [A record of my recollections]. Seoul: Saemt'ŏ, 1975.

Cho, Chang-Hyun. "The Politics of Local Self-Government in South Korea." In *Korean Public Administration and Policy in Transition,* vol. 1, ed. Kwang-woong Kim and Yong-duck Jung. Seoul: Jamgwon Publishing, 1993.

Cho, Jae Hong. "Post-1945 Land Reforms and Their Consequences in South Korea." Ph.D. diss., Indiana University, 1964.

Ch'oe Hyŏn-sŏp et al. *Kodŭng hakkyo sahoe munhwa* [High school society and culture]. Seoul: Hansaem Ch'ul'pan, 1995.

Choe, Yong-ho. *The Civil Examinations and the Social Structure in Early Yi Dynasty Korea, 1392–1600.* Seoul: Korean Research Center, 1987.

———. "Commoners in Early Yi Dynasty Civil Examinations: An Aspect of Korean Social Structure, 1392–1600." *Journal of Asian Studies* 33, 4 (August 1974).

Chŏn Tok-kyu, Han Pae-ho, Kim Hak-chun, Han Sŏng-ju, and Kim Tae-hwan. *1950 nyŏndae ŭi insik* [Understanding the 1950s]. Seoul: Han'gilsa, 1981.

Chŏng Chae-ch'ŏl. *Ilche ŭi taehan'guk singminji kyoyuk chŏngch'aeksa* [A history of imperial Japan's colonial education policy toward Korea]. Seoul: Ilchisa, 1985.

Chŏng Mi-suk. "Han'guk mun'gyo chŏngch'aek ŭi kyoyuk inyŏn kusong e kwanhan kyoyuk sahoe hakchŏk punsŏk, 1948–1953" [Educational and social analysis of Korean educational structure and ideology, 1948–1953]. Master's thesis, Yonsei University, 1987.

Chŏng Yŏng-su et al. *Han'guk kyoyuk chŏngch'aek ŭinyŏn yŏn'gu 1960–1979* [An examination of educational ideals in major educational policies in Korea, 1960–1979]. 3 vols. Seoul: Han'guk Kyoyuk Kaebalwŏn, 1986.

Chŏngmyohoe. *Paek Nak-chun: Hakhoe kirok* [Record of Paek Nak-chun]. Seoul Chŏngmyohoe, 1952.

Chōsen Nenkan [Korea yearbook]. Keijō (Seoul): Keijō Nippo-sha, 1937–1945.

Chu Ki-yong. "Kyoyuk chaegŏn" [Educational reconstruction]. *Sae kyoyuk* 2, 2 (March 1949).

Chung Tai-si. "Problems Facing the Enhancement of the Status of Teachers in Korea." *Korea Journal* 6, 7 (July 1966).

Chungang Hakto Hoguktan. *Hakto hoguktan sipnyŏnji* [Ten-year record of the Student Defense Corps]. Seoul: Chungang Hakto Hoguktan, 1959.

Chungang Taehakkyo Pusŏl Han'guk Kyoyuk Munje Yŏn'guso. *Mun'gyosa* [History of the Ministry of Education]. Seoul: Chungang Taehakkyo Pusŏl Han'guk Kyoyuk Munje Yŏn'guso, 1974.

Cole, David C., and Princeton N. Lyman. *Korean Development: The Interplay of Politics and Economics.* Cambridge, Mass.: Harvard University Press, 1971.

Cumings, Bruce. *Korea's Place in the Sun: A Modern History.* New York: W. W. Norton, 1997.

————. *The Origins of the Korean War.* Vol. 1: *Liberation and the Emergence of Separate Regimes, 1945–1947.* Princeton, N.J.: Princeton University Press, 1981.

————. *The Origins of the Korean War.* Vol. 2: *The Roaring of the Cataract, 1947–1950.* Princeton, N.J.: Princeton University Press, 1990.

Deyo, Frederic C., ed. *The Political Economy of the New Asian Industrialism.* Ithaca, N.Y.: Cornell University Press, 1987.

Diamond, Larry, and Byung-Kook Kim, eds. *Consolidating Democracy in South Korea.* Boulder, Colo.: Lynne Rienner, 2000.

Dodge, Herbert Wesley. "A History of U.S. Assistance to Korean Education: 1953–1966." Ph.D. diss., George Washington University, 1971.

Dong, Won-mo. "Japanese Colonial Policy and Practice in Korea, 1905–1945." Ph.D. diss., Georgetown University, 1965.

Drake, Henry Burgess. *Korea of the Japanese.* London: John Lone and the Baldy Head, 1930.

Duke, Benjamin. *Japan's Militant Teachers.* Honolulu: University of Hawai'i Press, 1973.

Eckert, Carter. *Offspring of Empire.* Seattle: University of Washington Press, 1991.

————. "Total War, Industrialization, and Social Change in Late Colonial Korea." In *The Japanese Wartime Empire, 1931–1945,* ed. Peter Duus, Ramon H. Myers, and Mark R. Peattie. Princeton, N.J.: Princeton University Press, 1996.

Educational Planning Mission to Korea. *Rebuilding Education in the Republic of Korea: Report of the UNESCO–UNKRA Educational Planning Mission to Korea.* Paris: UNESCO, May 1954.

Fisher, James Ernest. *Democracy and Mission Education in Korea.* New York: Columbia University Press, 1928.

Fukuyama, Francis. "Falling Global Trends and U.S. Civil Society." *Harvard International Review,* Winter 1997/1998, 60–64.

Goslin, Williard E. *Han'guk kyoyuk e issŏ ŭi munje wa paljŏn* [Development and problems of current Korean education]. Seoul: Combined Economic Board, 1958.

Government-General of Chosen. *Annual Reports on Reforms and Progress in Chosen.* Keijō (Seoul): Sōtokufu. Annual, 1910/1911–1937/1938.

Grajdanzev, Andrew. *Modern Korea.* New York: Institute of Pacific Relations, 1944.

Haggard, Stephan, and Chung-in Moon. "Institutions and Economic Policy: Theory and a Korean Case Study." *World Politics* 17, 2 (January 1990): 210–237.

Han, Sung-joo [Han Sŏng-ju]. *The Failure of Democracy in South Korea.* Berkeley: University of California Press, 1974.

Han Yŏng. *80nyŏndae han'guk sahoe wa haksaeng undong* [Korean society and student movements in the 1980s]. Seoul: Chungnyunsa, 1989.

Han'guk Hyŏngmyŏng Chaep'ansa P'yŏnch'an Wiwŏnhoe. *Han'guk hyŏngmyŏng chaep'ansa* [History of the Korean Revolutionary Tribunal]. 3 vols. Seoul: Han'guk Hyŏngmyŏng Chaep'ansa P'yŏnch'an Wiwŏnhoe, 1962.

Han'guk Kyoyuk Chaejŏng Kyŏngje Hakhoe. *Kwaoe wa sa kyoyukpi* [Tutoring and private educational fees]. Seoul: Han'guk Kyoyuk Chaejŏng Kyŏngje Hakhoe, April 1997 and June 1997.

Han'guk Kyoyuk Kaebalwŏn (Korean Educational Development Institute). *Han'guk ŭi kyoyuk chip'yo* [Index of Korean education]. Seoul: Han'guk Kyoyuk Kaebalwŏn, 1996.

————. *Research Abstracts 1996*. Seoul: Han'guk Kyoyuk Kaebalwŏn, 1996.

Han'guk Kyoyuk Sipnyŏnsa Kanhaenghoe. *Han'guk kyoyuk sipnyŏnsa* [Ten-year history of Korean education]. Seoul: Han'guk Kyoyuk Sipnyŏnsa Kanhaenghoe, 1959.

Han'guk Kyoyuk Yŏn'guso. *Han'guk kyoyuksa kŭnhyŏndae p'yŏn* [Studies of modern and recent Korean educational history]. Seoul: Han'guk Kyoyuk Yŏn'guso, 1994.

Hanyang Hagwŏn P'yŏnch'an Wiwŏnhoe. *Hanyang hagwŏn osipnyŏnsa* [Fifty-year history of the Hanyang Educational Foundation]. Seoul: Hanyang Taehakkyo Ch'ulp'ansa, 1989.

Helgesen, Geir. *Democracy and Authority in Korea: The Cultural Dimension in Korean Politics*. New York: St. Martin's Press, 1998.

Henderson, Gregory. *Korea: The Politics of the Vortex*. Cambridge, Mass.: Harvard University Press, 1968.

Hong, Sung Chick [Hong Sŭng-jik]. "Values of Korean Farmers, Businessmen and Professors." In *International Conference on the Problems of Modernization in Asia: Report*. Seoul: Asiatic Research Center, Korea University, 1965.

Hong Ung-sŏn. *Kwangbokhu ŭi sin kyoyuk undong, 1946–1949, chosŏn kyoyuk yŏn'gu rŭl chungsim ŭro* [The New Education Movement after liberation, 1946–1949, centered on the Chosŏn Education Research Society]. Seoul: Taehan Kyogwasŏsa, 1991.

Hood, Christopher P. *Japanese Education Reform: Nakasone's Legacy*. London: Routledge, 2001.

Hwang Sok-chun, ed. *Yoktae kukhoe ŭiwŏn ch'ongnam* [Comprehensive biography of former lawmakers]. Seoul: Ulchisa, 1982.

Hwang Ŭn-yuk. "*Ipsi-pŏp ŭi chindan kwa haekyŏl ch'ak ŭl wihan mosaek*" [The evil influence of the entrance examinations and its solutions]. *Sae kyoyuk* 20, 4 (April 1968): 47–54.

Hyojae Kungmin Hakkyo. *Hyojae kusibinyŏnsa* [Ninety-two-year history of Hojae Elementary School]. Seoul: Hyojae Kungmin Hakkyo, 1987.

Ihm, Chon Sun. "South Korean Education." In Morris and Sweeting, eds.

Im Hanyong. "Korean Private Education." In Korean Commission for UNESCO.

International Monetary Fund. *International Financial Statistics* 14 (January 1961).

"Ipsi munje" [The entrance exam problem]. *Sae kyoyuk* 8, 2 (February 1956): 27–43.

Johnson, Chalmers. "Political Institutions and Economic Performance: The Government-Business Relationship in Japan, South Korea, and Taiwan." In Deyo, ed., 136–164.

Joon, Park. "Hwasin Village." In Mills, ed.

Kang Kil-su. *Kyoyuk haengchŏng* [Educational administration]. Seoul: P'ungguk Hagwŏn, 1957.

Kang, Kun Pyung. "The Role of Local Government in Community Development in Korea." Ph.D. diss., University of Minnesota, 1966.

Kang Mu-sŏp et al. *Kyoyuk ŭi sekyehwa kusang* [Envisioning globalized education in Korea]. Seoul: Han'guk Kyoyuk Kaebalwŏn, 1995.

Kang Sang-gyun et al. *Kodŭng hakkyo sahoe munhwa* [High school society and culture]. Seoul: Tusan Tonga, 1995.

Kehoe, Monika. "Higher Education in Korea." *Far Eastern Quarterly* 7 (February 1949): 184–186.

Kennedy, Edgar S. *Mission to Korea*. London: Derek Verschoyle, 1952.

Kim, C. I. Eugene, ed. *A Pattern of Political Development: Korea*. Seoul: Korea Research and Publication, 1964.

Kim Ch'ong-su. "Chibang chunghaksaeng ŭi sŏul chŏnip e kwanhan yŏn'gu" [Study of middle school transfer students in Seoul]. Master's thesis, Yonsei University, 1976.

Kim, Choong Soon. *The Culture of Korean Industry: An Ethnography of Poongsan Corporation*. Tucson: University of Arizona Press, 1992.

Kim Hak-chun. "*Taegu maeil sinmun* p'isŭp sagŏn" [The *Taegu maeil sinmun* attack incident]. In Chon Tok-kyu et al.

Kim, Hee-don. "The Social Mobility and the Effects of Schooling in Korea." Ph.D. diss., Korea University, 1988.

Kim, Heung-ju, "Korea's Obsession with Private Tutoring." *Korea Focus* 8, 5 (September–October 2000): 76–89.

Kim In-hoe et al. "Han'guk kyoyuk 1980 nyŏndae ŭi kwamok" [Topics for Korean education in the 1980s]. *Sae kyoyuk* 32, 1 (January 1980): 24–55.

Kim, Jin Eun [Kim Chin-ŭn]. "An Analysis of the National Planning Process for Educational Development in the Republic of Korea, 1945–1970." Ph.D. diss., Harvard University, 1975.

Kim, Jongchol [Kim Chong-ch'ŏl]. *Education and Development: Some Essays and Thoughts on Korean Education*. Seoul: Seoul National University Press, 1985.

———. "Higher Education Policies in Korea." *Korea Journal* 23, 10 (October 1983).

———. "Impact and Problems of the Middle School No-Examination Admission Policy." *Korea Journal* 11, 10 (May 1971).

Kim Ki-ok. "Kajŏng kyosa wa pumo wa kyosa" [Tutors, parents, and teachers].

Kim Kuk-hwan. "Ilche singminji ha kodŭng kyoyuk chŏngch'aek e kwanhan yŏn'gu" [Study of higher education policy under the imperial Japanese colonial rule]. Master's thesis, Yonsei University, 1977.

Kim Kyu-taik. "Decision Making in an Inter-Departmental Conflict: The Case of the Revival of Educational Autonomy in Korea." In *Inter-Group Conflicts and Political Decision Making in Korea*. Seoul: Social Science Research Institute, Yonsei University, 1968.

Kim, Myung Han. "The Educational Policy-Making Process in the Republic of Korea: A Systems Analysis." Ph.D. diss., North Texas State University, 1974.

Kim, Shin Bok. "Educational Policy Changes in Korea: Ideology and Praxis." In G. Lim and W. Chang, eds., 383–403.

Kim Sŏng-jin. Ch'oesin ilban sahoe [General social studies]. Seoul: Minju Segwan, 1974.

Kim, Sunhyuk. "Civil Society in South Korea: From Grand Democracy Movements to Petty Interest Groups?" Journal of Northeast Asian Studies (Summer 1996): 81–97.

Kim, Sung-il. "A Study of Certain Aspects of Educational Policy in Korea." Ph.D. diss., Syracuse University, 1961.

Kim Tong-gil. "Minjok minjujuŭi ranrŭn inyŏm" [The educational ideology known as democratic nationalism]. Sae kyoyuk 13, 2 (1964).

Kim Ŭn-ju. "Taehan chegugi ŭi kyoyuk kŭndae kwa kwajŏng e kwanhan yŏn'gu" [Study of the process of modernization of education during the Taehan Empire period]. Master's thesis, Yonsei University, 1987.

Kim Yŏng-ch'ŏl et al. Kodŭng hakkyo p'yŏngjunhwa chŏngch'aek ŭi kaesŏn pangan [Plans for the reform of the high school equalization policy]. Seoul: Han'guk Kyoyuk Kaebalwŏn, 1996.

Kim Yŏng-hwa. Han'guk ŭi kyoyuk pul p'yŏngdŭng [Education and inequality in Korea]. Seoul: Kyoyuk Kwahaksa, 1993.

Kim Yŏng-hwa et al. Kukka paljŏn esŏ ŭi kyoyuk ŭi yŏkhal punsŏk yŏn'gu [The role of Korean education in national development]. Seoul: Han'guk Kyoyuk Kaebalwŏn, 1996.

Kim Yong-il. Han'guk kyoyuksa [History of Korean education]. Seoul: Sungmyŏng Yŏja Taehakkyo Ch'ulp'ansa, 1984.

Kim, Yong Rae. "Emerging Civil Society in the Development of Interest Group Politics in Korea." Korea Observer 30, 2 (Summer 1999): 247–268.

Koo, Hagen, ed. State and Society in Contemporary Korea. Ithaca, N.Y.: Cornell University Press, 1993.

Korean Commission for UNESCO. Korean Survey. Seoul: Tonga Publishing, 1960.

Korea Newsreview. Seoul. Weekly since 1974.

Korea Review. Seoul. Monthly, 1900–1906.

Kukhoe Samuch'ŏ. Kukhoesa [History of the National Assembly]. 2 vols. Seoul: Kukhoe Samuch'ŏ, 1971.

———. Kukhoe sokkirok [Minutes of the National Assembly]. Seoul: Kukhoe Samuch'o.

Kungmin Taehakkyo Samsipnyŏnsa P'yŏnch'an Wiwŏnhoe. Kungmin taehakkyo samsipnyŏnsa [Thirty-year history of Kungmin University]. Seoul: Kungmin Taehakkyo Ch'ulp'ansa, 1976.

Kwak Byong-sun. "Examination Hell in Korea Revisited: An External Malady in Education?" Koreana 5, 2 (1991): 45–55.

Kyŏnghŭi Isipnyŏn P'yŏnch'an Wiwŏnhoe. Kyŏnghŭi isipnyŏn [Twenty years of Kyunghee University]. Seoul: Kyŏnghŭi Taehakkyo Ch'ulp'ansa, 1969.

Kyoyuk (Education). Seoul: Sŏul Taehakkyo Sabŏm Taehak Kyoyukhoe. Since 1954.

Kyoyuk sinbo (Education news). Seoul: Taehan.

Kyoyuk yŏnhaphoe. Weekly, 1957–1960.

Lee, Ha Woo [Yi Ha-u]. "The Korean Polity under Syngman Rhee: An Analysis of the Culture, Structure and Elite." Ph.D. diss., American University, 1973.

Lee, Man-gap, and Herbert R. Barringer. *A City in Transition: Urbanization in Taegu, Korea.* Seoul: Hollym Corporation, 1971.

Lee, Namhee. "The South Korean Student Movement, 1980–1987." *Chicago Occasional Papers on Korea* 6, 6 (1994): 204–225.

Lee, Yung Dug. *Educational Innovation in the Republic of Korea.* Paris: UNESCO, 1974.

Lett, Denise Potrzeba. *In Pursuit of Status.* (Cambridge, Mass.: Harvard University Press, 1998.

Lim, Gill-chin, and Wook Chang, eds. *Dynamic Transformation: Korea, NICs and Beyond.* Urbana, Ill.: Consortium on Developmental Studies, 1990.

Mason, Edward S., Mahn Je Kim, Dwight H. Perkins, Kwang Suk Kim, and David C. Cole. *The Economic and Social Modernization of the Republic of Korea.* Cambridge, Mass.: Harvard University Press, 1980.

McCune, George, and Arthur L. Grey, Jr. *Korea Today.* Cambridge, Mass.: Harvard University Press, 1950.

McGinn, Noel F., Donald Snodgrass, Yung Bong Kim, Shin-bok Kim, and Quee-young Kim. *Education and Development in Korea.* Cambridge, Mass.: Harvard University Press, 1980.

Meyer, John W., Francisco O. Ramirez, Richard Robinson, and John Boli-Bennett. "The World Educational Revolution, 1950–1970." In Meyer and Hannan, eds., 37–55.

Meyer, John W., and Michael T. Hannan, eds. *National Development and the World System.* Chicago: University of Chicago Press, 1979.

Migdal, Joel S. *Strong Societies and Weak States: State–Society Relations and State Capabilities in the Third World.* Princeton, N.J.: Princeton University Press, 1988.

Mills, John E., ed. *Ethno-Sociological Report of Three Korean Villages.* Seoul: United Nations Command, Community Development Division, Office of the Economic Co-ordinator for Korea, 1958.

Morgan, Robert M., and Clifton B. Chadwick, eds. *Systems Analysis for Educational Change: The Republic of Korea.* Tallahasee, Fla.: Department of Education Research, Florida State University, 1971.

Morris, Paul. "Asia's Four Little Tigers: A Comparison of the Role of Education in Their Development." *Comparative Education* 37, 1 (March 1996): 95–109.

Morris, Paul, and Anthony Sweeting, eds. *Education and Development in East Asia.* New York and London: Garland Publishing, 1995.

"Musihŏmje" [The no-exam system]. *Sae kyoyuk* 11, 5 (May 1959): 8–30.

Nam, Baek Kyu. "Napunto Village." In Mills, ed.

Nam, Byung Hun. "Educational Reorganization in South Korea under the United States Army Military Government 1945–1948." Ph.D. diss., University of Pittsburgh, 1962.

Nathan, Robert R., Associates. *An Economic Report for Korean Reconstruction*. New York: United Nations Korea Reconstruction Agency, 1954.

No In-hwa. "Taehan cheguk sigi kwanhan hakkyo, kyoyuk ŭi sŏngyŏn'gu" [Study of the characteristics of education in the schools of the Taehan Empire]. Ph.D. diss., Ewha University, 1989.

O Ch'ŏn-sŏk. "Chŏngyunyŏn kyoyukkye ŭi chŏnmang" [The prospects for the education of the world in 1957]. *Sae kyoyuk* 9, 1 (January 1957).

———. *Han'guk sinkyoyuksa* [A history of the new education in Korea]. Seoul: Hyŏndae KyoyukChipsa Ch'ulp'ansa, 1964.

———. *Minju kyoyuk ŭl chihyang hayŏ* [Toward a Democratic Education]. Seoul: Hyŏndae Kyoyuk Ch'ulp'ansa, 1960.

OECD (Organization for Economic Cooperation and Development). *Reviews of National Policies for Education: Korea*. Paris: OECD, 1998.

Oh, Byung-hun. "Students and Politics." In *Korean Politics in Transition,* ed. Edward Reynolds Wright. Seattle: University of Washington Press, 1975.

Oh, John Kie-chiang. *Korea: Democracy on Trial*. Ithaca, N.Y.: Cornell University Press, 1968.

Osborne, Cornelius. *The Koreans and Their Culture*. New York: Ronald Press, 1951.

Pae Chŏng-gun. "Ilbon-ha minjok kyoyuk ŭi pyŏngch'ŏn e kwanhan yŏn'gu" [A study of changes in Korean national education under Japan]. Master's thesis, Yonsei University, 1984.

Paek Hŏn'gi. *Kyoyuk haengjŏng-hak* [Educational administration]. Seoul: Uryu Munhwasa, 1962.

Paek Nak-chun. *Han'guk kyoyuk kwa minjok chŏngsin* [Korean education and the national spirit]. Seoul: Han'guk Munhwa Hyŏphoe, 1954.

Pak, Chi-young. *Political Opposition in Korea, 1945–1960*. Seoul: Seoul National University Press, 1980. Institute of Social Sciences, Korean Studies Series 2.

Pak Mun-ok. *Han'guk chŏngburon* [Principles of Korean government]. Seoul: Pakyongsa, 1958.

Palais, James. *Politics and Policy in Traditional Korea*. Cambridge, Mass.: Harvard University Press, 1975.

Park, Bu Kwon. "The State, Class and Educational Policy: A Study of South Korea's High School Equalization Policy." Ph.D. diss., University of Wisconsin–Madison, 1988.

Park, Sung Jae. "Physical Education and Sport as an Instrument of Nation Building in the Republic of Korea." Ph.D. diss., Ohio State University, 1974.

Reeve, W. D. *The Republic of Korea: A Political and Economic Study*. London: Oxford University Press, 1963.

Republic of Korea, CERI (Central Education Research Institute). *A Study for Solving the Problems of Compulsory Education*. Seoul: CERI, 1967.

Republic of Korea, MOE (Ministry of Education). *Education in Korea*. Seoul: Mun'gyobu. Annual, 1963–1996.

———. *Entrance Examination Policy for Colleges and Universities in Korea*. Seoul: Mun'gyobu, 1981

———. *Kodŭng hakkyo kyoryŏn* [High school ethics]. Seoul: Mun'gyobu, 1995.

———. *Kyoyuk kibon t'onggye* [Basic statistics on education]. Seoul: Mun'gyobu, 1974.

———. *Kyoyuk t'onggye yŏnbo* [Statistical yearbook of education]. Seoul: Mun'gyobu, 1964–1995.

———. *Mun'gyo kaeyo* [Outline of schooling]. Seoul: Mun'gyobu, 1958.

———. *Mun'gyo sasimnyŏnsa* [Forty-year history of the Ministry of Education]. Seoul: Mun'gyobu, 1988.

———. *Mun'gyo t'onggye yoram* [Outline of educational statistics]. Seoul: Mun'gyobu, 1963.

Republic of Korea, National Statistical Office. *Statistical Indicators in Korea 1995*. Seoul: National Statistical Office, 1995.

Republic of Korea, Office of Information and Research. *Korean Report: Reports from the Cabinet Ministries of the Republic of Korea*. Vol. 1, 1948–1952. Vol. 3, 1954. Vol. 4, 1955. Vol. 5, 1957. Vol. 6, 1958. Washington, D.C.: Korea Pacific House, 1952–1959.

Rettig, Solomon, and Benjamin Pasamanick. "Moral Codes of American and Korean University Students." *Journal of Social Psychology* 50 (1959): 65–73.

Rhee, Yoo Sang [Yi Yu-sang]. "Korean Education, 1956–1965." *Journal of Social Sciences and Humanities* 31 (December 1969): 25–45.

Rim, Han Young [Im Han-yŏng]. "The Development of Higher Education in Korea during the Japanese Occupation." Ph.D. diss., Columbia University, 1952.

Sae kyoyuk [New education]. Seoul: Taehan Kyowŏn Yŏn'haphoe. Since 1948.

Sasanggye [World of thought]. Seoul: Sasangyesa. Since 1946.

Seki, Eiko. "An Endeavor by Koreans toward the Reestablishment of an Educational System under the U.S. Military Government." *East–West Education* 5, 1 (Spring 1986): 39–47.

Shin, Doh C. *Mass Politics and Culture in Democratizing Korea*. New York: CambridgeUniversity Press, 1999.

Shin, Yong-ha [Sin Yong-ha]. "The Establishment of the First Modern School in Korea." *Korean Social Science Journal* 5, 1 (1978): 127–141.

Sŏ Ton'gak. Chŏngch'i-kyŏngje [Politics and economics]. Seoul: Pŏpmunsa, 1974.

Son In-su. *Han'guk kaehwa kyoyuk yŏn'gu*. [A study of Korean enlightenment education]. Seoul: Ilchogak, 1980.

———. *Han'guk kyoyuksa* [History of Korean education]. 2 vols. Seoul: Munŭmsa, 1987.

———. *Han'guk kyoyuk undongsa* [History of the Korean educational movement]. Seoul: Munŭmsa, 1994.

———. "Yŏktae mun'gyo changgwan ŭi chuyo sich'aek kwa ŏpchŏk" [An outline of achievements and policies of successive ministers of education]. *Kyoyuk p'yŏngnon* 2 (1972).

Sŏng Chŏng-a. "Kodŭng hakkyo kuksa kyogwasŏ ŭi ch'eji wa naeyong punsŏk yŏn'gu" [The study and analysis of the content and structure of Korean high school history textbooks]. Master's thesis, Ewha University, 1993.

Sorensen, Clark W. *Over the Mountains Are Mountains: Korean Peasant Households and Their Adaptation to Rapid Industrialization.* Seattle: University of Washington Press, 1988.

Sŏul Taehakkyo Sabŏm Taehak. *Chung hakkyo kyoyuk* [Middle school ethics]. Seoul: Sŏul Taehakkyo Sabŏm Taehak, 1995.

Sŏul T'ŭkpyŏlsi Kyoyuk Wiwŏnhoe (Seoul Board of Education). *Taehan kyoyuk yŏn'gam* [Yearbook of Korean education]. Seoul: Sŏul T'ŭkpyŏlsi Kyoyuk Wiwŏnhoe, 1948–1961.

Spencer, Robert F. *Yŏgang: Factory Girl.* Seoul: Royal Asiatic Society–Korean Branch, 1988.

Taehan Kyoyuk Yŏnhaphoe (Korean Federation of Educators' Associations). *Han'guk kyoyuk yŏn'gam* [Yearbook of Korean education]. Seoul: Taehan Kyoyuk Yŏnhaphoe. Since 1962.

———. *Han'guk ŭi kyoyuk* [Korea's education]. Seoul: Taehan Kyoyuk Yŏnhaphoe, 1956.

———. *Taehan kyoryŏn sasipnyŏnsa* [Forty-year history of the Korean Federation of Educators' Associations]. Seoul: Taehan Kyoyuk Yŏnhaphoe, 1987.

———. *Taehan kyoyuksa, 1947–1973* [History of Korean education 1947–1973]. Seoul: Taehan Kyoyuk Yŏnhaphoe, 1974.

Takahashi, Hamakichi. *Chōsen kyōiku shikō* [Survey of Korean education]. Keijō [Seoul]: Chōsen Sōtokufu, 1927.

Tan'guk Samsipnyŏnsahoe. *Tan'guk samsipnyŏnsa* [Thirty-year history of Tan'guk]. Seoul: Tan'guk Taehakkyo, 1978.

Tonga Taehakkyo. *Tonga hakkyo samsipnyŏnsa, 1948–1978* [Thirty-year history of Tonga University, 1948–1978]. Pusan: Tonga Taehakkyo Ch'ulp'ansa, 1976.

Tsurumi, Patricia. "Colonial Education in Korea and Taiwan." In *The Japanese Colonial Empire: 1895–1945,* ed. Ramon H. Meyers and Mark R. Peattie. Princeton, N.J.: Princeton University Press, 1984.

Umakoshi Toru. "Dokuritsugo ni okeru kankoku kyoiku no saiken to amerika no kyoiku enjo" [Rebuilding Korean education after independence and U.S. educational assistance]. *Han* 112 (1988): 67–100.

Underwood, Horace H. *Modern Education in Korea.* New York: Columbia University Press, 1926.

UNESCO (United Nations Educational, Scientific, and Cultural Organization). *Bulletin of the UNESCO Regional Office for Education in Asia.*

———. *Long-Term Projections for Education in the Republic of Korea.* Bangkok: UNESCO Regional Office for Education in Asia, 1965.

———. *Statistical Yearbook 1993.* Paris: UNESCO, 1993.

United Nations Statistical Office. *United Nations Statistical Yearbook 1961.* New York: United Nations, 1962.

United States Department of the Army. *Educator's Guide to Korea*. Seoul: Reports and Analysis Branch, Civil Affairs Division, 1 April 1948.

———. *Report of the Staff of the Teacher Training Center*. Seoul: Reports and Analysis Branch, Civil Affairs Division, 1 April 1949.

United States Operations Mission/Korea. *Technical Assistance in Public Administration*. Seoul: United States Operations Mission/Korea, 1967.

USAMGIK (United States Army Military Government in Korea) *Official Gazette*.

———. *Summation of the U.S. Army Military Government Activities in Korea*. Nos. 6–22, March 1946–July 1947. Seoul: General Headquarters, Commander-in-Chief, U.S. Army Forces, Pacific.

Vicante, Russell Anthony. "Japanese Colonial Education in Korea, 1910–1945: An Oral History." Ph.D. diss., State University of New York at Buffalo, 1987.

Voice of Korea. Washington, D.C.: Korean Affairs Institute, April 1946–April 1960.

Watanabe, Manabu. *Kintai chōsen kyōiku kenkyū* [Study of the modern history of Korean education]. Tokyo: Yuzankaku, 1969.

Wells, Kenneth M. *New God, New Nation: Protestants and Reconstruction Nationalism in Korea, 1896–1937*. Honolulu: University of Hawai'i Press, 1990.

———, ed. *South Korea's Minjung Movement*. Honolulu: University of Hawai'i Press, 1995.

Wilson, Elizabeth Cecil. "The Problem of Value in Technical Assistance in Education: The Case of Korea, 1945–1955." Ph.D. diss., New York University, 1959.

Woo, Jung-en. *Race to the Swift: State and Finance in Korean Industrialization*. New York: Columbia University Press, 1991.

Wood, C. W. "Post-Liberation Problems in Korean Education." *Phi Delta Kappan* 39 (December 1957): 116–118.

World Bank. *The East Asian Miracle: Economic Growth and Public Policy*. Oxford: Oxford University Press, 1993.

Yang, Sung Chul. "South Korea's Top Bureaucratic Elites, 1948–1973: Their Recruitment Patterns and Modal Characteristics." *Korea Journal* 34, 4 (Autumn 1994): 8–19.

Yi Chae-o. *Haebang hu han'guk haksaeng undongsa* [A history of the Korean student movement after liberation]. Seoul: Hyŏngsŏngsa, 1984.

Yi Chang-wŏn. "80nyŏndae ŭi kyosa undong" [The 1980s teachers' movement]. In *Minjung kyoyuk* [Minjung education], ed. Kim Chin'gyŏng et al. Seoul: P'urŭn Namu, 1988.

Yi Chin-jae et al. *Uri nara sihŏm chedo ŭi p'yŏnch'ŏnsa* [The history of the change in Korean school entrance examination systems]. Seoul: Chungang Kyoyuk P'yŏngkawŏn, 1986.

Yi Chŏng-sik. *Haksaeng undongsa* [History of the student movement]. Seoul: Tosŏ Ch'ulp'ansa, 1993.

Yi Hae-sŏng. "1950 nyŏndae ŭi kukka kwalyŏk kwa kyoyuk kwa hakkyo kyoyuk: Saeroŭn iron chongnip ŭl wihan nonjaeng koridŭl" [National authority in the

1950s and education]. In *Han'guk kyoyuk-ŭi hyŏndankye* [Current stage of Korean education], eds. Kim Sin-il et al. Seoul: Kyoyuk Kwahaksa, 1990.

————. "T'ongch'i ch'eje ŭi musun gwa hakkyo kyoyuk ŭi chŏngch'i sahoehwa kinŭng" [Contradictions in the political system and the ability to politically socialize school education]. Ph.D. diss., Yonsei University, 1987.

Yi Hae-yŏng. "Taehak iphak chŏngwŏn kyŏlchŏng ŭi sahoejŏk tongan e kwanhan yŏn'gu" [An analytical study of the social dynamics determining higher education enrollment quota]. Ph.D. diss., Seoul National University, 1992.

Yi Hŭi-gwŏn. "Chosŏn chŏn'gi ŭi konggwan yŏn'gu" [Student protests in early Chosŏn]. *Sahak yŏn'gu* 28 (December 1978): 1–30.

————. "Chosŏn hugi ŭi konggwan kwŏndang yŏn'gu" [Student protests and strikes in early Chosŏn]. *Sahak yŏn'gu* 30 (June 1980): 31–64.

Yi Ki-ha. *Han'guk chŏngdang paldalsa* [A history of Korean political party development]. Seoul: Uihae Chongchisa, 1961.

Yi Kwang-ho. "Han'guk kyoyuk ch'eje chaep'yŏn ŭi kujujŏk t'ŭksŏng e kwanhan yŏn'gu, 1945–1955" [Study of the special characteristics of the reorganization of Korean education, 1945–1955]. Master's thesis, Yonsei University, 1990.

Yoo, Jong Hae [Yu Chong-hae]. "The System of Korean Local Government." In *Korea under Japanese Colonial Rule: Studies of the Policy and Technique of Japanese Colonialism,* ed. Andrew Nahm. Kalamazoo, Mich.: Western Michigan University, Institute for International and Area Studies, Center for Korean Studies, 1973.

Yoon, Eul Byung. "Naejongja, Hampyong-gun, Cholla Namdo," in Mills, ed., 6–8.

Yu Sang Duk [Yu Sang-dŏk]. "Korean Teachers' Struggle for Educational Reform." Unpublished manuscript, March 1996.

Yu, Si-joung. "Educational Institutions." In Man-gap Lee and Barringer, eds., 423–453.

Yu Sŏk-ch'ang. *Choyanghan hyŏngmyŏng ŭi hayŏ* [For a quiet revolution]. Seoul: Tosŏ Ch'ulp'ansa, 1987.

Yun, Seongyi. "Contributions and Limitations of Student Movement in South Korea Democratization, 1980–1987." *Korea Observer* 3, 3 (Autumn 1999): 487–506.

Yun Tae-yong. "Chunghakkyo ipsi munje" [The problems of the middle school exam system]. *Sae kyoyuk* 2, 2 (March 1949): 52–59.

Index

About the Author

Michael J. Seth is assistant professor of history at James Madison University in Harrisonberg, Virginia. Seth, who received a Ph.D. in history from the University of Hawai'i in 1994, spent several years living and working in Nigeria, Taiwan, Japan, and South Korea. While in South Korea, he taught English at Han'guk University of Foreign Studies and participated as an English instructor in several in-service training programs for middle and high school teachers. He has published several articles on Korean social history and is currently working on a study of the impact of the Korean War on East Asian history. *Education Fever* is his first book.

Production Notes for Seth/EDUCATION FEVER

Interior design and composition by inari.

Jacket design by Wilson Angel.

Text and display type in Granjon.

Printing and binding by The Maple-Vail Book Manufacturing Group.

Printed on 50 lb. Glatfeter Hi-Opaque, 440 ppi.

CPSIA information can be obtained
at www.ICGtesting.com
Printed in the USA
BVHW050025250322
632253BV00010B/266/J